The Administrative Professional
PROCEDURES AND SKILLS

THIRD CANADIAN EDITION

The Administrative Professional
PROCEDURES AND SKILLS

THIRD CANADIAN EDITION

Patsy Fulton-Calkins
Ph.D., CPS

Diane Blaney
M.Ed., CPS

NELSON
EDUCATION

The Administrative Professional, Third Canadian Edition

by Patsy Fulton-Calkins, Diane Blaney

VP, Product and Partnership Solutions:
Anne Williams

Publisher, Digital and Print Content:
Amie Plourde

Senior Marketing Manager:
Alexis Hood

Content Development Manager:
Courtney Thorne

Photo and Permissions Researcher:
Jessica Freedman

Senior Content Production Manager:
Imoinda Romain

Production Service:
Cenveo Publisher Services

Copy Editor:
Mariko Obokata

Proofreader:
Pushpa

Indexer:
BIM Creatives, LLC

Design Director:
Ken Phipps

Managing Designer:
Franca Amore

Interior Design:
Dave Murphy Design

Cover Design:
Dave Murphy Design

Cover Image:
Phil Boorman/Getty Images

Compositor:
Cenveo Publisher Services

Library and Archives Canada Cataloguing in Publication

Fulton-Calkins, Patsy, 1934–, author:

The administrative professional : procedures and skills / Patsy Fulton-Calkins,

Diane Blaney. — Third Canadian edition.

Includes index.
ISBN 978-0-17-653206-2 (paperback)

1. Office management—Handbooks, manuals, etc. 2. Administrative assistants—Handbooks, manuals, etc. 3. Office management—Textbooks. I. Blaney, Diane, 1944–, author II. Title.

HF5547.F84 2015
651   C2015-906111-3

ISBN-13: 978-0-17-653206-2
ISBN-10: 0-17-653206-4

Interior Image Credit:LCD screen/tablet, © CostinT/iStockphoto.

As always,
To my longest and best love, Roy; you were missed this time around.
And
To my pride and joy, my children Keri-An and Ryan; and,
To the lights of my life, my grandchildren, Riley and Connor.

Diane

Brief Contents

Contents

Preface

To the Administrative Professional

Whether your title is administrative assistant, administrative secretary, executive assistant, or executive secretary, as an administrative professional you are a respected and valued member of a team in business, industry, hospitality, government, education, law, medicine, science, or the arts. As "Information Central" for a department, you are depended on by employees throughout the organization to ensure that the office has the resources needed to remain productive. When you coordinate repairs to office equipment and order new equipment and supplies, you ensure that the office is organized and able to operate efficiently. As the "voice" and "face" of the organization, you will meet and greet visitors and customers; schedule meetings and appointments; share information with others through social media and by email, correspondence, reports, faxes, and telephone; maintain records; create presentations; and manage many other administrative details.

You may work as part of a team, providing administrative support to several managers, or you may work with an individual executive. In either situation, your role in the workplace will be constantly evolving and changing. Advances in technology are occurring at an exponential rate, and the ability to be constantly connected and to perform tasks with greater speed and sophistication means that you face a challenging and exciting future. While the work itself can be very rewarding, it can also serve as an introduction to a business or industry; provide you with opportunities to demonstrate your leadership ability; allow you to move to other positions or occupations; or enable you to assume greater responsibility through promotion. In offices all around the world, the demand for administrative professionals is strong and growing, and both women and men are choosing office administration as a career and as a means of advancing within a company or field.

The globalization of business and the diversification of the Canadian population mean that, in addition to keeping your technology skills current, you must possess the broad range of human relations, communication, and critical-thinking skills outlined in *Employability Skills 2000+*. It is important that you not only recognize and understand how diversity affects the workplace but also practise diversity-competent behaviours. As you begin this challenging and rewarding career as an administrative professional, realize that, while it may be the hard skills you possess that initially land you the job, the soft skills you develop will help you keep your job, and the leadership capabilities you demonstrate will move you forward. To keep up with the pace of change in the Canadian workplace, you, as an administrative professional, must commit to continuous learning.

What you learn in this and other courses in your program of study will equip you to find opportunities for meaningful employment wherever you wish to go. I know firsthand how valuable my administrative skills have proven to be and how they have provided me with the ability to support myself when travelling around the world. When I was very young, I couldn't decide whether I wanted to be a "secretary" or a teacher. How fortunate I have been in my career to have accomplished both goals. My administrative skills opened doors and provided opportunities to lead. As an educator, helping students like you acquire the knowledge and skills to change your life is one of **my** most rewarding experiences. I wish you all the very best in your current studies and in achieving your goals in work and life.

Diane Blaney

New to This Edition

Thanks to the reviewers and working administrative professionals whose insightful suggestions prompted some of the following changes.

Part 1: The Workplace and You
Chapter 1: Entering the Workforce and Becoming a Professional—This chapter introduces the concept of becoming diversity-competent and practising diversity-competent behaviours that promote equity and inclusion. A new section has been added on emotional intelligence as a quality for success and the job responsibilities of the administrative professional have been updated. Looking ahead, this chapter includes a section on future career paths and outlines the core competencies required to become Medical Office Assistants, Legal Administrative Assistants, and Executive Assistants.

Chapter 2: Managing and Organizing Yourself, Your Time, and Your Workspace—This chapter expands on the topic of ergonomics and consolidates the guidelines for creating a safe and healthy physical workspace that reduces the risk of repetitive stress injury. Tips and illustrations have been added on designing and keeping a neat, well-organized, and professional-looking work area that will maximize efficiency.

Chapter 3: Working Ethically—Updates in this chapter include changes in employment standards legislation, health and safety standards, due diligence, and an expanded definition of sexual harassment. A new optional case study has been added to examine ethical dilemmas.

Chapter 4: Mastering Technology—This chapter has been significantly edited to reflect developments in technology, such as the growing use of the "cloud" for both workplace collaboration and accessing software applications.

Part 2: Communication—The Key to Your Success

Chapter 5: Improving Communication Skills—Added to this chapter are the concept of diversity competency and an optional project to help develop behaviours that promote equity and inclusion.

Chapter 6: Creating and Preparing Business Documents—Images in this chapter have been updated to reflect recent developments in technology.

Chapter 7: Developing Effective Presentations—To reflect changes in technology, this chapter updates the description of the interactive electronic whiteboard (IWB). A PowerPoint presentation file is included as a new optional project to enable students to focus on presentation skills without the necessity of learning the features of the software.

Part 3: Administrative Support—Your Responsibilities

Chapter 8: Using Telecommunications and Workplace Collaboration Tools—This chapter is updated with the inclusion of an organization's formal email policy and the advantages and practical use of instant messaging in business.

Chapter 9: Handling Mail and Using Reprographic Equipment—This chapter details changes to Canada Post services. Mail processing has been reorganized into two broad categories to improve chapter flow and understanding. Other additions include new images and key terms, updated content on copiers, and information on the protection of privacy in reprographics. The chapter also expands on the use of postal meters and procedures for refilling postage, and it introduces a new description of the use of laminators and binders.

Chapter 10: Maintaining Financial Records—A new topic in this chapter is the ability to make deposits remotely.

Chapter 11: Managing Physical and Electronic Records—The chapter has been renamed to more adequately describe the contents, which now include the administrative, legal/legislative, and historic value of records to an organization. Updated images have been added. Managing electronic records has been significantly updated and reorganized, and the limitations and concerns of businesses regarding online "cloud" storage have been expanded.

Chapter 12: Developing Customer Focus—The focus of this chapter is the customer—internal and external—and the Disney customer-service philosophy that businesses are adopting. The content discusses customers' use of Web resources and social media to provide feedback and express their concerns to organizations, and includes the administrative professional's responsibility to monitor and provide preliminary responses. Images have been updated to reflect changes in technology. Examples of electronic scheduling software have been added and electronic calendaring content has been updated.

Chapter 13: Planning and Organizing Meetings and Other Events—New to this edition is the use of electronic invitation and polling software. Additional tips have been added on note taking at meetings, and the accompanying images have been updated. The chapter introduces the use of event management software to track details when planning events.

Chapter 14: Arranging Business Travel—This chapter's updates include airline security (Nexus and TSA Pre✔ programs), flight classifications (new premium economy), online travel arrangements (mobile itinerary apps), and travel documentation (ePassports, electronic boarding passes). Images have been updated to reflect changes in technology.

Part 4: Planning for Your Future

Chapter 15: Seeking Employment—This chapter provides links to new job boards and updates the guidelines for submitting a résumé electronically.

Chapter 16: Becoming a Virtual Assistant—As a virtual assistant, you are in control of where, when, and how you work. This chapter introduces the use of an always-on video portal that connects office spaces and facilitates natural unscheduled face-to-face communication among team members.

Chapter 17: Leading with Confidence—Different leadership styles—autocratic, democratic, and laissez-faire—are introduced, and management responsibilities have been updated.

Text Features

- *Professional Profiles* open each of the four parts of the textbook. The four profiles, three of which are new to this edition, introduce four administrative professionals who, not too long ago, were students just like you. They share their stories of career advancement and success.

- *Do I Qualify?* At the beginning of each chapter, actual job postings introduce you to some of the topics in that chapter, and illustrate how the chapter objectives relate to your future career as an administrative professional. The job postings illustrate the skills required by prospective employers and help you to see how the courses in your program of study apply to the day-to-day duties, tasks, and responsibilities you will be expected to perform on the job.

Do I Qualify?

Executive Assistant

Highly organized and professional, you will report to the President providing administrative support to the executive team. Booking appointments for all executive officers, preparing confidential materials, and assisting with board and industry meetings are some of the functions that will require your expertise.

Your strong interpersonal and communications skills make you confident liaising with a wide range of stakeholders, from executive personnel and board members to government officials, clients, and personnel at all management levels. Your attention to detail, computer proficiency with Microsoft Office applications, ability to multi-task, and strong team commitment will make you the successful candidate.

- *Learning Outcomes*, updated and revised to reflect new content, are provided at the beginning of each chapter. They are related to the skills required in the *Do I Qualify?* job postings and reveal the expected outcomes to be achieved from studying each chapter. Because of the importance of soft skills to the administrative professional, the related learning outcomes appear in *italics*.

- *Soft Skills* (such as critical thinking, teamwork, interpersonal skills, and leadership) are consistently identified by organizations as critical skills that all employees must possess. You will be directed to include your reflections on these soft skills in your e-portfolio. You'll find the following *Soft Skills* boxed features in the text:

PART 1: The Workplace and You
Chapter 1 Critical Thinking
Chapter 2 Conflict Resolution
Chapter 3 Business Ethics
Chapter 4 Continual Learning

PART 2: Communication—The Key to Your Success
Chapter 5 Value Clarification
Chapter 6 Ethical and Legal Considerations
Chapter 7 Creativity

PART 3: Administration Support—Your Responsibilities
Chapter 8 Email Ethics
Chapter 9 Teamwork
Chapter 10 Committed to the Community
Chapter 11 Effective Decision Making
Chapter 14 Maintaining a Positive Attitude

PART 4: Planning for Your Future
Chapter 15 Living Your Values
Chapter 16 Self-Management
Chapter 17 Earning the Right to Lead

- *Self-Checks* in each chapter allow you to test your understanding of the content. The appropriate responses to some of these features are included at the end of the chapter.

SELF-CHECK

1. After what length of time will the bank no longer accept a cheque for deposit? What term refers to a cheque that has exceeded this time limitation?
2. What steps should you take prior to initiating payment of an invoice? Prior to filing a monthly statement?
3. Why should a cheque not be written out to "Cash"?
4. What type of endorsement provides the highest degree of protection?

- Three different *@ Work* feature boxes are included in each chapter.

  Skills @ Work boxes focus on the Conference Board of Canada's **Employability Skills 2000+** and stress new techniques in technology and the importance of effective interpersonal, personal management, and communication skills.

  Professionalism @ Work boxes emphasize topics and professional habits, attitudes, and actions that will help you discover what is needed and wanted in the workplace.

  People @ Work boxes introduce you to people you will interact with on the job, from reception to the Chairperson of the Board.

- *Key Terms* are highlighted in orange font within each chapter, listed at the end of each chapter, and then defined in the Glossary at the end of the text for ease of reference.

- *Chapter Summaries* reinforce the major points in each chapter.

- *Discussion Items* are included to provide opportunities to reflect and discuss with your classmates the key topics found in each chapter.

- The *Critical-Thinking Activities* provide cases based on real-life situations that demand the use of critical-thinking skills.
- In *Building Workplace Skills*, career-focused projects are tied to the chapter's Learning Outcomes to help you apply the key concepts you've learned in each chapter. These projects will build your workplace skills and direct your research to maintain currency. Some projects are collaborative and provide opportunities to work with classmates in developing team-building skills, while others ask you to use the Student Course Data files or require online research.
- Begin the creation of an **e-portfolio** using some of documents you create by completing end-of-chapter workplace skill-building projects. You will have the option of uploading the completed documents to a website where they can be easily maintained and kept up to date, to use when you initiate a job search, to print out, or to save to a suitable medium so that they can be left with a prospective employer.
- Updated and expanded *Weblinks* for each chapter, which will help you in your research on new and emerging technologies, have been added to the MindTap for the textbook.

Ancillaries

Instructor Resources

The **Nelson Education Teaching Advantage (NETA)** program delivers research-based instructor resources that promote student engagement and higher-order thinking to enable the success of Canadian students and educators. Visit Nelson Education's **Inspired Instruction** website at www.nelson.com/inspired/ to find out more about NETA.

The following instructor resources have been created for *The Administrative Professional*, Third Canadian Edition. Access these ultimate tools for customizing lectures and presentations at www.nelson.com/instructor.

NETA Test Bank

This resource was written by Arlene Koteff, George Brown College. It includes over 160 multiple-choice questions written according to NETA guidelines for effective construction and development of higher-order questions. Also included are over 130 true/false questions, over 80 matching questions, and over 50 short-answer questions.

cognero
Full-Circle Assessment®

The NETA Test Bank is available in a new, cloud-based platform. **Testing Powered by Cognero®** is a secure online testing system that allows instructors to author, edit, and manage test bank content from anywhere Internet access is available. No special installations or downloads are needed, and the desktop-inspired interface, with its drop-down menus and familiar, intuitive tools, allows instructors to create and manage tests with ease. Multiple test versions can be created in an instant, and content can be imported or exported into other systems. Tests can be delivered from a learning management system, the classroom, or wherever an instructor chooses. Testing Powered by Cognero for *The Administrative Professional* can also be accessed through www.nelson.com/instructor.

NETA PowerPoint

Microsoft® PowerPoint® lecture slides for every chapter have been created by Sherri Veilleux, Lambton College. Each chapter has an average of 25 to 30 slides, many featuring key figures, tables, and photographs from *The Administrative Professional*. NETA principles of clear design and engaging content have been incorporated throughout, making it simple for instructors to customize the deck for their courses.

Image Library

This resource consists of digital copies of figures, short tables, and photographs used in the book. Instructors may use these jpeg files to customize the NETA PowerPoint or create their own PowerPoint presentations.

TurningPoint® Slides

TurningPoint® classroom response software has been customized for *The Administrative Professional*. Instructors can author, deliver, show, access, and grade, all in PowerPoint, with no toggling back and forth between screens. When using JoinIn on TurningPoint, instructors are no longer tied to their computers. Instead, instructors can walk about the classroom and lecture at the same time, showing slides and collecting and displaying responses with ease. Anyone who can use PowerPoint can also use JoinIn on TurningPoint.

NETA Instructor Guide

This resource was written by Christine Doody, Algonquin College. It is organized according to the textbook chapters and explores the main ideas of the chapter with suggested classroom activities, additional discussion items, and optional projects. Other features include answers to activities, and keys to discussion items.

DayOne Slides

DayOne—Prof InClass is a PowerPoint presentation that instructors can customize to orient students to the class and their text at the beginning of the course.

MindTap®

Offering personalized paths of dynamic assignments and applications, **MindTap** is a digital learning solution that turns cookie-cutter into cutting-edge, apathy into engagement, and memorizers into higher-level thinkers. MindTap enables students to analyze and apply chapter concepts through relevant assignments, and allows instructors to measure skills and promote better outcomes with ease. A fully online learning solution, MindTap combines all student learning tools—readings, multimedia, activities, and assessments—into a single learning path that guides the student through the curriculum. Instructors personalize the experience by customizing the presentation of these learning tools to their students, even seamlessly introducing their own content into the learning path.

Student Ancillaries

MindTap®

Stay organized and efficient with *MindTap*—a single destination providing access to all the course material and study aids you need to succeed. Built-in apps leverage social media and the latest learning technology. For example, you can use **MindTap** to access the following features:

- MindTap Reader, which you can use to highlight text and make notes. Your notes will flow into Evernote, the electronic notebook app that you can access anywhere when it's time to study for the exam.
- ReadSpeaker, an application that will read the text to you
- Student Course Data (SCD) files that can be downloaded
- Electronic files for many of the sample forms mentioned in the textbook, which you can open in Adobe Acrobat® and print for easy reference
- Additional projects and worksheets for each chapter
- Flashcards that are pre-populated to provide you with a jump-start for review—or you can create your own
- Self-quizzing that allows you to assess your understanding
- *In-Basket : An Office Simulation* is a capstone project that sees you working as a temporary employee at the engineering firm of Paterson, Hall & Marklinger. You will review, prioritize, and complete a series of realistic tasks found in the in-basket of the firm's administrative professional, Pat Gartman, who has taken leave to deal with a family emergency. The tasks in the simulation provide an opportunity to develop confidence dealing with a variety of challenging tasks within the familiar setting of your classroom and are designed to allow you to experience a real-life office situation.

- A *Records Management Simulation* that provides you with an opportunity to use your decision-making skills as you set up an alphabetic filing system and apply correct procedures in preparing records for filing. You will inspect, index, code, sort, and store a series of mini-letters and cards in folders placed in a file box.
- A *Reference Guide* that serves as a review of grammar and punctuation rules
- A *Business Document Formatting Guide* that provides detailed instructions and fully formatted, labelled model documents that illustrate how to correctly format memos, letters, and reports

Visit www.nelson.com/student to start using **MindTap**. Enter the Online Access Code from the card included with your textbook. If a code card is *not* provided, you can purchase instant access at NELSONbrain.com.

Acknowledgments for the Third Canadian Edition

Firstly, I would like to acknowledge the author of the original text, Patsy Fulton-Calkins, whose 12th edition of *The Administrative Professional: Technology and Procedures* was the basis for the first Canadian edition of *Office Procedures for the Administrative Professional*. I felt very fortunate indeed to be asked to adapt this text for the Canadian market and pleased at the increasing adoption of it by postsecondary institutions across Canada. It has always been one of my favourite courses. I have taught it often and believe it is a very important component of any administrative professional program. I was excited then, as I am now, to be able to work on bringing it to you and to be able to contribute value-added features such as my Business Document Formatting Guide, In-Basket: An Office Simulation, and the Records Management Simulation.

Thanks also to the talented and dedicated staff at Nelson Education: Maya Castle, publisher, who got the ball rolling on this third edition before commencing maternity leave; and Amie Plourde, publisher, who picked up the project and who, along with Courtney Thorne, content development manager, encouraged and supported me along the way, especially when I thought I just couldn't do "IT." I am indebted to them both for their generosity in lending me a helping hand when I was overcommitted and feeling overwhelmed, for their quick responses when I had a question, and for gently keeping me on track throughout the whole process. Thanks also to Mariko Obokata, a very skilled copy editor, for working her magic with the content, improving both readability and understanding; she has made this edition a better product. Also, thanks to Lynn McLeod and Jessica Freedman for researching appropriate images to enhance the content and for obtaining permission to use them; to Imoinda Romain and to Sangeetha

Vijay and Ezhilsolai Periasamy for their attention to detail in the content production phase; and to Alexis Hood and her marketing team for bringing the final product to you.

I am especially thankful to the following working administrative professionals

Karen Esplen, B.Comm, CMA, CGA, CPA

Roxanne Florentine, Legal Administrative Assistant, Talisman Energy Inc.

Sarah Steinke, BA, CHRP, Human Resources Leader, Garibaldi Glass

Kate Weiss, (Adv. Dipl. Bus.), Company Secretary, Bedakaro Consulting Ltd.

for their time, their detailed review, and their suggestions and input into various chapters. It is their contributions to this textbook that helps to ensure it is both current and real.

Thanks also go to the following reviewers and users who provided valuable feedback through their in-depth and thoughtful comments and suggestions, ensuring this third Canadian edition is relevant, instructive, and up to date:

Nancy Breen, Nova Scotia Community College

Patricia Gaudreault, Camosun College

Kellie Hayward, Sheridan Institute of Technology and Advanced Learning

Julie Ivanchenko, Mohawk College

Cynthia MacDermid, Nova Scotia Community College

Sean McCorkell, Red River College

Margaret VanBlarcom, Nova Scotia Community College

Benita Worley, Sprott Shaw College

The Authors

Dr. Patsy J. Fulton-Calkins' experience in the field is extensive. Her past experience in the workplace includes working as an administrative professional for large corporations for six years. Early in her career, she completed the CPS certification. Her teaching experience includes over 13 years at the university, community college, and high-school levels. In addition to her teaching experience, she has worked as an administrator in the following positions:

- Chancellor of Oakland Community College (the chief executive officer), Oakland County, Michigan
- President of Brookhaven College, Dallas, Texas
- Vice-President of Instruction at El Centro College and Cedar Valley College, Dallas, Texas
- Division Chairperson of Business and Social Science, Cedar Valley College, Dallas, Texas

Her present position includes working with Tom Monaghan Associates, Inc., as a senior consultant in institutional advancement work with clients across the United States. Additionally, she is an adjunct professor at the university level.

Her educational credentials include a B.B.A., an M.B.Ed., and a Ph.D. Honors. She has also received the following recognitions: Outstanding Alumnus, University of North Texas; Transformational Leader in Community Colleges; Who's Who in America, Outstanding Woman in Management; Paul Harris Fellow of Rotary International; Beta Gamma Sigma, National Honorary Business Fraternity; and Piper Professor.

Diane Blaney began her career as an administrative assistant in the Music Department of the Edmonton Public School Board. From there she travelled north to Inuvik, east to Ottawa, and south to Bermuda before finally heading west and settling in Vancouver, British Columbia. In every location, her administrative skills ensured that she would find challenging and rewarding employment opportunities.

After working for ten years as an administrative professional, she completed the CPS certification and, soon after, began teaching at Capilano College (now Capilano University) in North Vancouver. She has taught a variety of technology courses in the Applied Business Technology department as well as the Administrative Procedures course.

Additionally, she has been coordinator of the Legal Secretarial and the Applied Business Technology Online programs at Capilano College, department chair for Applied Business Technology, and chair of various college committees. She has served as chair of the provincial Business Educators Coordinating Committee and as president of the Capilano College Faculty Association, and represented faculty for nine years as a governor on the college board. She is especially proud of her work on the steering committee for the provincial Applied Business Technology collaborative online programs. Her work in the community includes a term as president of an internationally recognized private recreational facility, and a year working as a volunteer member of the Board with the 55+ Games in North Vancouver.

Diane obtained her M.Ed. in administrative leadership from Simon Fraser University in Vancouver, British Columbia, and her instructor's diploma from the University of British Columbia.

The Workplace and You

In this first part of the text, you are introduced to the challenging world of office administration and the use of telecommunications equipment and services that are an integral component of most business transactions. You will learn about different organizational structures and the management of business and organizations, and identify what makes an organization ethical. The qualities associated with being a professional, such as maintaining a professional image through appearance, good communication and teamwork skills, and the employability skills that will be expected of you as a new employee, along with your responsibility to your employer—and theirs to you—are presented. Working ethically as an administrative professional and some steps to take in making ethical choices are outlined. You will discover methods for managing your workload, strategies for prioritizing and adjusting priorities as needed, and different approaches to managing relationships, handling stress, and maintaining a healthy work/life balance. The concept of ergonomics is introduced and guidelines are provided to help you create a safe and healthy physical workspace that reduces the risk of repetitive stress injury. Also provided are several tips on keeping a neat, well-organized, and professional-looking work area so that you can work efficiently. You are entering a diverse workforce and this first part of the text will help ensure your entry into the workplace is a positive one.

not only understand but also effectively handle cultural differences in the workforce.

Telework/Remote Employment and the Virtual Assistant

Today, many workers have traded in the traditional work environment for **telework**—work that can be performed at any place and at any time using technology. *Teleworking* is the term that broadly describes a working arrangement using telecommunications to work from a home office, a client's office, or some other location. *Teleworkers* refers to those individuals who are employed full- or part-time by an organization and work from home or some other mobile type of work environment for part or all of the workweek.[3]

Also, **remote employment** (any working arrangement in which the worker performs a significant portion of work at some fixed location other than the traditional workplace) and the **virtual office** (the operational domain of any organization that includes remote workers) are terms used in describing the concept of work done through technology in which an individual is physically present in one location and virtually present in another. Instant messaging, virtual meetings, and email have created a niche for freelance administrative

assistants, also called **virtual assistants**. These self-employed administrative assistants work from a home office to provide off-site administrative and/or personal assistance to clients. This arrangement is popular with individuals and small start-up companies that may not require the services of a full-time administrative assistant. You can find out more about this arrangement in Chapter 16.

Quality Focus

Whether an organization is national or international, its effectiveness and long life depends on the production of a quality product or service. Based on the concepts of Dr. W. Edwards Deming, an American statistician who developed the quality concept, workforce teams have become an important part of producing quality work. Deming first introduced his ideas to businesses in the United States but failed to receive support. In the 1950s, he took his ideas to Japan. Significant increases in productivity resulted, and Japan began to surpass the United States and Canada in certain areas of production, such as technology and cars. As a result, North American businesses began to apply Deming's principles, which stressed the principle of continued improvement through **total quality management (TQM)**. This approach is also referred to as **continuous quality improvement (CQI)**. Deming's main principles are briefly listed in Figure 1-1.

Telework can be performed from virtually anywhere at any time using technology.

© Paul Vasarhelyi/Shutterstock

FIGURE 1-1
Deming's Total Quality Management Philosophy

1. Create constancy of purpose for improving products and services.
2. Adopt the new philosophy.
3. Cease dependence on inspection to achieve quality.
4. End the practice of awarding business on price alone; instead, minimize total costs by working with a single supplier.
5. Improve constantly and forever every process for planning, production, and service.
6. Institute training on the job.
7. Adopt and institute leadership.
8. Drive out fear.
9. Break down barriers between staff areas.
10. Eliminate slogans, exhortations, and targets for the workforce.
11. Eliminate numerical quotas for the workforce and numerical goals for management.
12. Remove barriers that rob people of pride in their work and eliminate the annual rating or merit system.
13. Institute a vigorous program of education and self-improvement for everyone.
14. Put everyone in the company to work to accomplish the transformation.

Source: Used with permission of Business Excellence E-Zine, http://www.bexcellence.org/deming-total-quality-management-philosophy.html, accessed February 2011.

TQM affects the administrative professional in several ways. You may find that you are

- More involved in decisions that affect the direction of the organization
- Part of a workforce team (perhaps even leading a team) that is responsible for improving a service or product
- Expected to be a productive member of a team, making unique contributions that assist the company in improving the quality of its goods and services
- More involved in helping to solve the problems of the organization

Downsizing and Outsourcing

Two cost-cutting measures used extensively by large corporations are reducing the number of full-time employees in an organization (downsizing) and contracting with an outside company or a consultant to assume responsibility for a project or some part of an organization's business (outsourcing). By reducing overhead costs (salary and benefit costs), large businesses are able to streamline their procedures to create an organizational structure that can be more easily managed.

For example, an outside payment-processing firm might be contracted to perform the payroll operations of a company, which can save the organization the money that would have been spent in salaries and other benefits such as health insurance and retirement options.

Temporary agencies may be contracted to provide the services of accounting assistants, administrative assistants, and human resources assistants, when and as needed by an organization.

Skills @ Work

Leadership Skills

Set a goal to become an expert in the most common software your group uses (e.g., word processing, spreadsheet, presentation, or email/calendar) so you can be a leader supporting people by answering their questions, solving problems, and making their documents look professional.

When the group upgrades software or acquires a new program, become an expert user. Be proactive in learning to use new software and office equipment. Because of your central role, people will ask you for help and expect you to be able to provide it.

The Workweek

The traditional 9-to-5 workday and five-day workweek have both undergone some changes. Hours in the workday may be flexible, and the workweek may be compressed, or may involve job sharing with another individual.

With a compressed workweek, employees work the usual number of hours (35 to 40); however, the hours are compressed into four days (three nine-hour days and one eight-hour day).

Flextime enables an employee to work the full quota of time but at periods mutually determined by the company and the individual. Flextime helps to reduce traffic congestion at the traditional peak hours and allows employees to have some flexibility in their schedules. A job sharing arrangement allows two part-time employees to perform one job that otherwise would be held by one full-time employee.

Workplace Organization

Learning about the culture, structure, and management of the organization you work for will help you perform your job better. It will help you understand

- Your position in the organization; your position relative to others
- Acceptable behaviours and actions
- How the organization is run; why things are done the way they are
- What to expect

Office Culture and Language

Every organization has its own culture, which reflects the key values, beliefs, and attitudes that drive the organization and define its style of doing business. The culture may be formal and strict or casual and laid-back. Most cultures are somewhere in between. You will absorb this atmosphere as you work, but by paying careful attention, you can learn about it more quickly and more quickly fit in.

Culture is expressed in symbols such as the dress code and unwritten rules that may not be discussed but that show up in employees' attitudes. WestJet Airlines, for example, is known for having a relaxed, informal culture. Employees have an upbeat attitude and are dedicated to helping each other and to providing excellent customer service.

You will also find that every office has its own terminology. If you are working in a law or medical office, you will need to learn legal or medical terms. The same is true of working for an architect, an engineer, or a performing artist. Make it your goal to acquire and maintain a good working knowledge of the field.

Business Organizations

The businesses you work for as an administrative professional may be organized in different ways. The three basic forms are a sole proprietorship, a partnership, and a corporation.

- A sole proprietorship is owned and controlled by an individual. The owner receives all the profits and is responsible for all the debts.
- A partnership is an association of two or more people as co-owners of a business. Business decisions, profits, and losses are shared among the partners according to the terms of the partnership agreement.

- **Corporations** are legal entities formed by following a formal process of incorporation established by federal or provincial statutes and associated regulations. Corporations may be publicly or privately owned. If public, they are owned by investors called **shareholders** (or **stockholders**) who have purchased stock that represents a portion or share of the company.

The investment of shareholders may be affected by the actions, decisions, policies, or practices of the business. For example, if the business is mismanaged or has financial problems, the stock price may decrease, and the shareholder may lose money on the investment.

Formal Organizational Structures

Large companies usually are under the control of a board of directors that is charged with looking after the interests of shareholders. Boards of directors guide the management of the organization by establishing policies and setting goals that are implemented by the chief executive officer (**CEO**) of the corporation. The directors typically meet monthly or every two or three months. Directors may not put themselves in a position in which their private interests and duties conflict with the duties they owe the company. When these interests and duties differ, a director is said to have a **conflict of interest**.

In addition to the CEO, a company may have a **CFO** (chief financial officer), **COO** (chief operating officer), and **CIO** (chief information officer). These top executives may have presidents and vice presidents reporting to them. In large organizations, managers at lower levels, such as the human resources director and the director of engineering, are responsible for day-to-day operations and for carrying out upper management's strategies and decisions and achieving the goals that have been set for the organization.

Management Responsibilities

Every organization has leaders and managers. The top executives described above are the company's key leaders, who set the direction for the organization.

Management is considered a subset of leadership, and the responsibilities associated with these two roles overlap. Although the textbook covers the characteristics of effective leaders separately from the responsibilities of effective managers, most effective managers are also effective leaders. You will learn more about effective leadership in Chapter 17. See Figure 1-2 for an example of management responsibilities depicted on an organizational chart.

FIGURE 1-2
Organizational Chart of CanAsian Airlines

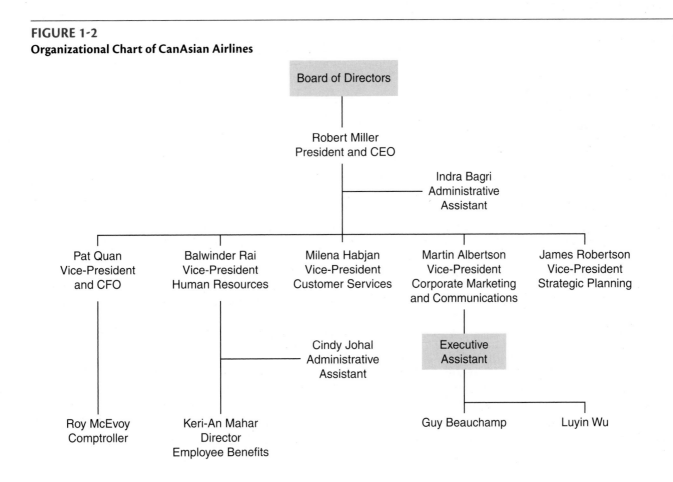

The Administrative Professional's Responsibilities

With the availability of technology and the emphasis on greater efficiency and productivity through **flattened organizational structures** (fewer management levels than the traditional structures of the past) and teams, administrative professionals of today and tomorrow will find that their role is continually shifting. This shifting role generally leads to greater responsibility.

Administrative assistants support organizations in many ways. Figure 1-3 lists some of their most common responsibilities.

Job responsibilities of the administrative professional have increased in complexity and accountability and will vary depending on educational level, work experience, and even employee initiative. Many executives now answer their own voice mail and email, key in certain correspondence directly on the computer, and handle much of their own scheduling using electronic calendars. This change frees the administrative professional to take on more responsibility and become a valued member of the office team.

For years, the administrative professional's title was confined to *secretary, receptionist,* and such specialized titles as *legal secretary* and *medical secretary.* Although these titles are still used to a limited extent, today's emerging titles reflect the shifting role of the administrative professional: *administrative assistant, executive assistant, marketing assistant, payroll assistant, human resources assistant,* and *office manager.*

Although job roles and responsibilities differ among the various positions, certain skills and knowledge sets are essential in all administrative professional roles; these will be emphasized throughout this course. The terms **administrative professional** and **administrative assistant** will be used consistently throughout the text to denote this workplace support person.

The administrative professional today may have the responsibility of training colleagues and/or managers in new technologies.

FIGURE 1-3
Typical Job Tasks and Responsibilities of an Administrative Professional

- Schedule appointments, and meet and greet visitors and clients
- Answer, screen, and transfer incoming phone calls
- Compose and key written responses to routine inquiries
- Prepare and modify documents (correspondence, reports, drafts, memos, and emails)
- Process (open, sort, and distribute) incoming mail
- Process (fold, seal, and stamp) outgoing mail
- Manage social media and update website information
- Maintain electronic and physical filing systems and retrieve documents and/or data as requested
- Schedule and coordinate meetings, appointments, and travel arrangements for managers or supervisors
- Prepare agendas for meetings, and record, compile, transcribe, and distribute minutes of meetings
- Resolve administrative problems and respond to inquiries

- Perform general support duties, including photocopying, faxing, and mailing
- Maintain office supply inventories
- Recommend equipment and software purchases
- Coordinate maintenance of office equipment
- Perform calculations related to expense reports, budgets, invoices, purchase orders, and petty cash
- Work with outsourcing companies
- Interview prospective office support personnel and recommend the employment of suitable candidates
- Train and supervise office support personnel
- Conduct research as directed by the supervisor; prepare accompanying presentation visuals
- Administer computer networks and provide computer and software training
- Solve day-to-day problems within the role of the administrative professional

---

4. *Empathy* is the ability to understand how others are feeling and to use this knowledge to respond appropriately.

5. *Motivation* is an incentive to act—a move to action. This incentive can be either an intrinsic motivation (internal) or an extrinsic motivation (external). The emotionally intelligent person is generally intrinsically motivated—seeking ways to improve, to learn, and to grow rather than extrinsically motivated by external recognition or monetary rewards.

Integrity and Honesty

Integrity is defined as "the adherence to a code of behaviour." In the workplace environment, the code of behaviour means in part that you must be honest. It means you do not take equipment or supplies that belong to the company for your personal use. It means you spend your time on the job performing your job duties—not making and receiving personal phone calls or writing personal emails. It means you uphold high standards of ethical behaviour. You do not engage in activities in which your morals or values may be questioned. The focus of Chapter 3 is on the ethical organization and the ethical employee.

Initiative

Initiative is defined as "the ability to begin and follow through on a plan or task." Initiative is taking the tasks you are given and completing them in an appropriate manner. It means having the ability to set appropriate work goals for yourself. The most highly valued administrative professional has the ability to analyze a task, establish priorities, and see the work through to completion. The professional who takes the initiative to make suggestions to the employer about needed changes or revisions and is truly worth his or her weight in gold.

Flexibility and Adaptability

Earlier in this chapter, you learned about the importance of being able to work with a diverse workforce. You also learned that globalization, downsizing, outsourcing, and telework can and often do make our work environment very different from workplaces of the past. All these continuing changes demand flexibility (being responsive to change) and adaptability (capable of making adjustments).

What Is a Professional?

A professional looks, speaks, writes, and behaves in a manner that reflects well on both the employer and the employee. A professional sets an example for others through a strong work ethic, positive attitude, and dedication to continuing improvement.

Strong Work Ethic

One of the most valued traits in an administrative assistant is a strong work ethic. A person with a strong work ethic does not need to be externally motivated. Arriving at work on time and meeting deadlines are two of the basic values behind a strong work ethic. Your employer should be able to rely on you to take the initiative to begin and complete projects with little supervision. Employers value administrative professionals who stick with a project until it is done and done well. Always give your employer your best effort, no matter what may be going on in your personal life.

A strong work ethic does not mean that you avoid social interaction in the workplace, but that you keep it under control. Your relationships with co-workers are essential to your success, so you want to be friendly and sociable without letting such interactions keep you from your work.

Positive Attitude

Human resources experts know that a worker's attitude is as important as skills for success on the job. If you come to work in the wrong frame of mind, your negative attitude can affect your performance all day. It can also influence those around you. Others want to be around you when you have a positive attitude. They are more likely to cooperate with a positive co-worker than with one who brings a negative attitude to work. Think about jobs you have had or group class projects on which you have worked. You probably preferred working with others who were enthusiastic and positive about the task.

Everyone has occasional complaints about work or co-workers, but it is important not to let any resentments you have affect your work. Such behaviour only perpetuates problems. It can also make matters worse. No one wants to listen to the worker who seems to be always complaining about problems instead of trying to fix them. You may encounter problems you cannot solve, but they should not affect your overall attitude and performance.

Find ways to accept situations you cannot change. Your workplace may not be perfect, but you can overcome many problems by taking pride in yourself, your work, and your organization, doing everything in your power to make it better. Be part of the solution, not part of the problem.

Self-Confidence

Having self-confidence means you believe in yourself and your abilities. Most of us become self-confident over time through learning, growing, and refining new skills. When you are constantly striving to improve, you will have small successes that will build your self-confidence. Give yourself credit when you do something well. Everyone makes mistakes and everyone has weaknesses. Both are part of the learning process. Forgive yourself when you make mistakes.

When you do not understand something, it is important to ask questions rather than to hide your confusion. When you are open to learning new information, new procedures, and new skills, you will not need to impress others with how much you already know. You can share your knowledge with others without feeling that you need to impress them by knowing everything. No matter how long you have been on the job, the people and situations around you can always teach you something that will make you a better worker.

Your Professional Image

Presenting a professional appearance to your co-workers and outsiders is essential to your success. Your appearance, speech, writing, and conduct all have an impact on how professional you appear.

Appearance

You should arrive at work every day looking clean, tidy, and well-groomed. Being *well-groomed* generally means the following:

- Your hair is clean, trimmed, and combed. Avoid hair that is overdone—such as excessive use of colour or product.
- Your fingernails are neat, clean, and trimmed.
- Your teeth are brushed and breath is fresh. Use mouthwash or a breath mint if needed.
- You are freshly bathed and use deodorant.
- You use scented products sparingly or not at all.
- If you are a woman, you use makeup sparingly.
- If you are a man, you are either clean-shaven or your moustache or beard is neatly trimmed.

It may not seem fair, but people often judge others by how they look. We form first impressions during the first few seconds of meeting someone. Because not much can be said in this short time, this early judgment is based mostly on appearance. Whether or not they realize it, people may think that the quality of a person's work will match the quality of the person's appearance. Your appearance may be seen as reflecting your attention to detail, your level of motivation, and your sense of commitment and professionalism. The clothes you wear may also shape your own attitude and confidence level. For example, when you dress more casually, you may also tend to behave more casually.

You and your clothing should always be neat, tidy, and inconspicuous. Stick to comfortable, practical, simple, and professional shoes and attire. Your shoes should be shined, and any jewellery and other accessories should not be too large or too flashy. If you have tattoos or other body art, wear clothing that conceals it. If you have lip, brow, or nasal piercings for facial jewellery, leave the jewellery at home. You have a right to express your own individuality, but not in this way on the job.

The administrative professional dresses in appropriate business attire and is always well groomed.

You should never wear tight or revealing clothes to work, no matter how casual the dress code may be. If your workplace has no written code, observe how others dress in the workplace, and if you are still in doubt, ask.

Typically, inappropriate attire includes the following:
- T-shirts
- Tank tops, halter tops, or midriff tops
- Tops with bare shoulders or revealing necklines
- Shirts or blouses with words on them
- Sweatshirts and sweatpants

A professional image is more than dressing appropriately, however. A positive personal appearance without the necessary skills and qualities is meaningless. If the administrative professional expects to succeed, he or she must combine an appropriate personal appearance with the necessary skills and qualities presented in this chapter. A professional image is a combination of all of these areas.

Understanding Your Organization

The most valuable administrative professionals know a great deal about the company or organization they work for and the department or group they support; they begin to accumulate this knowledge even before they are hired. A variety of sources are available for acquiring this knowledge and some basic information about the industry in general: company publications (brochures and annual reports), the company website, the business section of local newspapers, and articles in financial publications. Chapter 15 describes information you should gather about a company or organization before applying for a job. Once hired, observe your supervisor and co-workers; they are valuable resources for learning about the culture and structure of your organization and about the group or department you support and your role in the group.

Professional Growth

With the workplace constantly changing, you must be willing to continue to learn and to commit to continual professional growth by
- Attending classes at a college or university (either on-site or online)
- Attending seminars and workshops provided by your company, outside firms, or professional organizations
- Finding a mentor
- Reading business and/or professional periodicals
- Participating in professional organizations
- Volunteering your time and expertise to organizations in your community

Professional Organizations and Certifications

Participating in a professional organization can enhance your career by giving you opportunities to network; you can learn valuable information from interacting with colleagues in your field. Local chapter meetings, national conferences, online forums, and other venues offer opportunities for professional growth. Through organizations such as the *International Association of Administrative Professionals (IAAP), the Association of Administrative Assistants, or ARMA International, administrative professionals can attain certification attesting to their skills and knowledge in given areas.* The largest and best-known association for office and administrative professionals, *IAAP,* may have a local chapter in your area. This international organization offers opportunities to become accredited as a Certified Administrative Professional (CAP). Figure 1-5 provides details on both the CAP certification process and the Organizational Management (OM) optional additional specialty certification.

ARMA International is an association for information management professionals. This association sponsors the Certified Records Manager (CRM) designation, a certification designed for experienced professionals with management-level responsibilities.

The *Association of Administrative Assistants* is a Canadian association that offers certification as a Qualified Administrative Assistant (QAA) through programs offered at several post-secondary institutions across Canada.

Professional organizations often provide access to websites, articles, newsletters, and seminars that can help you improve your skills. Links to several administrative and other industry related associations can be found on the MindTap site that accompanies this textbook.

FIGURE 1-5
IAAP Certification: Certified Administrative Professional (CAP) and Organizational Management (OM)

WHY CERTIFICATION?
- *Improve professional qualifications*
- *Build invaluable personal and professional confidence*
- *Open new doors in the job market*
- *Advance your career to the next level*
- *Allow you to become the "go-to" resource in your office*
- *Give you the potential to earn a higher salary or receive a promotion or bonus*

WHO IS ELIGIBLE?
Before applying for the CAP exam, you must have administrative experience that has been earned within the past 10 years. Of that, and within the past five years, you must have 12 months of continuous experience with the same employer.

Education	Experience Required
No college degree	4 years
Associate degree	3 years
Bachelor's degree or higher	2 years

WHEN AND WHERE IS THE EXAM GIVEN?
The CAP and OM are both single 3.5-hour computer-based examinations administered each March and August through authorized testing centres around the world.

WHAT IS ON THE EXAM?
The CAP exam includes 300 questions that focus on eight categories:
- Communication
- Organization and Planning
- Information Distribution
- Records Management
- Physical and Information Resources
- Document Production
- Financial Functions
- Human Resources

The OM exam includes 175 questions that focus on four categories:
- Organizational Planning
- Advanced Communication
- Advanced Administration
- Team Skills

Source: International Association of Administrative Professionals site, Columbus, OH, http://www.iaap-hq.org/certification. Accessed June 10, 2010.

Looking Forward

The procedures you learn and the skills you acquire in this course and other courses in your program of studies can form the basis of a future transition to working in other specialized fields. You can build on these core competencies through on-the-job experiences and by participating in online or continuing education studies. Office and administrative professionals often pursue a field of specialization after completion of their initial certification, for example, to become a Medical Office Assistant, Executive Office Manager, or Legal Secretary/Legal Administrative Assistant.

Legal Secretary/Legal Administrative Assistant

Working in the legal field, whether in a law office or the legal department of a large corporation, can be both fascinating and challenging. Legal secretaries/legal administrative assistants provide valuable administrative support to ensure that law firms function efficiently. Responsible for liaising with clients, they schedule appointments and respond to questions from clients, perform conflict searches, diarize or record court dates, transcribe notes from dictation, and prepare legal and court documents. Legal secretaries/legal administrative assistants are in high demand, which means they often command the highest salaries of all administrative professionals. Some will build on their knowledge and experience by continuing their studies to eventually become a paralegal.

Medical Office Assistants

Knowledgeable about medical terminology and doctors' practices, medical office assistants (MOAs) perform administrative, clerical, and in some cases clinical duties in a doctor's office, clinic, or other medical setting. Responsible for liaising with patients, they schedule appointments, gather and verify patient information, collect specimens, and may also take patients' vital signs. MOAs also file charts, keep patient records up-to-date, use specialized billing programs to invoice local government health services, and, depending on the environment, may also perform medical transcription. Because of our aging population, this specialized field is expected to continue to grow and expand.

Executive Assistant/Executive Secretary

Responsible for carrying out the administrative duties of executive management, executive assistants may support the work of directors, executives, or many managers all at once. They may be responsible for coordinating meeting plans from start to finish, including preparing agendas and taking minutes, organizing and coordinating the creation and publishing of correspondence; preparing departmental budgets, and liaising between executives, management, and clients. The duties of the executive secretary may include planning and organizing events, from a small department lunch up to a large holiday party or even an extensive four-day conference, which requires competency in event planning. Computer proficiency at the advanced level will provide executive assistants with the superior knowledge required for such positions as office manager or even executive assistant to the company president or CEO.

For administrative professionals who have already acquired competencies in keyboarding, numeracy, communications, computer applications, and customer service, the specialized courses outlined here will provide the core competencies to work professionally in these specialized fields. For the core competencies for legal, medical, and executive assistants, see Figure 1-6.

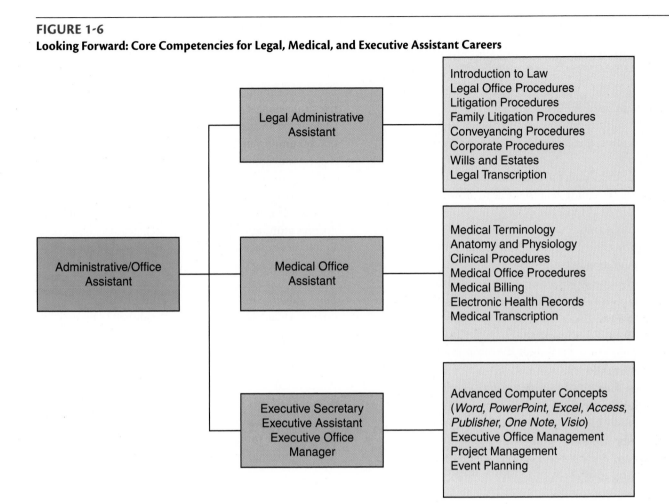

Chapter Summary

The summary will help you remember the important points covered in this chapter.

- Working in today's diverse workplace requires that you are aware of and sensitive to the various differences in culture, gender, age, and backgrounds of the people around you and that you respect their different perspectives.
- Teamwork, based on the quality concept developed by W. Edwards Deming, will continue to grow; the ability to work effectively as part of a team is important for administrative assistants.
- Downsizing and outsourcing will continue to be used to cut organizational costs.
- Opportunities for telework—becoming a virtual assistant—may be a choice for some administrative professionals.
- Flexible working arrangements that vary from the traditional 9-to-5 workday include the compressed workweek, flextime, and job sharing.
- Businesses take one of three basic forms: a sole proprietorship, a partnership, or a corporation.
- Boards of directors are responsible for establishing policies and setting goals that guide the management of the organization; top executives and managers are responsible for implementing those policies and working to achieve those goals.
- Largely as a result of changing technology, administrative professionals are assuming more responsibility and performing a wide and expanding range of tasks to keep offices running efficiently and smoothly.
- A successful administrative professional works with integrity, respects confidentiality, displays initiative, is honest, dependable, flexible, adaptable, and open to change. She or he is self-confident and possesses a strong work ethic, a positive attitude, and emotional intelligence.
- Employers expect administrative assistants to apply critical-thinking skills when solving problems and making decisions.
- *Employability Skills 2000+* identifies the fundamental, interpersonal, and teamwork skills required to be successful as an administrative professional.
- To be seen as professional, you must be appropriately dressed and well-groomed every day.
- Professional growth can occur through attending classes or seminars/workshops, reading business periodicals, and participating in professional organizations.
- Careers of the future will be built on a commitment to lifelong learning.

Key Terms

knowledge age p. 5
multicultural p. 5
stereotype p. 6
telework p. 7
remote employment p. 7
virtual office p. 7
virtual assistants p. 7
total quality management (TQM) or continuous quality improvement (CQI) p. 7
downsizing p. 8
outsourcing p. 8
compressed workweek p. 8
flextime p. 8
job sharing p. 8
sole proprietorship p. 8
partnership p. 8
corporations p. 9
shareholders (stockholders) p. 9
CEO p. 9

conflict of interest p. 9
CFO p. 9
COO p. 9
CIO p. 9
flattened organizational structures p. 10
administrative professional p. 10
administrative assistant p. 10
Employability Skills 2000+ p. 11
critical thinking p. 12
leadership skills p. 13
dependability p. 14
confidentiality p. 14
emotional intelligence p. 14
intrinsic motivation p. 15
extrinsic motivation p. 15
integrity p. 15
initiative p. 15
professional p. 15
work ethic p. 15

Responses to Self-Check

The most appropriate answers are as follows:

1. Yes
2. Yes
3. No
4. Yes
5. No

6. Yes
7. No
8. No
9. Yes
10. No

Discussion Items

These discussion items provide an opportunity to test your understanding of the chapter through written responses and/or discussion with your classmates and your instructor.

1. Explain how the workforce and workplace are changing. What do these changes suggest for you as a future employee?
2. How is our current work environment changing? How is the administrative professional's role changing?
3. Identify the three basic types of business organizations. Brainstorm what you consider to be the advantages and disadvantages working in each of these types of environments.
4. Why are interpersonal and communication skills especially important for someone in an administrative assistant role?
5. Describe the qualities that make a worker a professional.
6. Explain why critical-thinking, decision-making, and problem-solving skills are essential to an administrative assistant.
7. Describe a professional appearance, and give examples of clothing or grooming that are inappropriate in the workplace.

Critical-Thinking Activity

CanAsian Airlines has introduced total quality management (TQM) in an effort to improve quality and productivity. You were asked to be part of a team that looks at the improvement of internal communication, and you took the assignment seriously. Before the first meeting, you had identified several communication problems that seem to be ongoing in the organization. At the meeting, you raised several issues: failure to respond promptly to email, failure to respond to voice mail, and airline ticket customers who have long waits when attempting to buy tickets by phone. Two of the individuals who work in your department became upset. They assumed that your statements referred to situations you had encountered with them. They exploded in the meeting, making these comments:

I can't answer the email you send me within the hour. Get off my back.

The next time you have a complaint about me, talk with me personally.

The manager in charge of the airline ticket sales department asked exactly what you meant by customers having "long waits" when attempting to buy tickets. He did not seem upset but was merely asking for clarification of your comment.

You responded to the two individuals in your department by stating that you were not talking about individual cases; you were attempting to identify problems that needed to be addressed so that customers can be better served. You answered the manager's question with, "I don't know the exact length of time; I have just heard complaints." Since the meeting did not get off to a good start, you feel responsible. You want to be a contributor to the process. What should you do? Think through the following items and prepare your responses.

- What is the problem?
- Do the upset employees have cause to be concerned about your behaviour?
- Should you talk to these employees before the next meeting? If so, what should you say?
- Did you have enough information about the customer ticket issue to mention it at the meeting? How should you handle this type of issue in the future?
- How should you identify problems/issues that are negatively affecting office communication?
- How can you present problems/issues at the next meeting without causing the volatility you experienced at the last meeting?

Remember, your task is to critically analyze the situation given here. Before you attempt to answer the questions, review the section Think and Solve Problems, starting on page 11.

Building Workplace Skills

The Company

While completing projects throughout this course, you will be working for CanAsian Airlines, 2300–888 3rd Street SW, Calgary, AB T2P 4C4. CanAsian was formed as the result of a merger in March 2015 between CanAir, founded in 2000 in Calgary, Alberta, with only 30 employees, and China Airlines, founded in 2005 in Beijing, China, with 40 employees. Figure 1-2, earlier in the chapter, shows the organizational chart of CanAsian Airlines. Both airlines had grown, and after the merger, CanAsian Airlines now employs more than 39 000 people. The Canadian head office is located in Calgary at the address given above. The China head office is in Beijing.

Net earnings have experienced a slight drop from the combined net earnings of the two companies before the merger. The company is currently developing strategies to increase its overall market share by decreasing labour costs and providing certain incentives. It is looking at adding a frequent flyer program for the China operation and improved in-flight customer service for the total company.

Your Role

Your job title is executive assistant. You report directly to Martin Albertson, vice-president of corporate marketing and communications in Calgary. Since the merger, executives in both companies have been discussing how they might assume more social responsibility in the head office cities. They intend to take an active role in the educational, environmental, and social concerns of the community, in both Canada and China. Before the merger, each community saw the airline as a good corporate citizen, and the executives want to ensure things stay that way. Although their profitability picture has been good since the merger, there has been a slight downturn. As a result, the Calgary head office has laid off 50 employees in the corporate office. The result has been a lowering of staff morale; however, steps have been taken to make the employees feel more a part of the decision making through TQM.

Your duties are extremely varied. They include assisting Martin Albertson to set up meetings with government and educational leaders within the local communities to determine issues of common concern. At one point, you travelled to China with your employer and two other support staff to help set up a community conference. This trip was the only time you have travelled outside the company; however, you do communicate frequently with staff at the China office through fax, email, and computer conferencing. Your other duties include the following:

- Researching and preparing all types of correspondence
- Participating in TQM teams
- Organizing your employer's schedule
- Scheduling meetings
- Making travel arrangements
- Handling the mail
- Filing correspondence
- Supervising two assistants

You have two assistants who report to you—Guy Beauchamp (who has been working for CanAsian Airlines for just over a year) and Luyin Wu (who has been working for CanAsian Airlines for six months).

Project 1-1 (Learning Outcome 1)

Online Project

Browse the Web for the following information:

- Articles on the changing office; at the IAAP website (www.iaap-hq.org), check the magazine *OfficePro*.
- Diversity statistics in your province, as reported in the most recent Statistics Canada documentation (www.statcan.ca). Prepare a short summary of the articles, giving the Web addresses; submit your summaries to your instructor.
- Information on standard legal forms that might be used when an organization requires employees to sign a confidentiality agreement.

Project 1-2 (Learning Outcomes 1 and 3)

Collaborative Project

In teams of two or three, interview two administrative professionals. You do not need to interview these people in person; you may choose to do it by email. Ask the following questions:

- What are your roles and responsibilities?
- What skills and qualities do you need to be successful?
- What types of technology changes have occurred in your organization in the past five years? Two years?
- Describe the diversity of personnel within your organization. Have there been any issues in dealing with this diversity? If so, what were those issues and how were they handled?

Report your findings verbally to the class.

Project 1-3 (Learning Outcome 2)

Business Organization

Select a business to research. The business can be one with which you have some familiarity, such as a local company, or a large, nationally known company. If possible, talk to employees, read newspaper or magazine articles, or search the Internet to find information about the company. Create a short report that gives the following information:

Time Wasters	Example	Result
Ineffective Communication	You misunderstood or did not clarify your supervisor's instructions about a letter to a client.	You required additional time to rewrite the letter; the client is unhappy and an account could have been lost.
Poor Telephone Techniques	You were unprepared when taking a message.	Your supervisor will not know what action to take in response to the message or, worse yet, will call the wrong person or the wrong number and will then need you to resolve the issue.
	You were unprepared when placing an outgoing call—you do not have the necessary details at hand.	You waste not only your time but that of the person called because you must locate the necessary information and replace the call.
	You take or place personal calls during work hours.	You do not demonstrate your professionalism.
	Using the telephone when email or an instant message would be a better choice.	You do not demonstrate your ability to choose an appropriate communication medium.
Inadequate Planning	On Friday afternoon, your supervisor gives you what appears to be a brief report with a Monday afternoon deadline. You do not immediately review the project; by the time you get started early Monday afternoon, you quickly realize the job involves more than you had anticipated.	You are embarrassed, and your supervisor is disappointed when you must advise her that you are unable to meet the deadline. This oversight has a domino effect, first affecting your supervisor's plans, which then leads to her disappointing her supervisor or a client.
Interruptions	A client who is well known to you arrives at the office a few minutes early for an appointment and begins to chat about a recent function you both attended; or, a co-worker stops by your workspace to discuss a work-related issue but once his concerns are addressed, he remains and begins to chat about his weekend mountain biking trip.	In both cases, the task you were working on has been interrupted, and you may need to take some additional time to refocus.
Disorganization	Your desk has a pile of folders on it with their contents spilling out; material for half-finished projects are scattered across the top of your desk; or a stack of documents to file are piled on top of the filing cabinet.	You are unable to locate required information in a timely manner. Deadlines are not met, and decision-making is hampered and/or delayed.
Procrastination	You are assigned a large project that seems overwhelming. Because you worry about the size of it, you postpone getting started.	Leaving your work to the last minute creates stress for everyone involved.

Step Two—analyze your time log to discover ways in which you can improve the management of your time. Each day ask yourself these questions.

- What was the most productive period of the day? Why?
- What was the least productive period of the day? Why?
- Who or what accounted for interruptions?
- Were these interruptions expected? Did they occur at an expected (daily or weekly) time? An example of an expected weekly interruption is the need to make copies of a report for a weekly meeting.
- Can the interruptions be minimized or eliminated?
- What activities needed more time?
- On what activities could I spend less time and still get the desired results?

Step Three—prepare an action plan. The purpose of the plan is to set goals for yourself as to how you will increase your time management efficiency. Using some of the following techniques will help you.

FIGURE 2-1
Time Log

DAILY TIME LOG		
Name_____ Day_____ Date_____		
Time	Activity/ Interruptions	Comments
8:30–8:45	Retrieved messages	
8:45–9:15	Aaron stopped by to discuss staff luncheon	Could have had a 10-minute chat online

Establish Priorities

Many times, you will not be able to do everything you are asked to do in one day. To distinguish between the more important and lesser important jobs and determine the order in which they should be completed, you need to establish priorities. A **priority** is something that merits your attention ahead of other tasks. When prioritizing your work, it can be helpful to organize tasks into one of three categories—A, B, or C—to reflect their level of importance and urgency. When asked to perform a task, ensure you confirm the required deadline so that you can establish the appropriate category of priority.

- *A-level* tasks require immediate attention; a significant negative impact could result if these tasks are not completed today.
- *B-level* tasks are tasks on which you or your company places a high value but a significantly negative impact would not occur if these tasks were not completed today.
- *C-level* tasks are tasks that would have no negative impact if they were not completed today.

When you are new to a job, you may need help from your supervisor to determine which tasks are the most important. Then, when you learn more about your position and your supervisor, you should be able to establish priorities on your own.

It is not unusual for established priorities to change from day to day and from hour to hour, depending on the needs of your company and your department. Your top priority may have been completing the sales report; however, if your supervisor asks you to do something he or she considers more urgent, realign your tasks and priorities to match those of your supervisor. Move that sales report down a notch. Finish your supervisor's priority as efficiently as you can and then refocus on the sales report.

Skills @ Work

Developing your organizational skills will help you to get and stay in control of your workday. Scheduling some time each day to complete important but routine tasks such as filing—putting it on your task list and checking it off when completed—ensures records are up-to-date. Consider ways to simplify repetitive tasks—create a template of a frequently used "master" document, create a "contact group" for an email distribution list you use frequently, or store telephone numbers in the memory redial on your telephone. Some time is needed initially to organize these tasks but you will reap dividends later in time saved.

You can ease boredom by varying repetitive tasks—filing, mail processing, updating distribution lists. You can help to control your level of stress by saying "yes" to the things that matter and "no" when appropriate or by delegating to others if you realize you cannot complete a task within the time allotted. Take a few moments at the end of the day or just before going to lunch to organize your desk. You will feel much better about returning to it if it is well organized.

Prepare Daily To-Do Lists

Making lists of tasks you need to address can be a very effective way of organizing your work. A daily to-do or task list is a simple and invaluable tool. You can tell at a glance what you need to accomplish that day, in what order, and which tasks can wait until another day if necessary. A simple paper list works well for many people. Others like to keep a list in their word processing or personal information management software so they can use program features to easily reorder items.

Review and adjust your task list periodically during the day and again before you leave work at the end of the day, taking a few moments to prepare your task list for the next day. To create this list, randomly record all the tasks, activities, and projects that you need to accomplish. Then review your list. Identify the most urgent and important items and mark them "A," the less important items "B," and those remaining "C." Use your list, with priorities in place, to

- Arrange papers on your desk in priority order, with the A's in one pile, the B's in another pile, and the C's in still another pile
- Prioritize telephone messages as well, marking them A, B, or C
- Establish a ranking for the papers in each pile (starting with the A pile) by determining the order in which you

Choose the method that works best for you.

will deal with each (1st, 2nd, 3rd, etc.) Do the same with the telephone messages

- The next day, work through the tasks in order of priority—A-1, A-2, A-3 until all A tasks are completed. Then proceed through the B's and C's. Determine a specific interval of time (once an hour or so) to periodically review the remaining items to see whether they need to be moved up in order

Try to organize your to-do list to include variety in the tasks you are completing. Build in opportunities for regular breaks. As you complete the tasks on your to-do list, mark them off. Doing this will give you a sense of accomplishment and call your attention to what still needs to be completed. When preparing your task list for the next day, transfer any items not completed, and use it as the basis for your next day's list. A sample to-do list is shown in Figure 2-2.

Use a Planner

Few people have such good memories that they do not need to make notes about tasks and appointments. That's why nearly everyone needs a planner. You have probably used a planner in your personal life, at school, or at previous jobs. If not, take some time to explore the various options that are available. If you are responsible for tracking appointments and other commitments for your supervisor or others, a planner, paper-based/manual or electronic, is an essential tool.

Your organization may require that you use a certain type of planner or planning software. It may be as simple as a calendar form or paper-based planning system such as a Day-Timer where you can record daily, weekly, monthly, and annual appointments and tasks in addition to contact details. Blank pages for recording goals or tasks delegated to others are also often included. Using a paper-based system has one advantage to consider—it can be accessed quickly by anyone during an emergency absence.

FIGURE 2-2
Planning Calendar and To-Do List

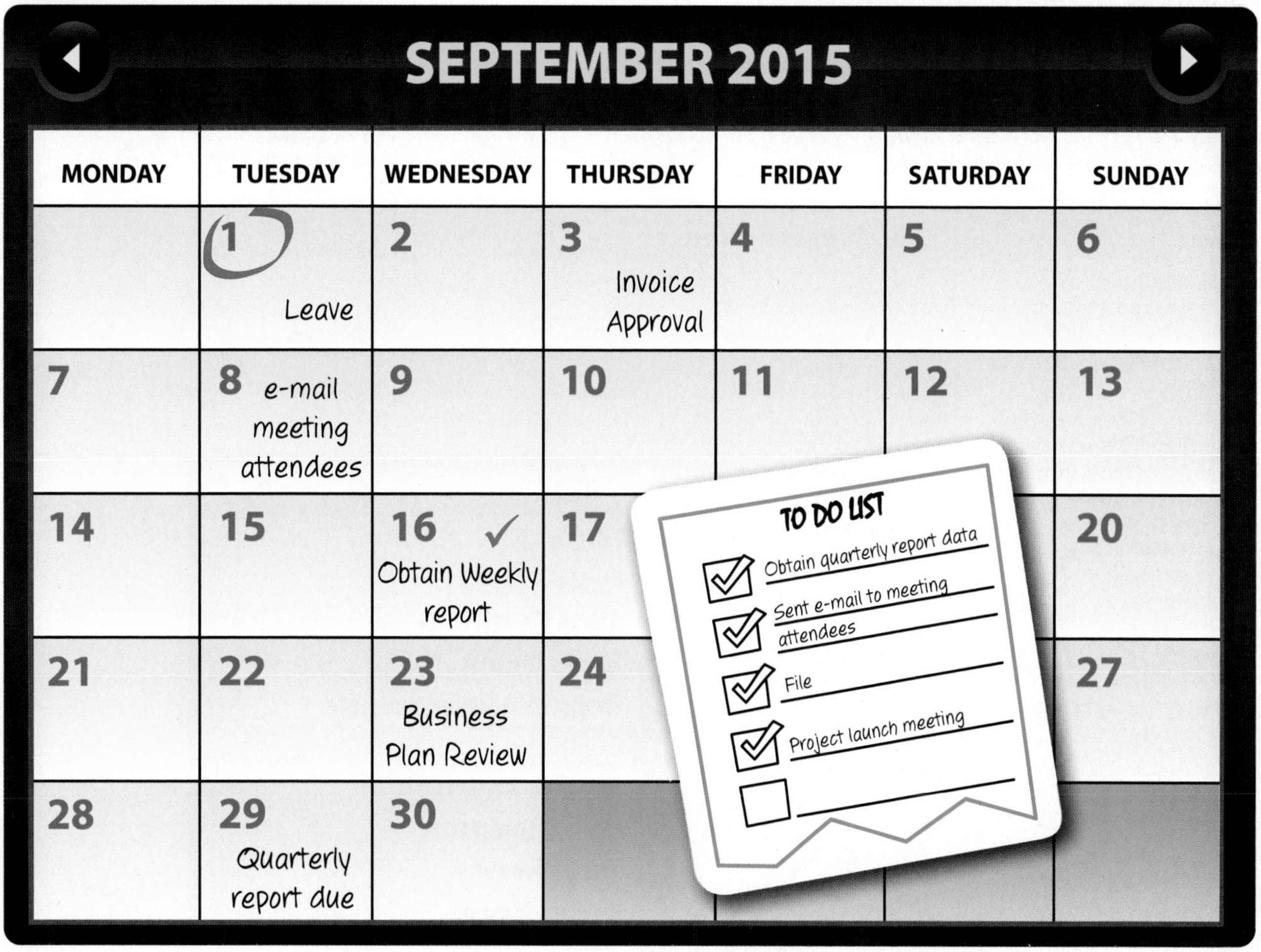

CHAPTER 2: Managing and Organizing Yourself, Your Time, and Your Workspace

Electronic planners are applications that are a component of PIM or personal information management software. Once installed on your computer network or mobile device, it can be used to do much more than categorize, colour-code, and track your task list—it can also be shared. In addition it can also manage your schedule, track and keep detailed histories of your business contacts, and handle documents you have downloaded from the Internet or from other sources. Documents sent as PDF attachments or web links can be easily attached to calendar entries or flagged for follow up. Reminders for recurring activities and tasks can be stored easily with one entry, filtered or sorted into categories, and then viewed by day, week, or month. With scheduling features and built-in reminders, electronic calendars, when used to their full potential, lend themselves very well to computer desktop organization. File folders for electronic files, web shortcuts, etc., can be placed on the computer desktop, which creates a paperless bring-forward file that can be easily deleted or moved when tasks are completed.

Most offices today are networked for file sharing. Calendars and tasks can be quickly and easily "shared" (see Figure 2-3) with various people as required and can be accessed on mobile devices. When sharing a calendar, owners control and determine the levels of access to be granted to others. For example, in a large office you could choose to "share" your calendar details with your supervisor and perhaps two other administrative professionals in your team. For you to be able to see the details of their calendars, they would need to grant reciprocal sharing rights to you. Extending sharing rights means that specific details of appointments could be viewed and anyone with shared access could add, revise, or delete appointments; create new or delete existing contacts; and add notes or other details to these calendars. If you suddenly had a personal emergency and had to leave work, a printout of the calendar and task list would assist your co-workers in terms of determining the tasks on which they should focus.

FIGURE 2-3
A Shared Task Resource Folder in OfficeCalendar

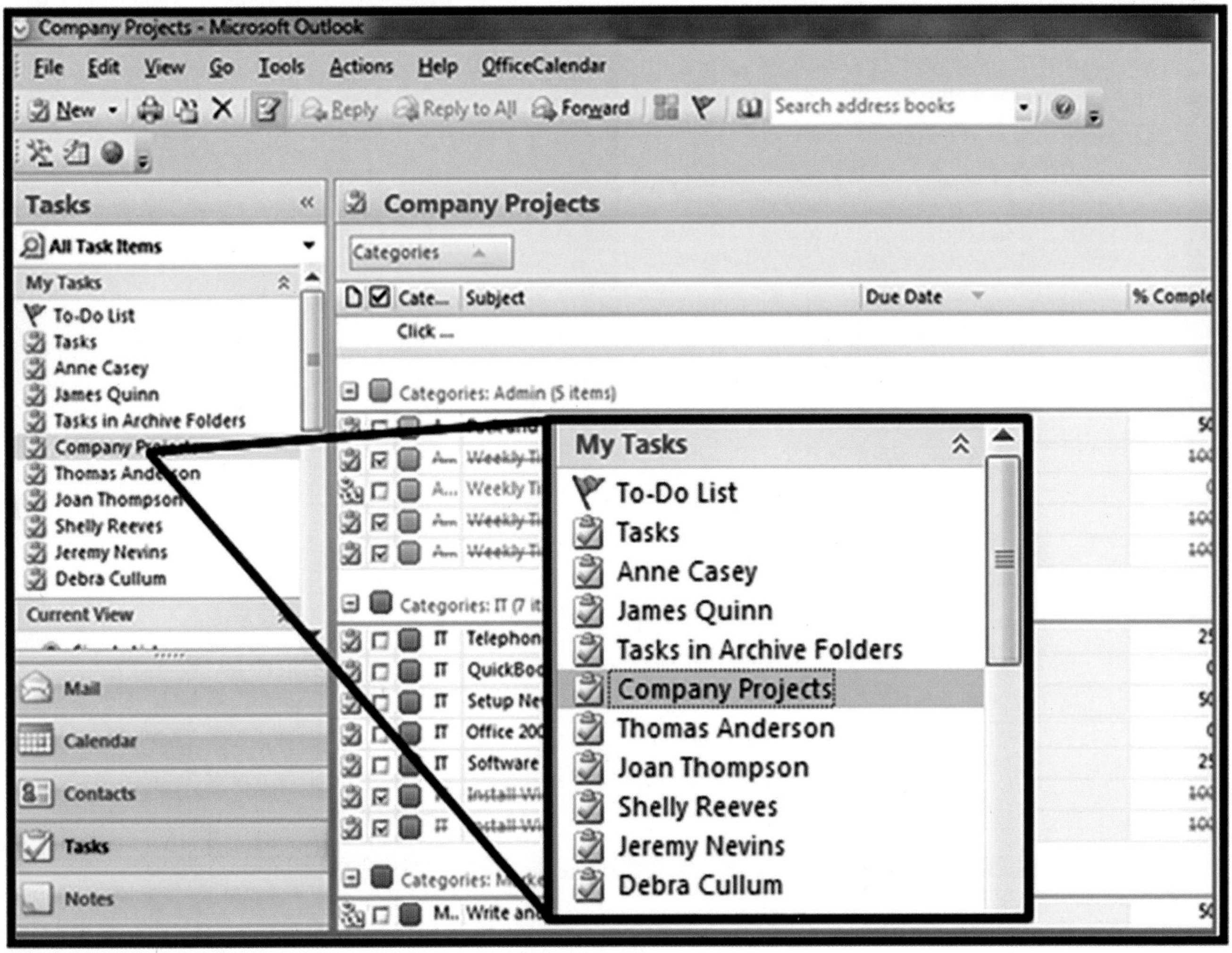

Courtesy of OfficeCalendar

Two popular and widely used PIM software packages are Microsoft Outlook (calendar and contact management software that comes as part of the Microsoft Office suite) and Google Calendar. Planning templates are also available in the Microsoft Office suite. Other planner software available for download from the Web for a trial period is known as shareware or trial software. This option gives you a limited period of time to try it and determine whether the program meets your needs. See Figure 2-4 for an image of a planner page in Microsoft Outlook. Planner templates are also available in word processing and spreadsheet applications.

Your personal preference may be a paper planner, instead of an electronic planner on your workstation or mobile device. Or, perhaps a combination of these would be your choice. Use your planner to record appointments, meetings, tasks, and reminders. Enter important dates and tasks as soon as you become aware of them so that you will not forget to enter them later. The simple activity of recording upcoming tasks and activities means you do not have to think about them again until your planner reminds you at the appropriate time. Recording these activities can help reduce stressors in your life.

If you use an electronic planning system such as those mentioned here, invest some time in learning about their many features. Take a course at your local college or university, use the software help feature, take an online tutorial or webinar, or check out a book from the library.

Make a backup copy of your planner data. If you use a paper-based planner, photocopy the essential pages. When deciding how often to make a backup, consider the impact if you lost the data, including the time and effort it would take to replace it. What is most important is that you find or create a system that works for you and that you will use regularly.

Conquer Procrastination

Procrastination is the postponement or needless delay of a necessary project or task. Procrastinators arrive late for meetings, put off starting projects, and do not return telephone calls. Procrastinators may be such relaxed, easygoing people that their procrastination does not bother them as much as it bothers others but their last-minute efforts, and the stress they put on other members of their work group can be significant. Many of us are guilty of procrastination. We do so for a variety of reasons—worrying about the size of the project, being afraid of failing, or lack of interest. We do not want to admit to any of these reasons, so we make excuses, such as having no time to get started, having too many other projects, lacking the necessary materials to complete the job, needing

FIGURE 2-4
Calendar Software

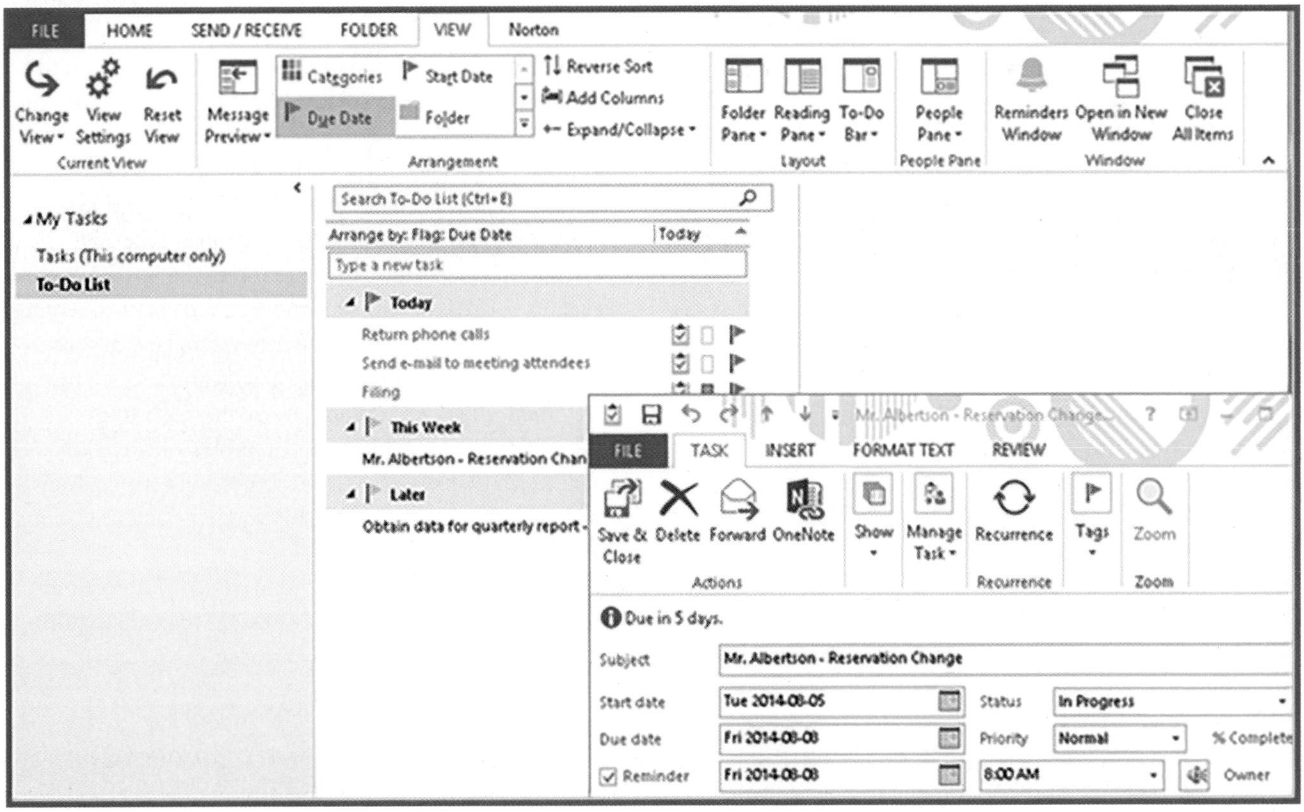

additional advice from a supervisor, or believing there is more than sufficient time and therefore no rush to begin.

The first step to getting something done is starting. Pick one area where procrastination plagues you and conquer it. If you always put off filing, and too often find yourself with two or three weeks of filing stacked on your desk and/or have difficulty locating documents in a timely fashion, you need to specifically include filing in your list of priorities. Make an appointment with yourself in your calendar so that this important task does not get out of hand.

Recognize that you have developed the habit of putting things off, then take steps to correct the habit. Even if you know you cannot finish a project that you have been postponing, give yourself a deadline and promise yourself that, until it is finished, you will dedicate yourself to it for half an hour a day, or some other length of time that suits your schedule and your attention span. If possible, blocking time in your calendar daily may help—such as first thing in the morning prior to when your supervisor arrives or prior to the time your daily duties begin. The main idea is to find time when you expect to have the least interruptions.

When planning to work on a large project, try to anticipate what could go wrong and what you might do to prevent problems along the way. Break the project into smaller tasks and focus on one at a time so that tasks seem more manageable and you get the reward of making progress. Set some deadlines, then tackle the most difficult ones first.

Do not let perfectionism paralyze you; do not be afraid to make mistakes. Any job has its difficult and boring tasks. Try to think of more efficient ways to manage them. Discipline yourself to work on them a little at a time.

Controlling Paper

Piles of letters, memos, and other documents can accumulate quickly. If you have ever found yourself rereading a piece of paper or shuffling it from the top to the bottom of the stack several times, you are not alone. Most of us have done the same thing. You open a piece of mail and put it in a pile, thinking, "Oh, this can wait." The document quickly grows into an overwhelming mountain of items you thought could wait.

Many time management experts claim that handling paper over and over is the biggest paperwork time waster. They advise that you should handle each piece of paper just once. Read it, route it, file it, or answer it. Get it off your desk as quickly as possible. While this advice is helpful, it is not always possible, practical, or even desirable. What you should do when you receive a document is to decide how you will handle it.

- Act on it at once if it needs immediate action or if you have the time.
- Keep it on hand if you will deal with it later that day.
- If it doesn't need to be dealt with that day, and if you have more pressing priorities, determine a time when you will

handle it and note it in your to-do list or planner. You may find it helpful to have an action file for items that won't be dealt with immediately but will be addressed in the next few days.

- If the document isn't your responsibility, forward it to someone who can handle it.
- If the document needs to be stored, do so at once, if possible. Non-urgent filing can wait, but set a specific time for it so it doesn't accumulate. Place it in a sorting strip or in a "pre-file" folder where documents are partially organized according to the master file list. Then if it is needed, you can quickly locate it in the sorting strip or pre-file area. Think before you create a new folder for a document or before you add it to an existing folder. Will you really need to refer to it again? An illustration of a sorting strip is shown in Chapter 11, Managing Physical and Electronic Records, on page 197.
- If you don't need the document, destroy it.

Controlling Your Email Inbox

The volume of email we receive can quickly become overwhelming. Some of the techniques described for controlling paper can be adapted to your electronic documents. Experts in the field say that staying on top of your email can be accomplished by emptying your inbox every day. How, you may ask? You can do the following:

- Process each message once, by asking yourself, is this message "actionable"? Am I being asked to do something? If the answer is "yes" and you can respond quickly, do so. Be courteous, direct, and specific. If you cannot respond immediately, defer it to later by tagging it, moving it to a follow-up folder or by forwarding it to someone who can deal with it. If the answer is "no," delete it, or file it if you think you will need it later.
- Create a filing system for electronic folders that parallels your paper records management system and/or a system that complements the categories you use for establishing priorities. Use it for any sent and received emails and other document files that need to be deferred to later or saved.
- Most email programs have a "rules" feature. Use it to automatically filter, sort, and move messages to predetermined email folders. For example, solicited bulk mail, such as newsletters from professional associations, requires no action but are items you will want to save for reading later.
- Spend a few minutes at the end of each day or week to review tagged or saved email messages that still require action or no longer have any purpose.

Organize Your Work Area

When you are working on a project, clearing your desktop of materials that relate to other projects helps to keep you

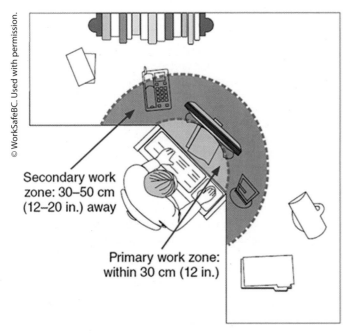

Secondary work zone: 30–50 cm (12–20 in.) away

Primary work zone: within 30 cm (12 in.)

Place frequently used items in the primary work zone and infrequently used items in the secondary work zone.

focused. Put these materials in a file folder, label the folder with the name of the project, and put the folder in your drawer.

Keep "in" and "out" trays on your desk, and label the trays for incoming and outgoing material. If space permits, you may wish to have a tray, your pre-file folder, or sorting strip on your desk for material to be stored. Keep frequently used supplies and equipment such as pen, stapler, telephone, and telephone message pad close at hand. Make neatness a habit. Not only will neatness demonstrate your professionalism, it will help you feel relaxed and in control.

Minimize Interruptions

Interruptions are a normal part of the day for an administrative professional. They come from a variety of sources—email, telecommunications, and visitors—and can become frustrating time wasters. Your responsibility is to maintain positive relationships with colleagues and clients, which can involve some personal finessing on your part. Making visitors feel comfortable and welcome does not mean you must "entertain" them while they are waiting to see your supervisor. The same is true for co-workers who stop by your workspace to visit. Certainly if a co-worker comes by on a work-related errand, engage briefly in pleasantries such as "Good morning. How's your day going?" But try to not spend a lot of time in excessive chatting. Controlling or minimizing these types of interruptions is crucial to using your time effectively. See Figure 2-5 for some suggestions.

Use Good Communication Techniques

When your supervisor asks you to do something, be sure you understand exactly what it is that you are to do and the time frame in which it needs to be completed. If you are not clear what is being asked, paraphrase what you believe your supervisor said. Do not be afraid to ask questions. Transmit ideas in simple, clear terms. Define terms if necessary. It is better to ensure clarity at the outset rather than wasting time later when you must interrupt your supervisor for direction.

Listen carefully when someone is talking. When you are communicating with an individual face to face, look at her or him. Be sensitive to the person's body language and to the words the person is saying. Keep your mind open to new ideas; refrain from passing judgment on what the speaker is saying.

Your Ergonomic Workspace

Derived from the Greek words *ergos* ("work") and *nomos* ("natural laws"), the term ergonomics refers to the study of the fit between people, the tools they use, and the physical setting in which they work. Ergonomics can help in the design of furniture and equipment that is physiologically sound so you remain healthy as you use it. When your workspace is set up correctly, you may be less likely to suffer from headaches, neck and back pain, and the resulting stress that can accompany these symptoms. A comfortable and ergonomically designed workspace can help you to be more productive and reduce injury, which can be caused by placing your body in awkward positions. While no solution is "one-size fits all," the following basic guidelines can help you design a workspace that "fits" you.

Furniture and Equipment

Much of the workplace furniture today is modular. Desktops, shelves, and cabinets attach to partitions or walls. These units can be adjusted for height and efficiency. Other areas to consider as you organize your workspace are your chair and your desk; the position of your monitor, your keyboard, and your mouse; and ambient lighting and task lighting.

The Chair

Some recent studies suggest that chronic sitters are at an increased risk of cardiovascular disease, obesity, and metabolic disorders. If you sit at a computer keyboard every day for more than two hours, you should take special care to ensure your workstation is user-friendly. While no single body position can be recommended for everyone, a fully adjustable

FIGURE 2-5
Controlling and Minimizing Interruptions

Email

- If your email program is not set to notify you each time a new message is received, check it regularly but not constantly. Determine an appropriate interval to check your email (hourly, every other hour, or as frequently as you and your supervisor determine is necessary).
- Respond to emails courteously, clearly, and concisely. Be direct and specific.
- Do not let emails take the place of personal contact unless that is the preferred choice of your supervisor and colleagues.

Telephone

- Give and record correct information during telephone calls.
- Identify yourself or your supervisor and state the reason for your call.
- Group multiple outgoing calls and make them when people are most likely to be available.
- If the person called is not in, ask when he or she will return or leave a concise voice mail message, identifying yourself and providing a brief summary of the reason for your call.

- When taking a message or screening incoming calls for your supervisor, determine who is calling (repeat the name and phone number) and the nature of the call. Confirm accuracy by spelling the caller's name and repeating the message to the caller.
- During work hours, make personal calls only when they relate to an emergency.
- Use email and fax as an alternative to leaving and receiving phone messages.

Visitors

- Set up appointments for visitors. Discourage people from dropping by unexpectedly to see you or your supervisor.
- Make visitors welcome but continue with your work as soon as you can.
- Discourage co-workers from dropping by to socialize. For example, you can stand when they enter your workspace, or keep your hands over your keyboard or pen in your hand to silently indicate your responsibility to work during working hours.

---

chair helps to minimize awkward postures that could lead to potential health problems. Some options to consider as you adapt your workstation for your individual body and workspace are forward-sloping, kneeling, and sit-stand chairs and height-adjustable and treadmill desks.

The Desk

You can contribute to a well-organized and safe workstation by placing your keyboard and mouse approximately 5 cm below your desk top, close together and at the same level as one another; and positioning hardcopy documents and other frequently used items within easy reach and proximity to one another. A desk that is height-adjustable with an adjustable keyboard pad offering keyboard and mouse support provides the option of alternating between sitting and standing at your workstation.

The Monitor

Ideally the monitor should be placed at the same height as the keyboard. Research in this area indicates that the eyes naturally assume a straightforward and slightly downward cast of between 15 and 30 degrees.[3] When the monitor, an integral part of a computer workstation, is incorrectly placed, you force your body to work in a variety of awkward positions. You could be tilting your chin upward, and/or bending the head and upper body forward or sideways. These forced working positions will contribute significantly to your

personal discomfort, and can lead to work-related injury such as headaches, aches and pains in the neck and shoulders, and/or eyestrain.

Lighting

Working in an environment with improper lighting can cause headaches, eye fatigue, neck and shoulder strain,

Ergonomic workstation

FIGURE 2-8
Problem-Solving/Decision-Making Steps

1. **Define the "Problem" or the Purpose**
    This first step may sound simple, but it is usually the most difficult of the steps. When attempting to define the purpose or problem, ask yourself:
    *   What problem am I trying to solve?
    *   Why is this decision necessary?
    *   What will be the outcome of this decision?

2. **Establish the Criteria**
    The next step in the decision-making process is to determine the criteria you need to make a sound decision. When setting your criteria, ask yourself:
    *   What do I want to achieve?
    *   What do I want to preserve?
    *   What do I want to avoid?

3. **Generate Alternatives or Possible Solutions**
    The next step in the decision-making process is to begin generating alternatives or possible solutions. What do you think you can do to solve the problem or make the decision? What alternatives are available to you?

4. **Test the Alternatives and Make the Decision**
    The effective decision maker will test each alternative using this system:
    *   Eliminate alternatives that are unrealistic or incompatible with the needs of the organization.
    *   Select the alternative that appears to be the most realistic.

5. **Evaluate the Decision**
    The last step in the decision-making process is evaluating the decision. In evaluating the decision, ask the following questions:
    *   What was right about the decision?
    *   What was wrong about the decision?
    *   How did the decision-making process work? What improvements are necessary? What changes need to be made for the future?

Chapter Summary

The summary will help you remember the important points covered in this chapter.

- Time is a unique resource; it cannot be bought, sold, borrowed, rented, saved, or manufactured. It is the only resource that must be spent the minute it is received.
- Time wasters include ineffective communication, poor telephone usage, inadequate planning, interruptions, disorganization, and procrastination.
- Good time management techniques include analyzing how we use our time, and establishing effective routines.
- Time management systems such as calendars and PIM software can help us manage ourselves in relation to our time.
- Stress is the body's response to a demand placed upon it. Chronic stress occurs when a distressful situation is prolonged, allowing no rest or recuperation for the body.
- Stress reducers include balancing work and play, knowing the difference between achievement and perfection, recognizing limits, exercising, eating right, getting enough sleep, and managing anger and time.
- Conflict resolution skills are always important in workplace situations. Attitudes that help resolve conflicts include openness, empathy, and equality.
- Anger is a growing corporate problem; incidences of violence in the workplace have increased.
- Techniques to help manage your anger include relaxing, engaging in positive self-talk, walking away either physically or emotionally from an anger-provoking situation, talking to a friend about the situation, and solving the problem that is making you angry.
- The following are the steps in problem solving:
  1. Define the problem or the purpose.
  2. Establish the criteria.
  3. Generate alternatives or possible solutions.
  4. Test the alternatives and make the decision.
  5. Evaluate the decision.

Key Terms

goal p. 25
time p. 26
time management p. 26
priority p. 28
PIM (personal information management) p. 30
shareware or trial software p. 31
procrastination p. 31
ergonomics p. 33
RSI (repetitive stress injury) p. 35
carpal tunnel syndrome p. 35

computer vision syndrome p. 35
downsize p. 36
rightsize p. 36
stress p. 36
chronic stress p. 36
conflict resolution p. 37
empathy p. 38
perfectionism p. 38
achievement p. 38
sleep hygiene p. 39

Discussion Items

These discussion items provide an opportunity to test your understanding of the chapter through written responses and/or discussion with your classmates and your instructor.

1. Identify and describe five time wasters.
2. What is PIM software, and how can it help you manage your time?
3. What is meant by ergonomics? Give five ergonomic guidelines to follow to avoid RSIs when establishing a new workstation or adapting an existing workstation.
4. What is stress, and what causes it? Identify three ways of managing stress.
5. Is all stress unhealthy? Explain your answer.
6. List and explain five ways you can manage your anger.

Critical-Thinking Activity

Keri-An Mahar has worked in human resources at CanAsian for five years. She is in charge of employee benefits. Keri-An is an excellent employee—very competent, knowledgeable about human resources (she holds an MBA, with a specialty in management), loyal, dependable, and respected by her colleagues. Two years ago, a new vice-president of human resources was hired. Keri-An has tried to work with him, but the situation does not seem to improve; in fact, it worsens. He gives her inadequate information. He asks her at the last minute to prepare reports. He lies to her about company policies and directions. Then, he yells at her about violating the directions of the company. On several occasions, Keri-An has yelled back at him; she never felt good about the situation when she allowed this outburst to happen. She has talked with him repeatedly about the issues from her perspective. He seems to listen but never responds. He has never complained about her performance; she believes he is satisfied with her work. Keri-An has considered leaving the job; however, she has two more

years until she is vested in the retirement system. If she leaves now, she loses all of her retirement benefits. Recently, Keri-An began to have health problems. She went to her physician, who said her illness was the result of stress. He also recommended that she take at least three months off. Keri-An did so. The three months have passed, and Keri-An is ready to come back to work.

What suggestions would you make to Keri-An to decrease the stress on her job?

Building Workplace Skills

Project 2-1 (Learning Outcomes 1 and 2)

To access the MindTap site, use the printed access card on the inside cover of your textbook. Student Course Data file SCDP2-1a is a screen in your PIM software, and file SCDP2-1b is an email message from Martin Albertson. After considering both of these documents, put your task list in priority order, adding the necessary items from Martin Albertson's memo. Assign a category A to the items you must attend to immediately, a B to the items you should deal with this week, and a C to the items you should begin work on as soon as possible but that have no immediate deadlines. Then rank each task in the categories by assigning a 1, 2, 3, etc., to each item to place it in order within each category. This number will indicate the order in which you should proceed to work on the items. Submit your new prioritized task list to your instructor.

If available, use Outlook or another calendar software to complete this project by first entering the details from the screen image into your calendar. Next, update the calendar with the details provided in the memo. Your instructor will provide specific submission instructions.

Project 2-2 (Learning Outcome 1)

In your work with Martin Albertson, you have shared access to his planner to update his contacts and schedule. He hands you four business cards that he received at the recent national marketing conference he attended in Ottawa and asks you to enter them.

While he was out of town, you received several requests for appointments. After discussing the requests with him and receiving his approval, you enter them into his schedule.

Two data files are to be used to complete this project. The file SCDP2-2a, a PDF file, contains the business cards; the file SCDP2-2b, a list of appointments. Using Outlook or another calendar software, complete all entries and make any revisions that arise due to conflicts. Prepare the contact list and a copy of the calendar in monthly format, and submit both to your instructor.

Project 2-3 (Learning Outcome 1)

On the MindTap site, file SCDP2-3a is a time log form. Print out or create a page for each of the next five days. Use the hard copy forms or create a document to log the time you spend on various activities. If you are a student and employed, log the time you spend on school, part-time work, and personal activities. If you are not employed, log the time you spend on school and personal activities. Create as realistic a picture as possible.

After you finish that part of the project, analyze the way you spent your time during the five days. File SCDP2-3b contains questions to help you. File SCDP2-3c contains a Time Effectiveness Questionnaire, which provides general questions concerning the use of time. Respond to these items. After you have analyzed the way you use your time and considered your answers to the Time Effectiveness Questionnaire, prepare an action plan using the form in file SCDP2-3d. Indicate how you will make more effective use of your time. Submit a copy of your action plan to your instructor.

Project 2-4 (Learning Outcomes 4 and 6)

A friend of yours, Indra, works in an office in your building. She is having problems. Her situation is described in file SCDP2-4. Analyze her case. Follow your instructor's directions to respond to the questions following the case description. You may use the memorandum form file SCDP2-4a or some other document as directed to by your instructor submit your responses.

Project 2-5 (Learning Outcomes 4 and 6)

Ahmad, a friend of yours who has worked for CanAsian for two years, is extremely unhappy in his job. He has confided in you about the office situation and has asked for your analysis of what is happening. His situation is described in file SCDP2-5. Follow your instructor's directions to respond to the questions following the case description. You may use the memorandum form file SCDP2-5a or some other document as directed by your instructor to submit your responses.

Project 2-6 (Learning Outcomes 4 and 6)

Collaborative Project
Online Project

Work with three of your classmates on this project. Using the Web, search for a recent article on each of the following topics:

- Conflict resolution
- Controlling stress
- Managing anger

Summarize the articles and present your findings to the class. Turn in a written report of your findings to your instructor; cite all of your references.

Project 2-7 (Learning Outcome 3)

As an administrative professional, you are likely to spend a lot of time working at a computer. If you follow ergonomic guidelines in arranging your workstation and using your computer equipment, you will work more comfortably and will be less likely to develop medical problems such as back pain and carpal tunnel syndrome.

Visit the Canadian Centre for Occupational Health and Safety (CCOHS) and/or the equivalent website for your province or territory to learn about ergonomics for computer workstations. Links to the CCOHS and CanOSH sites are provided on the MindTap site. Follow the guidelines at these sites to arrange your workstation at school, work, or home to follow ergonomic guidelines. Create a report summarizing your findings and describing the results. Submit your report to your instructor.

Project 2-8 (Learning Outcomes 1 and 2)

Your company recently hired a new administrative assistant, Maryam Arjmand. On her first day, you stopped by her desk to meet her. During your conversation, you told her that if you could do anything to help her in settling in, just to let you know. Since then, Maryam has called you whenever she has a question. Sometimes the questions are about items that are urgent; but on other occasions, they are not. Assisting her usually takes just a few minutes, but sometimes it takes longer.

Maryam probably calls you about eight times a day. Helping her so much is affecting your ability to get your work done. Two administrative assistants work in Maryam's department, and you know they would be happy to help her. Maryam, however, doesn't know them very well and is more comfortable asking you. How can you continue to assist Maryam and to encourage her to ask questions about things she doesn't understand while limiting the inroads that her interruptions make on your time?

Discuss this situation with two of your classmates and brainstorm some solutions. Share your ideas with the class.

Project 2-9 (Learning Outcome 2)

Take an online tutorial for software that you use in school or at work. Identify at least three things you learn from the tutorial that will help you do your work more efficiently. Make a list of these items.

Project 2-10 (Learning Outcome 6)

Share with your classmates some methods of relieving stress that you have found effective in your own life. Then add to your e-portfolio that you began in Chapter 1 by describing how you plan to control your stress and manage your anger in the future. In preparing this plan, do the following:

- Identify the stressors that you currently have in your life. These stressors may be at home, at school, or at the office.
- Identify ways you can relieve these stressors.
- Identify situations that currently make you angry.
- Identify ways you can manage that anger.
- Identify ways you will seek to control stress and manage anger in the future.
- Identify some of the ideas that you have heard from your classmates that you will consider implementing.

Save this document in your "Reflections folder" under an appropriate file name.

Endnotes

1. "Managing to Manage Workplace Stress," The Psychology Foundation of Canada, http://psychologyfoundation .org/pdf/publications/managing_to_manage.pdf, accessed January 3, 2015.
2. The Sanofi Canada Healthcare Survey 2014" Sanofi Canada, http://www.sanofi.ca, accessed January, 2014.
3. "OSH Answers: Office Ergonomics," Canadian Centre for Occupational Health and Safety site, http://www.ccohs .ca/oshanswers/ergonomics/office/ , accessed January 3, 2015.
4. Andrea Atkins, "Laughing Matters," *World Traveler*, November 1997, pp. 53–56.

Working Ethically

LEARNING OUTCOMES

After studying this chapter, you should be able to …

1. Explain the importance of ethical behaviour in the workplace.
2. *Identify characteristics of ethical businesses and organizations.*
3. List and describe basic workplace standards as found in the Canada Labour Code.
4. Identify traits of an ethical administrative professional.
5. Define the steps necessary for ethical change.

Do I Qualify?

Administrative Assistant

National nonprofit organization seeks assistant to support the work of its legal affairs department. The ideal job candidate must have:

- Excellent written and oral communication skills
- Understanding of and commitment to the mission and philosophy of the company
- Excellent interpersonal skills
- Flexibility and adaptability
- Ability to maintain confidentiality of sensitive information
- Effective time management skills, organizational abilities, and attention to detail
- Experience with federal, provincial, and municipal lobbying and gift/gratuities rules

The ethics of business enterprises affects our society greatly. Highly successful business leaders are quoted in the news, and their behaviour is observed and often emulated by others, not only in the business world but also in the nation and the world at large.

The influence of business on society and the influence of corporate leaders on individuals are not always positive. For example, poorly run businesses and leaders who misuse their power and authority can lead to inferior products and services, environmental pollution, unsafe working conditions, unfair treatment of employees, and various other unethical behaviours. When business leaders behave irresponsibly, our society and individuals within it are often the losers. For example, in the early 2000s, respected corporations such as WorldCom and Enron, to name just two, were found guilty of mismanagement and criminal activity that led to the loss of millions of dollars of shareholder money and resulted in jail terms for many high-level executives. In 2010, mechanical failure as a result of cost-saving measures is said to have caused an oil spill in the Gulf of Mexico that some say is the worst environmental disaster the United States has ever faced.

Ethics is a systematic study of moral conduct, duty, and judgment. Ethics can be thought of as guidelines or accepted beliefs about what is right or wrong, good or bad. These beliefs are reflected in business ethics, which applies these principles to day-to-day decisions and activities in the workplace.

People's decisions and actions each day affect how others perceive them. Can others depend on you to act fairly? Do they consider your decisions to be based on a thoughtful process? Do they count on you to do the right thing? In a similar way, the reputation of a business is affected by the decisions and actions of its employees, managers, and owners.

Certainly, ethical behaviour has always been important for organizations and individuals, and understanding business ethics is especially important for administrative professionals because of the nature of this trusted position. Administrative assistants are knowledgeable about confidential information and sensitive issues. The use of technology and the level of connectedness existing today through social and other forms of media means that we are now more immediately aware of unethical practices. For example, if an airline crash kills hundreds of people and the cause is faulty equipment due to improper maintenance by the airline, we learn those facts almost immediately; similarly, news travels quickly when a company puts a food product on the market with an additive that may cause illness or even death. And when Enron filed for bankruptcy in 2001, secretive insider partnerships were disclosed that had been used to hide millions of dollars in corporate debt. This disclosure was due in part to ethical employees who "blew the whistle" on the illegal activities. The term "whistleblower" now applies to ethically minded employees who bring to light the indiscretions of their organization.

Technological advances in medical science have expanded to the point that ethics now represents a major consideration. Some of the ethical questions being debated include the following.

1. Does an individual have the right to determine when he or she dies and to seek assistance with death?
2. How long should a seriously ill patient be kept alive through artificial means?
3. Is it ethical to use stem cells derived from embryos and fetuses in medical research?

These questions have implications for various health professions, pharmaceutical businesses, and individuals.

Obviously, these ethical questions represent only a few of the many issues we face. As technology opens new vistas, ethical questions will continue to occur. The point here is that we require, now and in the future, wisdom on the part of business leaders and individuals who are employed by businesses to face and solve the ethical issues that will confront us. An important aspect of this wisdom is **morality** (a set of ideas of right and wrong). All of us must strengthen our own ethical understandings and moral **integrity** (consistently adhering to a set of ideas of right and wrong), both within and outside the workplace.

In this chapter, ethics is considered a **pragmatic** topic—one not only to be understood conceptually but also to be practised on a daily basis. This chapter will help you to understand the significance of ethics in the workplace and the responsibility you have as an administrative professional.

The Ethical Organization

Ethics has become so important that it is the topic of numerous books, the subject of seminars, the basis for consulting businesses, and a daily concern of executives. A company can succeed or fail as a result of its ethical behaviour.

Every year, *Fortune* magazine prints a list of the "Global 500"— 500 of the most admired companies around the world. George Weston Limited is a Canadian company consistently ranked in the top ten; its website includes statements that support this recognition. These statements do not address the size of the company or the amount of profit it makes, but rather its ethical nature:

- We are committed to giving back to the communities where our customers, employees and shareholders live and work—locally, regionally, and nationally.*

* George Weston Limited website, "Corporate Responsibility," http://www.weston.ca/en/George-Weston-Ltd.aspx, accessed April 20, 2011.

- George Weston Limited and its subsidiaries are focused on improving the quality of life in the communities where our employees live and work. Weston is committed to contributing a minimum of 1% of pre-tax profits to charitable organizations in Canada and to encouraging employee engagement.[1]

These statements show a commitment to employees and to community involvement, both characteristics of ethical organizations.

Characteristics of Ethical Organizations

Employees are more likely to enjoy going to work each day when they know they will be treated fairly, they will not be harassed, and the other workers will play by the rules. Employees expect their employer to pay them well and treat them fairly. Companies that do neither can expect to have a high turnover rate, which adversely affects the business. Owners, including shareholders, have an interest in the company showing a profit. Investors expect the company to be open and honest about its financial condition. Customers who buy the company's products and services provide the financial resources for making a profit. Pleasing its customers with an excellent product or service and standing behind that product or service are top priorities for successful businesses. You can see that maintaining an ethical climate is frequently in the best interests of a business or organization.

Several characteristics distinguish ethical organizations. They include being honest, visionary, and environmentally and socially responsible; being committed to diversity and intolerance of discrimination within the organization; providing a safe and healthy environment for workers; offering fair and equitable pay; and respecting the law. Many organizations today have written vision or mission statements that clarify the directions and values of the organization. Such statements let the employees know the directions of the organization, what it values, how it intends to live those values, and what is and is not considered to be ethical behaviour within the organization.

Sun Life Financial, another Canadian organization consistently on the *Fortune* 500 list, has a Code of Conduct that applies to all employees and directors (see Figure 3-1); each year, they are asked to reaffirm their commitment to comply with the Code and to confirm that they have complied with it over the previous year. In part the Code aims to ensure that employees "come to work every day with a commitment to the highest standards of honesty and integrity in the way we treat our employees and serve our customers. Acting ethically is more than how we work, it's how we *think*."[2]

FIGURE 3-1
Sun Life Advice to Employees

Applying the spirit of the Code to situations encountered at work, Sun Life provides this advice to employees if they encounter a difficult situation.

Ask yourself the following questions:
- is this legal?
- is this permissible under Sun Life policies?
- is this fair and ethical?
- am I confident that Sun Life would not be embarrassed if this situation became public knowledge?
- would I approve of this situation if I were a co-worker, a customer or shareholder?

You should be able to answer "Yes" to each question. Use your best judgment and common sense, keeping in mind that you are required to comply with both the content and spirit of the Code. If you have any questions as to how to apply the Code in any situation, consult your manager, human resources, a compliance officer or a member of the law department.

Source: Sun Life Financial, Acting Ethically: Code of Business Conduct (2013). Sun Life Assurance Company of Canada website. http://cdn.sunlife.com/static/global/files/Code%20of%20business%20conduct/pa_e_code_of_business_conduct.pdf (Accessed September 2015).

Being Socially and Environmentally Responsible

Social responsibility refers to the obligation of a business to contribute to the greater good of the community. Communities rely on the support of local companies for financial stability and growth. Businesses have a legal and ethical obligation not to harm the citizens of the community. This obligation includes properly disposing of harmful wastes and using pollution controls for factories. An ethical company is a good neighbour.

Businesses make choices about pollution, employee health and safety, the sponsorship of charitable endeavours and employee volunteer programs, and other issues and needs. As is the case with both George Weston and Sun Life, they may choose to give employees time off for volunteering or a convenient way to financially support worthy causes. After the September 11 attacks, the flooding in New Orleans following Hurricane Katrina in 2005, and the 2011 earthquake and tsunami in Japan, corporations were among the first to send millions of dollars in aid for people in need.

Business executives who are socially and environmentally responsible are constantly aware of the possible dangers in their businesses and take all necessary precautions to see that the environment is not polluted. They pay attention to government regulations that address the careful disposal of hazardous materials and implement programs to recycle paper, plastics, electronics, and other items. Ethical organizations work to preserve the environment for future generations by reducing the impact of their operations on the environment. When involved in new construction, they give top priority to cutting down as few trees as possible and protecting wetlands and other areas that are environmentally important. They adopt alternative energy sources, such as solar, wind, or methane, and may use hybrid or electric vehicles in their fleets.

Being Committed to Diversity

A diverse workforce benefits companies in several ways. It helps them meet the needs of their global customers and an increasingly diverse Canadian population. Studies have shown that groups and teams with diverse members are more creative and make better decisions. Diversity also helps a company attract and retain talented employees.

Ethical organizations go farther than the law requires. They make hiring decisions based on merit and are committed to providing equal employment opportunities. They create environments that are attractive to all employees. They provide diversity training for their employees, and hold managers accountable for consistently supporting and ensuring diversity.

Being Intolerant of Discrimination

Businesses are made up of people; people who bring their own particular prejudices to the workplace. **Prejudice** is defined as "a system of negative beliefs, feelings, and actions." These beliefs, feelings, and actions are based on *learned* categories of distinctions, *learned* evaluation of these categories, and *learned* tendencies to act according to certain beliefs and feelings. Prejudice can lead to acts of **discrimination** (treatment or consideration based on class or category rather than individual merit). Discrimination may occur in many forms; some of the most commonly seen forms of discrimination are based on race or ethnicity, gender, sexual orientation, and age. Discrimination may also involve sexual harassment.

Racial/Ethnic Discrimination

Racial/ethnic tensions will always exist in a multicultural country like Canada. All organizations must comply with laws that promote equal treatment and prohibit discrimination. The Canada Labour Code (CLC) and subsequent regulations form the primary source of federal employment and labour law. Additionally, at the provincial and territorial level, numerous statutory provisions govern the employer/employee relationship. Human rights codes established at the provincial level state that every person has a right to equal treatment with respect to employment without discrimination based on race, ancestry, place of origin, colour, ethnic origin, citizenship, creed, sex, age, record of offences, marital status, family status, sexual orientation, or handicap. Figure 3-2 lists areas of prohibited discriminatory practices identified in federal law.

FIGURE 3-2
Prohibited Discriminatory Practices

- Discriminatory hiring, firing, or treatment in the course of employment
- Discriminatory employment applications, advertisements, or inquiries
- Discriminatory membership practices by employee organizations
- Discriminatory policies or agreements by employee or employer organizations
- Maintenance of gender-based wage differentials
- Freedom from sexual and other kinds of harassment in the workplace

Gender Discrimination

The federal Employment Equity Act provides for employment equity for women, Aboriginal peoples, people with disabilities, and members of visible minority groups. We recognize in our society today that very few occupations are gender-specific. Employers may not advertise a job specifically for a man or woman unless bona fide occupational requirements require a person of a specific gender—for example, if the position involves modelling men's clothing. Hiring decisions must be based on whether the individual has the knowledge and skills needed for the job, not on whether the person is male or female.

Also, employee pay cannot be based on whether a person is male or female. Provincial and territorial employment standards legislation and the federal CLC prohibit pay discrimination on the basis of gender. Men and women performing work in the same establishment under similar conditions must receive the same pay when their jobs require equal skill, effort, and responsibility.

Provincial human rights codes also prohibit discrimination based on sexual orientation. Gay, lesbian, bisexual, and transgender organizations have become active in helping to ensure that the rights of individuals are not violated on the basis of their sexual preference.

Age Discrimination

No distinction can be made in age, either in the advertising or hiring process or after an employee is on the job. For example, an organization cannot print a job vacancy notice that specifies a particular age or age range for applicants. At one time, many companies in Canada had a mandatory retirement age. Forcing an employee to retire by reason of age is considered to be a human rights issue. From 2006 through 2008, various provinces and territories adopted legislation prohibiting mandatory retirement. Figure 3-3 lists steps for handling harassment or discrimination.

FIGURE 3-3
Steps for Handling Harassment or Discrimination Issues

- Know your rights and know the laws. Know your organization's position on discrimination and harassment, the activities considered to be legal under your provincial human rights code, and your employer's responsibility towards you.
- Keep a record of all harassment and discrimination infractions, noting the dates, incidents, and witnesses (if any).
- File a formal grievance with your company. Check your company policy and procedure manual or talk with the director of human resources concerning the grievance procedure. If no formal grievance procedures exist, file a formal complaint with your employer in the form of a memorandum describing the incidents, identifying the individuals involved in the harassment or discrimination, and requesting disciplinary action.
- If your employer is not responsive to your complaint, your province may have human rights offices that can assist you. Search online for the address and telephone number of the Human Rights Commission office nearest you where you can file charges of discrimination.
- Talk to friends, co-workers, and relatives. Avoid isolation and self-blame. You are not alone; harassment and discrimination of all types occur in the workplace.
- Consult a lawyer to investigate legal alternatives to discriminatory or harassing behaviour.

Maintaining a Policy against Harassment

Harassment in the workplace may be present in several forms. It is generally defined as conduct that demeans, humiliates, or embarrasses a person, leading to a hostile work environment. Bullying is one form of harassment that has moved from the school playground into the office. Both the Canadian Human Rights Act and the Canada Labour Code protect employees from harassment in the workplace.

Sexual harassment, a specific type of harassment, has been defined in the Canada Labour Code as "any conduct, comment, gesture or contact of a *sexual nature* that is likely to cause offence or humiliation or that might, on reasonable grounds, be perceived as placing a condition of a sexual nature on employment or on any opportunity for training or promotion." Three criteria can be used to determine whether sexual harassment exists:

1. Submission to sexual conduct is either implicitly or explicitly a condition of employment.
2. Employment decisions affecting the recipient are made on the basis of the recipient's acceptance or rejection of sexual conduct.
3. The conduct has the intent or effect of substantially interfering with an individual's work performance or creates an intimidating, hostile, or offensive work environment.

Division XV.1 of Part III of the Canada Labour Code makes the organization responsible to "make every reasonable effort to ensure that no employee is subjected to sexual harassment"[3] by issuing and publishing to all employees a policy statement concerning sexual harassment.

The organization is liable for the behaviour of its employees whether or not management is aware that harassment has taken place. The organization is also responsible for the actions of non-employees on the company's premises. Because of these liabilities, many organizations have published policy statements that make it clear to all employees that harassment of any kind is a violation of the law and of company policy. These statements generally include a clearly defined grievance procedure so an employee has a course of action to take if harassment does occur.

Supervisors can help to create a workplace free from sexual and other forms of harassment by

- Applying and promoting high standards of integrity, conduct, and concern for all employees.
- Leading by example. Social behaviour should not become confused with behaviour that is considered appropriate in the workplace.
- Ensuring employment decisions are based on merit.
- Educating employees as to the activity that constitutes sexual harassment; let everyone know that sexual harassment will not be tolerated. Sexual jokes, teasing, or innuendo should not become a routine part of the work environment.

- Ensuring that employees who feel they are victims of sexual harassment are aware of the options available to them in addressing these issues. They should not fear punitive action or retaliation against them as a result of lodging their complaint.
- Identifying a person that employees can contact confidentially with any concerns and complaints about sexual or other harassment issues.
- Investigating every complaint promptly and thoroughly.
- Observing the language and behaviour of fellow supervisors and advising them if their actions may be perceived by others as sexual harassment.

People @ Work

Sexual Harassment Compliance Officer

If you work for an organization that provides training for employees on the activities that constitute sexual harassment, you may receive your training from a sexual harassment compliance officer. Sexual harassment compliance officers provide policy information and guidance when an organization responds to incidents of sexual harassment. An officer takes complaints of sexual harassment and sex discrimination and investigates each complaint thoroughly. She or he provides remedies and works with external representatives regarding complaints. The sexual harassment compliance officer also works with management to provide a working environment free of sexual harassment and sexual discrimination.

Providing for Persons with Physical Handicaps

Persons with physical handicaps can face biases based on their physical challenges and may be treated differently due to their disabilities. The ethical organization abides by federal, provincial, or territorial human rights statutes, acts, or policies in fulfilling their "duty to accommodate." The objective of the statute, act, or policy is to eliminate barriers that prevent full participation of existing and potentially new employees in the workforce. In addition to physical barriers, other barriers to employment include unnecessary job requirements and unequal access to training and development. The ethical organization

- provides access to all facilities for people who have physical challenges
- provides the proper equipment, workspace, and training and development
- ensures that initial employment practices do not discriminate against people who have physical challenges

"Duty to accommodate" requires the employer to make every effort to accommodate employees with disabilities, unless to do so would create undue hardship on the employer. In determining undue hardship, an employer may take into consideration the health of the employee, safety, and costs.

Involvement in the Community

The ethical organization recognizes the needs of its community and assists with meeting these needs when possible. For example, the organization might

- provide tutors for elementary and high-school students
- engage in mentoring programs for troubled youth
- work with colleges and universities in providing intern experiences for students
- provide computers (or other technology the business manufactures) to schools
- serve on community boards and commissions
- participate in the local chamber of commerce
- contribute to community charities
- provide leadership to solicit funds for worthy causes, such as for children who have disabilities, health care for people who are indigent, and shelters for people who are homeless
- assist with arts and other programs by providing leadership and/or monies

Respect for the Needs and Rights of Employees

Promoting employee productivity is important to the ethical organization. An ethical organization understands that employees have needs, such as the need to know the values and directions of the company, what is expected of them, and so on. Figure 3-4 illustrates some ways the organization can meet the needs of employees.

FIGURE 3-4
Meeting the Needs of Employees

- Provide employees with a copy of the values and goals of the organization; ask that managers review these documents with their employees
- Encourage managers to consistently distribute important information about the organization
- Help employees set achievable goals that are consistent with the goals of the organization
- Administer employee performance evaluations fairly
- Support employees in learning new skills
- Reward employee creativity
- Challenge employees to generate new ideas
- Encourage collaboration and cooperation among employees
- Establish teams to work on significant organizational issues

---

An ethical organization also understands that employees have rights. Three such rights are the right to due process, the right to organize, and the right to privacy.

Right to Due Process

Generally, employees make a conscientious effort to contribute to an organization. In return, they expect to be treated fairly by an organization. People would not choose to work for an organization if they did not think they were going to be treated fairly. Employment at will (the doctrine that allows employees to be fired for good cause or for no cause) has been and still is an employment doctrine upheld by some organizations. In an unethical organization, adherence to such a doctrine can cause irreparable harm to employees. For example, companies have been known to call long-time employees into a supervisor's office, tell them they no longer have a job, and send them home immediately with no severance package and loss of all benefits. The doctrine of employment at will has come under considerable attack and, in most organizations, is being replaced by the right to due process. Due process means that managers impose sanctions on employees only after offering them a chance to correct the organizational grievance. An ideal system of due process is one in which employees are given

- a clearly written job description
- organizational policies and procedures
- the assurance that all policies and procedures will be administered consistently and fairly without discrimination
- a commitment by top management that managers will be responsible for adhering to the values and morals of the organization
- a fair and impartial hearing if the rules are broken

Right to Organize

Approximately one-third of the Canadian labour force is represented by a trade union. Under federal, provincial, or territorial labour relations legislation, every person is free to join a union of his or her own choice and to participate in its lawful activities. With more than a half-million members, the Canadian Union of Public Employees (CUPE) is Canada's largest union.

Labour unions are instrumental in ensuring that the rights and benefits of employees are upheld. Employees join unions in order to have a stronger, collective voice in resolving the issues that arise in the workplace. They resolve such issues through negotiations and by creating collective agreements, without which many employees could be at an economic disadvantage. These collective agreements enhance existing federal, provincial, and territorial employment standards.

Right to Privacy

Canada's Personal Information Protection and Electronic Documents Act (PIPEDA), or similar legislation implemented provincially or territorially, provides the ethical organization with guidelines regarding the individual employee's right to privacy. Certainly, an organization has the right to information about an employee that affects that individual's performance. For example, if a physical illness no longer allows an employee to perform his or her job, the employer has a right to know about it. However, the employer does not have the right to know about illnesses that do not affect job performance. Similarly, an employer does not have the right to know about a person's political or religious beliefs. In fact, in a job interview, the employer cannot ask questions about marital status, age, organizations to which the person belongs, where the person was born, the spouse's employment status, and so on. These questions are illegal. If an organization acquires information about an employee's personal life while doing a legitimate investigation, the organization has an obligation to destroy the information, especially if the data would embarrass or in some way injure the employee. Also, an organization must give employees the right to give or withhold consent before any private aspects of their lives are investigated.

Adherence to Workplace Standards

Occupational health and safety legislation in Canada outlines the general rights and responsibilities of the employer, the supervisor, and the worker. In addition to federal legislation that applies to employees across the country employed by the federal government, each province and territory has its own legislation.[4] You can read more about the specific legislation in your province or territory by accessing the CanOSH (Canadian Occupational Safety and Health) website from the link provided on the MindTap site.

An ethical organization abides by the Canada Labour Code and other statutory provisions at the provincial or territorial level that confer upon employees certain minimum standards of employment. Figure 3-5 (on page 52) provides an overview of the topics covered by employment standards legislation. Specific requirements may vary by province or territory.

Establishing and Living Organizational Values

Many organizations today establish vision and value statements and make these statements available to their employees and to the public by posting them on websites and distributing them in organizational publications. Here are excerpts of mission/vision/value statements from two organizations—Horizon Health Network in New Brunswick and Sun Life Financial.

Horizon Health Network*

Our Vision: Exceptional care. Every person. Every day.

Horizon, through our staff, physicians and volunteers must seek to be more than simply adequate…to exceed the expectations for every person who looks to us for service and to do this for each and every interaction with our patients and visitors…. Nothing short of

aspiring to give exceptional care will allow us to do our very best.

Our Mission: Helping People Be Healthy

…We achieve best results through placing our patients and clients at the centre of our health delivery system.

Our Values: At Horizon, the following values guide how we work together and serve our patients, their families and each other
- We show empathy, compassion and respect.
- We strive for excellence.
- We are all leaders, yet work as a team.
- We act with integrity and are accountable.[5]

Sun Life Financial†
- Mission is to help customers achieve lifetime financial security
- Vision is to be an international leader in protection and wealth management.
- Values are the foundation of our day-to-day business operations. At Sun Life we are about integrity…engagement…customer focus…excellence…and value….[6]

Once you know the company mission/value statement, it is your responsibility to behave in ways that support the mission. If you find yourself in a company where you cannot support the mission/values, it is time for you to find another position.

Maintaining a Safe and Healthy Environment

The public expects an organization to behave in ways that protect and maintain a safe and healthy environment for its customers and the community it serves. Additionally, the ethical organization is committed to providing and maintaining a safe and healthy environment for its employees.

Over the past few years, incidences of violence in the workplace have increased. In fact, workplace violence has become such a large problem in North America that the Occupational Safety & Health Administration in the United States and the Canadian Centre for Occupational Health and Safety have both published specific guidelines on this issue, and legislation exists in both countries. This legislation in Canada, known as "due diligence" legislation, when applied to occupational health and safety means that an employer shall take all reasonable precautions to prevent injuries or accidents in the workplace. Due diligence is defined as that level of judgment, care, prudence, determination, and activity which a person would reasonably be expected to exercise under particular circumstances. This duty applies to all situations that are not covered by other, specific workplace legislation.[7]

* http://en.horizonnb.ca/media/616051/horizon_strat_plan_english_jan28. pdf, accessed February 2015.

† Sun Life Financial website, Mission, Vision and Values," www. sunlife.com, accessed April 2015.

FIGURE 3-5
Topics Covered by Employment Standards Legislation

MINIMUM WAGES

The minimum wage rates payable to most workers varies from province to province. In 2015, the minimum wage rate in Alberta and Saskatchewan was $10.20; in Nova Scotia, $10.60; and in Ontario and Nunavut, $11.00.

HOURS OF WORK

While some provinces may authorize hours in excess, generally the legislation provides that no employee shall work more than eight hours per day or 48 hours per week. In Quebec, the Act defined 40 hours per week to be a regular workweek for any employee.

OVERTIME

Overtime generally at a rate of one-and-a-half times the regular rate of pay is paid to employees who work in excess of approximately 40 hours per week. At the request of an employee, some employers may provide time off in lieu of overtime pay.

PUBLIC HOLIDAYS

Under federal, provincial, and territorial law, employees are entitled to five paid public holidays each year: New Year's Day, Good Friday, Canada Day, Labour Day, and Christmas Day. Federal employees also receive paid days off for Easter Monday, Victoria Day, Thanksgiving Day, and Boxing Day; many non-federal employees also get these holidays. Some provinces recognize Remembrance Day in November, a civic holiday in August that is known by specific names in each province, and a Family Day in February.

VACATION PAY

After one year of service with an organization, an employee is entitled to two weeks' vacation with pay (except in Saskatchewan where it is three weeks and Quebec where it is one day per month worked). At the employer's discretion, this vacation may be taken at a time mutually convenient to the employee and employer, and may occur within 10 months of commencement of employment.

MATERNITY LEAVE

Provincial and territorial laws vary, but upon four weeks' written notice, female employees are entitled to 17 weeks of unpaid maternity leave, provided the employee has been employed for a minimum number of weeks immediately preceding the estimated delivery date. Unemployment insurance benefits are available to employees on maternity leave. On her return, the employee is entitled to reinstatement in her former position, or be given a comparable position in the same location and with the same wages and benefits.

PARENTAL LEAVE

Upon four weeks' notice, an employee who has been employed a minimum number of weeks is entitled to 37 weeks of parental leave. This leave is available to male and female employees, and, in the case of a female employee, may immediately follow a maternity leave. At the end of the parental leave, an employee is entitled to be reinstated to the same or comparable job at the same rate of pay, and with the same benefits and seniority accrued as of the date of the commencement of the leave.

COMPASSIONATE CARE LEAVE

Compassionate Care Benefits are a component of Employment Insurance. Benefits may be paid up to a maximum of eight weeks to a person who needs to be absent from work in order to care for a family member who is gravely ill and at risk of dying. No provision is made for paid leave as the Code provides job security only. However, some financial support may be available through the Employment Insurance Act to qualified employees.

EQUAL PAY FOR EQUAL WORK

Employees who perform substantially the same kind of work in the same establishment where the performance of duties requires the same skill, effort, and responsibility shall see no difference in their rate of pay. Difference in pay rates may exist where the differential is based on any factor other than sex such as seniority or meritocracy.

BENEFIT PLANS

When in place, they must be furnished to all employees with no differences based on age, sex, or marital status.

Sources: Compiled from various sites, including "Statutory Holidays in Canada," www.statutoryholidays.com/index.php; "Minimum Wages in Canada," Canada Online, http://canadaonline.about.com/od/labourstandards/a/minimum-wage-in-canada.htm; "The Canada Labour Code," http://laws-lois.justice.gc.ca; "The Canadian Human Rights Commission," www.chrc-ccdp.ca, accessed August 2011.

Many organizations have workplace violence prevention programs, which include helping individuals learn how to deal with and de-escalate conflict. Why is this happening? No one has all the answers to this question, but experts suggest that the following issues may contribute to increased anger and violence:

- ignorance of other cultures
- belief that one is being treated unfairly

An ethical organization upholds the provincial or territorial regulations and/or acts that require employers to furnish a place of employment free from recognized hazards that can cause death, injury, or illness to employees. Such is the case with smoking and substance abuse.

Smoking

Studies have shown that smoking can be extremely dangerous to an individual's long-term health, and that exposure to second-hand smoke can cause emphysema and lung disease. All provinces and territories in Canada have legislation that prohibits smoking in indoor public spaces and workplaces. Because this legislation is not federally enacted, differences do exist at provincial, territorial, and/or municipal levels in terms of the provision of ventilated smoking rooms and the distance from a building's entrances and exits at which smoking is banned.

Substance Abuse

Substance abuse refers to the use of alcohol or drugs to an extent that is debilitating for the individual using the substance. Drug and alcohol users are absent an average of two to three times more than other employees and perform at about two-thirds of their actual work potential. Their absence and reduced performance affects all employees, by reducing overall productivity in the workplace. Shoddy work and material waste are evident, and mental and physical agility and concentration deteriorate with substance abuse. Even small quantities of drugs in a person's system can cause deterioration of alertness, lack of clear-headedness, and slower reaction speed, which often result in serious workplace accidents.

CCOHS has a sample safety inspection checklist that can be modified for your particular workplace. Some of the questions it asks are detailed in Figure 3-6.

FIGURE 3-6
Sample Safety Checklist for Offices

Ask these safety questions about your workspace:
- Floors
  Is there loose material, debris, or worn carpeting?
  Are the floors slippery, oily, or wet?
- Equipment
  Are sound-dampening devices in place and effective?
  Is furniture in good condition (i.e., are there worn or badly designed chairs; any sharp edges on desks and cabinets)?
  Is the workspace configured ergonomically (i.e., is the keyboard at the proper elevation, is the chair adjustable)?
- Dangerous Substances
  Are there any controlled substances (i.e., products that comply with the standards of the Workplace Hazardous Materials Information System, or WHMIS)?
  If yes, are the products properly labelled?
  Does each product have a corresponding material safety data sheet (MSDS)?
  Are workers trained in how to use these products safely?
- Sanitation
  Are washroom and food preparation areas clean?
  Are measures in place to prevent the spread of disease?
- Material Storage
  Are materials neatly and safely piled?
  Are storage shelves overloaded or beyond their rated capacity?
  Are large and heavy objects stored on lower shelves?
- General
  Are electrical or telephone cords exposed in areas where employees walk?
  Are wall and ceiling fixtures fastened securely?
  Are file cabinet drawers overloaded?
  Are file cabinets loaded with the heaviest items in the bottom drawers?

Providing an Ergonomically Sound Environment

An organization's management has a responsibility to ensure employees are provided with an environment where ergonomic factors are carefully considered to avoid RSIs. Chapter 2 detailed several principles to apply when setting up an ergonomically sound workstation, which you may wish to review now (refer to page 35).

Acoustics and colour can also affect the workplace environment. Sound in the workplace can be good or bad. Soft background music and subdued conversations do not disrupt the workday; however, street sounds and loud machines interfere with communication, make concentration difficult, and cause fatigue. Noise can be controlled by installing carpet, draperies, and acoustical ceilings, and by using partitions with acoustical panels between workstations.

Thoughtful use of colour in the workplace can stimulate collaboration, creativity, and cooperation, and minimize fatigue. Attractive, cheerful, and efficient-looking workplaces tend to inspire confidence and trust. Warm colours (such as yellow, red, and orange) create cheerful surroundings, while tones of grey tend to put people to sleep. Cool colours, such as green and blue, produce a calm and tranquil atmosphere. Determining the function of the workspace can help in establishing the best colour scheme.

Being Honest

An ethical organization is honest. It makes its policies and procedures clear to both its customers and its employees. For example, its pricing policies are made clear to buyers; its product warranty is upheld. Employees understand salary and promotion policies. Executives within the organization are forthright and truthful. The ethical executive does not appropriate excessive and lavish perks for himself or herself. The ethical executive's word can be taken seriously; employees know and understand the direction of the company.

Being Visionary

The visionary organization can look beyond day-to-day activities. Executives within the ethical organization can help managers and employees understand where the company will be in 5, 10, or 15 years, and assist others in formulating policies and objectives that will help the company achieve its goals. The organization, through its leadership, consistently articulates the vision of the company and constantly evaluates the daily operations of the company in relation to meeting the vision. Refer to Self-Check A.

The Ethical Administrative Professional

At work, you will face many ethical choices. Some of these choices will be easy to make. The right or wrong answer will be clear. For others, the answer will not be so easy. Many of the characteristics of an ethical organization are also considered ethical characteristics of employees within the organization. People rely on their personal values when making ethical decisions. While each person has his or her own core values, values that are widely shared by ethical employees include respect (for the organizational structure, diversity, clients and customers, and the privacy of others), honesty, fairness, responsibility, and compassion.

Respect for the Organizational Structure

While organizations today have fewer layers than in the past, an organizational structure and a reporting line are usually identified in an organizational chart. Being respectful of the organization means that when you have issues or concerns you do not go over your supervisor's head—that is, you do not consult his or her superior. If you have an idea that you believe will help the productivity of the office; if you cannot meet a deadline on a project; or if you have problems with someone who reports to you, talk with your supervisor. Keep him or her informed on all significant items.

Respect for Diversity

Just as the ethical organization is committed to diversity, so too is the ethical employee. The ethical employee accepts and respects the diversity of all people—whether that diversity is in ethnicity, race, gender, or age. The ethical employee understands that there is no place in the office for telling jokes that have racial, ethnic, or gender overtones.

Respect for Clients and Customers

As an administrative professional, you must be respectful of your clients and customers. In business, follow the adage "The customer is always right." While you should not take this statement literally—a customer may be wrong; after all, everyone makes mistakes—in the context of service to the customer, he or she is always considered to be right. Advocate within the company on behalf of your client, to gain the needed information or, if at all possible, provide the service your client needs. Value the client's time; do not waste it by keeping him or her on the phone for too long or by being late for an appointment. Treat every client and customer as a VIP (very important person). Remember, without clients and customers, the company would not be in business and you would not have a job.

If you have occasion to help entertain customers and clients—you may be asked to take an out-of-town customer to dinner—keep the situation on a purely professional basis. If gifts from clients and customers are offered to you, check the policy of your organization before accepting. Certainly a small gift may be appropriate, and you can accept it graciously; however, as a matter of ethics, you should not accept an extremely expensive gift.

Respect for the Privacy of Others

Respect the privacy of others within the office by maintaining the confidentiality of information that is formally protected in federal and provincial or territorial legislation and information that is not formally protected but that people assume is private. For example, if someone confides a personal matter to you, do not spread the "juicy gossip." If you have access to personnel files that contain confidential information about others, keep the information confidential. You may at times be given information that is not specifically labelled "confidential," yet should not be passed on to others. Be sensitive

Do not go over your supervisor's head; talk with him or her about issues.

to the handling of this information. Do not hide behind the rationale "But I was not told it was confidential." Use your common sense. Ethical conduct dictates that you are always discreet. Remember the Golden Rule: Treat others as you would want to be treated.

Forwarding someone's email to another reader without first getting permission from the writer is an example of unethical behaviour. While breaches of confidentiality are sometimes intentional, they can also occur through ignorance and carelessness. Take the time to make yourself thoroughly aware of the ways in which confidentiality needs to be protected in your office. Learn the requirements of the law, and always follow standard company procedures for storing, maintaining, and releasing confidential data.

Professionalism @ Work

Accept Constructive Criticism

Your supervisor is just that—your supervisor, with the responsibility to help you do your job well. Be willing to accept constructive criticism—that is, criticism that can help you learn and grow. If your supervisor recommends that you do something differently, do not view his or her remarks personally.

For example, assume you recently set up a meeting for your employer at a hotel where lunch was served. This was the first time you planned such a meeting, and you thought you did a good job. However, after the meeting, your employer told you the room arrangement was not satisfactory and the food was not good. How do you respond to such criticism? First of all, deal with the issues at hand. You might say, "Can we talk about it further? How else could the room have been arranged? What type of meal would you suggest?" Keep an open mind; realize that you have much to learn and that everyone makes mistakes. You might also suggest reviewing the arrangements with your supervisor before the next meeting.

Always avoid an emotional response to criticism. Try to separate the issue from the critic; consider that the critic is probably concerned with improving the situation. If you respond emotionally to the critic, you may succeed only in upsetting yourself (and possibly the critic). Do not dwell on criticism and carry it around with you. Learn what you can from the situation, determine never to make the same mistake again, and then move on.

Honesty

Dishonesty at work is a common ethical problem. Dishonesty means not only lying but also withholding information or misrepresenting the truth. These actions are always unethical; they can also be illegal.

Employee theft costs companies billions of dollars each year. Most people would never consider stealing something from a friend. Yet taking from an employer is a common ethical problem. Taking home notebooks, copy paper, staplers, and other office supplies is stealing. So is using an office copier for personal copying. Duplicating company software to use at home is not only unethical, it is illegal. Using the company mail system to mail personal packages is stealing from the company and is highly unethical.

The importance of attending to company business while at work was discussed in earlier chapters. Surfing the Internet, reading or writing personal email, browsing through catalogues, and reading the newspaper during paid working hours is akin to stealing time from your employer; these activities should be done at a time away from work. While occasional personal phone calls are usually permissible, and short communications with other employees on matters that are not related to work are appropriate, abuse of that privilege is unethical.

Calling in sick when one is not is a common unethical practice. Attendance is extremely important. When employees are not at work, their work does not get done. Other people may need to do it for them. Employee absences affect co-workers and supervisors. Coming in late and leaving early can become a habit—a very bad habit—as can taking long breaks or extended lunch hours.

Being honest means the employee does not take anything (time or product) that belongs to the company, is conscientious about using time wisely, and gives the company productive work for the whole workday.

Skills @ Work

How can you apply ethics in your workplace writing? Here are several suggestions:
- Make sure your content is accurate. Check and recheck your facts.
- Honesty is important. Avoid questionable language.
- Under no condition should your writing contain obscenities or off-colour language.
- Use the editing process as a means of ensuring your messages are courteous and professional. Setting aside a document and reviewing it later will help you from sending messages that you will later regret.
- Take pains not to offend any group in your writing, and avoid language that could be perceived as sexist.
- Don't use humour, unless you know your correspondent well. Keep in mind that many jokes can be offensive to different people or groups.

Dealing with Workplace Politics

In a truly ethical world, office politics would not exist. Unfortunately, we do not live in such a world and probably never will. Workplace politics are fed by networks of individuals where whom you know can be more important than what you know. Favours may be handed out on the basis of the existing networks.

So what do you do about workplace politics? When you begin a new job, notice what is happening around you. Be aware of the power bases. Be aware of who knows whom and their relationships. Then hold on to your own value system. Do your job to the best of your ability. Do not gossip about office politics. Use your awareness of the power bases to get your job done. In other words, do not fight a power base when you know you cannot win. Spend your energies in doing what is right. Generally, when you hold on to your values and perform your job extremely well, you will be recognized and respected for who you are.

Making Ethical Decisions

Your own ethics are influenced by the following:
- your religious beliefs
- your philosophical beliefs
- the culture in which you grew up

The convergence of these factors plus the culture and expectations of the business organization where you are employed can make it difficult to determine what truly is right and wrong in a particular situation. Asking these questions can help you decide what is ethical.
- What are the facts in the situation?
- Who are the stakeholders, or who will be affected by my decision?
- What are the ethical issues involved?
- Are there different ways of looking at this problem? If so, what are they?
- What are the practical constraints?
- What actions should I take?
- Are these actions practical?

If you are still unclear about what you should do, ask yourself these questions.
- If my actions appeared in the newspaper, would I feel all right about everyone reading about what occurred?
- Is what I anticipate doing legal?
- Could I proudly tell my spouse, my parents, or my children about my actions?
- Will I be proud of my actions one day, one week, and one year from now?
- Do my actions fit with who I think I am?

Dependability

Do what you say you will do, when you say you will do it. Do not make excuses for poor performance. Your employer and peers are not impressed with excuses.

Take a few minutes now to complete Self-Check B. When you finish, check your answers with those given at the end of the chapter.

SELF-CHECK B

Respond to the following statements with "Always," "Sometimes," or "Never."

1. I accept constructive criticism. ___
2. I respect the privacy of others. ___
3. I become involved in office politics. ___
4. I am dependable. ___
5. I make excuses when I cannot finish a job. ___
6. I give credit where credit is due. ___
7. I am honest with customers. ___
8. I use the telephone for personal conversations. ___
9. I believe it is all right to accept gifts from clients. ___
10. I talk with my employer first about any job-related issues. ___

Working Ethically

Most people want to work ethically. They want to do the jobs they have been hired to do and to live up to the expectations of their supervisors, co-workers, and customers. When things are going well, working ethically can be easy. It's when circumstances are not ideal that the temptation can arise to lie, cut corners, or cover up. Making ethical decisions in your personal life will help you make ethical decisions in your professional life. Ethical and unethical behaviours tend to be consistent. In addition, ethics can and do become better and stronger with repeated ethical decisions and actions. The more people make ethical decisions, the easier they are to make. Unfortunately, the reverse is also true: the more people make unethical decisions, the easier it is to make them again. Making unethical decision can become a bad habit and can build a poor character.

Working ethically also means not taking credit for work that is not one's own. When someone takes credit for another person's words or ideas, it is known as plagiarism. Like breaches of confidentiality, plagiarism is sometimes intentional, but it can also occur through carelessness or lack of understanding. When you are overburdened with work or are under a deadline, it is easy to hastily copy material and forget to make note of the source. And people are often not aware, for instance, that copying and pasting material from the Internet is plagiarism and can also be a violation of the Canadian Copyright Act. Always provide the source for the following kinds of information, regardless of the medium in which it is provided:
- direct quotations
- paraphrasing, or restating material in your own words
- factual information that isn't widely available or generally known

Ethical Change

We do not live in a world in which all individuals and organizations are ethical. Such a statement is not meant to be negative. It merely suggests the inevitable—we do not live in a perfect world. We do live in a world in which employees make ethical mistakes but, in the majority of instances, consistently strive to improve themselves and the organizations in which they work. Ethical organizations require that people within the organization behave ethically, including top management and all individuals throughout the organization. The process of achieving ethical change requires understanding, a systematic approach, commitment, cooperation, and hard work.

Factors Impeding Ethical Change

Our backgrounds and beliefs often stand in the way of ethical change. As you read the statements in Self-Check C, ask yourself whether you believe these statements to be true or false. Now examine each of these statements individually.

SELF-CHECK C

Answer "True" or "False" to each of the following statements on the basis of your personal beliefs.

Organizations are amoral. ___

Organizational leadership is unethical. ___

Values cannot be changed. ___

Labels accurately describe individuals. ___

"Organizations Are Amoral"

Amoral is defined as "lacking moral judgment or sensibility, neither moral nor immoral." Generally, we readily accept that individuals should have ethics, but we are not so clear about what that means within the organizational framework. You may hear a statement such as "The organization has no right telling me how to behave." Yet if an organization is to be ethical, its employees must be ethical. The two are inexorably linked—the organization is the people who make up the organization, and the people within the organization are the organization. Managers have a right and an obligation to hold employees responsible for upholding the ethics of the organization, and to hold them accountable for maintaining the skills required to produce the product or service of the organization.

"Organizational Leadership Is Unethical"

Certainly there are organizations in which the leadership does not behave ethically. However, to assume automatically that all management is bad is to negatively stereotype management. If we do not want to behave ethically, it is easy to shift the blame for our lack of ethical behaviour to management. Your first obligation is to uphold the organizational ethics yourself. Then, if you find through repeated incidents that management does not uphold the organizational ethics, you may decide to leave. When management does not embrace organizational ethics, the organization may not be a good place to work.

"Values Cannot Be Changed"

Clearly, we have difficulty changing our values, since they are our personal beliefs about what is right and wrong. Generally held since childhood, our values are derived from our parents and other family members, religious groups, education, and the media. Culture affects values. If you belong to a culture that considers the development of personal relationships important, you may tend to try to establish such relationships with customers and with fellow employees. If, on the other hand, you belong to a culture in which people tend to keep others at a distance, you may be more reserved and less likely to attempt to form close associations on the job. When people enter the workforce, they bring with them their value system and integrate it into the employer's value system, rules, and policies. As situations arise that require judgment, employees rely on their sense of right and wrong to choose how to react. These decisions continue to shape their values.

However, change is possible. Consider this example. Edgar learned at an early age that gender roles are fixed in our society—a female holds menial positions and a male, the management positions. Edgar has a female supervisor and has discovered that women can indeed hold high-level positions and be extremely competent. As a result, he has altered his view of women. Organizations, by upholding a set of values and giving support to changes a person makes, can help an individual change or redefine his or her values.

"Labels Accurately Describe Individuals"

When we attach a label to someone, we are usually not describing that individual accurately. For example, to describe a person as a "computer nerd" or a "party animal" is restrictive of the whole person's qualities and traits. Remember that labelling hinders rather than helps the change process. Labelling individuals often restricts our view of them. We begin to see them only as the label we have attached. We ignore their other qualities. If we are committed to ethical change within an organization, we must avoid the use of restrictive labels.

Factors Supporting Ethical Change

The organization and individuals committed to ethical change can take certain practical steps to produce the change. These steps include the following:
- Determine the ethical change needed.
- Determine steps required to achieve the objective.
- Practise the new behaviours.
- Seek feedback on the change.

- Reward the individual or group involved.
- Evaluate the effects of ethical change.

Ethics—The Choice Is Yours

Although you cannot influence the ethics of an entire organization unless you are in upper management, you can carefully check out an organization's ethics before you accept a position. How do you check out an organization's ethics? Here are a few suggestions:

- Read the organization's Web page information. Does it mention the ethics of the organization? Does it mention a commitment to diversity? Does it mention a commitment to the external community? What types of programs does it offer for employees?
- Check the history of the organization. Has the organization ever made headlines for behaving unethically?
- Talk with acquaintances who work for the organization. Ask them to describe the ethical environment of the company.

As an individual employee, you can commit to behaving in an ethical manner. You can decide to follow the ethical stances mentioned in this chapter. You will

- respect the organizational structure
- respect diversity
- respect clients and customers
- respect others' privacy
- be honest
- accept constructive criticism
- consider office politics
- make ethical decisions
- be dependable

You can also promise yourself that if for some reason (beyond your control) your organization begins engaging in grossly unethical behaviours, you will seek employment in another organization. Peter M. Senge, in his book *The Fifth Discipline*, tells the story of the frog: If you put a frog in a cup of tepid water, it will not jump out; the temperature is comfortable. If you continue to turn up the heat gradually over a period of time until the water is boiling hot, the frog will continue to stay in the water and die. The frog adjusts to the temperature as it increases and does not notice the difference in the environment or the threat to its safety. The moral of the story is this: Unless you are committed to observing the ethical behaviour of an organization and behaving in an ethical manner yourself, you may stay in an organization that becomes unethical and find yourself supporting those unethical behaviours to the detriment of your own value system and career growth. Commit now to "jumping out" of unethical waters before you "die" in them.

A Case Study

Consider this example of a setting in which ethical change is needed and is addressed within the organization.

Determine the Ethical Change Needed

As an administrative professional, you have two people reporting to you—Guy Beauchamp and Luyin Wu. You have been asked to lead a 10-person team that will be looking at the hiring practices of administrative professionals. Presently CanAsian's number of minorities employed in this category is not consistent with the number of available minorities in the area. Of the administrative professionals presently working for CanAsian, 7 percent are Indo-Canadian, 3 percent are Latin-American, and 2 percent are Asian. The statistics for Calgary show that the availability of administrative professionals is Indo-Canadian, 25 percent; Latin-American, 10 percent; and Asian, 5 percent. The task of the team is to examine how CanAsian might change these statistics to be more representative of the area. You ask both Guy and Luyin to work with you on the team.

At the first meeting, Guy makes several statements that are interpreted by the team as being negative concerning the need for change. Luyin says nothing but exhibits body language that suggests she is upset with Guy. You believe you must try to help them modify their behaviours or the team will not be successful. You determine that the following ethical changes are needed:

- Guy needs to demonstrate greater acceptance of all diversity.
- Luyin needs to state her opinions in meetings in an open but non-confrontational manner.

Determine the Steps Required to Achieve the Objective

After thinking through the situation, you decide to approach each person individually and discuss the following:

Guy—Discuss with Guy the importance of CanAsian improving its diversity statistics and ask his opinion of how this might be done. Ask him to prepare his ideas before the next team meeting and to review his ideas with you. In this example, the team leader recognized that the approach to Guy must be positive, not negative. The team leader did not berate him for his behaviour, but asked for his help on the completion of the team report.

Luyin—Discuss with Luyin the importance of stating her opinions in an open manner at the team meetings. Let her know you value her opinions and want to hear from her. Remember that Luyin is Chinese, and it may not be easy for her to state her opinions openly.

You also decide to clarify the objectives with the entire group at the next meeting, presenting the objectives positively.

Practise the New Behaviours

Give Guy and Luyin a chance to behave differently from their behaviour in the last meeting by asking Guy to share his suggestions for improvement (that you have reviewed together before the meeting). If Luyin does not voice her opinions, ask for her response. Reward Guy and Luyin for doing a good job by publicly praising both of them.

After clarifying the objectives for the group, ask whether anyone has questions and discuss whatever issues are raised.

Seek Feedback

Ask a trusted member of the committee to evaluate both your behaviour and the behaviour of the team, and to then make suggestions for changes. If necessary, you might have a consultant observe the group and offer suggestions to team members for successfully completing their tasks. The team leader may also engage in team-building exercises with the group.

Reward the Individuals and the Group

Assuming Guy and Luyin show positive changes in their behaviour, reward them for their growth. Let them know you appreciate their work on the committee, that they did a good job, and that the results of their work will make CanAsian a better place to work. In addition, reward yourself for your work with the team. You deserve to be proud of your insights and willingness to work with the individuals. Mentally add this success to your list of strengths.

Evaluate the Effects of the Ethical Change

Observe whether the team's recommendations result in greater diversity in the numbers of administrative professionals who are employed. If not, you might want to discuss the problem with the human resources director.

Chapter Summary

The summary will help you remember the important points covered in this chapter.

- Ethics are guidelines or accepted beliefs about what is right or wrong, good or bad. Business ethics apply these principles to day-to-day decisions and activities in the workplace.
- The lack of ethical behaviour by a business can affect our society and the individuals within it.
- Advances in technology and the immediate coverage of business practices through social media have resulted in higher awareness of ethical standards.
- The ethical organization respects the needs and rights of employees, is honest, visionary, committed to diversity, and socially and environmentally responsible.
- The ethical employee is honest, dependable, and cooperative; respects the organizational structure, diversity, others' privacy, clients, and customers; and makes ethical decisions.
- Mistaken perceptions that impede ethical change include beliefs that organizations are amoral, organizational leadership is unethical, values cannot be changed, and labels accurately describe individuals.
- People apply their own core values when making ethical decisions.
- Ethical change activities include identifying the change and the necessary steps to achieve it, practising the new behaviours, seeking feedback, rewarding the individual or group involved, and evaluating the effects of ethical change.
- As an individual, commit to behaving ethically; and, when necessary prepare to leave an organization that is unethical.

Key Terms

ethics p. 46
morality p. 46
integrity p. 46
pragmatic p. 46
prejudice p. 47
discrimination p. 48

sexual harassment p. 49
employment at will p. 50
due process p. 50
substance abuse p. 53
amoral p. 57

Responses to Self-Check A

An ethical organization
- Is socially and environmentally responsible
- Is committed to diversity
- Is intolerant of discrimination
- Maintains a policy against harassment
- Provides for the physically challenged
- Is involved in the community
- Respects the needs and rights of employees
- Adheres to workplace standards
- Establishes and lives organizational values
- Maintains a safe and healthy environment
- Provides an ergonomically sound environment
- Is honest
- Is visionary

(Responses should include any six of the above characteristics.)

Responses to Self-Check B

The most appropriate answers are as follows:
1. Always
2. Always
3. Never
4. Always
5. Never
6. Always
7. Always
8. Never
9. Sometimes (If the gift is small, it may be appropriate; each situation needs to be analyzed. Some organizations do not allow an employee to accept any gifts.)
10. Sometimes (On some issues, you may not need to involve your employer; but never go to his or her supervisor.)

Discussion Items

These discussion items provide an opportunity to test your understanding of the chapter through written responses and/or discussion with your classmates and your instructor.

1. Why is ethical behaviour important for businesses?
2. List and explain six characteristics of the ethical business.
3. List and explain six characteristics of an ethical employee.
4. Can ethical change occur? If so, how?
5. What factors often impede ethical change?

Critical-Thinking Activity

Martin Albertson, your supervisor at CanAsian, gives his expense accounts to you each month. Your responsibility is to put the information on a form and return the form to him. Once he reviews and signs the form, you send it to the president for signature. Last month, you noticed Mr. Albertson included alcoholic beverages on the expense report (under the category of food and beverage). This month you noticed he did it again, and you remember the same thing occurring several months ago. Company policy specifically states that an employee cannot be reimbursed for purchases of alcohol. You believe it is merely carelessness on the part of your supervisor; you believe in his honesty. However, you are beginning to wonder whether you are engaging in unethical behaviour by not calling his attention to these items. Mr. Albertson has always been clear about your responsibility for knowing and adhering to the policies and procedures of the company.

- What is the problem?
- What is your role in the issue?
- How should you handle the situation?
- Have you been behaving ethically by not calling it to his attention? If your answer is yes, explain your position.

Building Workplace Skills

Project 3-1 (Learning Outcome 1)

In this project, you are to examine your own ethics. Instructions are provided in file SCDP3-1 on the MindTap site, access to which is provided with the printed access card on the inside cover of your book. This project is a continuation of your e-portfolio. Save your project in your "Reflections" folder under an appropriate file name.

Project 3-2 (Learning Outcomes 1, 2, and 4)

Collaborative Project

Along with three of your classmates, interview two executives concerning the following:

- The importance of ethical behaviour
- The characteristics of an ethical organization
- The traits of ethical employees

As you are interviewing the executives, determine whether their organizations have a vision or mission statement or code of ethics. If so, ask if you may have a copy of the statement or code. Present your findings to the class. Take notes during the interviews so you can report your findings accurately.

Project 3-3 (Learning Outcome 5)

Read the case study for this chapter, which can be found in the document SCDP3-3a, and respond to the questions given. Submit your answers to your instructor in a short memorandum using the memorandum form provided in file SCDP3-3b.

Project 3-4 (Learning Outcome 4)

Locate the sound file SCDP3-4, Exchange from the Student Course Data files, on the MindTap site. Play the file to hear a short conversation between Mark and his supervisor, Ms. Ramirez, and a second conversation between Mark and his co-worker, Courtney. What unethical workplace behaviours are taking place? Did Mark make the right decision?

Project 3-5 (Learning Outcome 2)

At CanAsian, employees can propose volunteer projects that the company will sponsor through funding and inviting employees to participate. Choose a volunteer project that you think is important. Write an email to Mr. Albertson in which you propose the project to the company. Use your persuasive skills to convince the company that the project is worthwhile. Be sure to do any research that is needed to give Mr. Albertson an accurate idea of the work to be done and the cost. Use the email form in file SCDP3-5 or the address provided by your instructor.

Project 3-6 (Learning Outcome 4)

At CanAsian, the offices open at 8:00 a.m. and close at 5:00 p.m. each day. All office personnel are required to punch in and out on a time clock. You have noticed that some people stop working at 5:00, go to the restroom or chat, and then punch out at 5:08. In this way, they get paid for an extra quarter hour. You do not feel this is right. What do you do? To decide, use one of the methods described in the "Making Ethical Decisions" section of the chapter.

Project 3-7 (Learning Outcome 4)*

You are responsible for maintaining the supply cabinet. You have noticed that some supplies are diminishing at a rate more quickly than seems reasonable. You suspect that they are being taken for personal use. Additionally, you have noticed that a few of the staff are consistently arriving to work a few minutes late. They appear to feel that it doesn't matter. Locate the file SCDP3-7. Create a spreadsheet in Microsoft Excel. Enter the data provided and complete the calculations to see how much these types of employee theft could cost a fictitious company of 30 employees over the course of one week. Over the course of a year? Does this change your opinion?

Prepare a report for Mr. Albertson that can be circulated to all staff. Attach your spreadsheet.

Project 3-8 (Learning Outcome 2)

Use library resources or the Internet to find *Maclean's* magazine's most recent annual listing of the 10 best companies to work for in Canada. Pick three of the companies and write a paragraph on each one explaining why it was picked as one of the best companies to work for.

Make the Grade with MindTap

MindTap®

Stay organized and efficient with **MindTap**—a single destination with all the course material and study aids you need to succeed. Built-in apps leverage social media and the latest learning technology. For example:

- ReadSpeaker will read the text to you.
- Flashcards are pre-populated to provide you with a jump-start for review—or you can create your own.
- You can highlight text and make notes in your MindTap Reader. Your notes will flow into Evernote, the electronic notebook app that you can access anywhere when it's time to study for the exam.
- Self-quizzing allows you to access your understanding.

Visit http://www.nelson.com/student to start using **MindTap**. Enter the Online Access Code from the card included with your text. If a code card is not provided, you can purchase instant access at NELSONbrain.com.

Endnotes

1. "Corporate Responsibility," George Weston Limited website, http://weston.ca/en/George-Weston-Ltd.aspx, accessed September 2015.
2. "Acting Ethically: Code of Business Conduct (2013)—Message from the CEO," Sun Life Financial website, http://cdn.sunlife.com/static/global/files/Code%20of%20business%20conduct/pa_e_code_of_business_conduct.pdf, accessed September 2015.
3. "The Canada Labour Code", Part III, Division XV.1, http://laws-lois.justice.gc.ca, accessed April, 2015.
4. CanOSH (Canada's National Occupational Health and Safety) website, www.canoshweb.org/en/legislation.html, accessed August 2015.
5. "Strategic Plan 2015–2020," Horizon Health Network website, http://en.horizonnb.ca/media/616051/horizon_strat_plan_english_jan28.pdf, accessed February 2015.
6. "Mission, Vision and Values," Sun Life Financial website, www.sunlife.com, accessed April 2015.
7. "OSH Answers: OH&S Legislation in Canada—Due Diligence," Canadian Centre for Occupational Health and Safety website, www.ccohs.ca/oshanswers/legisl/diligence.html, accessed August 2015.

Mastering Technology

Do I Qualify?

Administrative Assistant

Seeking an administrative assistant with excellent communication and technology skills. Job duties include:

- Maintaining IM and email links with remote offices
- Working collaboratively with co-workers and managers
- Processing and sharing data via a company intranet and an extranet
- Performing research using the Internet
- Assisting staff in resolving network and applications software related issues

The ideal candidate will have demonstrated abilities in:

- Effective time management and multitasking
- Innovative and conceptual thinking
- Organizational skills and a keen attention to detail

LEARNING OUTCOMES

After studying this chapter, you should be able to …

1. Explain the functions of computer hardware components.
2. Explain the difference between operating system software and application software.
3. Use the Internet to research information.
4. Troubleshoot software problems.
5. Identify ethical computer behaviours.
6. *Demonstrate a commitment to continual learning in our technological age.*

Today in both our personal and business lives, Canadians are constantly connected to the Internet of Things. Smartphones, which have replaced single-function cellphones, are used to talk, text, tweet, shop, bank, and so much more. Accessing the Internet using mobile devices as a telecommunication tool has grown exponentially each year, with more than 1.2 billion Internet-capable mobile devices[1] being sold in 2014. Constantly changing computer technology enables users to stay connected and to work faster and with greater portability. Just as new advances will continue to occur with all telecommunication tools, so too will new advances continue with the Internet and the Web. The task today and for the future is to fully utilize these changes to make our work and home lives more productive and efficient.

Telecommunication Tools

Telecommunications is defined as the transmission of electronic information (text, data, voice, video, and images) from one location to another. Having accurate and timely information is essential for businesses wishing to remain competitive in today's global economy. As an administrative professional, you will use telecommunication tools for many of your daily tasks—gathering data, processing data into usable information, and then sharing the information with your supervisor, co-workers, suppliers, and customers. Computers in business come in all shapes and sizes—from **supercomputers** used in organizations that process huge amounts of data, such as the Canadian census, to personal computers. Desktop and laptop computers are used extensively by administrative professionals in the workplace. Laptops are smaller in size than the desktop computer, and their power, capabilities, and portability make them a lightweight viable alternative to the desktop computer. Using a laptop or notebook to take notes at a meeting means the administrative professional can quickly and efficiently format the notes into meeting minutes and almost immediately distribute them to attendees.

Mobile Devices

As the demand for worker mobility in the workplace continues to increase, portable devices such as laptop/notebook computers, netbooks, tablets, and smartphones will help mobile workers take their computing power with them wherever they go. For those employees who travel frequently or spend significant time out of the office, laptops have replaced the desktop computer. The ability to fold up their computer, put it in a carrying case, and access their files while away from the office improves accessibility and increases effectiveness and efficiency. With cloud computing and offline storage, files are always accessible and the opportunity exists to work collaboratively with colleagues from various locations.

Tablet computers such as the Apple iPad or comparable systems from Acer and Asus are lightweight, small, and easy to carry. Using touch technology, a virtual onscreen keyboard can be used to input data, browse the Web, check email, listen to music, read books, play games, and download applications. For some people, tablets are the device of choice when travelling for business or pleasure.

A **smartphone** is a full-featured cellphone equipped with an operating system making it more like a handheld computer than a cellphone. This device combines a cellphone with functions previously available on a personal digital assistant, which enables users to send and receive email; maintain a calendar, an address book, and a task list; and make and receive calls. Using apps developed for mobile devices, users can watch movies, listen to music, browse the Web, and access cloud storage to view and edit documents. **Wi-Fi** (short for "wireless fidelity") technology connects users to the Internet, and **GPS (Global Positioning System)** services make it possible to map a location. An Internet connection known as a hotspot can be created with a smartphone so that other mobile devices are able to connect to the phone wirelessly and share its Internet connection.

Input Devices

The keyboard, mouse, touchpad, and touch screen are input devices that are used daily. Other input options include scanners, microphones with voice recognition technology, and digital cameras. The keyboard and a mouse may be connected physically to a port on a desktop computer or cordlessly by a wireless connection. Laptop/notebook or netbook computers use a **touchpad** to control the mouse pointer with some additional buttons available that can be used to execute commands. Text, drawings, graphics, and photos can be converted into electronic documents using a **scanner** as an input device. Once a document has been stored on the computer, it can be edited, copied, and printed.

Speech recognition software such as Dragon NaturallySpeaking by Nuance provides an alternative input method for people who have difficulty using their hands to operate a keyboard, mouse, or touchpad. Using a headset microphone, speech recognition systems reduce wrist strain, thereby helping to prevent repetitive stress injuries such as carpal tunnel syndrome.

Touch screen monitors using either *capacitive* or *resistive* technology are the input interface of choice for tablets, e-readers, and smartphones. Capacitive technology allows you to use your finger to touch and select an item on the screen, to zoom in or out when stretching or shrinking an image, to scroll from page to page when reading a document or from photo to photo in your media gallery, and to enter items for purchase at a self-serve kiosk. Resistive technology uses a stylus—a pen-like instrument—to sign on a screen when completing the purchase of goods at some retail outlets.

SELF-CHECK A

1. What are the two types of technology available with touch screens and how is each one used?
2. What devices are used to input information into a computer?

Data Storage

Computers use two types of data storage—primary storage (or main memory) and secondary storage. The three types of primary storage are **random access memory (RAM)**, **read-only memory (ROM)**, and **flash memory**. RAM storage, which works very fast, is used to temporarily store and run software program instructions and to store data currently in use. Purchasing the highest RAM capacity you can afford ensures that, as new applications come on the market, your computer will be able to handle them. When the computer is turned off, RAM contents are lost.

ROM storage holds basic operating instructions needed when a computer is turned on. The computer battery ensures

FIGURE 4-1
Data Measurement Chart vs. Size

Data Measurement	Size
Bit	Single Binary Digit (1 or 0)
Byte	8 bits
Kilobyte (KB)	1,024 Bytes
Megabyte (MB)	1,024 Kilobytes
Gigabyte (GB)	1,024 Megabytes
Terabyte (TB)	1,024 Gigabytes
Petabyte (PB)	1,024 Terabytes
Exabyte (EB)	1,024 Petabytes

that these necessary instructions are not lost when the computer is turned off. Some computers and devices such as cellphones and smartphones use flash memory to store these basic start-up instructions.

A **bit** (the term derived from combining **b**inary and dig**it**) is the basic unit of information in computer storage; a **byte** is eight bits. Memory capacity has expanded significantly over the years; terms that are now commonplace, such as gigabyte, were unheard of in early years. Each new term is an expansion on that original term "byte," as illustrated in the data measurement chart in Figure 4-1.

Your computer uses secondary storage memory the same way you use a file cabinet—to organize, store, save, and retrieve software and data files. A hard disk drive is an internal storage device physically mounted into your computer console that is intended to remain in place indefinitely. The amount of storage you need depends on the programs and type of data with which you intend to work. The amount of memory available has steadily increased in direct relation to its declining cost.

Do Self-Check B to determine the storage capacities of your computer.

SELF-CHECK B

Take a few minutes to go to your computer and check out how much RAM and hard disk storage you have.

* Depending on the version of Windows you have installed, to find out how much working memory you have, find the "My Computer" or "This PC" icon on your desktop or the "Computer" or "System" link in the Start Menu. Right-click with the right mouse button and select Properties. The General tab in the top left-hand corner or the "System" section will show you how much RAM you have.

* To find out how much hard disk storage you have, find the "My Computer" or "This PC" icon on your desktop and double-click with the left mouse button; or, open the Start Menu and select the "Computer" or "File Explorer" link with the left mouse button in. Right-click on the C: drive icon; then left-click on Properties to see how much used and free space you have on your hard drive.

If you require additional storage capacity, you can plug one or more external hard drives into a USB port on your computer. Two secondary storage devices that allow you to remove data from the hard disk but still retain data files are optical disk and flash memory devices. An optical disk is a thin, round, plastic disk that can be read from or written to using laser technology; two examples of optical disks are CDs and DVDs, both of which are available in two options: read-only (CD- or DVD-ROM) and read/write (CD- or DVD-RW).

A flash drive, also known as a jump drive, keychain drive, pen drive, or thumb drive can be used on any computer by plugging it into a **USB** port. This small, portable secondary storage device is about the size of a package of gum with storage capacities that range from 4 to 128 Gigabytes (GB). With a flash drive's read/write capability, data can be stored, retrieved, and deleted from this storage device as easily as from a hard drive.

Cloud storage is like having another hard drive—one that can access files from any computer with an Internet connection. Files can be backed up to the cloud or uploaded to share and work collaboratively with other users. Microsoft OneDrive and Google Drive are two examples of cloud storage.

Output Devices

Flat screen **LCD** (liquid crystal display) and **LED** (light-emitting diode) monitors are output devices for a soft copy (copy shown only on the monitor). Monitors are available in various sizes and are typically mounted on a stand. Lightweight and slim, monitors can be raised, lowered, tilted, swivelled, and rotated to provide maximum ergonomic flexibility in positioning. When a hard copy (printed on paper) is required, an inkjet, laser, or photo printer is used.

Photo printers produce a high-quality image on photo paper directly from a digital camera, computer, or mobile device. Inkjet printers are relatively inexpensive and produce graphics and text, with quality and speed close to that of a

© Pieter Beens/Shutterstock

Touch screen monitors are the input interface of choice for tablets, e-readers, and smartphones.

laser printer. They are an excellent choice for home and small businesses.

Laser printers generally have faster printing speeds than inkjet printers, which make them a primary choice of larger businesses. By connecting printers to a local area network, businesses can minimize the cost of producing hard copy. These networked printers can be accessed through the local network or through Wi-Fi technology, and may be shared among individuals and departments within the organization.

A multifunction peripheral is a popular choice for a home or small office since it can produce more than one type of output: generally, it can print, fax, copy, and scan. This one device takes up far less space than the multiple machines it replaces and can be installed more easily, since a single hookup or Wi-Fi connection takes care of numerous functions.

Take a few minutes now to respond to the items in Self-Check C. Once you have answered the questions, turn to the end of this chapter and check your answers.

SELF-CHECK C

1. List the external computer storage devices.
2. What are the major types of printers used today?

Software

The hardware components that make up a computer system could not function without the instructions it receives from operating system software and application software.

A *computer's operating system* provides the connection between you, the computer's hardware, and the application program. In understanding how an operating system works, consider this analogy. When you turn the key in your car, the motor starts. You merely perform the one function, without being aware of the various electronic parts and the interrelationships among them that are needed for the motor to start. Once the motor starts, you are ready to perform a whole series of other steps—putting the car in gear, stepping on the gas, turning on the heat or air conditioning, and so on.

Operating system software works in a similar manner. It translates your instructions—entered by keyboard, mouse, or touch—into a form that can be understood by the computer. When you turn on your computer, the operating system gets the computer ready to receive your additional commands, which generally come from application software programs. Without an operating system, you are unable to use any application software program. Existing operating systems—such as Microsoft Windows, Android, Linux, and iOS for Macs—are continually being modified and revised, and new ones developed.

Application software works with operating software to perform specific tasks. For example, you can use a word processing program to produce a report with graphics, add tables to it using a spreadsheet program, and create a presentation that includes graphics with presentation software. These applications are available separately or bundled together in packages known as application or productivity suites. In a suite, components of the individual applications have a consistent user interface, making it easier to learn new features and to share content between files that have been created by separate applications. As an administrative professional, you should select and use the application most appropriate to the task. For example, using a spreadsheet program to write a letter would be inappropriate and inefficient.

Some of the software programs that can be purchased for installation on your computer and are available from Microsoft, Corel, and IBM include the following:

- *Microsoft Office.* Available by annual subscription or one-time purchase. The subscription version includes the full suite of Word, Excel, PowerPoint, Access, Outlook, OneNote, and Publisher as individual applications. The one-time purchase version for PC or Mac each include some but not all of these applications.
- *WordPerfect Office.* Available in four versions. The Professional version includes WordPerfect, Quattro Pro, Presentations, Paradox, Publisher, and Lightning as individual applications. The Standard, Home and Student, and Legal versions each include some but not all of these applications.
- *Quicken.* A financial management program for personal and small business use.
- *Sage 50 Accounting.* An accounting software program used by small businesses for managing cash flow and monitoring expenses, creating invoices, making bill payments, and generating a payroll.

Software application programs such as these are continually revised and updated. In addition to the application programs that can be purchased and installed on single workstations or local networks, thousands of free software packages available on the Web. As an administrative professional, you may be asked to review and test new or free versions to determine their suitability for your organization.

Using cloud computing eliminates the need to install, maintain, and upgrade software applications on individual computers, networks, or mobile devices. Access to the cloud, a series of computers called servers connected to the Internet, is done through a Web browser. The trend to using the cloud is growing. Users are able to access and share the resources and applications they need paying only for the applications they use. Microsoft to copy software for their personal use. In Canada, computer software is defined as a literary work, and is therefore covered by the Copyright Act that protects original literary, artistic, musical, and dramatic works.

In addition to the copying of software being unethical and illegal, it can bring viruses into the computer system. Companies and individuals that copy software deprive themselves of both the benefits of technical support provided by many software companies and the ability to buy upgrades at reduced rates. There is, however, one legal exception to copying—one backup copy of software may be made. In Canada and the United States, organizations and individuals that are caught illegally copying software can be tried and fined. Penalties can include imprisonment and/or fines for the unauthorized reproduction or distribution of software.

It is unethical to use a computer to gain entry into a company's databank; in fact, it is theft. You might ask, "If I produced the data for the company, isn't it my property to do with as I please?" The answer is no; it is not your property unless you have specifically negotiated an arrangement with your company that allows you to retain the rights to the property. The property rights belong to the company whose resources have been used to develop the product—in other words, they have paid you or others within the company a salary or a commission to develop the product. To usurp any property rights, including the right to use the property, is a form of property theft and is unethical.

Professionalism @ Work

Employees sometimes believe that after the workday has ended, it is acceptable to use a computer for personal use or to take a few minutes during the day to email a friend or shop on the Internet. It is not okay unless permission is granted by the organization. Many businesses publish computer and Internet use policies. However, never assume that the absence of a policy regarding acceptable behaviour implicitly gives you the right to do as you please.

Unless you have permission to do so, you should not send and receive personal email, shop, play games online, download non–work-related files, or take an online class without company authorization.

The Future of Telecommunications

Alexander Graham Bell, who is credited with inventing the first practical telephone, could never have imagined how this communication device would change our world. Twenty years from now, today's solutions and scenarios will likely be irrelevant, as fibre-optic networks and cloud computing expand.

The evolution of telecommunications promises to continue, with access to all types of data, video, audio, text, and graphics at faster speeds than we are currently experiencing. In addition, telecommunication companies will continue to both merge and expand their services, delivering telecommunication services that connect people to people and people to machines in a multitude of ways.

Soft Skills   Continual Learning

This chapter reinforces the importance of continual learning in our technological age. Changes in technology occur at a rapid pace. Even though great care has been taken to include the latest information here, it may soon become outdated. As a result, we must all be continual learners if we are to be productive workers and citizens in our society. Years ago, Alvin Toffler said in his book *Future Shock* that the educated person of tomorrow is the person who has ***learned how to learn***. That statement is particularly relevant today and will continue to be relevant for many years. Here are some suggestions for you as you commit yourself to continual learning:

- Since none of us can keep all the newly emerging information in our heads, learn how to find and where to look for what you need—take time to explore the Internet, computer periodicals, and books.

- Develop an inquiring mind. When you do not understand something, ask questions. Do not be afraid to admit that you do not have all the answers. Part of ongoing learning is accepting what you do not know and being willing to do something about it.
- Commit to continuing your formal education. Take classes offered by your organization or classes offered at a college or university. Take a course online—many colleges and universities now offer a wide variety of these courses that you can complete at a location of your choice and at a time that is convenient for you.
- Devote time to learning. Learning does take time, but the results are well worth it.

Chapter Summary

The summary will help you remember the important points covered in this chapter.

- When telecommunication tools such as laptops, tablets, and smartphones are connected to a network, they make sharing information fast and affordable.
- The most frequently used input devices are the keyboard, mouse, touchpad, and touch screen.
- In addition to hard drives, flash drives, and optical disks, the use of cloud storage is a growing trend.
- Computer output is handled by monitors or touch screens (soft copy) or inkjet, laser, and networked printers (hard copy).
- An intranet is a private network available for internal users only; an extranet is a private network with access provided to selected external users.
- Operating system software enables a computer to read and write data to storage media and to accept commands from application software, while application software tells the computer how to perform a specific task.
- Software packages are available online by subscription or for free by downloading from the Web.
- Users should be aware of security risks and take steps to reduce exposing themselves to viruses and other risks.
- Be aware of ethical computer behaviour and appropriate etiquette when using telecommunication devices.
- Make a commitment to continual learning.

Key Terms

telecommunications p. 63
supercomputers p. 64
tablet computers p. 64
smartphone p. 64
Wi-Fi p. 64
GPS (Global Positioning System) p. 64
touchpad p. 64
scanner p. 64
touch screen p. 64
random access memory (RAM) p. 64
read-only memory (ROM) p. 64
flash memory p. 64
bit p. 65
byte p. 65
USB p. 65

LCD p. 65
LED p. 65
cloud computing p. 66
intranet p. 67
extranet p. 67
Web browser p. 67
broadband p. 68
digital subscriber line (DSL) p. 68
hotspot p. 68
spam p. 69
computer virus p. 69
malware p. 69
phishing p. 69
spyware p. 69
firewall p. 70

Responses to Self-Check A

1. Touch screens use either resistive or capacitive technology as an input method. Resistive technology requires the use of a pen-like instrument know as a stylus, such as entering your signature to verify a credit card transaction when purchasing items at a retail outlet. With the capacitive technology you use your fingers to tap a screen icon to select an item or to pinch or expand the size of images on the screen.

2. Devices that are used for inputting information into a computer include the computer keyboard, mouse, scanners, voice recognition technology, touch screens, and digital cameras.

Responses to Self-Check C

1. External computer storage devices include external hard drives, flash drives, optical disks, and the cloud.

2. The two major types of printers used today are inkjet and laser.

Discussion Items

These discussion items provide an opportunity to test your understanding of the chapter through written responses and/or discussion with your classmates and your instructor.

1. Explain the differences among the Internet, an intranet, and an extranet.
2. List and describe computer input devices.
3. Explain the difference between operating system software and application software.
4. How does a smartphone differ from a regular mobile phone?
5. Describe the differences between computer viruses, worms, and Trojan horses.
6. What are some steps you can take to combat security risks and keep computer data secure?
7. Describe two ethical problems involving computers that may occur in organizations.

Critical-Thinking Activity

(Learning Outcome 5)

Guy has been working at CanAsian Airlines as your assistant for slightly over a year. When he started with the company, you gave him the Policy and Procedures Manual for CanAsian, which includes a section on computer ethics. This section makes clear that all computers are the property of CanAsian and are not to be used for the personal use of employees. Yesterday, your supervisor, Martin Albertson, asked you why Guy had worked overtime the evening before. Mr. Albertson said that as he was leaving, at about 7 p.m., he noticed that Guy was still at his desk. He walked over to say goodnight and noticed that Guy was working on some type of project that did not appear to be related to CanAsian work. You had to answer that you knew nothing about it but that you would look into it. This afternoon, you asked Guy why he had worked late the evening before. He stated he had volunteered to prepare a mailing list for a community organization of which he was a member but he did not have a computer at home. You thanked him for giving you the information and left to mull over what you should do. Guy has been an exceptional employee—he never misses work; he is always on time;

his work is done promptly and accurately; he is polite and understands confidentiality. In fact, in his yearly review last month, you gave him an outstanding rating.

When you gave him the Policy and Procedures Manual, you did not go over it with him, but you did ask him to read it. After thinking about it overnight, you went back to Guy the next morning and asked him if he had read the Policy and Procedures Manual. When he answered yes, you asked him why he had violated the company policy on using computers for personal business. Guy told you the manual did not discuss personal use of computers. He pulled it from his desk and showed you that there was no section on computer ethics. Now you are in a real quandary. Address the following items:

- Do you believe you made a mistake in giving Guy an incomplete Policy and Procedures Manual? Do you believe Guy is lying to you? Explain your answers.
- How should you handle the situation?
- How can you be certain in the future that employees understand and adhere to the Policy and Procedures Manual?
- After talking with Guy, what will you report to Mr. Albertson?

Building Workplace Skills

Project 4-1 (Learning Outcome 3)

Online Project

Using one of the search engines listed in this chapter, research the status of speech recognition systems. Write a short summary of your findings, identifying your sources. Submit your summary to your instructor.

Project 4-2 (Learning Outcomes 1, 2, and 3)

Online Project

Search the Web for information on one of the following topics:

- The newest office suite software available and the latest antivirus package available

- Current operating systems in use for mobile devices
- The latest developments in smartphones. Prepare a table to compare the features of three different models, including manufacturer or brand, price, and features.
- Developments in touch screen technology
- Developments in cloud computing
- Passwords managers

Write a summary of your findings, identifying your sources. Submit your summary to your instructor.

Project 4-3 (Learning Outcome 4)

Refer to the instructions in file SCDP4-3 on the MindTap site, access to which is provided with the printed access card on the inside cover of your textbook. Numerous changes must be made to SCDP4-3a. If you do not know how to make the changes, use the Help icon on your software package to troubleshoot. Print out a copy of the document with the changes you made. Using the memorandum form SCDP4-3b on the CourseMate site, write a memorandum to your instructor and provide the readability level. This project could be added to your e-portfolio as evidence of your ability to revise a document and use the help feature of your software package.

Project 4-4 (Learning Outcomes 3 and 5)

Collaborative Project
Online Project

CanAsian plans to write two ethics policies to be distributed to the staff. For the first assignment, work with two or three of your classmates and surf the Web for companies' business ethics policies that may be available and articles on business ethics. From your research and information in the textbook, write a draft of a business ethics policy for CanAsian. Submit your draft policy with a cover memorandum to Mr. Albertson. Use the memorandum form SCDP4-4 on the MindTap site.

For the second assignment, research what other organizations are doing concerning policies on computer ethics for a section to be included in the Policy and Procedures Manual. Using the Web, see what you can find on the subject. Summarize your findings, citing your sources, and submit your findings to your instructor.

Project 4-5 (Learning Outcome 6)

Prepare another section of your e-portfolio; describe how you will commit to continual learning throughout this course. Refer to the suggestions in your text on continual learning before you prepare your plan. Save your self-improvement plan in your e-portfolio under an appropriate file name.

Make the Grade with MindTap

MindTap®

Stay organized and efficient with **MindTap**—a single destination with all the course material and study aids you need to succeed. Built-in apps leverage social media and the latest learning technology. For example:

- ReadSpeaker will read the text to you.
- Flashcards are pre-populated to provide you with a jump-start for review—or you can create your own.
- You can highlight text and make notes in your MindTap Reader. Your notes will flow into Evernote, the electronic notebook app that you can access anywhere when it's time to study for the exam.
- Self-quizzing allows you to access your understanding.

Visit http://www.nelson.com/student to start using **MindTap**. Enter the Online Access Code from the card included with your text. If a code card is not provided, you can purchase instant access at NELSONbrain.com.

Endnotes

1. Brett Molina and Marco della Cava, USA TODAY (3 March 2015). "Apple beats Samsung in Q4 smartphone sales," accessed March 2015.

2. Internet World Stats: Usage and Population Statistics, June 30, 2014, www.internetworldstats.com, accessed March 30, 2015.

Determine to improve your communication skills throughout this course. Commit to carefully studying the concepts presented in this chapter and to using the effective communication techniques presented.

Our global business environment, increasing technology, and the greater diversity of the people who comprise the workforce are some of the forces that contribute to the complexity of communication in the workplace.

This global business environment demands that we be globally literate—that we see, think, and act in ways that are culturally mindful of the vast differences in our world. Our contacts with others may be through telecommunications— the Internet, fax, telephone, and virtual conferencing—in addition to our face-to-face communication. Regardless of the form the interaction takes, practising effective communication techniques is imperative. Effectiveness assumes that you are

- Clear concerning your own values and attitudes
- Sensitive to cultural differences
- Aware of gender and age issues

Values and Attitudes

Generally, we do not give much thought to how our values may differ from other people's values. We sometimes assume that everyone has the same values and then operate from this assumption. Obviously, that assumption is not true, and it can cause communication difficulties if it is not understood.

Just as you need to understand what you value, you also need to be clear about the attitudes you reflect to others. **Attitude** is defined in the dictionary as "position, disposition, or manner with regard to a person or thing." In the workplace, a great deal of attention is paid to the attitude of employees. In fact, during the formal evaluation process, an individual is often evaluated on his or her attitude. A positive attitude is always an asset, whereas a negative attitude is always a detractor.

Cultural Differences

Our diverse population and multinational organizations require that we be alert to and tolerant of the differences between the people with whom we work. We cannot expect that all people will react to situations in the same way. Diversity can mean that significant differences exist among our values, our assumptions, and our attitudes. Consider some of these cultural differences between people.

Trust is earned differently in various countries. If an employee in Canada or in the United States performs well on his or her job, he or she earns trust quickly. Superior performance equates to trusting the individual to do the job well. In Japan and Germany, trust is earned over a long period of time; trust may in fact be a result of an individual's family relationships or long-term knowledge.

Respect also is viewed differently in various cultures. In Asian countries, great respect is given to the older generation and to people in authority, such as political officials. In Canada, we tend to believe that respect must be earned; it is not automatically given to specific people or groups of people.

Canadian students learn from the time they enter school that class participation is important; we are taught to give our opinions. If students do not participate in class, they are considered to be uninterested or even unprepared for the class. Asian students regard teachers so highly they find it difficult to voice their own views in class. Doing so is almost a sign of disrespect to the teacher.

North Americans are considered to be demonstrative. Generally, we show our feelings easily. If we are happy, we

The word *value* comes from the French verb *valoir*, meaning "to be worth." Values are our beliefs. They determine how we live on a day-to-day basis. For example, knowledge is a value. You probably would not be taking this course if you did not value knowledge. You want to learn. We may or may not spend much time thinking about what we value, but the decisions we make each day are influenced by the values we have.

Our early values are learned from significant people in our environment—our parents and other family members—and from our educational, social, and religious structures, such as our schools and places of worship. Our values are not static; that is, as we grow and change, our values may change. Like the roots of a tree, the roots of our values are the people and social and religious structures that have helped shaped them. The branches of the tree are like the values by which we operate. As we continue to grow and change mentally, psychologically, and physically, our expanded root system may include other factors that reshape our individual values—resulting in new values (like new branches) being added to the tree and even old values being removed. As you study the material in this course and perform the tasks given, you should come to understand your own value system. Your value system shapes what you believe, how you live and work, and how you relate to others.

Values are not inherently good or bad. However, the way in which you live your values may involve behaviours that are either acceptable or unacceptable in our society. If we encounter someone who is not behaving appropriately for the values we hold, we sometimes say, "That person has no values." Such a statement is incorrect; everyone has values. The values a person holds simply may not match our values or may not match those of the society in which we live.

One of your values might be to become economically independent. To accomplish this value, you might decide to obtain an education and then seek a job in an organization that gives you the opportunity to move to higher levels of responsibility. Conversely, you might decide to rob a bank, get involved in drug trafficking, or engage in some other type of criminal behaviour to satisfy your need to become economically independent. In other words, the principles that you hold, the attitudes that you exhibit, and the behaviours that you demonstrate in living your values are either legally and socially acceptable or unacceptable.

Complete Self-Check B now.

SELF-CHECK B

Stop for a moment and think about your values. List your top five values.

1. _____
2. _____
3. _____
4. _____
5. _____

smile a lot. If we are sad, we seldom smile. We are taught from an early age to make eye contact with people. We have certain concepts of time and space—it is important to be on time for business appointments; a certain amount of space or distance is maintained between people in a conversation. Figure 5-1 highlights how these same behaviours are viewed very differently in certain other countries.

Diversity can mean that significant differences exist in our values, our assumptions, and our attitudes.

FIGURE 5-1
Cultural Differences

- In Korean culture, smiling can signal shallowness and thoughtlessness.
- Asians, Latin Americans, and Caribbeans avoid eye contact as a sign of respect. Avoidance of eye contact in Japan means that the person is being polite and non-confrontational. Mothers often scold their children for staring into people's eyes when they speak.
- In France and Mexico, being 30 minutes late to an appointment is perfectly acceptable.
- Latin Americans stand very close to each other when talking; the interaction distance is much less than in North America.
- Open criticism should be avoided when dealing with Asian employees, as this may lead to loss of face.
- In Japan and China, "yes" does not always mean "yes." Avoid asking "yes/no" questions which often results in misleading answers. Some Asian cultures consider it rude to say no and will go to extremes to avoid doing so.
- Japanese are taught to withhold their personal opinions. An old Japanese proverb says "Silence is a virtue."

Source: Norine Dresser, *Multicultural Manners: Essential Rules of Etiquette for the 21st Century* (New York: John Wiley & Sons, 2005). Reproduced with permission of John Wiley & Sons, Inc.

Businesses that lack an understanding of our global cultural differences can easily make mistakes. Here are some examples that were costly to business:

- McDonald's took 13 months to realize that Hindus in India do not eat beef. When it started making hamburgers out of lamb, sales flourished.
- In Africa, companies show pictures of what is inside bottles so that illiterate customers know what they are getting. When a baby food company showed a picture of a child on its label, the product did not sell very well.
- A U.S. television ad for deodorant depicted an octopus putting antiperspirant under each arm. When the ad flopped in Japan, the producers realized that, in Japan, octopuses do not have arms; they have legs.
- A U.S. firm sent an elaborate business proposal to Saudi Arabia bound in pigskin. Since Muslims consider pigs to be unclean, the proposal was never opened.
- Kentucky Fried Chicken's "Finger-Lickin' Good" translated to "Eat Your Fingers Off" in Chinese.[1]

In the future, remind yourself not to expect people from different cultures to behave as you do. Become diversity-competent—educate yourself about other cultures by reading books that are available in bookstores and/or your local library; by joining a global chat group on the Internet; and by talking with your colleagues from different cultures about their life and the differences they see in various cultures.

Gender Issues

In all societies, the gender of an individual holds significant importance in terms of job roles, social responsibilities, family responsibilities, and even education and socialization. We are taught values, attitudes, behaviours, and roles on the basis of what is considered right and appropriate for being male or female. These roles and behaviours vary, depending on where we are born and the societal position of the group teaching the behaviours (their professional role or occupation, education attainment, and so on). Roles and behaviours also vary within a particular part of the country or within various ethnic communities. The diverse populations that exist in any city may mean that men and women are socialized in very different ways; boys and girls who grow up in large cities may be socialized differently from those who grow up in rural environments.

Gender roles are not static but change in response to events in our world. For example, women's experience of working outside the home, which became essential during World War II, changed not only the way many women viewed work roles but also changed the way many businesses and industries viewed the role of women in the workforce. Today we have greater numbers of women in the workforce than ever. An important concept that business and industry learned about more women being in the workforce is that different gender voices are present, which allows the organization to meet the needs of a greater number of people.

Before moving on, take a few minutes to reflect on gender roles in your own community. Using Self-Check C, respond to the items given.

SELF-CHECK C

1. List the different professional roles carried out by men and women in your community.

_____

_____

_____

2. List the professional roles you identified in point 1 in order of status in your community.

_____

_____

_____

3. In your opinion, does one gender carry more status in professional roles than the other? If so, explain how.

_____

_____

_____

4. List the home activities carried out by men and women—for example, cooking, cleaning, or child care.

_____

_____

_____

5. Is one gender responsible for more home activities than the other? If so, what activities are men more responsible for, and what activities are women more responsible for?

_____

_____

_____

6. If you could change the way your community views gender, what would you do?

_____

_____

_____

Age Issues

Since the requirement of mandatory retirement at age 65 was eliminated for all but a few specific occupations in certain provinces in Canada, the workforce has become more diverse and now consists of people ranging in age from 19 to those in their 70s. In coming decades, labour analysts predict that as many as six generations could be working alongside one another. Just as people who grow up in different cultures and environments have different values and expectations, so do people who are of different ages. These diverse generations and some of their characteristics have been variously labelled by writers in the field as shown in this table:

Birth Dates	Generation Name
before 1946	Silent Generation or Traditionalists
1946–1964	Baby Boomers
1965–1980	Generation X
1981–1999	Millennials or Generation Y
after 2000	Generation Z

As writers have categorized these generations by age group, they have also studied how these generations behave and have assigned certain values and characteristics to each. Tom Brokaw, in his best-selling book, *The Greatest Generation*, discussed the common values held by the men and women of the Silent Generation as duty, honour, courage, service, and responsibility for oneself.

Baby boomers, skeptical about politics and the status quo, have grown up in an era of reform. They are confident, independent, and self-reliant. Possessing a strong work ethic and commitment to their workplace, they often remain with a single employer throughout their working lives. They are optimistic and team-oriented but are neither afraid of confrontation nor hesitant to challenge established practices.

In contrast, the values and characteristics of Generation X identify this generation as more tolerant and more open to diversity and alternative lifestyles than previous generations. They readily embrace differences in religion, race, and ethnicity. They are spiritual and relational, and value good friends. They are more willing to change jobs to get ahead and less committed to one employer. They appreciate a work/life balance—they work to live; they do not live to work.

Millennials have grown up with technology, and their values and characteristics have been shaped by the technological revolution. They are entrepreneurial, goal-oriented, and adept at multitasking, and they expect immediate feedback and rewards. They seek meaningful work and, like Generation Xers, appreciate a work/life balance.

Generation Z is the newest generation to be classified. What we can expect from them has yet to be determined. They are likely to be more independent, needing less direction because of their immediate access to information and the answers they need. At young ages, they were already highly connected through mobile devices in a seamless cloud-based world of friends, data, and entertainment; they will likely expect to be able to work, learn, and study whenever and wherever they wish.

Individuals who grow up in different times may have different values. Recognizing these different values does not give anyone the right to characterize or make judgments about individuals on the basis of their ages. What is important is that, in the workforce, we must recognize possible differences due to age and then address these differences in positive ways.

As you work in this diverse world comprising multiple values, cultural differences, and gender and age issues, your challenge is to develop diversity competence by doing the following:

- Recognizing that these differences occur
- Constantly seeking to understand these differences
- Understanding their implications for communication
- Growing your ability to communicate with all people

In order to grow in your ability to communicate, you must understand the communication process and the barriers to effective communication. Additionally, you must continually practise effective communication techniques.

The Communication Process

Communication occurs when a message is sent by one person and received and understood by another person. Communicating effectively is essential to successful business operations and is the first skill listed in the Conference Board of Canada's *Employability Skills 2000+*. As an administrative professional, you must communicate with co-workers, clients, and vendors to achieve the company's goals. Advertisements and product information on websites must be current, correct, and sensitive to the needs and attitudes of customers of different cultures, interests, and abilities. Customer requests and questions must be answered clearly and promptly to maintain goodwill.

Improving your communication skills will help you create messages that are clear and effective. Good communication skills may also help you get and keep a job. Employers understand the importance of these skills. When discussing job candidates, "By far, the one skill mentioned most often by employers is the ability to listen, write, and speak effectively. Successful communication is critical in business."[2]

Do you consider yourself a good listener? Complete Self-Check D to determine your present listening effectiveness. Rate yourself by answering the statements with "Always," "Sometimes," or "Never."

The communication process involves a message, an originator, a channel, a receiver, and feedback.

- A **message** is the idea being presented by the originator of a communication. It is a symbol or group of symbols that conveys meaning, such as a thought or idea. For example, a letter contains words that are written symbols. These words convey a message to the reader.

Responses to Self-Check D

The most effective listeners would have responded with "Never" on the first eight items and "Always" on the last two items.

Discussion Items

These discussion items provide an opportunity to test your understanding of the chapter through written responses and/ or discussion with your classmates and your instructor.

1. What is meant by value clarification? Do all individuals have values? Explain.
2. What is a communication barrier? Give examples of internal and external communication barriers.
3. List five effective techniques to improve your communication skills.
4. List and explain three elements of nonverbal communication.

Critical-Thinking Activity

Yuan Liang is a manager for CanAsian Airlines. He was transferred from China shortly after the merger of the two companies. He speaks English; however, he has never lived outside China, although he had visited Canada several times before his transfer. He is having difficulty understanding the culture. Although you do not report to Mr. Liang, your employer, Mr. Albertson, has assigned you to work on a quality team chaired by Mr. Liang. In the first team meeting, you made several suggestions to Mr. Liang and the committee. Mr. Liang smiled and nodded in agreement with your suggestions; the team also voiced agreement. However, when the minutes from the meeting were sent out, you found no indication that your suggestions would be implemented. During the second meeting, Mr. Liang started the discussion with the same problem as was discussed at the last meeting— the one you thought had been resolved. After some discussion within the group (without your participation), you stated that you did not understand why the topic was being discussed again since you thought the group had agreed on a resolution at the last meeting. Mr. Liang only smiled and continued the discussion. However, after the meeting, he contacted your manager and told him you had embarrassed him before the group. Mr. Albertson called you in and asked you to explain the situation; he stated that you should have told him your concerns about the meeting. You are angry and also defensive—angry with Mr. Liang because he did not talk with you and angry with your supervisor because he seems to be questioning your integrity.

Using several of the critical-thinking techniques presented in the first chapter, ask yourself these questions:

- Am I recognizing the cultural differences that are involved?
- Is my position on this issue reasonable and rational?
- Have I tried to understand the situation from Mr. Liang's point of view?

With those critical-thinking concepts in mind, answer these questions:

- How should I have handled the situation?
- What can I learn from this situation?
- Should I talk with Mr. Liang about my feelings?
- What should I say to Mr. Albertson?

Building Workplace Skills

Project 5-1 (Learning Outcome 2)

Online Project

Browse the Web for articles on the culture of Asians and Latin Americans. Summarize two articles, giving the Web addresses, and submit your summaries to your instructor.

Project 5-2 (Learning Outcomes 2 and 3)

Collaborative Project

Open and read file SCDP5-2a on the MindTap site, access to which is provided with the printed access card on the inside cover of your textbook. With a team of three or four of your classmates, discuss the case provided; then answer the questions given at the end of the case by writing a memorandum to your instructor, using the memo form in file SCDP5-2b. List the members of your team in the From section.

Project 5-3 (Learning Outcome 4)

Keep a five-day log of the time you spend speaking and listening. You cannot be accurate to the minute, but make a concentrated effort to record the amount of time spent on both speaking and listening. Also, record the effective and ineffective behaviours you engage in while listening and speaking. At the end of the five-day period, analyze your log. How much time did you spend speaking? How much time listening? What effective behaviours did you engage in? What ineffective behaviours occurred? Determine ways in which you can improve your communication. Write a report identifying improved communication techniques you plan to follow. Submit your report to your instructor.

Project 5-4 (Learning Outcome 4)

Test your informative listening skills. Locate the sound file SCDP5-4 from the data files. Play the file to hear some assignments from your supervisor. Play the file only once. Take notes as you listen, but do not pause the recording or replay the file. Working from memory and your notes, list everything you can remember from listening to the instructions. List any questions you would ask your supervisor about the assignments if you were given the opportunity.

Make the Grade with MindTap

Stay organized and efficient with **MindTap**—a single destination with all the course material and study aids you need to succeed. Built-in apps leverage social media and the latest learning technology. For example:
- ReadSpeaker will read the text to you.
- Flashcards are pre-populated to provide you with a jump-start for review—or you can create your own.
- You can highlight text and make notes in your MindTap Reader. Your notes will flow into Evernote, the electronic

Now play the sound file again. Were you able to list all parts of the assignments? Were any of your questions answered as you heard the instructions again?

Project 5-5 (Learning Outcome 1)

In this chapter, you were asked to list your five top values. Add to this list your next five values. When you finish, you will have 10 values, listed in order of importance to you. Next, list the attitudes you think you demonstrate to others. Once you have listed your attitudes as you understand them, check with a trusted friend or family member. Ask that person to tell you what attitudes he or she believes you demonstrate. Format the document appropriately and save a copy on your e-portfolio. Title your list "Values and Attitudes." Save it under an appropriate file name.

Here is a list that may help you complete your top 10 values.
- Knowledge
- Honesty
- Dependability
- Cooperation
- Tolerance
- Justice
- Honour
- Responsibility
- Peace
- Sharing
- Freedom

MindTap®

notebook app that you can access anywhere when it's time to study for the exam.
- Self-quizzing allows you to access your understanding.

Visit http://www.nelson.com/student to start using **MindTap**. Enter the Online Access Code from the card included with your text. If a code card is not provided, you can purchase instant access at NELSONbrain.com.

Endnotes

1. Robert Rosen, Patricia Digh, Marshall Singer, and Carl Phillips, *Global Literacies: Lessons on Business Leadership and National Cultures* (New York: Simon & Schuster, 2000), p. 174.
2. Randall S. Hansen and Katharine Hansen, "What Do Employers Really Want? Top Skills and Values Employers Seek from Job-Seekers." Quintessential Careers, http://www.quintcareers.com/job_skills_values.html, accessed May 22, 2011.
3. Robert Louis Stevenson, "On Listening & Writing," Quotations, The International Listening Association, http://www.listen.org, accessed May 22, 2011.

Creating and Preparing Business Documents

CHAPTER 6

Do I Qualify?

Marketing Administrative Assistant

Marketing and research company seeks candidate with good organization and communication skills to assist management team. Candidate must

- Demonstrate effective written communication skills
- Work independently with minimal supervision
- Complete word processing tasks (correspondence, reports, memos, proposals, charts, agreements, etc.)
- Record, key, and distribute minutes without supervision
- Be able to conduct effective Internet searches
- Meet multiple and often competing deadlines
- Possess strong people skills

LEARNING OUTCOMES

After studying this chapter, you should be able to ...

1. Identify the characteristics of effective written communications.
2. Compose letters and memos.
3. Use proper email communication techniques.
4. Research and write a business report.
5. Identify skills and equipment required for transcription and dictation.
6. Observe ethical and legal obligations in written correspondence.

Written Communication Skills

Is written communication as important in the workplace today as it was in the past? The answer is a resounding yes. In fact, because email is so widely used in today's offices, administrative professionals probably compose more original written communications now than in the past. Written communication in all of its forms remains extremely important.

Emails, letters, memos, and reports are among the major communication documents in the workplace. Depending on the effectiveness of the writer, these documents may create goodwill or ill will for the organization—and the writer. To be a truly effective administrative professional, you need to add another communication skill to your list of qualifications—the ability to compose effective business documents.

As you begin your career, you may be asked to prepare emails, interoffice memoranda, and routine correspondence such as a letter requesting information. As you learn more about the organization and demonstrate your writing skills to your employer, the complexity and number of your writing assignments will probably increase, and your employer may ask you to compose letters in draft or final form for his or her signature. No matter what type of position you hold, written communication skills are invaluable to both you and the organization. You should establish a goal now to become an excellent communicator through the written word.

The basic types of written messages that the administrative professional prepares are emails, memoranda, letters, and reports.

- **Emails.** An email is generally a very short communication—it should be no longer than one computer screen.
- **Memoranda.** Although email has become the communication vehicle of choice for most interoffice correspondence, memoranda are still written, particularly when the message is longer than a paragraph or two.
- **Letters.** Letters are more formal than memos and email. They represent the company to customers, clients, and prospective customers and clients.
- **Reports.** The reports that are prepared in the workplace may be informal reports of two or three pages, or they may be formal reports containing a table of contents, the body of the report (with footnotes or endnotes), appendixes, and a bibliography.

Organizational Skills

Writing effectively is a process that involves planning, composing, editing, proofreading, and publishing messages. Each stage of the process is important in creating an effective message.

Planning

Before beginning to write any message, take time for some planning, which will save time and reduce frustrations. Ask yourself the "W" questions: Who? What? When? Where? Why?

- Who needs to receive the communication?
- What is the objective of the communication?
- What information is needed before writing the communication?
- When will the information be provided or required?
- Where should the information be sent?
- Why is the communication being written?

If you are working on a formal report, make an outline before beginning. If you are new to writing letters, you can help organize your thoughts by making random notes on a notepad or on your preferred computer note-taking program, such as Microsoft OneNote (Figure 6-1). Just as you would work with your to-do list, jot down ideas randomly; place them in order when you begin to compose the message. As you become more experienced in writing letters and informal reports, you may need to create only a mental outline of what you want to write; a formal report, however, will likely require an outline.

Determine the Objective

Next, determine the objective. What do you hope to accomplish? Is to inform the reader, to request an action or information, to persuade the reader to take action or accept an idea, or simply to promote goodwill? Some business messages have

FIGURE 6-1
Microsoft OneNote

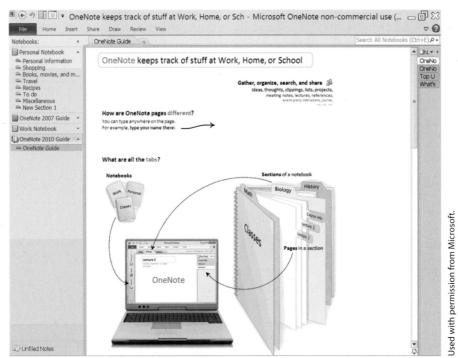

Used with permission from Microsoft.

more than one objective; for example, they may aim both to inform and to persuade. Once you have identified the objective, list the main ideas to include in the message and identify supporting details to explain or reinforce the main idea. If your task is to persuade someone to accept an offer, consider what it would take to convince the person to say yes.

Adjust the Message for the Reader

Your communication will be more effective when you adjust the message for the reader. Consider the reader's needs, wants, and interests as they relate to the message. Then state your message in a way that addresses these needs or interests. To help you identify the reader's needs or wants, ask questions such as these:

- What are the ages, genders, backgrounds, and biases of the readers?
- Do the readers have any knowledge or experience related to the message topic?
- Will the readers consider the message to be positive, neutral, or negative news?

Writing with the reader's needs and interests in mind is called the **you approach**. The *you* approach involves the use of **empathy** (mentally entering into the feeling or spirit of a person). Such writing emphasizes *you* and *your* and de-emphasizes the *I, we, mine,* and *ours.* When using the *you* approach for email messages, memos, and letters, be sincere. This means being genuine, honest, and empathic with the reader. When applying the *you* approach to your writing, the first paragraph of the message typically begins with *you, your,* or the person's name. The first example shown here is not written with the *you* approach. The second example is and will likely be more appealing to the reader.

> **Example 1** *We have decided to approve the loan application for a mortgage on the home at 234 Dollarton Highway.*
>
> **Example 2** *Your loan application for a mortgage on your new home at 234 Dollarton Highway has been approved.*

Composing

Composing is writing a message based on the objectives and plan developed for the message. A complete business message typically has an opening, one or more developmental paragraphs, and a closing.

- The opening paragraph identifies the subject of the message.
- The developmental paragraphs supply supporting details.
- The closing paragraph ends a message. This paragraph may summarize earlier points of the message, ask the reader to take some action, or try to build goodwill.

Organize the Message Content

Message content can be organized using the direct, indirect, or persuasive approach, depending on the anticipated reader reaction. Use the direct approach when the message, such as a job offer or congratulations on a promotion, is one the reader will be pleased to receive; or when the message is expected to have a neutral effect on the receiver, such as a message requesting or relaying information. Use the indirect approach when reader is expected to react negatively, and use the persuasive approach when attempting to prompt the reader to take some action.

Direct Approach

When using the **direct approach** the message content will:

- Begin with the reason for the correspondence.
  Do you sell an all-in-one printer, scanner, telephone, and copier?
- Continue with whatever explanation is necessary so the reader will understand the message.
  If so, please provide me with the capabilities of your product and the price.
- Close with a thank you for action that has been taken or with a request that action be taken by a specific date.
  I need the information by January 15; please respond using the address given in the letterhead. Thank you for your assistance.

The checklist presented in Figure 6-2 will help you as you begin to write messages using the direct approach.

Indirect Approach

At times, you must write messages refusing either a request or an appointment or in some way saying no to a person. Using an **indirect approach** will help the recipient accept the decision and understand your concern. You can leave the recipient with a positive impression when writing indirect messages if you:

- Begin with an opening statement that is pleasant but neutral.
  Your plan to build a fund for a new arts centre in the community is commendable. I hope you are able to meet your goal.

FIGURE 6-2
Direct Message Checklist

1. Did you begin the first paragraph with the reason for the correspondence?
   Yes ❑   No ❑

2. Did you continue with whatever explanation was necessary?
   Yes ❑   No ❑

3. Did you close with a thank you for action or with a request that action be taken by a particular date?
   Yes ❑   No ❑

4. Did you use the *you* approach?
   Yes ❑   No ❑

5. Did you ask the W questions?
   Yes ❑   No ❑

- Review the circumstances and give the negative information.

  Every year CanAsian contributes several thousand dollars to important causes. However, even though your proposal is a worthy one, we have already expended this year's budget. If you are still in need of our help next year, please let us know. We will be happy to consider a proposal from you.

- Close the message on a pleasant and positive note.

  Good luck in your efforts. Our town needs more civic-minded groups such as yours.

The checklist presented in Figure 6-3 will help you when writing messages using the indirect approach.

Persuasive Approach

When you want to convince someone to take a specific action, such as persuading a busy executive to speak at a conference or, when you want to change an indifferent or negative reader reaction, the persuasive approach is appropriate. By using this indirect approach with its special characteristics you can, ideally, change the reader's initial negative or indifferent attitude to a positive one.

Using the *you* approach to do so, you would:

- Begin with "you" or "your."

  Your role as an administrative professional is often challenging. You deal with conflict, unhappy customers, changing technology, and numerous other challenges daily. Would you like to know how to handle these challenges effectively and keep your frustration level down?

- Continue by creating interest and desire.

  If you answered yes to these questions, our monthly publication, The Effective Administrative Professional, will help you. It is packed with techniques and suggestions for handling office situations.

FIGURE 6-3
Indirect Message Checklist

1. Did you begin with a pleasant but neutral statement?
   Yes ❑   No ❑

2. Did you review the circumstances and give the negative information as positively as possible?
   Yes ❑   No ❑

3. Did you close on a pleasant note?
   Yes ❑   No ❑

4. If you had to say no to something, did you offer an alternative, if possible?
   Yes ❑   No ❑

- Close by asking for the desired action.

  You can have this publication in your office every month for only $48 per year. That is a very small amount to pay for lowering your frustration level and making your job more rewarding. Fill in the information on the enclosed card, and return it by January. Your early return will guarantee you one free month of the subscription. We look forward to counting you as one of our many satisfied subscribers.

An example of an indirect message is given in Figure 6-4.

Note that when you are in this initial phase of writing a document, do not be concerned about proofreading or formatting; these tasks can interrupt your creative thought processes. Get your ideas down; make corrections and do your formatting in the next phase, when you are editing the document.

Editing

Editing is reviewing and revising a message to improve its form and content. To be effective and to accomplish its goal, written communication in any form—instant message, email, memorandum, letter, or report—must be clear, concise, complete, courteous, and correct. Review your messages with these characteristics in mind.

Clear and Concise

Writing clearly means that your thoughts are well organized and expressed in words that are easily understood—you do not try to impress the reader with your vocabulary.

Conciseness in writing means that you express the necessary information in as few words as possible; you say what you need to say without cluttering your correspondence with irrelevant information, needless words, or flowery phrases. The reader should be able to easily determine the purpose of your communication. Figure 6-5 lists some principles to follow in creating clear and concise written communications.

Complete

A business document is complete when it gives the reader all the information needed so the intended results are achieved. To help you achieve completeness in your writing, ask yourself the "W questions."

Refer to Figure 6-6 for examples of ineffective writing when the "W" questions were not asked, and corresponding examples of effective writing when the "W" questions were asked.

FIGURE 6-8A
Letter with a Negative Tone

McBEE CONSULTING
218–450 Gostick Place
North Vancouver, BC V7K 3A4
604-555-1515

November 19, 20—

Ms. Cordelia Ramsey
CanAsian Airlines
2300–888 3rd Street SW
Calgary, AB T2P 4C4

Dear Ms. Ramsey:

Since we at McBee Consulting know that most people have trouble writing letters, we are having a one-day seminar on letter writing that you must not miss. We have put together a program that will be beneficial for you. After our seminar, you will have no trouble explaining to your reader exactly what you expect of him or her and getting what you want.

Give my office a call at 604-555-1515 to register. We are looking forward to your positive response to this letter.

Sincerely,

Rhonda Edwards

Rhonda Edwards
Training Consultant

RE:dgb

FIGURE 6-8B
Letters with a Positive Tone

McBEE CONSULTING
218–450 Gostick Place
North Vancouver, BC V7K 3A4
604-555-1515

November 19, 20—

Ms. Cordelia Ramsey
CanAsian Airlines
2300–888 3rd Street SW
Calgary, AB T2P 4C4

Dear Ms. Ramsey:

Do you write letters frequently? If so, are you sometimes unable to find the right words to let the customer know you care about her or him?

If you answered yes to these questions, you are certainly among the majority of writers. As you know, writing can be a difficult process. All of us sometimes have writer's block. We can't decide how to say what we mean or say it effectively.

Join us and a number of individuals who work in positions similar to yours for a writing seminar on Tuesday, October 25, from 9 a.m. until 3 p.m. in the conference room of our office on 450 Gostick Place. The cost for the day is $150—a small price to pay for hearing a noted communication theorist, Abraham Gassell, and having a chance to learn from your colleagues about their writing techniques. Lunch is included in the price.

Just mail the enclosed card by October 1. I hope to see you soon.

Sincerely,

Marvin Hanley
Marvin Hanley
Communication Consultant

MH:km

Coherence

A paragraph has **coherence** when its sentences are related to each other in content, in grammatical construction, and in choice of words. As illustrated in the following paragraph, repeating key words or using certain words for emphasis can achieve coherence.

> *The anthropologist Elena Padilla describes life in a squalid district of New York by telling how much people know about each other—**who** is to be trusted and **who** not, **who** is defiant of the law and **who** upholds it, **who** is competent and well and informed, and **who** is inept and ignorant.*

Parallel Structure

Parallelism helps achieve coherence in a paragraph. It is created when grammatically equivalent forms are used as seen in the following sentences.

Nonparallel: The position is prestigious, challenging, and also the money isn't bad.

Parallel: The position offers prestige, challenge, and money.

Appropriate Reading Level

Readability is the degree of difficulty of the message. Items that contribute to a greater reading difficulty include:

- long sentences
- words with several syllables
- technical terms

Readability formulas such as the Gunning Fog Index and the Flesch-Kincaid Index provide measures of readability. The higher the readability index is, the less readable the message. Business messages should be written to achieve a readability index between Grade 7 and Grade 11 levels. At this level, your email, letter, memo, or report should be clearly understood by most readers. Obviously, if the document is not understood, the message is ineffective.

Formal or highly technical reports may have a readability level of 14 or higher due to their complexity. However, these reports are not written for a general audience, but for an audience with the background and educational level to comprehend the report.

You can check the readability level of your writing by activating the spelling and grammar feature of your software program. Figure 6-9 shows readability and other statistics that are available in Microsoft Word.

Before publishing your message, use the checklist in Figure 6-10 to ensure your message will be effective.

Publishing

Publishing is sending a message to the receiver (as with a letter or email message) or making the message available to the receiver (as with posting information on a website). Selecting an appropriate method for publishing a message is important. For example, a message to a co-worker that contains sensitive or confidential information should not be sent in an email message. A personal conversation or a printed memo should be used instead. When choosing an appropriate communication channel, consider factors such as:

- The purpose/objective of the message
- The target audience
- The length of the message
- How quickly the information needs to be delivered
- The cost of distribution and the budget available

FIGURE 6-9
Readability Statistics for this Chapter

Counts	
Words	12532
Characters	67903
Paragraphs	518
Sentences	666
Averages	
Sentences per Paragraph	3.1
Words per Sentence	16.1
Characters per Word	5.1
Readability	
Passive Sentences	15%
Flesch Reading Ease	43.2
Flesch-Kincaid Grade Level	11.0
	OK

Used with permission from Microsoft.

FIGURE 6-10
Effective Message Checklist

1. Is the correspondence clear, concise, and simple?
   Yes ❑ No ❑
2. Is the correspondence complete, courteous, and correct?
   Yes ❑ No ❑
3. Is the correspondence prompt and positive?
   Yes ❑ No ❑
4. Is the correspondence timely?
   Yes ❑ No ❑
5. Do the paragraphs have unity, coherence, and parallel structure?
   Yes ❑ No ❑
6. Is the format correct?
   Yes ❑ No ❑
7. Did you proofread carefully?
   Yes ❑ No ❑
8. Is the readability level appropriate for the intended audience?
   Yes ❑ No ❑

Types of Written Messages

Emails

Have you ever not opened an email because the subject did not seem important or you didn't recognize the sender's name? With the number of emails we receive continually growing, it is important that they be well written. Although email is considered an informal means of communication, when composing business emails, you should apply the same effective writing techniques that you use when composing other types of messages. Since people receive dozens of emails every day, take care to write your emails effectively if you expect them to be read. Pay attention to all details—including the subject line—and consider the following guidelines:

- Know the purpose of your email and what you are trying to achieve before you begin writing.
- ALWAYS include a subject line; use it to state the purpose of the message. For example, if you are sending an email about a budget meeting, the *Subject* should read "Budget Meeting, 2:30 P.M., November 1," rather than "Meeting." If you are replying to a message but are changing the subject of the conversation, change the *Subject* line. Better yet, start a new message altogether.
- Keep the message short—one screen load is best. Be clear, concise, complete, and correct. Use complete sentences, capitalize and punctuate properly, and do not run sentences together; it is difficult to read email constructed in this manner. Insert a blank line after each paragraph. If your memo is longer than one screen, attach a separate document or send a hardcopy memorandum through the interoffice mail. A large attachment to an email can cause delivery problems. Check that the recipient has received it after sending or choose to share the attachment using the cloud.
- Edit and proofread carefully. Do not send an email that contains inaccuracies or incorrect grammar. Use the program's spelling and grammar check feature and delete unnecessary phrases, words, or sentences—be concise.
- Remember that email messages are not private. Never send confidential or sensitive information via email or as an attachment.
- Do not send or forward spam (electronic junk mail).
- Some mail programs do not keep an attachment together when a message is forwarded. Check to ensure both the message and attachment are being forwarded together.
- Be polite. Think of your email as a short letter and follow etiquette rules. Use *please* and *thank you.* Do not use all capital letters, which are considered as shouting. Do not send flames—angry or insulting messages.
- Emoticons can be perceived as casual interactions. In business communications, they have limited use (to soften a negative message or to clarify your tone and intent). They should be used only with people you know well.
- Be appropriately formal when writing emails. The rule of thumb is to be almost as formal in a business email as you are in other forms of written communications with your employer and/or co-workers.
- Always capitalize the appropriate words, be specific about your needs, and use a proper closing that includes your name and title in your signature (if appropriate). See the examples below; one is too informal and inappropriate for business and one is appropriate.

Inappropriate

jim, we need to have a meeting soon – can you arrange? i'm free next mon. thks.

Appropriate

Jim,

We need to meet to discuss our division's projected budget for the next six months. Are you available on Monday, November 14, from 9 a.m. until 10 a.m.? If so, let me know by this afternoon. We can meet in my office.

—Ed

- Include a standard text in your closing such as:
This email and any files transmitted with it are confidential and intended solely for the use of the recipient. If you have received this email in error, please notify me by return mail and delete this message from your system. Any unauthorized use or disclosure of this message is prohibited.
Or
Think green. Please consider the environment and do not print this email unless you really need to.
- Assign a high priority to the message only when truly needed.
- Assume that any message you send is permanent. Even if you and the receiver delete the message, it may not be deleted from everywhere the message was stored. The message could be sitting in someone's private file or in an archive. The receiver can also forward your email to others.
- Think carefully about what you say when you write an email. Reread it and double-check that any attachment mentioned in the message is actually attached before you hit "send."

A sample email message is shown in Figure 6-11.

Use appropriate email etiquette when writing email messages.

- Unless they serve a specific purpose, avoid using different fonts, colours, clip art, and other graphics in an email, which can clutter it and detract from your main message. Your message can take longer to send and receive as a result, particularly if you include numerous graphics. However, when replying to a message, using coloured text

FIGURE 6-11
Email Message in Direct Order

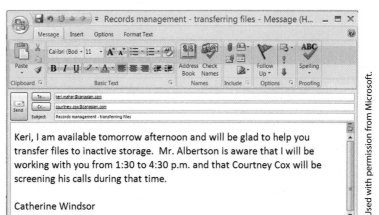

Used with permission from Microsoft.

to insert your responses to specific questions or comments is an effective method to use that can help to make your response more understandable.

- Do not key your message in ALL UPPERCASE, which connotes shouting. It is okay now and then to emphasize a word or phrase in all capitals, but use the Caps Lock key sparingly.

- Avoid sending messages when you are angry. Give yourself time to settle down and think about the situation before you send or reply to an email in anger. Take a walk around your office, drink a cup of hot tea to soothe your nerves, or wait 24 hours. Avoid expressions such as "You must be stupid if you do not understand that...." Such expressions constitute "flaming." In some cases, you may want to phone or have a face-to-face conversation with the person, rather than writing or emailing your response to a flaming email.

- Before you reply to an email, ask yourself whether you really need to reply. For example, a message to a group that says simply "I agree" should be sent only to the person who wrote the original email or perhaps not sent at all. If the message was only for your information, no reply is needed.

- If another person needs to know about the information contained in an email, send a copy of the email to that person.

- If you make a typo or regret sending a message, you can undo the action if the option is available in your email program. By enabling the "undo send" option in Gmail you have the option to take back a message you have just sent.

- Answer your email promptly. However, "promptly" does not generally mean you should respond within five or ten minutes. Your job involves more than answering your email. The general rule is to read and respond to your email at regular intervals as established by you and your supervisor.

Ethical behaviour is important. Ethics in regard to email means you do not misuse the organization's email system. Email ethics is the *soft skill* topic in Chapter 8. Turn to page 146 for some suggestions for maintaining a solid ethical stance in relation to email usage. Some organizations include an email usage policy in their Policy and Procedures Manuals. See the policy adopted by Central Washington University in Chapter 8 (Figure 8-6).

Instant Messaging

Instant messaging (IM), similar to email, is a cost-effective tool for written communications among employees of any organization. Text conversations between yourself and anyone using the same program on your contact list can happen in "real time" through a server connection. When you launch the program, you can see icons that indicate who on your contact list is online; who is online but not available for IM, and whether or not they are using a mobile device.

As the text version of a phone call, IM usage is growing in organizations, as a supplement to both email and telephone communications. Many of the guidelines and etiquette for email also apply to IM. Figure 6-12 lists ten rules for businesses using IM.

Memoranda

Although email is widely used in most organizations, memoranda continue to have a place in the work environment. The hardcopy memorandum (memo, for short) generally is written when the message is fairly long (more than one screen) or the information is confidential or sensitive.

FIGURE 6-12
Instant Messaging Best Practices

Instant messaging (IM) can be a quick and easy way to exchange information without having a significant impact on your time or someone else's. Follow these simple best practices when using IM.

1. **Know and follow your company's IM policies.** Is it appropriate to use IM when communicating with customers or clients? Or, is it to be used for internal communication only? If the policy allows personal IM, keep your business and personal contacts separate.
2. **Be aware of IM statuses.** Check the recipient's IM status before sending a message. If the person's status is set to "busy" or "away," don't send a message. Conversely, if you are unavailable, set your IM status to "busy" but don't leave it that way all day. Part of good business practice is to be available to provide help and support to colleagues. Mute or turn off the sound feature so that audio notifications do not provide unnecessary distractions.
3. **Be careful what you say.** Do not share confidential or sensitive information in instant messages. IM may not be as secure as other forms of communication. Know that IM messages can be copied and saved by a recipient. You may have deleted the conversation, but it may not be gone.
4. **Consider your message.** If your message is short and to the point and the recipient can answer your message quickly without the need for a long reply, instant messaging is the appropriate communication tool.
5. **Be professional.** Start with a short greeting and ask if the recipient has a moment to chat about a specific topic. Example: "Hi there. Do you have a minute to answer a question about this report?" This message politely lets the recipient know the nature of your request. End the conversation professionally. Saying "Thanks" is a polite way to do so.
6. **Use abbreviations sparingly.** IM in a professional setting should not include the abbreviations used in text messages. If you do use an abbreviation, make sure that both you and the recipient know what it means.
7. **Use good grammar, punctuation, and spelling.** Just like any other form of communication, IM between colleagues should be free of errors. It is a reflection of you and your professionalism.
8. **Do not use humour or sarcasm.** Like email, it's difficult to determine the tone of a message. What you think is funny may not be read that way on the other end of your message.
9. **Be positive.** IM is not the place to share bad news or negative feedback. Deliver this kind of information in person, when possible.
10. **Close the conversation.** Ending the discussion with a brief closing like "Thank you" will politely tell the recipient that the conversation has come to an end.

Source: Courtesy of Courtney Thorne

A word processing template that includes standard elements ensures that the same format is used throughout the organization. A variety of templates from Microsoft Word can be customized to include an organizational logo in addition to the heading *Memorandum* and the following required elements:

- *To* line
- *From* line
- *Date* line
- *Subject* line

When completing the "To" portion of the memo, know your company preferences and follow them. Follow these general rules:

- Use the first name (or initial) and last name of the individual.
- Use the job title of the individual if it is company procedure to do so; many organizations do not use titles in memos.
- Do not use courtesy titles such as *Ms.* or *Mr.*
- If you are sending a memorandum to more than one individual, list the names in alphabetical order or by hierarchical order within the company.

- If you are addressing a memo to a group (generally six or more people), use a generic classification, such as "United Way Fundraising Team." Include a distribution list at the end of the memo giving the names of the recipients. An example of a distribution list for a memo is shown in the Document Formatting Guide available on the MindTap site for this textbook.

When distributing memos, you may use specially designed "interoffice" envelopes. These envelopes are reusable and are generally large enough that standard-size stationery can be inserted without folding. An example of an interoffice envelope is illustrated in Chapter 9 on page 150.

The notation *pc* (photocopy), *cc* (courtesy copy), or *c* (copy) can be added at the end of the memo when copies are being sent to other individuals. List the names of the recipients alphabetically or hierarchically, whichever is company procedure.

As with all messages, before writing a memo, take time for some planning, then gather information and apply the characteristics of effective communication. In style, memos are slightly more formal than an email, but less formal than a letter. Consider your audience when setting the memo's tone (informal or formal). Memos to co-workers may be informal, while memos to managers or clients may be more formal.

If a memo is more than one page long, a heading should be placed on the second and subsequent pages. The heading should include the recipient's name, the appropriate page number, and the date. An example of a second-page heading is shown in the Document Formatting Guide, which can be accessed on the MindTap site.

Figure 6-13 illustrates a memorandum. Notice the memorandum uses side headings. This approach helps the reader scan the memo quickly and easily. Such an approach also helps the writer to focus on and clarify the message.

Letters

Although organizations communicate extensively with their customers, clients, and employees via telephone, memo, email, and perhaps IM, letters remain an important method of publishing a message. Letters are more formal than memos

FIGURE 6-13
Sample Interoffice Memorandum

CanAsian Airlines

Memorandum

TO:	Andrew Macino
FROM:	R. T. Vanderveen *rtv*
DATE:	October 12, 20--
SUBJECT:	Management Conference, December 1, Toronto

Purpose

Monaghan Consulting is holding a management conference on December 1 in Toronto. The main topic is developing empowered teams in an organization. I believe we can gain valuable information that will help us as we continue to build teams here.

Action

Please look over the information I am attaching to this memo and give me a call by November 1 if you and your staff are interested in attending.

Attachment
cc: Barbara Churchill

and email. A letter represents the company to the outside public—customers, clients, and prospective customers and clients. A well-written letter can win friends and customers. Conversely, a poorly written letter can lose customers and make enemies of prospective customers. One of your tasks as an administrative professional is assisting your employer with writing effective letters, or writing letters yourself for her or his signature.

Take a few minutes now to check your understanding of what you have learned about writing. Rewrite the sentences in Self-Check B so they are effective. When you have finished, check your responses with those given at the end of the chapter.

Ensuring Mailability

Since letters represent your company to outside individuals, in addition to writing them well and using correct grammar, spelling, and punctuation, you must also format them correctly. If you need a quick review on letter styles and folding letters, refer to the Reference and Business Document Formatting Guides on the MindTap site.

Increase your productivity when creating letters by using formatting and other features of your word processing software such as mail merge and envelope and label options. **Mail merge** is a feature that allows you to create personalized letters, labels, or envelopes for large mailings. The mail merge operation creates new documents that contain the text of a main file with data from a data file inserted at specified locations in the main document. Using mail merge is an efficient way to create letters for several recipients when only a small amount of data specific to each recipient changes with each letter.

By using your cursor to "select" the recipient's address in a letter, you can automatically generate envelopes or labels.

SELF-CHECK B

1. Your kind letter of October 8 was received today.
2. I wish to thank you for your recent order.
3. As per my letter of November 5, the modular furniture delivered to us that day is unsatisfactory.
4. Please send us the information at your earliest convenience.
5. The error I made was unfortunate.
6. Your claim that we made an error in your bill is incorrect.
7. A preponderance of businesspeople was consulted on this esoteric matter.
8. People's propensity to consume goods is insatiable.
9. You will receive the merchandise without any more delay.
10. You will not be sorry if you buy one of our washing machines.

Using this method to create an envelope saves times and ensures that exactly the same name and address appear on both the letter and the envelope. You can print the envelope or add it to the document for printing later. Similar procedures can be followed to create a mailing label. You will be given options to select the label size and to print a full page of the same label or a single label.

Your supervisor may, on occasion, return a piece of correspondence to you, informing you of an error that must be corrected before it can be mailed. Ensure your effectiveness as an administrative professional by paying attention to all details in correspondence before submitting it to your supervisor for signature.

Reports

The writing process for reports is the same as for other written messages—plan, compose, edit, proofread, and publish—with one exception. The writer may need to do research to find the information needed to compose the report.

The administrative professional's role in preparing reports varies:

- You may have the responsibility of keying and formatting the report, creating visuals such as charts or graphs, producing the final copies, and distributing the report.
- You may conduct some of the research.
- You may draft some or all of the report.

Since formal or long reports often require much time and effort to prepare, it is especially important that the objective of the report is clearly identified and the audience for the report has been considered (ask the "W" questions). For a long or complicated report, use your project management program, a spreadsheet, or the task application on your calendar program to develop a timeline that sets deadlines for the completion of various stages of the research and report composition.

With the initial planning completed, you can begin to determine the content of the report. Prepare a summary that identifies what should be included in the report and begin to gather information. To help organize your thoughts, create an outline—which may be informal notes that are either randomly created or very detailed.

Working from your outline, begin to draft the report. As with all written messages, the body of the report should begin with an introduction to help the reader understand the purpose of the report, then move to a main section that includes all the pertinent information, and close with a conclusion or findings and recommendations to help the reader understand the next steps. Create any necessary graphs, charts, and tables that you feel will enhance the reader's understanding of the content.

People @ Work

Skills @ Work

Finally, proofread and edit the report, prepare the executive summary if one is required, and publish the report.

Research for Reports

Most reports involve some type of research. The research may be primary research—the collecting of original data through surveys, observations, or reviewing and analyzing data. For example, suppose your manager asks you to create a report on the use of company sick days. You might need to review the attendance records for all employees for the past five years to determine whether use of sick days has been increasing or decreasing. Your report might include a graph that shows total sick days used for each of the last five years. The report might include other information that you calculate, such as the percentage increase or decrease in the use of sick days and the time of year when the most sick days are used.

The research also may be secondary research—finding data or material that other people have discovered and reported via the Internet, books, periodicals, and various other publications.

Suppose you are asked to conduct research for a marketing plan for a new product your company plans to sell. You could research the demographics of the target market area to find the number of people living in the area. You could also find information about the ages, races, gender, education, and income levels of the area residents. Using this information, the report writer can make recommendations for marketing strategies that will appeal to the target buyers. When using information discovered from secondary research, be sure to give proper credit to the source of the information by using footnotes or endnotes. Do not reprint copyrighted material without the consent of the copyright holder.

During your research, it is important to determine the credibility of the company or individual providing the information that you find and to note the date of the article or study. All information found in print or on the Internet is not necessarily reliable or current. Ask yourself these questions to help you evaluate the credibility of sources: Who wrote the information? What education or expertise does the person have? Is the person representing a respected organization? Is the information current? Is the information biased toward a particular viewpoint?

When using secondary research in reports, you must properly document your research sources. The Document Formatting Guide on the MindTap site includes a section on documentation. Information is also provided on MLA style (Modern Language Association), APA style (American Psychological Association), Web style, and traditional documentation styles.

Formats for Reports

An informal report may have only one or two parts, either just the body or the body and an executive summary (a one- or two-page summary of the report). An informal report may also be formatted as a memo. In the memo format, the name of the person requesting the report appears in the To line, the report writer in the From line, and the title in the Subject line. When the report contains more than one page, side headings, similar to those used in a formal report, may be used to identify the sections of the report. An informal report is written in a conversational style using personal pronouns such as *I*, *you*, *me*, *we*, and *us*.

The executive summary is useful for a reader who does not need a detailed understanding of all aspects of the report, but who does need to know the major findings and recommendations. Readers can use the executive summary to preview the report to determine whether they want to read a certain portion in its entirety.

The executive summary

- Describes the background—why the report was necessary and identifies the problem or issue
- Summarizes the report's major findings—what was discovered through the research
- Itemizes the recommendations being made as a result of the discoveries

The formal report normally deals with a more complex subject, is longer than the informal report, and requires more time and preparation. Formal reports are generally written in manuscript format and contain several parts, which may include an executive summary, title page, table of contents, body, bibliography or reference section, and appendix. Not all reports will contain all these parts.

Your company may have a particular format that you will be expected to use for formal reports. Refer to the company's style guide for documents if one is available. If a style guide is not available, review reports in the company files to see the formats that have been used for other reports.

Formal business reports usually follow these guidelines:

- **Title page.** The title page contains the title of the report; the writer's name and title; the organization, department, or division name; and the date the report is being submitted.
- **Table of contents.** A table of contents is optional, but is generally included when a report is long. The table of contents lists major sections and the first page number of each section. The table of contents helps the reader quickly locate specific sections of the report.
- **Manuscript style.** The body of the report includes a main title and side headings to identify parts of the report. Software features such as the Title and Heading styles in Microsoft Word or Corel WordPerfect are typically used to ensure consistency in the format of titles and headings.
- **Paragraph formatting.** Use 1 or 1.5 line spacing with 10 or 12 points of blank space between paragraphs. The paragraphs are not indented.
- **Visual aids.** Tables, charts, or other visual aids may be included in the report body or an appendix.
- **Footnotes, endnotes, or internal citations.** Ensure the report properly cites sources of material and the authors

of material used in the report. Footnotes appear at the bottom of the page where the reference is made. Endnotes are grouped at the end of the document. Internal citations appear within the context of the document.

- **Bibliography.** At the end of the report, a references page lists all sources used in writing the report. Each entry includes the complete name(s) of the author(s), the title of the book or periodical, the date of publication, the publishing company, and the page numbers.
- **Appendix.** Use an appendix to provide additional details or related information mentioned in the report.

A sample business report appears in the Business Document Formatting Guide found on the MindTap site for this textbook.

Productivity Tools for Preparing Business Documents

The preparation of all business documents can benefit from using software features such templates, macros, and building blocks.

A template is a model for creating similar items and can be used to create documents quickly and consistently. Word processing programs, such as Microsoft Word and Corel WordPerfect, provide templates for letters, memos, reports, brochures, and other documents.

A template file contains settings for margins, line spacing, formatting, and page layout that are appropriate for the type of document you will create. The template may also contain text and design elements, such as tables, borders, shading, or graphics. See Figure 6-14 - Microsoft Word's Report Cover Page Templates

Using a template file with these settings already in place saves time in creating a document and helps ensure that formats will be consistent. Once you have created a document or modified a template, you can create a new template based on the document. For example, you might start with a template for a product brochure. You could modify the template to add data, such as a company logo, name, address, Web address, and email address. Saving this document as a template and using it the next time you want to create a similar brochure will save time in creating the new document.

Macros are a sequence of actions or commands grouped together as a single instruction to accomplish a task automatically. For example, every letter that you create will have a signature block that includes a name and title for the sender. The complimentary close for the letter might also be included in the signature block. A macro might also include the company logo, name, and contact information, formatted as a letterhead. The keystrokes you enter to create this block can be saved. When needed, you "run" the macro by pressing a defined shortcut key or entering the macro name. All the saved keystrokes are automatically inserted into your document.

Building blocks are parts of a document or text that are often used in a particular type of document. The cover or title page for a report could be in a building block. Design elements, such as a text box, clip art, or formatted table, can also be placed in building blocks. Programs such as Microsoft Word contain galleries of building blocks that you can select and use in a document. Figure 6-14 shows Word's Report Cover Page Templates. You can also create a document part or **boilerplate text** (standard text used in documents) and add it to a gallery. The Quick Part Gallery available in Word is a gallery where reusable pieces of content can be created, stored, and reused.

Collaborative Writing

You have learned throughout this textbook that teams are used extensively in organizations today. Teams may write reports or prepare presentations as a group. To be an effective member of any team, you need to use the skills presented in Chapter 5, such as listening actively and understanding and accepting differences in cultural, gender, and age. Additionally, team writing and presentation assignments both require

FIGURE 6-14
Microsoft Word's Report Cover Page Templates

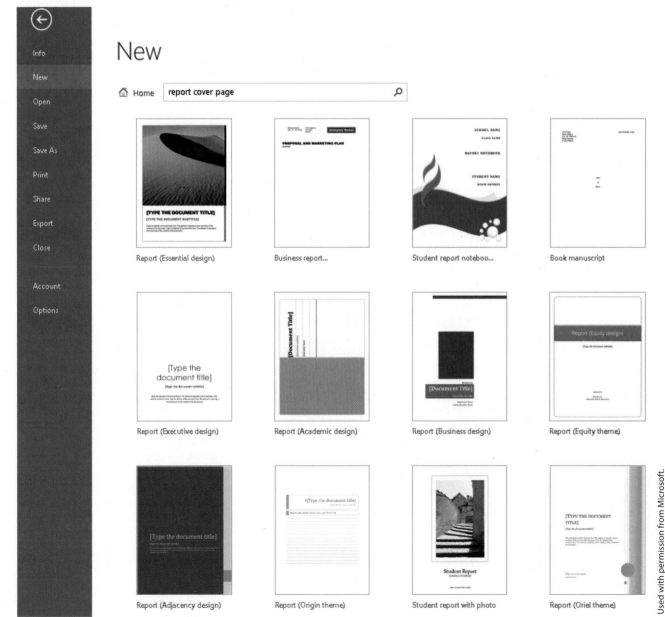

FIGURE 6-15
Brainstorming Techniques

- Say each idea aloud as it occurs to you.
- Have a recorder jot down each idea.
- Listen attentively to others' ideas.
- Piggyback on the ideas of others.
- Suspend judgment. Do not critique ideas as they are presented.
- Encourage an uninterrupted flow of ideas.
- Expect the outrageous to surface, which is perfectly okay in the brainstorming process; it encourages creativity.

collaborative planning. **Brainstorming** will help to determine the content to include in the report or presentation and how it will be presented. (See Figure 6-15 for how to brainstorm.)

Additionally, if you are engaged in a team writing or presentation assignment, the collaborative writing guidelines presented in Figure 6-16 will help you be successful.

International Communications

Throughout this course, you have been reminded of the global nature of business and what that means for you as an administrative professional. Chances are great that, at some point in your career, you will be communicating in writing with individuals from various countries. The part of this chapter that

FIGURE 6-16
Collaborative Writing Guidelines

- Determine the purpose of the writing assignment. What is the team to produce? What is the deadline? Must certain stipulations be met?
- Determine who the audience is. Who is to receive the final report? What is their background? How much do they know about the subject matter? In other words, determine what your style of writing should be and how much information to give the recipients.
- Select a team leader. The team leader is responsible for setting the procedures for the team writing meetings; facilitating the meetings; and helping the group meet deadlines, solve problems, and produce the document.
- Set a work schedule. Decide when and where you are going to meet. Set timelines and stick to them.
- Allocate the work. Define the tasks of each team member. Determine each team member's writing strengths, and use these strengths when assigning tasks.
- Monitor the progress. The group must stay focused and produce the written product by the deadline established.
- Reduce the chance of conflict by
  - Actively listening to each group member
  - Paying attention to cultural, age, and gender differences
  - Acknowledging the worth of the other group members and their points of view

focused on written communication dealt with the principles appropriate for North American firms. However, if you are writing to individuals outside of Canada, you must consider the differences in culture. You learned in Chapter 5 about various cultural differences. Although these differences vary from country to country, you need to be aware of them when communicating in writing. The result of such knowledge and understanding will be clear, concise, and appropriate communications with international businesses. Generally, communication must be more formal than what is used with Canadian businesses. To learn the particulars of a country, read about the country and its customs. General principles for international written correspondence are provided in Figure 6-17.

Transcription

While transcription was once a widely used method of creating business documents, and is still used regularly in medical or legal environments, fewer executives today use dictation as an input method for document production. Because of the user-friendly nature of word processing software, email, and IM, executives are able to draft messages and send the documents through the network to the administrative professional who is then responsible for proofreading and formatting the text of the documents.

For executives that do not possess keyboarding skills, however, dictating reports and other documents is often a preference, simply because they can speak more quickly than they can keyboard. It is possible, therefore, that as an administrative professional you may find yourself responsible for either

FIGURE 6-17
General Principles for International Written Correspondence

- Use relatively formal language. Phrases such as Very Honoured Professor Dr. Fruer and Your honoured servant are used in some countries.
- Do not use expressions unique to North America; do not refer to events that are common only to Canada.
- Use the dictionary meanings of words; do not use slang.
- Always use the title of the individual with whom you are corresponding. First names should not be used.
- Be extremely courteous; use thank you and please often.
- Be complimentary when appropriate (but always sincere).
- Ask questions tactfully.
- Do not use humour; it may be misunderstood.
- Respect all customs of the country (social, religious, and so on).
- Learn all you can about particular countries; read extensively.
- Translate correspondence into the native language of the country.
- Send business cards that are printed in the native language of the country.

transcribing notes made by your supervisor or dictating on behalf of your employer.

Equipment

A wide range of dictation and transcription equipment and software are available, from traditional cassette-based dictation/transcription units, to digital dictation systems and apps for smartphones. Executives who travel or whose job responsibilities are in the field may use handheld portable dictation devices or their smartphones to record reminders, documents, and instructions when not in the office.

Mobile and desktop digital dictation units are illustrated in Figure 6-18 along with the foot pedal and headset, which are used for transcription. These units contain adjustable volume, tone, and speed controls so that the playback can be modified for the individual transcriptionist. A digital display indicates the total dictation time, and audio tones sound to indicate the location of dictated instructions.

Computer-based systems are another option for dictation and transcription. Once the appropriate dictation software is loaded onto the computer or smartphone, the originator dictates using a computer, a portable handheld recorder, or other telecommunication device and then transmits the recordings via email, the Internet, or the company intranet. Transcription software, which includes features such as variable-speed playback, foot-pedal or hand-control operation, file management, and more, must be installed on the computer being used by a transcriptionist. This transcription software can be controlled using the keyboard (with **hot keys**—user-defined combinations of keystrokes that provide quick access to a command or menu) and/or a foot pedal or hand control as illustrated in Figure 6-19.

You can find out more about current dictation/transcription equipment and systems by keying *transcription systems* or *transcription software* into your search engine. Links to the following can be found on the MindTap site for this textbook.

- Start-Stop
- NextWave Solutions

FIGURE 6-18
Mobile and Desktop Digital Dictation Units with Transcription Headset and Foot Pedal

Photos/Videos: Speech Processing Solutions GMBH. www.philips.com/dictation

FIGURE 6-19
Ergonomic Transcription Hand Control—An Alternative to the Foot Pedal.

Photos/Videos: Speech Processing Solutions GMBH. www.philips.com/dictation

- Express Scribe
- Phillips Dictation Systems

Transcription Techniques

A headset and foot pedal or hand control are the necessary pieces of equipment used when transcribing dictated material. In the physical process of transcribing dictation, you will follow these steps:

1. Press the play forward section of a foot pedal or hand control to listen to the dictation.
2. Listen and keyboard as you hear the words spoken.
3. Raise your foot from the pedal or hand from the control bar to stop the forward play of the dictation while you complete keyboarding the phrase.
4. Press the foot pedal or hand control bar to continue, or press the reverse section to listen to words or phrases you may have missed.
5. Repeat steps 1–4 until the document is complete.

Some tips to increase your productivity when transcribing dictation are presented in Figure 6-20.

Dictation Techniques

An originator who is aware of the skills required for efficient transcription creates the most successful dictation. Like the writing process, planning, organizing your thoughts, and gathering necessary materials before beginning to dictate is the key to success. You learned in Chapter 2 the time management technique of batching your work—organizing and performing similar tasks at one time. Setting aside a specific time for dictation and assembling the necessary files before you begin contributes to efficiency on the job. Figure 6-21 presents some additional tips for effective dictation.

Improving Written Communication Skills

As you have learned in these sections, you should write in a conversational tone—one that is appropriate for the reader. You should write to express your thoughts—not to impress the reader. You should treat the reader with respect and friendliness;

FIGURE 6-20

Tips to Increase Your Productivity When Transcribing Dictation

Plan transcription activities	Identify the number of items to be transcribed.
	Determine the length of the items (how long will it take to transcribe each item).
	Prioritize the order of transcription for all items.
Special instructions	At the beginning of each dictated item check for special instructions such as:
	Number of copies
	Enclosures
	Special handling
	Distribution
	Draft or final form
	Optional: Listen to the complete document if the dictator is new to you or has a heavy accent. This step is not necessary when you are familiar with the originator's style of dictation and the vocabulary of the business.
Dating transcription	Date all documents. Documents may be revised several times. The date helps to identify the most current version.
	The date of transcription or the date the document will be signed—not the date of dictation—should be used on all correspondence.
	Adjust references to dates within the body of the document to conform with the date of transcription. For example, change "today" to "yesterday" when transcribing dictation created the previous day.
Listen actively	Concentrate while listening to the dictated material—eliminate as many distractions as possible.
	Listen ahead to the next few words as you keyboard. Eventually you should be able to listen and keyboard continuously.
	Do not make changes to what has been dictated unless it is an obvious error such as an incorrect personal name or date.
	Highlight words within the text that are unfamiliar to you or that you do not recognize. This highlighting will make it clear to your supervisor that you need some clarification before proceeding to produce the final version of the document.
Use precedents	Check your company procedures manual, reference book, or previous correspondence for formatting guidelines. Apply them to the dictated material as you are transcribing.
	Check correspondence previously dictated by the same person for words or phrases frequently used by them.
Proofread	Proofread as you keyboard; most word processing software programs will identify grammatical errors and automatically correct frequently misspelled words. Ensure you have set the default language for your system and application software to "English (Canada)."
	Run the spell checker when you have completed the transcription. Remember, it will not identify correctly spelled but incorrect words. See page 98 for proofreading tips.
	Proofread again for correctness of context, incorrectly used words, and inconsistencies. Ask, does it make sense? The dictator might indicate a date as Tuesday, February 14, when it should actually be Wednesday, February 14, or Tuesday, February 13.
	Some invaluable resources are reference sources such as a good dictionary, a word-division book, a thesaurus, and an office procedures handbook. Keep them close by, and use them in conjunction with the spelling and grammar checking features of your word processing software.

you should never show anger. By saying *please* and *thank you* and referring to the reader by name, you tell the reader that you care about him or her. By expressing statements in a positive rather than a negative manner, you help give the reader a favourable impression of you and your organization. If you carefully and consistently heed these guidelines, you will set a positive tone for the reader. In the process, you will have served your organization well.

FIGURE 6-21
Tips for Effective Dictation

Preparation	Book time for dictation in your calendar.
	Assemble all necessary information—files, reports, calendar.
	Annotate—make notes in the margin of a letter or report or on attachable Post-It notes—to help guide you.
	Think about what you want to say—organize your thoughts before beginning to dictate.
	Avoid interruptions—close your door or put a "Do Not Disturb" sign on your door.
	Turn off the radio and any music.
Instructions to the transcriptionist	Identify yourself—if necessary.
	Identify the type of message—email, letter, report, etc.
	Indicate priority—rush, required immediately, due next week.
	Indicate number of copies (in addition to file copy) required and to whom they are to be sent.
	Provide special formatting instructions if any.
Dictation	Avoid moving around while using a recording device.
	Do not eat or chew gum or play with anything that could create a noise that would be picked up by the recording device.
	Avoid dictating while on a plane or in a car.
	Hold the microphone approximately 20 centimetres from your mouth.
	Use your natural, conversational speaking voice.
	Provide the correct name and, if possible, the address of the addressee.
	Spell out personal names and other proper names.
	Spell out technical terms not known to the transcriptionist.
	Provide punctuation and paragraphing instructions.
	Provide the transcriptionist with the original copies of the documents being responded to, which should be arranged in the same order as the dictated items.

Soft Skills   Ethical and Legal Considerations

You were introduced to the importance of ethical behaviour in Chapter 3. Almost every day, we hear on television or read in a newspaper about business ethics. Ethical problems are difficult to resolve precisely because no rules exist to determine when something is ethical or unethical. Every organization and individual must make that determination independently.

In written correspondence, you, as an employee of an organization, must be honest, must maintain confidentiality (not divulge organizational business outside the organization), and must be loyal (act in the employer's interest). The organization must also act ethically in regard to its public responsibilities. Organizations must tell the truth about their products and services and not mislead the public. For example, airlines have an ethical obligation to the public to meet the scheduled flight times unless circumstances such as weather or mechanical problems arise. They also have an ethical obligation to be honest with the public as to why a flight is late. Automotive companies have an ethical obligation to the public to present

correct written specifications of all vehicles. Not-for-profit organizations have an ethical obligation to present in writing to the public how their dollars are spent in meeting the needs of the underprivileged.

In written correspondence (newspaper ads, TV ads, marketing letters, brochures, and so on), organizations have legal obligations that are covered by various laws, including copyright, trademark, contract, and liability laws. These laws are also applicable to email messages. For example, email users must abide by the "fair use" rule of copyright law when forwarding copyrighted materials obtained from the Web. The fair use rule is very specific about when something can and cannot be used and provides guidelines about materials used in a commercial or not-for-profit nature, the length of the copied work in comparison to the entire document, and so on. Unless the legal obligations of organizations are carefully observed in all written materials, the organization faces the consequences of costly lawsuits, loss of the public's goodwill, and loss of business.

Chapter Summary

The summary will help you remember the important points covered in this chapter.

- The basic business correspondence that the administrative professional prepares includes memoranda, email, letters, and reports.
- Effective correspondence is clear, concise, and simple; it should also be complete, considerate, correct, prompt, and positive.
- When planning correspondence, the writer should determine the objective, consider the reader, and gather the facts.
- Email is used extensively in businesses. When email messages are sent, email guidelines, ethics, and etiquette must be considered.
- Use the direct approach for letters and memoranda that are classified as favourable and routine (neutral). Use the indirect approach for unfavourable and persuasive messages.
- Use the *you* approach when writing letters. This approach involves the use of empathy, putting the reader uppermost in the mind of the writer.
- When planning a report, determine the purpose of the report and analyze the audience who will receive it.
- Primary research may be essential for a business report. This research may include observational research, survey research, and/or reviewing and analyzing data.
- Secondary research includes sources from the Web and from libraries.
- The parts of a formal business report include the title page, table of contents, body, footnotes/endnotes/internal citations, bibliography or reference section, and appendix.
- Reports are often written through a collaborative process that could include brainstorming.
- Instant Messaging (IM) is a cost-effective tool for written communications among employees of an organization.
- International correspondence is usually more formal than correspondence written to individuals within Canada. The writer must be aware of the customs and culture of the country to which he or she is writing.
- The writer and organization are responsible for ensuring that their written correspondence is both ethical and legal.
- Dictation may used by executives because they can speak more quickly than they can keyboard or handwrite.
- Providing instructions to the transcriptionist, dictating in a quiet environment using your natural conversational speaking voice, spelling out proper names and technical terms, and including punctuation and paragraphing instructions will all contribute to efficiency during transcription.
- Dictation/transcription systems range from traditional cassette-based dictation/transcription units to digital dictation and computer-based systems and apps for smartphones.
- Dictation units have a microphone; transcription units have a foot pedal or hand control and a headset.
- An effective transcriptionist possesses an extensive vocabulary, knowledge of business document formats, the ability to keyboard and proofread accurately, and a familiarity with the appropriate reference sources.
- Dictation productivity is increased when a specific time for dictation is set aside and all necessary materials are assembled before beginning.
- Transcription productivity can be increased by planning your activities, listening actively, following any special instructions, using precedents, proofreading, and dating all transcriptions.

Key Terms

you approach p. 93
empathy p. 93
direct approach p. 93
indirect approach p. 93
persuasive approach p. 94
editing p. 94
conciseness p. 94
tone p. 98
unity p. 98
topic sentence p. 98
coherence p. 101
parallelism p. 101
readability p. 101

emoticons p. 102
mail merge p. 105
primary research p. 107
secondary research p. 107
MLA style p. 107
APA style p. 107
executive summary p. 107
template p. 108
macros p. 108
building blocks p. 109
boilerplate text p. 109
brainstorming p. 110
hot keys p. 111

You or the individuals who asked you to speak may provide evaluation forms for the people in the audience. Ask to see copies of the completed forms; review them carefully. Do not let yourself become upset over a few negative comments. Know that there will always be some negatives. However, take seriously the points that are made in the critique. Before you speak again, concentrate on how you might improve your presentation techniques.

People @ Work

Marketing Manager

A marketing manager develops plans and strategies for how a company will promote and sell its products or services. Specific job duties may include directing or doing research, planning or conducting surveys on customer satisfaction, and estimating the expected demand for a product.

Marketing managers typically develop and give presentations to company managers, business partners, and customers. If you are an administrative professional who works with a marketing team, you may be asked to help do research and develop these presentations. If you work in another area of the company, you may be asked to provide information on products or services to the marketing team.

Giving Team Presentations

Teams are used extensively in businesses and other organizations. Team presentations require specific skills and offer some benefits that a single presenter does not have. Some of these benefits include the following:

- Having two or more people deliver parts of the presentation can increase and hold the audience's attention.
- Having more than one speaker brings greater experience and expertise to the presentation.
- If the audience works in small groups on a particular assignment, team members are available to mingle with the groups and provide expertise and leadership.
- One presenter can record comments or questions from the audience while another speaks.

Select the Team

Having the right combination of people on a team can make the team more effective. In some cases, you may be assigned to the team and have no input on who the other members will be. In other cases, you may be able to choose the people on the team. What should you consider when assembling a team? Here are a few suggestions to consider:

- What are the strengths and weaknesses of each person?
- What does the strength of each person add to the strength of the team?
- Do the team members collectively have a breadth of knowledge about the topic?
- What particular knowledge does each individual have? Do individual team members have the technical knowledge needed for the presentation?
- What people skills does each presenter possess? For example, is the person a team player? An effective communicator? A good listener?

A presentation team needs a strong leader who can make decisions and motivate the team. In some cases, the team may select its leader after a team discussion about the strengths and weaknesses of the group. Team members need to be willing to engage in this discussion non-defensively. If the team is going to work together for a longer period of time, management may appoint the leader. If the presentation will be delivered to an external group, the person who was initially contacted by the external group may be the leader. That person can assemble a team with members she or he chooses.

Work Together for Success

Each team member and the team collectively should know the purpose of the presentation(s). The team leader should facilitate this session. Certain questions need to be asked and answered: What do you want the audience to know or do as a result of the presentation? What is the best way to convey the message?

Identify duties for each team member related to planning, research, writing, developing visual aids, and presenting. Set deadlines for when each task should be completed and times for when the team will meet to work on or rehearse the presentation. When deciding who will be responsible for various duties, consider each team member's area of expertise, presentation style and skill, and understanding of the audience.

Not all team members need to speak during the presentation, but everyone should be present and available to answer questions and help during small group activities. All members should review the feedback and discuss ways to improve.

Chapter Summary

The summary will help you remember the important points covered in this chapter.

- Develop and use your creativity when preparing presentations.
- To help you release your creativity, have faith in your creativity, destroy judgment, look and listen, and ask questions.
- Bring your personal creativity to the office.
- As an administrative professional, your job may include helping to develop or deliver presentations. Developing your presentation skills is important for your professional growth.
- Many people experience presentation anxiety, commonly called stage fright. With proper planning and practice, you can develop effective presentation skills and overcome presentation anxiety.
- When planning a presentation, identify the goal of the presentation; consider the audience, the time and length of the presentation, and the location; and research the topic if needed.

- When writing a presentation, organize the material using a list or outline, develop an opening, create a strong message for the body, and write an effective closing.
- Using visual aids, such as posters, whiteboards, and electronic slides, can increase the amount of information the listeners remember from the presentation.
- Rehearse your presentation several times using your visual aids and, if possible, in the room where you will present.
- When delivering a presentation, focus on sharing your message with the listeners. Use the last couple of minutes of the session to repeat the main points or action you want the audience to remember as they leave the presentation.
- Teams are used extensively in businesses and other organizations. Team members should agree on the purpose of the presentation and work together to plan, research, write, and deliver the presentation.

Key Terms

creativity p. 118
demographics p. 120
visual aid p. 122
posters p. 122

flipcharts p. 122
interactive whiteboard (IWB) p. 122
credible p. 126

Discussion Items

These discussion items provide an opportunity to test your understanding of the chapter through written responses and/or discussion with your classmates and your instructor:

1. Why does an administrative professional need to develop presentation skills?
2. List the planning steps involved in developing a presentation.
3. What are some options you might use as an opening for a presentation? What points should you consider when selecting one of these options?
4. List some steps you might take to conquer your presentation fears.
5. Identify five techniques for preparing effective electronic presentations or slides that you consider most important. Explain why.
6. What are two benefits of giving a team presentation rather than an individual presentation?

Critical-Thinking Activity

You are a member of a local chapter of the International Association of Administrative Professionals (IAAP). You have been asked to speak at the IAAP national meeting, which will be held in Charlottetown this year. Your speech is not a keynote; you will be presenting at a session on the first afternoon of the conference from 2:00 p.m. to 2:40 p.m. You have been given the prerogative of choosing your own topic and whether or not you will present as an individual or make

it a team effort. The theme of the conference is Promoting Professional Growth. You decide you will do a team presentation; two members of your chapter have agreed to present with you. (Work with two of your classmates on this project.)

As a team, list the steps that you will need to take to select a topic and prepare the presentation. Select a topic and write an objective statement for the presentation. Develop a personal introduction for each person on the team.

Building Workplace Skills

Project 7-1 (Learning Outcome 1)

Collaborative Projects

Team Presentation

Do further planning, including needed research, to develop the team presentation on the topic you selected in the Critical-Thinking Activity. As a team, develop a strong opening for the presentation. Create an outline for the presentation body and write the body and closing for the presentation. Develop a list of five questions that might be asked during a question-and-answer session and write answers for each question.

Project 7-2 (Learning Outcome 2)

Visual Aids

Continue to develop your team presentation. Identify visual aids that will be helpful in giving the presentation. As a team, create the visual aids. Create a handout to accompany the presentation. The handout can be a printout of slides with space for taking notes or a sheet with additional details or related information.

Project 7-3 (Learning Outcomes 4 and 5)

Deliver a Presentation

Identify which part of the presentation will be delivered by each team member. Rehearse the team presentation, using the visual aids you created earlier. Deliver the presentation to your class or a group of classmates. As a team, write an evaluation of the presentation and the team's delivery, noting strong points and weak points to improve for future presentations. Use the Presentation Evaluation Form SCDP7-3a. Your instructor will collect the evaluation forms at the end of your presentation and give them to you for review. What can you learn from the evaluation forms? Write a memorandum to your instructor, using the memorandum form file SCDP7-3b. Detail the strengths and weaknesses of your presentation as revealed by the evaluation forms and as seen by your group. Use these headings in your memorandum: (1) Group Opinion of Strengths and Weaknesses of Presentation and (2) Class Members' Opinion of Strengths and Weaknesses of Presentation.

Project 7-4 (Learning Outcomes 1, 2, and 3)

You recently gave a presentation on "Ergonomics in the Office" at a local IAAP meeting. The goals of the presentation were to inform listeners about this important topic and to persuade them to apply ergonomic practices. The president of the IAAP chapter has asked you to provide the main points of your talk in an electronic slide show that can be posted online for IAAP members who were not able to attend your presentation.

- Do research on the topic using the Internet and other resources.
- Write an outline of the main points and the details you will include in the slides.
- Create an electronic slide show to include a title slide and at least nine additional slides. Use appropriate photos, pictures, or graphics and animation for the slides. For each slide except the title slide, record a voice file and attach it to the slide so users can hear your comments. The voice file for each slide should be one to two minutes in length.

Project 7-5 (Learning Outcome 3)

Feedback Form

As you waited for your dental appointment recently, you wrote a few notes about developing a form to request feedback from the listeners at your next presentation. Open file SCDP7-5. Review the notes in this file. Think of additional questions or information you might want to include on the form. Create and print an attractive form that you can use to get feedback from the audience when you give a presentation.

Project 7-6 (Learning Outcomes 2, 3, 4, and 5)

Add one or both of the presentations you created in Projects 7-3 and 7-4 to your e-portfolio as an example of the work you can do in preparing presentation visuals.

Make the Grade with MindTap

MindTap®

Stay organized and efficient with **MindTap**—a single destination with all the course material and study aids you need to succeed. Built-in apps leverage social media and the latest learning technology. For example:

- ReadSpeaker will read the text to you.
- Flashcards are pre-populated to provide you with a jump-start for review—or you can create your own.
- You can highlight text and make notes in your MindTap Reader. Your notes will flow into Evernote, the electronic notebook app that you can access anywhere when it's time to study for the exam.
- Self-quizzing allows you to access your understanding.

Visit http://www.nelson.com/student to start using **MindTap**. Enter the Online Access Code from the card included with your text. If a code card is not provided, you can purchase instant access at NELSONbrain.com.

Administrative Support— Your Responsibilities

As an administrative professional you will be "information central," a valued member of a team in a business or organization where everyone will depend on you to keep the office organized and operating efficiently. Your many administrative duties and responsibilities may include the following:

- Understanding the role an administrative professional commonly plays in creating and maintaining financial documents. This section stresses the confidential nature and importance of accuracy when preparing financial documents, and includes information about common employee benefits and required payroll deductions.
- Managing records is an important responsibility for every administrative professional. A working knowledge of common records systems— alphabetic, subject, geographic, and numeric—and the ability to determine which is appropriate will be invaluable to your organization. Choosing appropriate supplies, equipment, and media for physical and electronic records may also be your responsibility.
- You will be introduced to various types of business meetings and formats for meetings, and will learn the importance of your responsibilities as an administrative professional in assisting with meetings. Understanding the responsibilities of all meeting participants is important if meetings are to accomplish their business goals
- The role of an administrative professional often includes arranging for domestic or international travel—booking flights and hotel accommodations, researching travel and security alerts, handling issues while the executive is away, and completing follow-up activities after the trip.

Providing administrative support means anticipating your supervisor's needs—knowing what he or she wants or needs before he or she has requested it. In doing so, you can exceed expectations and help to create a professional atmosphere where everyone enjoys coming to work.

- Never answer the phone curtly or rudely.
- Do not speak in a monotone; vary your voice modulation.
- Be alert to what you are saying.

Be Attentive and Discreet

Listen carefully to what the other person says. During the conversation, avoid keyboarding or flipping through pages—these sounds are easily picked up and can be heard. Give the caller your undivided attention and do not interrupt. If the caller is unhappy about some situation, allow him or her to explain. Most of a person's anger may be dissipated in telling the story. It is easier to handle an unhappy person after you have listened to the problem. Use good listening skills to

- Listen for facts and feelings.
- Try to understand what the speaker is saying, both from the words and from the tone of voice.
- Search for hidden or subtle meanings.
- Be patient.
- Help the caller by responding to what the caller wants or asks. Do not just try—do it! As a customer, which response would you prefer to hear—"I will see what I can do" or "I will get the document faxed to you immediately"?
- If you need to access information on the computer, inform the caller of your activity. Remember, the caller cannot see what you are doing. When you are not speaking to him or her, you need to let them know what you are doing.

Be discreet when you must inform a caller that your supervisor is unavailable. Carefully explain why your supervisor cannot answer the telephone—but don't say too much. For example, you may say the following:

"Mr. Albertson is away from the office now. I expect him back in approximately an hour. May I have him call you when he returns?"

Avoid saying the following:
"Mr. Albertson is not here yet" (at 10 a.m.), "He's gone for the day" (at 3 p.m.), or "He's playing golf" (at any time of day).

A good rule to remember is to be helpful about when your supervisor is expected to return but avoid being specific about where he or she is.

Use Correct English and Avoid Slang

Pay attention to your English and pronunciation. Anyone with a good grasp of the language would be uncomfortable to hear "This is her" or similarly ungrammatical response. Slang

FIGURE 8-3
Slang and Replacement Words

Avoid Saying	Instead, Say
Yeah	Certainly
OK	Yes
Uh-huh	Of course
Bye-bye	Goodbye
Huh? I beg your pardon.	I did not understand. or Would you please repeat that?

is neither businesslike nor in good taste. Figure 8-3 gives you some suggestions to avoid using slang.

Take Messages Completely and Accurately

Although paper phone messages can get lost or misplaced, many offices still rely on them to manually record incoming messages or voice mail recordings. Two options that may be purchased from your local stationery supplier are single-sheet message pads and books with self-duplicating sheets. When using the book, a copy of every message is created and kept. This copy can be important in some organizations, such as law offices, where time attending to phone calls is considered billable. Whether the phone message is created manually or electronically, ensure that all the necessary information is captured (see Figure 8-4). Incomplete messages can be very frustrating for the recipient. If you are not given all the information, ask the caller. Repeat the message to the caller so you can be certain it is accurate.

Your organization may have a computer-based system for recording and delivering telephone messages. Similar in format to a single-sheet message pad, it can be completed and emailed to a recipient, and a copy is automatically generated and archived. PHONEslips (See Figure 8-5) is an example of a computer based message taking system. A program-specific toolbar gives instant

FIGURE 8-4
A Completed Telephone Message

When taking a telephone message, record the following information:
- The caller's name spelled correctly (If you are uncertain of the spelling, ask the caller to spell it. If the spoken letters are difficult to distinguish over the telephone, use words to help identify letters.)
- The caller's company's name
- The complete (7- or 10-digit) telephone number
- The date and time of the call
- The exact message
- Your initials or name so the recipient can contact you if there are questions

FIGURE 8-5
Computer-Based Messaging System

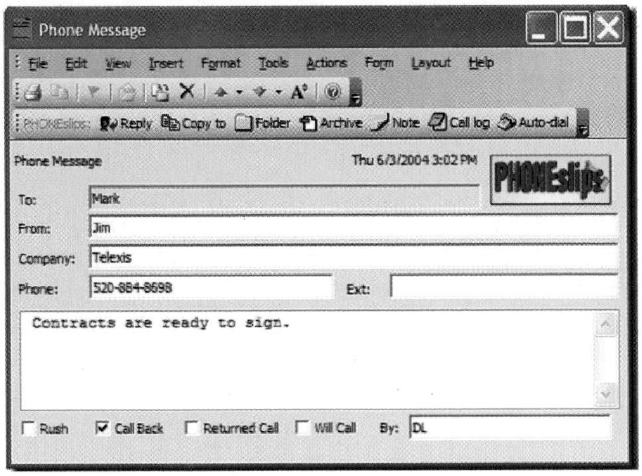

PHONEslips, an add-in application for Outlook, eliminates the need to use message pads.

access to all its features, and messages can later be instantly retrieved from the archive for follow-up and for scheduling reminders. Messages can also be automatically forwarded to a cellphone so an important message is never missed.

Use the Caller's Name

It is flattering to the caller to be recognized and called by name. Frequent responses such as "Yes, Mr. Valentine, I will be happy to get the information" and "It was nice to talk with you, Ms. Keiba" indicate to callers that you know who they are and that you care about them as individuals.

Ask Questions Tactfully

Care should be used in asking questions. Ask only necessary questions, such as "May I tell Mr. Albertson who is calling?" or "When Mr. Albertson returns, may I tell him who called?" Never ask, "Who's calling?" People can be offended by such a blunt question. If your employer is not in or cannot take the call, ask about the nature of the call, as you may be able to handle the call yourself or refer it to someone else. For example, you may say, "If you tell me the nature of your call, perhaps I can help you or refer you to someone who can."

Speak Distinctly and Clearly

Make sure the caller can understand what you say. You cannot speak distinctly with gum, candy, or a pencil in your mouth. Speak in a normal voice at a moderate rate—one that can be heard comfortably. You do not want to shout or whisper. If

you place the centre of the mouthpiece about 2.5 centimetres from the centre of your lips, the receiver firmly against your ear, and speak at a speed similar to the caller's, you provide the caller with a conversation at his or her comfort level. If your duties include considerable time on the telephone, a headset provides an ergonomic alternative to a regular telephone handset. Hands-free wireless headsets using Bluetooth technology are also available. They allow more freedom of motion and can be worn—and calls answered—when you are away from your desk.

Skills @ Work

If you have regular callers whose names are difficult to spell, store the names on your computer. When the person calls, you can look up the name quickly without having to ask for the spelling.

Use words to identify letters in the spelling of names and places when necessary.

Words to Use to Identify Letters

A as in **A**lice	**F** as in **F**rank
B as in **B**ertha	**G** as in **G**eorge
C as in **C**harles	**H** as in **H**enry
D as in **D**avid	**I** as in **I**da
E as in **E**dward	**J** as in **J**ohn

Handle Problem Calls

Most individuals are pleasant over the telephone, especially when you are courteous to them. Occasionally, you may have a caller who has had a difficult day or for some other reason is unhappy. Sometimes you can defuse an angry caller by taking the time to listen to the situation. Do not become emotionally involved in the situation. Remember that the caller is not angry at you, but at a situation or event.

After you have listened to the caller's story, try to help solve the problem. For example, you can suggest a solution or tell the call you will have someone who can solve the problem return their call. Do not put the person on hold or mishandle the call by transferring it to an individual who cannot help. Such actions may make the person angrier.

At times, a caller may refuse to give you his or her name. You should discuss this situation with your supervisor and understand exactly what you are expected to do. However, if you are unsure what to do, put the person on hold and explain the situation to your supervisor. He or she can then decide whether to speak to the caller.

Professionalism @ Work

Have you ever found yourself being nicer over the telephone to the president of the company than to a client you do not know? If the answer is yes, make a point of being friendly before you know who is on the other end. Before answering the phone, try saying to yourself, "A friend is calling."

Some people still assume that all assistants are female and all executives are male. If you answer the telephone and the voice on the other end is female, do not assume she is an assistant and ask to speak to her supervisor. When addressing anyone, use terms that connote respect. Do not refer to a woman as a "girl," a "young lady," a "beautiful young thing," or a "gal," or use any other term that might be construed as gender-biased. Do not refer to a man as a "boy," a "hunk," or a "guy."

Incoming Calls

The call management skills covered in the previous section apply to all calls. Here are some special techniques for handling incoming calls.

Answer Promptly

Never consider the telephone call an interruption in your workday. When your telephone rings, answer promptly—on the first ring if possible and certainly by the third. Consider the telephone call as your job calling. You may lose a potential customer if you are slow in answering the telephone.

Identify Yourself and Your Organization

Most businesses and supervisors have specific procedures for answering the telephone. If you work in a large organization, chances are you will not be the first person to answer any given call. In large businesses, calls are often routed first to a person whose job is to greet visitors, whether by telephone or in person. This person identifies the company and then routes the incoming call to the appropriate party, which may be a supervisor's administrative professional. For example, as the administrative professional for Mr. Albertson, you would answer his line with "Mr. Albertson's office, Rebecca Martin." If you are answering calls that have not been routed through a receptionist, you would identify the organization or department. You might say, "Good morning. CanAsian Airlines, Rebecca Martin." or "Good afternoon, Advertising Department, Rebecca Martin."

Transfer Calls Carefully

Each telephone system is different; be certain you know how to transfer calls on your system. Callers dislike being told their call will be transferred and then being disconnected due to incorrect transferring procedures. Before you transfer a call, explain to the caller why you must do so. Make sure the caller is willing to be transferred. For example, you might say, "Mr. Albertson is out, but Travis Figimara can give you the information. May I transfer you to Mr. Figimara?" If company policy permits, you may also want to give the caller the extension or complete number of the person to whom the caller is being transferred in case the transfer fails. The caller can then call that person directly without having to call you again.

Place Calls on Hold

A caller may sometimes request information that you do not have at your fingertips. You may need to check with someone else or access your files to get the information. You may be answering your supervisor's line because she or he is not available to take a call. If you must place the caller on hold until your supervisor is available or until you retrieve the necessary information, do so only with the caller's permission.

Do not assume that a caller is willing to be placed on hold. You may say, "I need to pull the information from my files. Would you like to hold for a moment while I get it, or shall I call you back?" or "Mr. Albertson is on another call, would you like to hold?"

If the caller agrees to hold, try to get back to the person as soon as possible. Nothing is more irritating to a caller than to be left on hold for a long time without an update on your progress. When you return to the line, let the caller know you are back by saying "Thank you for waiting." Some guidelines suggest you should check in and update the caller on your progress every minute. If you are delayed in getting the information, go back to the person on hold and ask if she or he wants to continue to hold or leave a message; apologize for the length of time it is taking.

Handle Multiple Calls

You may be responsible for answering more than one telephone line. If so, at times you will be answering a call on one line when another line rings. When this happens, you must remember that the caller on the second line does not know you are already on the phone. The caller is expecting to get an answer immediately. Excuse yourself politely by saying to the first caller, "May I put you on hold for a moment? I must answer another line." Be brief—ask the second caller to hold while you complete your first call or ask for a number so you can call back as soon as you finish the first call. Then return to the first caller with, "Thank you for waiting." Your responsibility is to handle all calls as quickly and efficiently as possible.

Defer Cellphone Calls

If you are working offsite with a client or customer and you receive a call on your cellphone, interrupting your work to answer may seem discourteous to the client or customer. Taking these calls conveys the impression that you have something more important to do than helping the client. When working with others, be courteous by setting your cellphone to silent mode. If you must keep your cellphone on due to an urgent call you are expecting, be sure your co-worker or client knows about it. You might say, "We may be interrupted by a call I must take, but I promise to be as brief as possible." If the call comes through, excuse yourself and do keep the conversation as brief as possible.

When you are in a meeting, do not use your cellphone to read messages, send email or text messages, or play games. The people in the room with you deserve your full attention. If your eyes stray to your phone, others will likely notice and may be offended.

Show your respect for others when using your phone in a public place or an open work area by keeping your voice low so as not to disturb others around you; by using discretion when discussing private matters or sensitive topics that may be overheard by others; and by turning your cellphone off or setting it to silent mode in one-on-one interactions and during meetings, classes, and other public events.

Screen Calls

Many executives have one telephone number that is published for callers and another, inside number that is not published. The executive typically uses the inside number to make outgoing calls; the number may also be given to close friends or family members. In an activity commonly referred to as "gatekeeping," the administrative professional may be expected to screen calls that come from the published number, by determining who is calling and why, and then diverting those calls the executive will not take, such as unsolicited sales calls. If your supervisor is not in or cannot take the call, ask about the nature of the call so you can handle it or refer it to someone else. For example, you may say, "If you tell me the nature of your call, perhaps I can help you or refer you to someone who can."

If someone else in the organization can handle the call, transfer it to that person, but only after first requesting permission from the caller to do so. If no one is available to take the call, either take a message, or courteously let the person know that your employer is not interested. One response might be, "I appreciate the information; however,

Mr. Albertson is not interested in pursuing the matter at the present time."

Remember to be tactful when asking a caller questions. Avoid blunt questions that may offend the caller.

Leave a Message When You Leave Your Desk

Technology offers several options for handling calls when you are away from your desk. For example, you can record a message on your system and set it to automatically forward your calls to your voice mail. Your voice mail greeting should be customized and updated regularly to include the current date and a message that informs callers when they can expect to receive a return call. You can also set your system to forward your calls to a cellphone, a pager, or a co-worker. If a co-worker will be taking your calls, let him or her know where you can be reached and what time you will be back. If your supervisor is also away, tell the co-worker in general terms where your employer is and when he or she will be back. For example, you might say, "Mr. Albertson is in a meeting and will be available around 3 p.m."

Follow Up

If you say to a caller that you will call back with information, do so. You can also help your supervisor to remember to follow up on phone calls. Following through enhances your reputation for reliability and trustworthiness; when you fail to follow up, the result may be a cancelled order or a lost customer. Use your chosen reminder system to keep track of these items and, when necessary, provide a tactful reminder to your supervisor to follow through. Your assistance will be appreciated.

Outgoing Calls

As an administrative professional, you will often be responsible for placing calls for your supervisor; you will also be making business calls yourself. Handling outgoing calls professionally is just as important as handling incoming calls professionally.

Place Calls Properly

Supervisors usually place their own calls to save time and to create a favourable impression. However, some people may prefer that you place calls on their behalf. If so, identify your supervisor before you transfer the call. For example, you might say, "Mr. Albertson of CanAsian Airlines is calling." Then transfer the call to Mr. Albertson's line.

Ensure that your supervisor is available to take the call before you place it and that he or she has not placed another call in the interim. For example, before you place the call, you might say, "Mr. Albertson, are you going to be available for a few minutes? I want to place the call you requested to Mr. Chen."

Plan Your Call

Before picking up the phone, take a few minutes to plan your call. Keep in mind its purpose and what you intend to say. You can avoid an unnecessary follow-up call by assembling beforehand any necessary files or reference documents that you might need during the call.

Your call may be answered first by a receptionist or the administrative professional to the person you are calling. Identify yourself and your organization and state your purpose clearly and concisely. For example, you might say, "This is John Chin of CanAsian. I'm calling to verify Dr. Lee's attendance at the committee meeting tomorrow at 3 p.m. in Conference Room A." If you are transferred to the person you are calling, be prepared to identify yourself again and to restate the purpose of your call. You may exchange pleasantries with the individual you are calling; however, the main purpose is to get your message across without wasting the other person's time. Complete Self-Check C.

SELF-CHECK C

In Self-Check B on page 134, you considered some of your own telephone errors. Take a few minutes now to consider the mistakes others have made with you over the telephone. List those mistakes here, along with correction suggestions.

Frequently Called Numbers

A file of frequently called numbers is an excellent time saver. For quick reference, program these numbers into your phone system or store them in the contacts section of your personal information management software.

Note the Time Zone

The multinational nature of business means that calls are made frequently to various locations across the country and around the world. Time zone differences must be taken into consideration when placing these calls. Canada has six time zones—Newfoundland, Atlantic, Eastern, Central, Mountain, and Pacific, which are shown in Figure 8-6. The World Clock website gives times for locations around the world. The MindTap site has a weblink to this site.

Voice Mail

Most workplace telephone systems today use voice mail or voice messaging. It has been estimated that only 25 percent of all calls placed reach the person for whom they are intended on the first try, making voice mail an efficient method of managing incoming calls when call recipients are unavailable and when broadcasting messages (sending the same message) to multiple voice mailboxes.

Incoming callers hear a recorded announcement, after which they can record a voice message. Voice messages are delivered to a call recipient's voice mailbox, from which they can be retrieved, forwarded, and erased. A voice mailbox is generally set up with a private code that provides access for the owner to retrieve recorded messages while at the same time preventing anyone else from listening to, forwarding, or erasing messages.

The owner of a voice mailbox usually accesses her or his voice mailbox from a phone inside the workplace. Many voice mail systems also permit access from a phone outside the workplace. Some voice mail systems provide automatic notification that messages are waiting via the recipient's mobile device. Some voice mail systems provide a return-to-operator feature that allows callers to talk with a person when they prefer not to leave a voice mail message.

The proper use of voice mail in the workplace increases productivity and saves time and money. For example, consider the following situations:

- Workers can leave a voice message instead of placing repeated calls to someone who is not available.
- Voice messages are to the point, eliminating extraneous conversation.
- Business travellers can communicate with the workplace at any time.
- Message delivery speed can be increased even between different time zones because a voice message can be left at any time of the day or night.

Caller Instructions

As an administrative professional, you may be assigned the task of setting up your telephone system's voice mail announcement—the first message a caller may hear when calling your company.

- Begin by identifying the company.
- Provide the most important information or answer the most frequently asked questions, such as hours of operation, fax number, website, street address, and postal code.
- If your voice mail system has multiple levels of call routing, give callers no more than four options. Callers strongly dislike trying to follow a maze of instructions to record their messages.
- Keep caller instructions short—aim for less than 15 seconds.

FIGURE 8-6
Canadian Time Zone Map

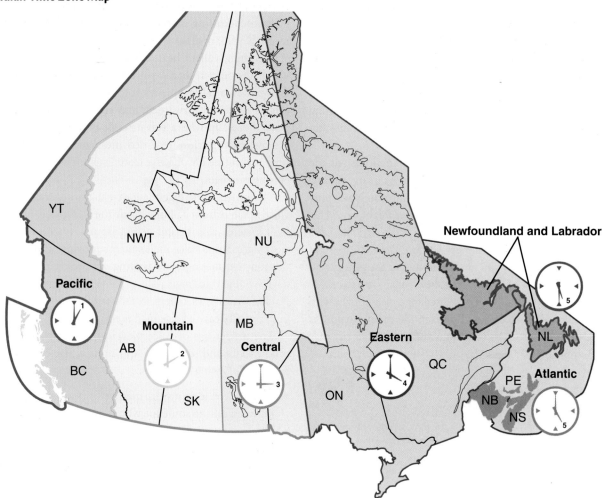

- When recording step-by-step instructions, refer to the end result first—then explain what action to take. For example, you may say, "To transfer your call to our receptionist, press zero."
- Be certain your instructions tell the caller how to reach a person. Callers dislike becoming lost in a voice message system that never allows them to speak to a person.

Your voice mail's outgoing message is very important, as it can create either a favourable or an unfavourable impression. A well-crafted announcement succinctly provides key information, such as your name, in-office or out-of-office information, and whom to contact if the call is urgent. The sound and tone of your voice message greeting should make a favourable impression. When recording your outgoing message, vary your vocal tone; do not talk in a monotone and try to eliminate background noise that could interfere with your message.

Keep It Current

The message your callers hear represents you in your absence. Your voice mail message should be timely and professional. During extended absences, if appropriate, provide sufficient details to ensure effective customer service. Hearing an outdated message is very frustrating for a caller. Change the message frequently; if your schedule changes from day to day, change your message daily; if your schedule changes during the day, periodically update it so that callers have some idea when they might expect to receive a return call.

Leaving a Message

When leaving a voice message, keep your message short and to the point. Include your name and company, a number where you can be reached, and a brief statement of the purpose of the call. Ask for a return call if that is what you want. Speak slowly and distinctly. Do not include sensitive or confidential information in a voice message. Repeat your name and number at the end of the message so that the recipient will not need to replay the message to double-check the information.

People @ Work

Customer Service Representatives

New services are constantly being offered by telecommunications providers. Customer service representatives are trained in these new services and assist customers in effectively implementing them. These representatives are available by phone, email, or an instant message chat to answer questions and provide real-time assistance. Through remote access to your computer screen, they can troubleshoot problems with installation or setup and provide step-by-step instructions to clients and customers in solving problems and resolving implementation issues.

In addition to having advanced computer skills and office support skills, the most successful customer service representatives practise professional call management techniques.

Customer service representatives provide assistance using new services.

Workplace Collaboration Tools

As an administrative professional, you will spend many hours collaborating with others to accomplish a variety of tasks, such as creating and revising documents. Software productivity suites contain basic collaboration tools that allow you to schedule, host, and participate in electronic meetings, and

send and receive email. Productivity suites also include features for routing documents across a network to co-workers who can then review, revise, and return them.

Networks enable several other useful electronic tools essential for collaboration—email, shared workspaces, weblogs, wikis, and Web conferencing. The network, Web-based software, and cloud software used for workplace collaboration are commonly referred to as **groupware**. Groupware examples include, Microsoft SharePoint Services, Novell GroupWise, IBM Notes Google Apps, Jive Software, and EMC Documentum eRoom.

Electronic Mail

The most popular and indispensable workplace communication and collaboration tool is email. Email messages can be composed, sent, and delivered in minutes

- are sent when convenient to the sender and read when convenient to the recipient
- can be used to transfer files across the network as email attachments
- can be accessed from numerous locations and devices
- provide a low-cost method of communication
- can be saved as a permanent record of a business activity

To receive email, you must have an email address, an electronic mailbox, and a computer to access the network. An email address has three parts: a name or nickname that identifies the recipient, the @ sign, and a host name. The host name is the identifying name of the account that hosts the electronic mailbox. Martin.Albertson@hostname.net is an example of an email address. To access the email messages in an electronic mailbox, you can use email software or Web mail.

Email Software

Email software is used to store an electronic address book, and to create, send, receive, retrieve, reply to, and save email messages. Incoming messages are downloaded from the mail server to an "Inbox" folder on your computer. In addition to enabling you to create custom folders, by default it will also contain folders for temporarily storing outgoing messages, copies of sent messages, drafts of messages not yet sent, and messages you have deleted. Some examples of email software are Novell GroupWise, Microsoft Outlook, Windows Live Mail, Mozilla Thunderbird, and Qualcomm Eudora.

Web Mail

Another way to access email is through a Web browser. Popular Web-based email services include Gmail by Google, Yahoo! Mail, and EarthLink Web Mail. Web-based email has the advantage of portability. You can access a Web-based email account from any computer or mobile device that has a Web browser and access to the Internet.

You learned in Chapter 6 that when email messages are sent in the workplace, email guidelines and etiquette must be considered. Another important consideration is email ethics.

Email Use Policies

Email is a powerful business tool for increasing collaboration between co-workers and for communicating with clients, vendors, investors, and others. But email abuse also poses potential problems for a business.

Sending personal emails from workplace computers reduces employee productivity. Forwarding jokes, junk mail, and chain letters to others can stress the email system, which can result in reduced productivity. Offensive email content can place a company at risk for charges of workplace harassment. Many businesses protect themselves from these risks by using network software tools to monitor their employees' email and/or have a formal email policy such as the one at Central Washington University (see Figure 8-7) that each employee agrees to follow.

Any workplace email policy should outline the rules for email use, inform employees of the types of emails to save and file as company records, and remind employees that email is not private and may be reviewed by company personnel.

Another concern is the amount of storage space an employee is allocated for email. Limitations on information technology (IT) storage may require that users purge their email on a regular basis. One strategy for retaining important mail is to save it as a file item on a network drive so that it is still available to collaborate and share through Dropbox or another cloud-based collaboration tool.

Instant Messaging

An **instant message** is an electronic message that opens in a small window on a recipient's computer screen. Although instant messages are quick and easy to use, some workers find it a distraction to have instant messages popping up on their screen. However, as a workplace collaboration tool, it has some real advantages. Instant messaging usually leads a faster response than email and can be quicker than making a phone call. It also supports text, video, and audio messaging, and greatly enhances collaboration in the workplace through its ability to transfer electronic files as attachments or to remotely access the computer screen of a colleague to troubleshoot a problem or share data.

In terms of disadvantages, instant messaging has a limited ability to keep a record of messages, and organizations may be concerned by the possibilities of unauthorized interception of messages or of sending viruses within attachments. Also, exchanging personal messages during work hours can lead to lost productivity. As a result, businesses are increasingly establishing company-wide procedures for using instant messaging in the workplace. Some have installed network software to

FIGURE 8-7
Responsible and Ethical Use Guidelines

- Respect the intended use of all information technology resources for learning, teaching research and university business purposes.
- Respect other users by not sending unwanted email messages, maligning address information, flooding the system, sending frivolous messages, forging subscriptions, or tampering with accounts, files, or data that are not owned by your account.
- Use only the user credentials assigned to you; use it for the purposes which it was intended, and to not share it with others.
- Be sensitive to the public nature of shared resources, i.e. labs, modem pool, disk space, printers, bandwidth.
- Occasional unsolicited receipt of email should be deleted, report repeated unsolicited receipt of email as directed under *Misuse of Information Technology Resources.*
- Student use of email services is regulated by the Statement of Agreement between Central Washington University and the ASCWU Board of Directors which states "The Associated Students of Central Washington University recognize all use of email and internet services that is legal, *adheres to University policy,* and meets contractual obligations, as educational in nature."
- Observe all legal requirements specified in any software licenses, contracts and copyright.
- When using networks outside of the University (such as the Internet), comply with acceptable use polices and contracts of those systems.

Source: Courtesy of Central Washington University

monitor and secure employees' instant messages, while others have turned the attachment feature off and permit only short text messages to avoid these potential problems.

Just as with email messages, be careful about what you say and how you say it. Keep your instant messages short and to the point. Send instant messages only when you need a prompt reply to a question or need to send urgent information. Remember that you must not disclose private or confidential information or spread office gossip via instant messaging. To do so is both embarrassing and unethical. Being too casual with co-workers and supervisors in your instant messages may be viewed as unprofessional behaviour. Some instant messaging best practices can be found in Chapter 6 (Figure 6-12). You may wish to refer to it again.

Shared Workspaces

Using Microsoft OneDrive, Dropbox, or Google Drive, it is possible to create a shared workspace—that is, a virtual work area hosted by a Web server and accessed via a Web browser. Team members who have been granted access are

Throughout this course, we have emphasized ethics, with the hope that you will understand its importance and accept the responsibility of behaving ethically. A growing body of ethical issues are connected with the use of and responses to email. Here are some suggestions for maintaining a solid ethical stance:

- Do not send personal email from your office computer, as doing so takes time away from your work. Some companies have developed policies for email usage—be aware of the policy where you work.
- When people send you inappropriate email, let them know politely that you cannot receive it. You might say, "I would enjoy hearing from you, but please send any personal email to my home."
- Do not use email to berate or reprimand an employee.
- Do not use email to terminate someone's employment.
- Do not use email to send information that involves any type of legal action; third parties that should have no knowledge of the action may obtain the information.

- Do not forward junk mail or chain letters; both are inappropriate in an office setting.
- Do not forward unwanted or junk email to a mailing list. This practice is known as spamming, and some organizations have established email policies that result in loss of computer privileges for individuals who engage in spamming.
- Do not forward an email unless you know its message is true. For example, you may think you are being helpful by forwarding a message about a computer virus. However, when you receive 10 email messages concerning misinformation about the viruses, you understand the importance of being certain that an email message is true before forwarding it.
- Do not include credit card numbers in email messages. Email can be intercepted in transit; an unscrupulous individual can use a valid credit card number.
- Do not criticize or insult third parties.

Some organizations have even developed codes of ethics for using email.

---

able to work together in the shared workspace to create and revise documents, view the status of projects, and share project calendars. Features of a shared workspace include the following:

- Names and contact information for each team member
- Links to other Web-based information needed by the team members
- Document libraries containing stored documents related to the specific project
- Tasks assigned to each team member and each task's status

The application software in some productivity suites can be used as an interface to a shared workspace. The software works in combination with Web server technologies.

Online Discussion Groups, Wikis, and Blogs

A discussion group is an online forum in which participants discuss or monitor information on a specific topic. Discussion groups include newsgroups (virtual bulletin boards), mailing lists (email newsletters), and Web-based forums (messages posted via a Web browser). Businesses use mailing lists and Web-based forums to provide customer service and to make customers aware of products and services. Professionals can use discussion groups to connect with peers and stay updated with the latest information in their field.

A wiki is a website or group of Web pages on which anyone can add, edit, or delete content. An example of a wiki is Wikipedia, a popular Web-based free encyclopedia to which anyone can contribute. Contents of wikis may not necessarily

be supported by facts, so you should never use a wiki as your only source of information or data. Wikis can, however, provide a good subject overview and, when sources are provided, a starting point for further research. In the workplace, businesses host wikis on their secure intranets to enable work groups to build knowledge bases on specific work-related topics.

A blog, also called a *weblog*, is a Web-based journal in which participants express their opinions, thoughts, and feelings. Posting to a blog is called *blogging*. Although a wiki and a blog are both Web-based, they are used differently. Unlike postings to a wiki, postings to a blog are added chronologically and generally follow conversational threads or ideas. Postings to a blog may be monitored by a moderator and edited to remove inappropriate content. Examples of public blogs include those hosted by reporters and columnists at online news sites such as GlobalTVBC or Canada.com.

Businesses use public blogs and social media such as Facebook, YouTube, Google+, and Twitter to create forums for exchanging information. Some examples include the following:

- Private blogs hosted on a company intranet can help work groups manage their projects.
- A blog site hosted by an application software manufacturer enables users who are testing a manufacturer's latest software version to share their testing results with other testers; they also can share ways to use and troubleshoot the software and can suggest software updates and new features.

- A business can set up a Facebook account to present a "human face" to customers and to provide an opportunity for people who like the brand or product to share their opinions.
- Small business owners such as restaurants can use Twitter to connect with new customers through "tweets" and to update existing clients and customers on promotions and/or events.

Virtual Meetings

Virtual meetings use telecommunication technology tools to provide opportunities for workplace collaboration. By choosing to collaborate using teleconferencing, video conferencing, or web conferencing, users save time and money. See Chapter 13 for more details on these technologies.

Fax Communications

Workplace collaboration tools have forever changed the way tasks are accomplished in the workplace and how team members communicate with each other. But another more traditional workplace communication tool—a fax machine—still plays an important role.

A **fax machine** is often a multi-function machine, combining printing, faxing, copying, and scanning capabilities into one machine. A fax machine copies or scans a document containing text or pictures, treating both as an image. It can then send the image to a destination telephone number assigned to another fax machine, to a printer, or to a computer where it is printed or stored. The ability to scan hard-copy documents, store them on a computer, and then attach them to email messages has eliminated much of the need for sending faxes.

Securing Messages

Securing fax messages is important for protecting sensitive or confidential data. Fax messages are generally automatically printed at their destination. They can remain unsecured and available to anyone who walks by the fax machine. Always take the appropriate measures to secure any fax transmissions—both outgoing and incoming messages. Follow these guidelines to secure fax messages:

- Place the fax machine in a private area and limit the access to it.
- Use a fax cover sheet that includes the name, fax number, and phone number of both the recipient and the sender. Also indicate the number of pages in the fax and the date.
- Check the page count on incoming fax messages to ensure no pages are missing.
- When sending a fax containing urgent or sensitive information, request a confirmation that the fax has been received.
- Double-check the entered fax number before sending the fax.
- When you receive a fax is received in error, notify the sender.

Chapter Summary

This summary will help you remember the important points covered in this chapter.

- Using broadband connectivity and a wide range of telecommunication devices and pipelines, traditional telephone companies are transforming themselves and the type of connection services they provide.
- With IP telephony, the cost of long-distance calls is reduced when an Internet service provider also becomes a telephone service provider.
- Telephone equipment for the workplace includes standard and IP telephony sets, cordless sets, standalone conference call speakers, and headsets.

- Telephone systems support a wide array of call management features, including call forwarding, call waiting, call holding, call parking, and voice mail.
- When used effectively, voice mail is an efficient method of managing incoming calls when the call recipients are unavailable.
- Examples of workplace collaboration tools include instant messaging, email, shared workspaces, and virtual meetings.
- Businesses are using public blogs and social media such as Facebook, YouTube, Google+, and Twitter to create forums for exchanging information.
- Securing fax messages is important for protecting sensitive or confidential data.

Key Terms

POTS (plain old telephone service) p. 132
VoIP (voice over Internet protocol) or IP telephony p. 133
voice mail p. 139
groupware p. 141
instant message p. 142

spamming p. 143
wiki p. 143
blog p. 143
fax machine p. 144

Responses to Self-Check A

1. Traditional telephone providers are transforming themselves from delivering a service that not only connects people to people but also connects *people to people and people to machines* through a wide range of telecommunication devices.
2. Some advantages of using IP telephony include the following:
   - Users are not tied to one area code, and their service provider may even provide them with a choice of area codes.

   - Phone services do not need to be transferred when moving to new office space or a new city.
   - Voice mail can be routed to a computer's electronic mailbox.
   - Phone numbers kept in a user's contact management software can be dialled from a computer.
3. Two disadvantages to using IP telephony are the poor voice quality and unreliable connections.

Discussion Items

These discussion items provide an opportunity to test your understanding of the chapter through written responses and/or discussion with your classmates and your instructor.

1. What are some popular call management features of telephone systems?
2. Why is it important for an administrative professional to use good call management skills?

3. List 10 effective call management skills.
4. What information should be included when leaving a voice message?
5. Why is it important to consider time zones when planning a call?
6. What are some tools that you might use for workplace collaboration?

Critical-Thinking Activity

You have asked one of your assistants, Guy, to send an email to a group of managers to set up a meeting with Calgary's superintendent of schools to discuss a mentoring program that CanAsian wants to begin with the public school system. The meeting is to be held on Monday, January 20, in Conference Room C, beginning at 8:30 a.m. and lasting approximately one hour. The managers are to forward written suggestions for a mentoring program to Mr. Albertson on Thursday, January 16. You did not review the email Guy sent. His email, a response from one of the managers, and Guy's response to the manager are on the MindTap site, access to which is provided with the printed access card on the inside cover of your textbook (files SCDCTA8-1, SCDCTA8-2, and SCDCTA8-3).

Guy comes to you very upset. He says one of the managers is angry with him, and when he tried to handle the situation, it became worse. Review the email exchanges. Has Guy made errors? If so, what are they? How should the present situation be handled? What advice would you give Guy on preventing such a situation in the future? (You may wish to use the email section in Chapter 6 as a source of reference.)

Building Workplace Skills

Project 8-1 (Learning Outcomes 1 and 3)

Online Project

Search the Web for current information on one or more of the following:

- Suggestions of freeware available for IP telephony. Compare the features they offer for free with those they offer for a small cost.
- Characteristics of two or more shareware software programs. Compare their features and cost.
- Implementation of social media by businesses to connect with clients, customers, and employees.
- Several sites on the internet offer free blog services. Locate such a site by keying *free blog* in an Internet search engine. Review several sites from the list. Compare the individual features offered and the cost.

Present your findings orally to the class, or write a report of your findings, documenting your resources. Submit your report to your instructor.

Project 8-2 (Learning Outcome 2)

Four situations are provided on the MindTap site in file SCDP8-2. Respond to each. Print a copy of your responses to submit to your instructor.

Project 8-3 (Learning Outcome 2)

Collaborative Project

Choose a member of your class to work with on this project. Call each other, recreating situations 1, 2, 3, and 4 in Project 8-2, which are found on the MindTap site in file SCDP8-2. Complete each of the situations twice. First, one of you should take the role of the caller and the other, the administrative assistant; then switch roles and replay the situations. Print out a copy of the Telephone Voice Rating Form file SCDP8-3. Complete the form and submit it to your instructor.

Project 8-4 (Learning Outcomes 1 and 3)

Mr. Albertson is considering working from home one day per week. Before committing to this arrangement, he needs to consider the viability of this option. He needs to be able to access both the Internet and the company intranet. In addition, he will need a mobile device for working on reports and budgets for special projects. He has asked you to research these needs for him and to provide the costs involved and your recommendation of the best solution.

In completing this task for Mr. Albertson, consider the telecommunications pipelines available in your area. He needs to know what costs, if any, are involved in getting set up, maintaining the connection, and any contractual obligations to be undertaken with the provider. He is also looking for a recommendation on the most cost-effective and appropriate mobile device. He asks you to compare at least three different pieces of equipment and provide him with a list of features that will meet his needs and the cost of each.

Prepare a summary of the information you compile and a recommendation for Mr. Albertson. Be prepared to discuss it briefly with the class.

Project 8-5 (Learning Outcome 2)

At a recent management meeting, the managers present discussed ensuring all employees are aware of the importance of good call management skills. It was decided that a Web page should be created and uploaded to your company intranet. Mr. Albertson has asked you to create a document on effective telephone techniques that he can take to the next meeting for approval. Using the information in this chapter and any other information you gather from research, write a brief introductory paragraph about the importance of using the telephone effectively. Follow it with a list of guidelines for effective telephone use. Include an appropriate photo or other graphic on the page. Save the file as a document or single-file Web page.

Canada Post has responded by introducing several electronic options for customers. For example *epost*, a free, secure, online personal digital mailbox, allows individuals and businesses to access, view, and pay bills online. It can also be used as a digital safety-deposit box to store copies of important documents such as passports, insurance documents, and more.

epost Connect is a secure service that is linked to an *epost* account to provide the same private and confidential online secure communications services for business customers through *Bulk* and *Collaboration* options.

Does this mean we are sending less mail than in the past? Absolutely not. In fact, with the growth of online shopping and parcel shipment, we are sending more mail. But it does mean that we have drastically changed the way we communicate with each other and our expectations about effective communication. Electronic communication is a routine part of our everyday existence and while paper mail may continue to drop in volume, for many organizations, it is still an extremely important method of communication.

An administrative professional has numerous responsibilities related to mail handling—from preparing incoming mail for presentation to your supervisor to reviewing and preparing outgoing correspondence to be mailed. After studying this chapter, you will understand your role and responsibilities in regard to effectively processing all types of mail, both traditional and electronic. You will also become more knowledgeable about reprographics equipment and their functions. The soft skill you will focus on in this chapter is *teamwork*.

Incoming Mail

Unanswered or misplaced mail can represent a significant cost to an organization in lost business. Your job as an administrative professional is to ensure that incoming mail is well organized and presented to your supervisor in a timely manner. If you work in a large organization, the mail is likely delivered to a central mailroom where it is sorted according to the company's departments. In addition to sorting, the mailroom may offer additional services, such as opening the mail. If the mail is opened, correspondence is not taken from the envelope, since the envelope itself may have information that the receiver needs. Mail opened in mailrooms is often processed through automatic mail openers that also count the items. This step helps a company to analyze and justify its mail costs. Mail is usually either picked up at the mailroom by the administrative professional or delivered by a mailroom attendant at set times during the day (usually in the morning and the afternoon) so employees know when to expect it.

In some cases, mailrooms may also process incoming mail using imaging technology that scans and electronically stores the contents of documents, integrating them into an electronic communication system. Colleges and universities, for example, receive thousands of applications for admission from potential students; this mail can be electronically distributed to the inbox of the appropriate department or departments. Using this technology reduces the needless copying of documents for circulation.

In small offices, a Canada Post carrier may deliver the mail directly to the office, or the company may maintain a mailbox at the post office. If the organization maintains a post office box, you may have the responsibility for picking up the mail. Once you receive the mail in your office or department, you will sort, open, read, and possibly annotate, organize by priority, and present it to your supervisor. You will also determine which items, if any, should be copied and circulated to others; such items are then prepared for distribution by attaching a routing slip.

Canada Post's plans to replace daily residential delivery with community mailboxes by 2016 was placed on hold in the fall of 2015. If this change in delivery policies proceeds in the future, it is not expected to affect small businesses.

Sorting Mail

First, do a preliminary mail sort. If several individuals work in the department, sort the mail according to the addressee. An alphabetical sorter is handy if you are sorting mail for several individuals. Once the mail is sorted, place the mail for each individual into separate stacks.

When this preliminary sort is completed, sort each person's mail in this order:

- *Personal and confidential.* The administrative professional should not open mail marked "Personal" or "Confidential." Place this mail to one side to avoid inadvertently opening it.
- *Xpresspost, Registered, or Priority.* This mail has high priority and should be placed so it is the first mail the recipient sees.
- *Regular business mail (Lettermail).* Mail from customers, clients, and suppliers is also considered important and should be sorted so it receives top priority.
- *Interoffice communications.* This mail generally is received in the distinctive interoffice envelope shown in Figure 9-1.
- *Advertisements, newspapers, magazines, and catalogues.* These materials are considered relatively unimportant and can be handled after the other correspondence is answered. They should be placed at the bottom of the correspondence stack so they may be read at your supervisor's convenience.

Opening Mail

Mail may be opened in the mailroom or in the individual's office. Mail opened in an individual's office is usually opened

FIGURE 9-1
An Interoffice Envelope

INTER-DEPARTMENT DELIVERY				
Note—Cross Out Entire Line When Received and Re-use Until All Lines Are Full.				
Date	Deliver To:	Department	Sent By:	Department

© Costas/Shutterstock

by hand, using an envelope opener. When opening mail, follow these procedures:

- Have these necessary supplies readily available: an envelope opener, a date and time stamp, routing and action slips, a stapler, paper clips, sticky notes, and a pen or pencil.
- Before opening an envelope, tap the lower edge of the envelope on the desk so the contents fall to the bottom and cannot be inadvertently cut when the envelope is opened.
- Check the envelope carefully to be certain all items have been removed.
- Fasten any enclosures to the correspondence. Attach small enclosures to the front of the correspondence. Attach enclosures larger than the correspondence to the back.
- Mend any torn paper with tape.
- If a personal or confidential letter is opened by mistake, do not remove it from the envelope. Write "Opened by Mistake" on the front of the envelope, add your initials, and reseal the envelope with tape.

Stack the envelopes on the desk in the same order as the opened mail in case it becomes necessary to refer to the envelopes. A good practice is to save all envelopes for at least one day in case they are needed for reference; they can then be thrown away.

Certain envelopes should be retained. Keep the envelope when you notice one or more of the following things:

- *An incorrectly addressed envelope.* You or your supervisor may want to call attention to this fact when replying to the correspondence.
- *A letter with no return address.* The envelope usually will have the return address.
- *An envelope that has a significantly different postmark from the date on the document.* The document date may be compared with the postmark date to determine the delay in receiving the document.
- *A letter specifying an enclosure that is not enclosed.* Write "No Enclosure" on the letter and attach the envelope.
- *A letter containing a bid, an offer, or an acceptance of a contract.* The postmark date may be needed as legal evidence.
- An envelope that appears to contain any suspicious substance or materials. Follow your organization's procedures for handling suspicious mail.

In many organizations, incoming mail receives a hand stamp or a stamp from a small machine that imprints the date and time of receipt. This procedure can be an important step as it furnishes a record of when the correspondence was received. If mail arrives later than a predetermined deadline, the stamped date of receipt is a recorded confirmation of the date the letter was received. If the letter has no date line, the received date stamped on the letter indicates approximately when the correspondence was mailed. Also, when an invoice is received, which, in a large organization may require several days to process as it travels from department to department obtaining appropriate coding and approvals, the received date stamped on the item can be very important to the accounts payable department.

Reviewing and Annotating

Busy executives appreciate help with the large amount of mail that crosses their desks each day. As an administrative professional, you can help by visually scanning all received mail and underlining the important words and phrases with a coloured pen, pencil, or highlighter. You should also check mathematical calculations and verify dates that appear in correspondence.

The next step is to annotate (to make notations about previous action taken or facts that will assist the reader). You can annotate by writing notes in the margin of the correspondence or by using sticky notes. The advantage of sticky notes is that they can be peeled off and destroyed when you and your supervisor are finished with them and before filing the correspondence. Discuss with your supervisor which of these methods is preferred.

If an enclosure is missing from the letter, make a note of this omission. If an invoice is received, check the calculations. Indicate any discrepancies in a note. If the correspondence refers to a previous piece of correspondence, pull that item or the file and attach it to the new correspondence, noting the attachment. Annotations may also be used to remind your supervisor of a previous commitment. For example, suppose you open mail that requests a meeting at a time that conflicts with an existing commitment; when answering the letter, your supervisor needs to be aware of this conflict to avoid inadvertently agreeing to a meeting that would conflict with existing plans.

Organizing and Presenting

After you have completed the preliminary mail sorts and have opened, date- and time-stamped, read, and annotated the mail, you are ready to do a final sort and to place the items in their respective folders. Folders help maintain confidentiality; for example, someone walking into your supervisor's office will not be able to easily read the material. Colour-coding the folders also helps your supervisor to see at a glance which mail needs to be handled first. Here is one arrangement you might use:

- *Immediate action.* This mail must be handled on the day of receipt or shortly thereafter. (RED FOLDER)
- *Routine correspondence.* Such mail would include memoranda and other types of non-urgent mail. (BLUE FOLDER)
- *Informational mail.* Included in this folder are periodicals, newspapers, advertisements, and other types of mail that do not require answering but are for informational reading. (YELLOW FOLDER)

If you have been working with your supervisor for a period of time, you may have learned that he or she does not want to see some mail, such as certain types of advertisements or catalogues. Also, you may be authorized to answer routine requests for information. Discuss with your supervisor where the mail should be placed and how frequently it should be presented. Depending on how often mail is delivered, your supervisor may ask that you organize and present it approximately 30 minutes after you receive it. Never destroy mail (even what you consider to be junk mail)

Capital Trust Company

9 St. Clair Avenue West, Tornoto, ON M4 1K6
Telephone 416-368-8484

April 25, 20--

Mr. Arthur R. Channing, President
Astrolite, Limited
400 West Georgia Street
Vancouver, BC
V6B 1Z3

Financing approved

Dear Mr. Channing:

We have now received a final report on the financing of your proposed plant in Windsor, Ontario. It appears that no difficulty will be encountered in providing the amount you require on the terms you requested.

Mr. C. E. Cabot and Ms. R. R. Ashcroft have both signified their intention to serve on the Advisory Board of Capital Astrolite Ltd. The addition of these two prominent industrialists to your control body is a major achievement and should make much easier any further development plans you might have for operations in Canada.

Your interim account has been established at our main office in Montreal. Mr. Wells has been informed of this, and we have arranged a temporary credit for his use until such time as your account in placed on a formal basis. Please arrange to provide an opening deposit of $1,000.

Sincerely yours,

Names added to mailing list

I. A. Wilson

Cheque requisition attached for your signature.

I. A. Wilson, President

IA/ds

An annotated letter

FIGURE 9-2
A Routing Slip

ROUTING SLIP			
Description of Document:	Draft — Travel Policy and Procedures		
Date:	October 21, 20--		
Please circulate to:			

Order	Name	Date	Initial
	Guy Beauchamp		
2	Luyin Wu		
1	Keri-An Mahar		
3	Ryan Hughes		
	Return to:	Guy Beauchamp	

- Read the email, reply to the email (if appropriate), and forward it, if necessary, to appropriate individuals and copy your supervisor so that he or she is aware of the action you have taken.
- If the individual does not know that you routinely handle the email of your employer, be explicit in the email when you answer it. Say, for example, "Mrs. Florentine has asked that I respond to your email."
- If you cannot handle the email, send a note to your supervisor informing him or her of the email you have not been able to handle. If your employer needs to handle it immediately, tag your email as urgent.

When your employer is out of town, handle the email as usual, assuming you have been authorized to do so. If not, forward the email to the appropriate person who is in charge during your employer's absence. In Chapter 11, you will be introduced to some suggestions for organizing your email.

Handling Mail in Your Supervisor's Absence

In Chapter 14, you will be introduced to some of the responsibilities of an administrative assistant while an executive is out of the office and travelling on behalf of the company. One of your responsibilities will be to handle the mail. Talk with your supervisor before he or she leaves to understand your mail-handling responsibilities. Be specific with any questions so you have a clear understanding. Mistakes in handling mail can be costly to the company. Here are some general guidelines for handling mail:

- When you receive urgent mail (any mail, including email, that includes a matter that needs immediate handling), respond to the correspondence the same day. If you cannot answer the mail, send it to the appropriate person in your organization who can answer the correspondence. Your supervisor will usually have designated someone who is in charge in his or her absence. Make sure that person receives the urgent correspondence quickly.
- Promptly answer any mail that falls within your area of responsibility.
- File in a separate folder any mail that has been answered (with the answer attached); your supervisor may want to review it when he or she returns. Create a folder in your email system named "Mr. Albertson Out of Office Sept 1–15" to hold copies of all email you dealt with in his absence. This folder can be shared with your supervisor while he is out of town or left to discuss upon his return.
- Keep in a separate folder any mail that can wait for your supervisor's return. Retrieve and add to the folder any previous correspondence that will be needed when reviewing the mail.

unless your supervisor has given you the authority to make these decisions.

Routing

At times, more than one person may need to read a piece of correspondence or a publication. In the case of correspondence, if you feel it is urgent that all individuals immediately receive the information, scan or make photocopies of the correspondence and email or forward a hardcopy to each person on the list. If it is not urgent, route the actual correspondence, using a routing slip to save copying costs. A routing slip is also an effective method for circulating publications.

You can purchase routing slips or create your own (an example is shown in Figure 9-2). For example, if you regularly route correspondence to the same individuals, you can create a routing slip that already has the individuals' names printed on it. If you are circulating several publications to the same people at the same time, vary the order of the names on the list so that the documents do not always start their circulation with the same person.

Handling Email

Some executives expect the administrative professional to assist with their emails. If so, be certain that you understand how she or he wants you to handle them. You might be expected to answer routine email; if so, your employer needs to know that you have done so. Here are some suggestions for handling your supervisor's email:

- Check email regularly not constantly. For example, you may check it at 9 a.m., 11 a.m., 2 p.m., and 4 p.m., or more frequently, depending on your supervisor's preference.
- Do not open email marked "Confidential" unless your employer instructs you to do so.

Outgoing Mail

While an administrative professional's responsibilities for handling outgoing mail will vary, the primary role is to ensure that mail leaves the office in a timely manner using the most expeditious service available. In a large organization, you would be responsible for preparing the mail for processing by mailroom employees. Mailroom employees may pick up the mail at various times during the day (when delivering incoming mail, for example), or you may be responsible for taking time-sensitive outgoing mail to the mailroom.

Mailrooms today are automated. Multi-functional equipment is used to fold, sort, label, and attach postage to outgoing mail, and software is used for maintaining mailing lists. The photo here shows multi-functional equipment from Pitney Bowes.

In large companies, the outsourcing of mail services may be implemented as a cost-saving measure. Firms that handle mail services for organizations include Kelly Management Services and Pitney Bowes Management Services Canada Inc.

The Internet is used extensively to gather information relating to post office services, to access related associations, and to track delivery status (Canada Post and express carriers, such as Purolator and others, provide detailed delivery tracking information online). More details on mail services and mail-processing equipment can be found at:

- www.neopost.ca
- www.francotyp.ca
- www.pitneybowes.ca

In the mailrooms of large companies, computer applications allow staff to easily record the accountable items (express items), including registered mail and items sent via private courier. To establish the sender's identity and enter the recipient's name, a bar code on incoming items is scanned. Mail can then be easily sorted by whatever delivery scheme is being used—by floor, building, department, or division. Mailrooms also use software to track mail expenditures by departments or divisions within the organization. Such tracking allows department managers to control their postal budgets more effectively.

In a small company, the administrative professional usually has the responsibility of preparing and processing the mail, which may also involve taking it to the local postal office or calling the mailing service to arrange pickup. Whether you work in a large or a small company, your responsibilities may include preparing correspondence for mailing, adhering to automation requirements, sealing and stamping items not processed through the mailroom, and maintaining mailing lists.

Preparing the Mail

By following these procedures consistently and carefully, you can save your organization both time and money.

- Check that every letter is signed and that any enclosures noted are included. Your supervisor may require a file copy of the signed letter.
- If enclosures are too large to send with the letter and must be sent in a separate envelope, check to see that the address on the second envelope is correct. Mark it with the appropriate class of mail.
- Address envelopes carefully. Your word processing software can automatically generate a label or envelope based on the address you have keyed into the letter. As a result, you need only key and proofread the address once. Check the address against your records. When an organization's address changes, be sure to update your mailing list. Ensure you have chosen the correct envelope size so that the address placement will be correct. Figure 9-3 illustrates a correctly addressed envelope. Note the required blank space that MUST appear at the bottom of the envelope to accommodate the electronic postal equipment.
- Make sure any special mailing notations are included and correctly positioned on the envelope.
- If a mailroom employee seals your mail and applies postage, you may be requested to stack your envelopes with the flap up (piggyback style) to facilitate passing them through the postage meter.
- Insert all interoffice correspondence in appropriate envelopes (as shown in the image on page 150) with the name and department of the addressee listed on the envelope.

Adhering to Automation Requirements

As an administrative professional, you are responsible for properly preparing outgoing mail for the automated sorting equipment used by Canada Post and private services. Envelopes that are not legible or that do not show a postal code will require additional handling. Adhering to automation requirements

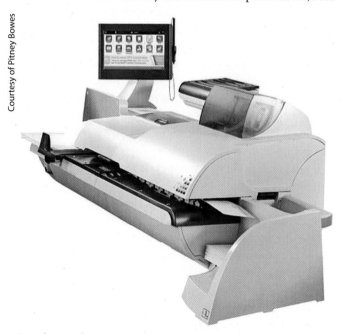

Courtesy of Pitney Bowes

Postal meter from Pitney-Bowes

FIGURE 9-3
A Correctly Addressed Envelope

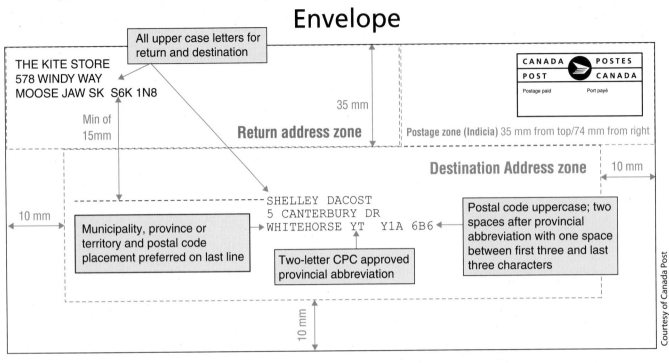

Envelope

All upper case letters for return and destination

THE KITE STORE
578 WINDY WAY
MOOSE JAW SK S6K 1N8

Min of 15mm

35 mm

Return address zone

CANADA POSTES
POST CANADA
Postage paid   Port payé

Postage zone (Indicia) 35 mm from top/74 mm from right

Destination Address zone   10 mm

10 mm

Municipality, province or territory and postal code placement preferred on last line

SHELLEY DACOST
5 CANTERBURY DR
WHITEHORSE YT   Y1A 6B6

Two-letter CPC approved provincial abbreviation

Postal code uppercase; two spaces after provincial abbreviation with one space between first three and last three characters

10 mm

Courtesy of Canada Post

ensures that mail is consistently delivered on time. In addition to being sorted by postal code, mail may also be scanned and sorted by bar code, using a **BCS** (bar code sorter). A bar code is similar to the UPC (Universal Product Code), which is found on everyday items such as groceries. When the bar code or UPC is scanned at the cashier, the price of the product is identified. When using Canada Post's parcel shipping service "Ship-in-a-click," a mailing label is generated, which includes a bar code. Private mail services, such as FedEx and UPS, also use bar codes to sort their large volumes of mail.

Dividing the country into 18 zones, Canada's six-character alphanumeric postal code system employs the following pattern: letter-number-letter (space) number-letter-number. The first letter represents the regional zone, usually an entire province or territory, with the exception of Ontario whose population size necessitates several major subzones. The two characters that follow, a number and a letter, provide additional division of the region by city, town, or municipality. The second group of characters identifies more specifically the location within a city, town, or municipality—whether the item is to be delivered to one side or the other of a street, or perhaps a specific building on a street or even a specific floor of a large building. In the case of CanAsian Airlines, the project company for this textbook, the postal code "T2P 4C4" represents the following:

- T designates the province of Alberta.
- 2 designates the city of Calgary.
- P designates an area within Calgary.

The next three-character group identifies the west tower of a large building known as the Bankers Hall. See Figure 9-4 for an illustration of Canadian geographic postal code regions.

The *Canadian Postal Code Directory* is no longer available for purchase. Locating a postal code is quickly obtained by visiting the CPC site at www.canadapost.ca. Click on the "Find a Postal Code" link on the home page and you are provided with a blank field. Begin keying a business name, address, or postal code, and CPC's Address*Complete* application will suggest results as the text is entered. If you require a postal code for a new address not yet in the Address*Complete* database, call Canada Post (1-900-565-2633 for service in English or 1-900-565-2634 for service in French) and, for a small fee, it will be provided. The option to locate an address when you know the postal code (formerly Reverse Search) is also available.

In the addressing of envelopes or packages, Canada Post requests the following:

- The address be keyed in ALL CAPITALS (using uppercase and lowercase letters is also acceptable)
- The attention line be keyed as the first line of the address
- No punctuation be used unless it is part of a name
- The CPC-approved two-letter provincial, territorial, or state abbreviations be used; see Figure 9-5 for approved Canadian abbreviations. A complete listing that includes U.S. abbreviations can be found in the Formatting

FIGURE 9-4
Canadian Geographic Postal Code Regions

The first letter in Canada's postal code system identifies each of the country's 18 regional zones.

Business Documents guide on the MindTap site for this textbook or the *Addressing Guidelines* on the CPC website.

- The municipality (city), province or territory, and postal code be keyed on the same line with one space between the municipality and province or territory, and two spaces before the postal code. If this line becomes too long, the postal code may be placed on the last line by itself.

FIGURE 9-5
CPC-Approved Two-Letter Provincial and Territorial Abbreviations

Province/Territory	Abbreviation	Province/Territory	Abbreviation
Alberta	AB	Nunavut	NU
British Columbia	BC	Ontario	ON
Manitoba	MB	Prince Edward Island	PE
New Brunswick	NB	Quebec	QC
Newfoundland and Labrador	NL	Saskatchewan	SK
Northwest Territories	NT	Yukon	YT
Nova Scotia	NS		

More detailed information about addressing mailable items is available in the "Addressing Guidelines" section of the *Canada Postal Guide* provided by Canada Post Corporation; it can be downloaded from the CPC website. A link to this section can be found on the MindTap site for this textbook.

Here you will find examples for correctly keying the following:

- Civic (street) addresses
- RR (Rural route) and General Delivery addresses
- Post office box addresses
- Bilingual addresses
- U.S.A. and international addresses

Skills @ Work

Electronic Postage

In the United States, **e-stamps** (electronic postage, also referred to as *PC postage*) are available through Stamps.com (www.stamps.com). With e-stamps, postage can be printed on labels or on envelopes, packages, mailing tubes, or anything else that needs mailing. Nothing similar is yet available in Canada for Lettermail.

Click-N-Ship allows U.S. users to download and print shipping labels with postage for packages. A similar service, "Ship-in-a-click," is offered by Canada Post for parcels. Using an online form, you enter the size and weight of the item you wish to ship; the postage is calculated, and payment can be made online against a credit card or through your business account. You print your shipping label, which includes a bar code, affix it to the parcel, and post at the nearest mailbox or postal outlet. A tracking number is provided so that a sender is able to track online the delivery status of the item—from pickup to the final destination—including the identity of the recipient.

The guide also provides other useful information, such as the following:

- Correct abbreviations for street types, directions, and designators
- Approved two-letter abbreviations for Canadian provinces and territories and for U.S. states
- English and French versions of country names

Bookmarking a link to this handy guide will ensure you are doing all you can to expedite your company's mail. The CPC website also provides videos that show the automated processing of the mail and explain the importance of adhering to these guidelines.

Sealing and Stamping

If you work in a medium-to-large office, you may not be responsible for sealing and stamping the mail; the outgoing mail is likely sent to a mailroom where these tasks are done using automated equipment. Envelopes are fed into the meter and stacked, sealed, weighed, meter-stamped, and counted in one continuous operation. The all-in-one metered mail imprint serves as postage payment, a postmark, and a cancellation mark. A postage meter prints directly on letter-sized envelopes or on adhesive strips that are then affixed to larger envelopes or packages.

If you work in a small office, using a postage meter to seal and stamp envelopes saves time and ensures faster delivery since, unlike stamps, metered postage does not need to be cancelled during processing by Canada Post. Postage is "cancelled" when bars, the date, the time, and the municipality where the mail has been processed are printed over the stamps. This "cancellation" prevents the stamps from being reused. (See the image of a cancelled stamp on next page.)

Organizations can lease postage meters from one of three approved private companies in Canada—Neopost Canada Ltd., Francotyp Postalia Canada Inc., or Pitney Bowes Canada. The **die** (an engraved metal stamp used for impressing the postage) on the meter may include business logos or other messages that are printed concurrently and in addition to the postage. Once an account has been created with the meter supplier, either a specified amount is prepaid into the account or arrangements are made to receive a monthly statement so that the digital meters can be "refilled" online or over the telephone 24/7 through your meter supplier. You may be responsible for monitoring the amount remaining in the meter to determine when postage refilling is necessary. Depending on the terms of your contract with your meter supplier, another payment on the account may also be required. It is important also to consider the issue of security around the postage meter (also known as the **franking** machine). Designating one person to be the keyholder and sole operator for the machine is a proactive action in preventing possible theft of postage.

Maintaining Mailing Lists

Most companies have correspondence they send to certain groups of individuals. As an administrative professional, your responsibility is to maintain a current mailing list. You must periodically update addresses and will occasionally add new names to the mailing list. By using the appropriate software, you can maintain mailing lists on your computer, updating them quickly and easily. You can print address labels and envelopes from your mailing lists.

Domestic Postal Services

The way we send and receive mail has changed with the advent of electronic technology. Canada Post, a Crown corporation, has committed to modernization, and in recent

Stamps are "cancelled" and prevented from reuse by printing bars and the date, time, and municipality over the stamps.

years has become more efficient. Reaching more than 15 million addresses through more than 6,000 post offices nationally,[1] Canada Post remains the main provider of a wide variety of mail services, only some of which are covered in detail here. Descriptions of these additional services can be located on the CPC website at www.canadapost.ca. The services offered and fees charged change periodically so it is important for administrative professionals to keep current and check the Canada Post website frequently.

Domestic postal services (mail delivered within Canada) provided by Canada Post generally fit into one of following three categories:

- Transaction Mail
- Direct Marketing
- Parcel Services

Postage meter suitable for a small office

Transaction Mail

Lettermail

Lettermail refers to any type of mail that measures no more than 156 by 245 millimetres and weighs 50 grams or less. It includes letters, cards, postcards, financial reports, and other promotional or non-promotional mailable items partly keyed or handwritten.

Incentive Lettermail

Delivery of large volumes of Lettermail at discounted prices can be arranged by signing an Incentive Lettermail Agreement with Canada Post. To be eligible for this rate, businesses must meet a required minimum number of items (1000 machineable or 500 presorted), mail must be presorted when delivered to a CPC outlet, all items must be of the same size, and all items must meet the CPC established machineability and readability guidelines. Canada Post provides an online "Do-it-Yourself Checklist" to assist businesses in avoiding common errors in mail preparation that could result in unnecessary delays or additional charges.

Direct Marketing

Admail

Admail enables businesses to promote their products and services by delivering their message directly to specific customers, neighbourhoods, or prospects. Two types of direct mail are available from Canada Post:

- Addressed Admail enables businesses to promote their products and services to specific delivery addresses.
- Unaddressed Admail or "householder mail" does not contain any specific delivery address and is delivered to locations based on demographics, consumer purchasing behaviour, or geographic location.

Business Reply Mail

A self-addressed, postage-prepaid business reply card or envelope is used by businesses and other organizations to request information, raise funds, or receive payments or subscription renewals.

Publications Mail

Periodical publications produced in Canada may be eligible for distribution at the Publications Mail rate. The periodical must be published at least twice a year, be mailed in Canada for delivery in Canada, be either individually addressed or bundled and unaddressed, and contain less than 70 percent advertising in at least half the issues mailed in a year. The maximum allowable weight varies from 50 grams for individually addressed items to 22.7 kilograms for bundled unaddressed copies. Rates are based on the weight of the piece and the distance from origin to destination.

Parcel Services

Parcel Services offered by Canada Post have grown to meet the evolving demands placed on businesses as a result of the exponential growth in online shopping. Offering a full spectrum of economical and timely services to urban and rural Canada, Canada Post provides delivery solutions, including delivery to a residential or business address, to a post office, or to a community mailbox. Canada Post's online tracking tool, Track, allows customers to go online or use their mobile device to determine where their shipment is at any time in the delivery sequence and, when returns are necessary, customers can access return labels from a business or the CPC website. For delivery of documents, packets, and parcels that do not exceed 30 kilograms in weight or 3 metres in combined length and girth (a measurement around the thickest part) businesses can choose from among several CPC parcel services, including Priority, Xpresspost, Xpresspost Certified, Expedited Parcel, and Regular Parcel.

Priority

Priority is the fastest mail service for time-sensitive documents and parcels. Delivery times are guaranteed and online confirmation is available at canadapost.ca/track. The service operates 365 days a year. Prepaid envelopes, available in different sizes, may be purchased in advance and used at any time.

Xpresspost

Xpresspost offers next-business-day delivery to local and regional destinations, and two-day service between most

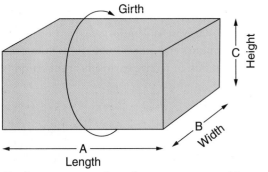

Total measurement of a package must not exceed 3 metres.

major Canadian destinations. Xpresspost envelopes, labels, and boxes are available at Canada Post outlets. Pickup service is available for a fee to Canada Post account customers only.

Xpresspost Certified

In addition to offering the same service as Xpressspost, this service captures the recipient's signature upon delivery of the item, making it suitable for important notices or legal or court documents. If the receiver refuses to accept delivery, the item is returned to the sender.

Expedited Parcel

Expedited Parcel is a cost-effective ground service that offers next-day local, three-day regional, and seven-day national delivery. Items are tracked, delivery is guaranteed, and status can be checked online.

Regular Parcel

Regular Parcel is the most economical shipping service offered by Canada Post. The standard delivery times are local delivery within two business days, up to five days regionally, and up to nine days between other Canadian destinations. Regular Parcel is used for mailing items such as books, circulars, catalogues, and other printed or non-printed matter that weighs no more than 30 kilograms.

Bill of Lading

A bill of lading is a document that itemizes a shipment's contents, quantity, and delivery destination. It accompanies items such as parcels or packages being shipped from a supplier to a customer. In addition to being a legal document between a supplier and a carrier, it also serves as receipt of the shipment when signed for by an authorized recipient.

Other Products and Services

Canada Post offers the following services that are beneficial in special situations: Collect on Delivery, Insured Mail, and Registered Mail.

Collect on Delivery (COD)

This service, available for a fee, allows mailers to collect the price of goods and/or postage on merchandise from the addressee when the item is delivered. The amount to be collected from the recipient may not exceed $1000.

SHIP FROM	Bill of Lading Number:
[Name] [Street Address] [City, ST ZIP Code] SID No.:	**BAR CODE SPACE**
SHIP TO	**Carrier Name:**
[Name] [Street Address] [City, ST ZIP Code] CID No.:	Trailer number: Serial number(s):
THIRD PARTY FREIGHT CHARGES BILL TO	**SCAC:**
[Name] [Street Address] [City, ST ZIP Code]	Pro Number: **BAR CODE SPACE**
Special Instructions:	**Freight Charge Terms** (Freight charges are prepaid unless marked otherwise): Prepaid ❑ Collect ❑ 3rd Party ❑ ❑ Master bill of lading with attached underlying bills of lading.

CUSTOMER ORDER INFORMATION

Customer Order No.	# of Packages	Weight	Pallet/Slip (circle one)		Additional Shipper Information
			Y	N	
			Y	N	
			Y	N	
			Y	N	
Grand Total					

Bill of lading template in Microsoft Word

Insured Mail

This service provides compensation to a mailer for loss or damage of mailable items. Coverage up to $1000 is available for Lettermail; up to $100 on Regular Parcel when delivery confirmation is purchased; and up to $5000 on Xpresspost. Items may not be insured for more than their value. To make a claim with Canada Post, a receipt or proof of value of the item being claimed is required. A detailed list of items not eligible for Insured Mail can be found in the *Canada Postal Guide*.

Registered Mail

Registered mail, which may include Lettermail and non-document materials such as coins or jewellery, provides proof of mailing and proof of delivery. The sender is given a date-stamped official registration receipt, and a signature is secured, free of charge, upon delivery. The sender can access, online and at no charge, a secured image of that signature usually by noon the following business day. A hardcopy of the signature is also available, for a fee, by contacting Customer Service.

Additional information, such as a list of items that are restricted or unacceptable for this service, may be found at www.canadapost.ca.

U.S. and International Mail Service and Requirements

As organizations continue to expand into international markets, you may need to send documents and parcels to the United States and internationally. The principal categories of international mail provided by Canada Post Corporation are USA or international Letterpost, Xpresspost USA or Xpresspost International, and International Incentive Letter-post.

U.S.A. or International Letterpost

Items posted in Canada bearing a Canadian return address are shipped by air and can include letters, cards, postcards, and self-mailers (items without a cover) weighing no more than 50 grams and oversize items no more than 500 grams.

Xpresspost U.S.A. or Xpresspost International

This service provides fast, guaranteed on-time delivery, with signature confirmation, of documents, packets, and parcels to the United States and other participating countries at a cost much less than a courier.

Advice of Receipt

An *Advice of Receipt* is, an option available for purchase when sending *Registered Mail–International*. The addressee's signature is obtained on the card at the time of delivery and then returned to the sender, thereby providing confirmation of delivery. *Registered Mail–U.S.A.* is automatically delivered as Xpresspost, which includes a recipient signature at no additional cost. An *Advice of Receipt* card is no longer necessary and the signature can be tracked on the CPC website at www .canadapost.ca/track.

International Incentive Letterpost

Similar to Incentive Lettermail in Canada, this classification of international service caters to Canadian businesses that send a large volume of commercial mail to the U.S.A. and/or other international destinations. The three service options are Premium, Per Item, and Standard Incentive service. *Standard Incentive* is the lowest cost choice with the longest delivery times. Unlike *Premium* or *Per Item* services, undelivered items are disposed of or recycled locally. *Premium* and *Per Item* services are airmail services that include, at no additional cost, the redirection of an item or the direct return of undeliverable mail.

Customs Requirements

All international mail is subject to the laws and customs regulations of both the originating and destination countries. Customs declaration forms must be completed for all international parcels but are not required for Letterpost items. In the case of Xpresspost U.S.A. and Xpresspost International, the customs declaration form is included in the shipping label.

The Canada Post website contains a vast amount of detailed information regarding domestic and international mailing and shipping; only a limited amount of that information has been included here. Regulations, services, and rates change regularly—check the CPC site frequently to maintain currency.

SELF-CHECK

Take a few minutes to check your understanding of Canada Post mail classifications. Answer the following questions:

1. Describe the following types of mail: Lettermail, Unaddressed Admail, Xpresspost, and Expedited Parcel.
2. Describe these special services offered by Canada Post: Advice of Receipt, COD, Insured Mail, and Registered Mail.

How did you do? Check your answers with the ones provided at the end of this chapter.

Alternative Delivery Services

Private Delivery Services

Canada Post cannot handle everything that needs to be shipped domestically or internationally. Several private companies in both Canada and the United States offer local, national, and international delivery services. Four major companies—Purolator Courier Inc., FedEx, United Parcel Service (UPS), and DHL Canada—offer Canadian business customers shipping solutions, tools, and applications that can be tailored to their individual needs.

Some of the services offered by these companies include the following:

- Overnight delivery of letters, documents, and packages
- Daily pickup services
- Online tools for selecting services, calculating rates, looking up addresses, validating and printing labels, creating a bill of lading, and tracking of shipping history.

You can find information about each of these companies and the many other services they provide at their websites:

- www.purolator.com
- www.fedex.com
- www.ups.com
- www.dhl.com

The UPS Store, which has many independently owned outlets across Canada, also provides packing and shipping services in addition to mailbox service. They pack the material, ship it through UPS, insure it, and make certain it reaches its final destination anywhere in the world. They will also stuff envelopes, meter mail, accept CODs, and hold and forward your mail while you are away.

Courier Services

When you require prompt local delivery of time-sensitive material, your best choice is likely to be a courier service. Within a matter of a few hours, courier services can have a messenger pick up the item and deliver it locally. Based on the size of the item and distance of delivery, the cost for this type of delivery service is generally higher than Canada Post. However, when rapid delivery is required, a courier service is your best option.

Ground Services

Some small rural communities in Canada may not have a postal outlet. Instead, bus, truck, or rail service, where available, can be used for parcel delivery. Most bus companies offer services every day of the week, and next-day delivery may be possible. Pickup service is also offered by some bus companies; check with their local offices for rates and delivery/pickup options.

Air Freight

Some of our most northern communities can be accessed only by air. The airlines that serve these locations have different rates depending on weight and the urgency of the delivery. Pickup and delivery options are also available with air services.

Managing Reprographic Equipment

Reprographics refers not only to the process of making copies but also to any piece of equipment that makes copies of an original. Most offices have digital multi-functional equipment that includes the features of a printer, scanner, fax machine, and copier. This equipment is available in different configurations and speed ratings. As an administrative professional, you may use this equipment to make copies of outgoing mail for filing or cross-referencing, to make copies of some incoming mail to route to others, or to make copies to use as working copies. It is important to make ethical decisions when doing so. Knowing the capabilities of copiers will help you understand the importance of ethical copying and avoid wasting resources by making unnecessary copies.

Copier Classifications

Copiers are classified into four basic categories, depending on their speed. The number of copies that are typically made each week or month will indicate whether you need a low-, mid-, or high-volume copier (see Figure 9-6). When purchasing or leasing a copier, you should consider the features you need; the cost of the copier, toner, and ink cartridges; and the availability and cost of maintenance and repairs.

If you work for a small company, you may be asked to research and recommend a copier for purchase by the company. Consider the following questions:
- How many people will use the copier?
- How many copies will be made per month? What size of paper will be used? What are the potential costs of consumables such as toner?
- Do you expect the volume of copies produced to increase or decrease?
- What type of materials will be copied?
- What features are needed? Collating and/or stapling of multi-page documents? Colour copying?
- Are there space limitations for the copier? (If so, the size of the copier may be an issue.)
- Will it be used as a networked printer for a group or department?

Copier Features

Office copiers have several features that can be helpful in your work. Learn to use the features of your particular copier by reading the product manual, viewing videos

FIGURE 9-6
Copier Classifications

Low-Volume Copiers	Produce copies in the range of 12 to 30 cpm (copies per minute) and 500 to 4000 ppm (pages per month)
Mid-Volume Copiers	Produce approximately 20 to 49 cpm and from 5000 to 80 000 ppm
High-Volume Copiers	Produce approximately 50 to 140 cpm and from 100 000 to 400 000 ppm
Copy/ Duplicators	High-performance machines generally found in specialized copy/duplication centres or in print shops

provided by the manufacturer, or attending training sessions. The following features are relatively standard in all categories of copiers:

- **Reduction and enlargement.** This feature allows you to make the copy larger or smaller than the original. Reducing the size of large documents (from legal size to letter size) ensures all filed copies are a uniform size. Enlarging an original allows the document to be magnified so that fine details on an original can be made more legible.
- **Automatic document feeding.** The automatic document feeder (ADF) allows you to copy multi-page documents without having to lift and lower the platen cover for every sheet.
- **Duplexing.** Copying on both sides of a sheet of paper is known as duplexing. On this setting, the copier automatically prints on both sides of the page, saving paper.
- **Editing.** Some copiers have built-in editing features. These features include border erasing, centring, colour adjusting, marker editing, and masking. Marker editing lets you change the colour of specific sections of a document to highlight these areas. Masking allows you to block out areas of sensitive or confidential information.
- **Collating and Stapling.** Collating means creating multiple sets of documents that are preassembled in the desired order. Depending on your needs and the equipment being used, you can program copiers to collate only or to collate and staple sets of materials.
- **Automatic Folding.** Some copiers include a feature that allows drawings and schematics to be folded into a convenient size for handling and distribution. The fold can also be offset (not folded to the edge of the paper) so that the folded materials can be placed in three-ring binders or envelopes.
- **Networking.** A digital copier that is routed through a network provides employees who are on the network with the capability to print, copy, fax, or scan directly from their workstation.

Multi-Functional Digital Copiers

Installing a multi-functional digital copier can result in savings for an organization by reducing the required dedicated equipment—fax machines, printers, scanners, and copiers. This type of equipment provides an economical alternative for smaller firms. Larger firms can analyze the needs of different departments in their organization and install multi-functional copiers in areas where documents are being printed, scanned,

People @ Work

The Sales Representative

When you are assigned the task of purchasing a new piece of equipment such as a copier, part of your research will be to meet with sales representatives. You should arrange to view demonstrations and obtain details from several different vendors so you can effectively compare their models to the list of your organization's specifications.

You might ask questions about the equipment.
- What is the quality of the copy?
- If it is a colour copier, are the colours clear?
- Is the machine easy to operate?
- How easy is it to remove jammed paper and replace toner?

You might ask questions about the company.
- How long has the company been in business?
- Is the company authorized to sell and service the models being considered?
- What is the purchase price of the machine?
- What is the cost of supplies, specifically the toner?
- What is the typical response time on a service request? What is the cost of service?
- Is a maintenance contract available? If so, what is the cost?
- Does the company offer training for a key operator (a person trained to operate and handle simple problems with the equipment)?

Lastly, you may want to check to determine whether any complaints have been filed against the vendor with the Better Business Bureau.

copied, and faxed. Dedicated equipment can then be installed where only one function is required.

Cost Control

Conserving paper is ecologically important (important to the relationships between human groups and their physical and social environments). Many organizations monitor the use of copiers in an effort to avoid the waste that occurs when employees make more copies of a document than are actually needed. The extra copies are often made "just in case"; but, more often than not, they are eventually discarded.

To curb abuses, many organizations use copy control devices. Every system operates a little differently, but they share the same basic features. The user is provided with either an account number or some other physical device that is used to access the copier. The number of copies made and the person (or the department) is recorded, so that copying costs can be

2. *Advice of Receipt* is an optional service that can be purchased when sending Registered Mail items to international destinations other than the United States. When the item is delivered, the addressee's signature is obtained on the Advice of Receipt card, which is then returned to the sender to provide confirmation of delivery.

Insured Mail service provides compensation to a mailer for loss or damage of mailable items. Items may not be insured for more than their value. Coverage up to $1000 is available for Lettermail; up to $100 for Regular Parcel when delivery confirmation is purchased; and up to $5000 for Xpresspost. Making a claim with Canada Post requires a receipt or proof of value of the item being claimed. Items not eligible for insurance coverage are listed in the *Canada Postal Guide*, available at www.canadapost.ca.

Registered Mail, which may include Lettermail and non-document materials such as coins or jewellery, provides proof of mailing and proof of delivery. The sender receives a date-stamped official registration receipt, and a signature is secured, free of charge, upon delivery. The sender can access, online and at no charge, a secured image of that signature usually by noon the following business day. A hardcopy of the signature is also available, for a fee, by contacting Customer Service.

A list of items that are unacceptable for this service may be found at www.canadapost.ca.

A *bill of lading* is a document that itemizes a shipment's contents, quantity, and delivery destination, and accompanies items such as parcels or packages being shipped from a supplier to a customer. In addition to being a legal document between a supplier and a carrier, it also serves as receipt of the shipment when signed for by an authorized recipient.

Discussion Items

These discussion items provide an opportunity to test your understanding of the chapter through written responses and/or discussion with your classmates and your instructor.

1. Why should you sort mail into categories before presenting it to the executive?
2. When reviewing incoming mail, what should you do when a letter lists an enclosure, but nothing is enclosed?
3. What is the purpose of annotating mail?
4. Identify the three categories of domestic postal services in Canada. Identify two of the mail classifications used by Canada Post in each of these categories.
5. Why might you select Regular Parcel for mailing a package with Canada Post rather than Priority?
6. What are two strategies a company might use to reduce copying costs?
7. List six characteristics of an effective team.

Critical-Thinking Activity

Mr. Albertson was recently out of town for two weeks. While he was out, you became sick and had to take three days off. You called in and talked with Adelaide Stein, another administrative assistant, who agreed to handle Mr. Albertson's mail and other items. You came back two days before Mr. Albertson returned. You did not have a chance to talk with Adelaide about the mail that was received in your absence; however, she left you a note about a few things. Mr. Albertson did not understand some of Adelaide's notes to him and asked you to explain. You could not explain since you had not yet talked with Adelaide. Mr. Albertson was upset and asked you to get the information immediately. You did so, but you know that Mr. Albertson thinks you did not perform your job well. Explain what you can do now.

Building Workplace Skills

Project 9-1 (Learning Outcome 1)

Below is a list of Mr. Albertson's incoming mail that you are to handle.

a) Explain how you would sort and place items in folders.
b) Prepare a list of the mail as it is to be arranged, listing the folder into which you would place each piece. If there are problems, explain how you would handle them. Submit your work to your instructor.

1. A confidential letter to Mr. Albertson
2. A copy of the *National Post*, a newspaper
3. A new product advertisement
4. A letter with enclosures
5. A letter sent by Xpresspost
6. A letter from China sent by courier
7. A catalogue of computer supplies
8. A letter with no letterhead address
9. A letter stating a cheque is enclosed; no cheque is enclosed
10. A letter referring to a letter written by Mr. Albertson two weeks ago
11. A copy of the magazine *Canadian Business*
12. A letter sent by FedEx for next-day delivery

Project 9-2 (Learning Outcome 2)

Access the MindTap site, using the printed access card on the inside cover of your textbook. Locate the Student Course Data file SCDP9-2a, a form letter, and SCDP9-2b, a mailing list. Make two changes to the letter:

1. The session has been moved to March 21.
2. The session will be held in CanAsian's Galaxy Room.

Make the following three changes to addresses on the mailing list:

1. Luther Maston of Vitale Furniture has moved to 1915–14 Avenue NE, Calgary, AB T2E 1G8.
2. David Sam of VosDan Construction has moved to 39–22 Street NW, Calgary, AB T2N 4W7.
3. Tien Wang of S & G Imported Car Parts has moved to 108 Prestwick Avenue SE, Calgary, AB T2Z 3S6.

Look up the postal codes for the other eight names given below, and add them to the mailing list.

Once you have made the changes to the letter and the mailing list, prepare letters and envelopes for only those individuals whose postal codes start with T2E. Use the letterhead form file SCDP9-2. Sign the letters for Mr. Albertson with your initials under the signature, fold the letters, and place them in the envelopes. Bundle the envelopes in alphabetical order; putting one copy of the revised letter on top. Print out a copy of the revised mailing list, sorted alphabetically by company name. Submit the package to your instructor. You may wish to place a copy of the letter, the mailing list, and the merged documents in your e-portfolio.

Mary Giovannetti, Hunt Manufacturing Corporation,
    135 MacLaurin Drive, Calgary, AB
Roxanne Florentine, Robinson Drugs,
    3407–26 Avenue SW, Calgary, AB
Brendan Mahar, The Roof Shop,
    6032–5th Street SE, Calgary, AB
Allan Argent, Kaczmarski Services Inc.,
    400–620 12th Avenue SW, Calgary, AB
Janet McDonald, Soft Warehouse,
    310–605 1st Street SW, Calgary, AB
Bruce Milley, Western Business Systems,
    3200–118th Avenue SE, Calgary, AB
Tony Kwok, Stampede Organic Foods,
    221–18th Street SE, Calgary, AB
Addas Abbah, Computers Unlimited,
    2807–36th Street SW, Calgary, AB

Project 9-3 (Learning Outcome 3)

Online Project

Using the Canada Post website (www.canadapost.ca), determine the appropriate class of mail and the mail services you would use to send the following items:

1. A package weighing 3 kilograms that must be at its Canadian destination within two days. The package is valued at $3000.

2. A letter that must be to the addressee before noon on the date after it is written.
3. Three books that weigh a total of 3 kilograms.
4. A package that weighs 5 kilograms, is worth $400, and must be to the addressee in the United States by the next day.
5. A letter that must reach its Canadian destination the next day and for which you need evidence of delivery.
6. A package weighing 5 kilograms that must be received in Japan within two days.
7. Valuables that are worth $5000.
8. A letter that must reach China within three days.

Project 9-4 (Learning Outcomes 4 and 5)

Collaborative Project

Work with two of your classmates on this task. Search the Web for the types of copiers available from two manufacturers; for example, copiers made by Hewlett-Packard and Canon. You work for CanAsian, and the copier is for your work area. Approximately 300 copies are made every week. It should print both colour and black-and-white copies and should have basic features such as reduction/enlargement, duplexing, and automatic document feeding. Recommend which copier the company should purchase and give your reasons. Submit your recommendations in memorandum form to your instructor, citing your Web references. Use the memorandum form file SCDP9-4. As you work on this assignment, use the effective teamwork characteristics you learned in this chapter. In your memorandum to your instructor, include a statement describing how you worked together as an effective team.

Project 9-5 (Learning Outcome 5)

Recently, your two assistants, Guy Beauchamp and Luyin Wu, have not been getting along well. Almost every day, one of them comes to you with a complaint about the other. You do not understand the problems; they seem to be petty and a waste of time. For example, Guy complained one day that Luyin was five minutes late getting back from lunch, which caused him to be five minutes late in taking his lunch. Luyin complained that Guy was pushing his work off on her. Your advice to both of them was to work together to handle the problem situations. However, the situation is getting worse, not better. You decide you need to help. You know they must work together as a team and with you as a team. What suggestions would you make to them? Submit your suggestions in a memorandum to your instructor. Use the memorandum form file SCDP9-5.

Project 9-6 (Learning Outcome 4)

You are friends with Josh Roland, another administrative assistant at your company. You have heard three people complain recently about Josh's behaviour. In one instance, he refused to let another person who needed to make only two copies interrupt his long copying job. Another time, he left the copier with a paper jam. Today, after Josh had finished using the copier, it was completely out of toner and paper, and he left it in that state. Since you are Josh's friend, you think you should approach him about his lack of courtesy regarding use of the copier. What can you say to Josh to encourage him to improve his behaviour while keeping his goodwill? Use the memorandum form file SCDP9-6.

Make the Grade with MindTap

Stay organized and efficient with **MindTap**—a single destination with all the course material and study aids you need to succeed. Built-in apps leverage social media and the latest learning technology. For example:

- ReadSpeaker will read the text to you.
- Flashcards are pre-populated to provide you with a jumpstart for review—or you can create your own.
- You can highlight text and make notes in your MindTap Reader. Your notes will flow into Evernote, the electronic notebook app that you can access anywhere when it's time to study for the exam.
- Self-quizzing allows you to access your understanding.

Visit http://www.nelson.com/student to start using **MindTap**. Enter the Online Access Code from the card included with your text. If a code card is not provided, you can purchase instant access at NELSONbrain.com.

Endnote

1. Parcel Services Customer Guide, November 15, 2013 with amendments up to June 23, 2014, http://www.postescanada.ca/cpo/mc/assets/pdf/business/parcelserviceguide_en.pdf, accessed September 2014.

Maintaining Financial Records

LEARNING OUTCOMES

After studying this chapter, you should be able to ...

1. Identify and describe basic business financial services, procedures, and software support.
2. Use and maintain various financial forms and documents.
3. Reconcile a bank statement.
4. Describe the basic elements of preparing employee payroll.
5. Establish and maintain a petty cash fund and register.
6. Prepare basic financial statements, including income statements and balance sheets.
7. *Demonstrate a commitment to community involvement.*

Do I Qualify?

Accounting Assistant

Small company seeks responsible and motivated worker to assist management and accounting staff. Attention to detail and ability to multi-task is an asset.

Duties include:

- Using accounting software to enter sales and purchase transactions and prepare financial statements
- Maintaining a petty cash fund and register
- Preparing payroll and maintaining payroll accounting records
- Ordering office supplies
- Preparing daily deposits and reconciling bank accounts
- Compiling monthly reports and preparing the monthly balance sheet

Every organization—no matter how large or small—must keep financial records. While you are working as an administrative professional, the type and size of the organization you work for will determine how much responsibility you will have for maintaining financial records. The time you spend on these activities each day will vary with the size of the organization and the degree of automation in place.

A large organization may have an accounting firm or department that handles the payment of all bills, reconciliation of statements, and preparation of payroll. The role played by an accounting department or firm in maintaining financial integrity is highly specialized.

In a smaller firm, you may be expected to maintain records of financial transactions. You need to know how to invoice clients and collect on accounts, prepare a deposit slip, reconcile a bank statement, and maintain a petty cash fund. Part of your responsibilities may include preparing the payroll, which requires knowledge of federal and provincial or territorial labour standards; regulations regarding minimum wages and deductions at source for taxes; workers' compensation; and medical and employment insurance premiums.

FIGURE 10-7
Completed Voucher Cheque

Rasmussen Realty Services
6030 – 5th Street SE
Calgary, AB T2H 1L4

156

July 1, **20--**

PAY   Twelve hundred eighty-two-----40/100   **DOLLARS** $1,282.40

TO THE ORDER OF

First Class Computers
210-605 – 1st Street SW
Calgary, AB T2P 3S9

Mark Rasmussen

0004 123 456 987   AUTHORIZED SIGNATURE

REMITTANCE ADVICE — PLEASE DETACH BEFORE DEPOSITING CHEQUE

DATE	DESCRIPTION		AMOUNT
June 23	Computer Accessories as follows:		
	2 - 19" TFT Flat Panel Monitor		650.00
	2 - Internal DVD CDRW Combo Drive		300.00
	2 - Optical Cordless Mouse		70.00
	1 - Security Screen		201.33
		GST	61.07
			$1,282.40

FIGURE 10-8
Cheque-Writing Guidelines and Tips

- Use ink to prepare all handwritten cheques.
- Date each cheque and stub.
- Using the fewest possible words, write out the amount of the cheque, starting at the extreme left of the line, putting an initial capital on the first word only.
- Write the amount in figures, starting close to the pre-printed dollar sign, and write the figures close together to prevent additional figures being added.
- If cheques and stubs are not already numbered, number them consecutively.
- Ensure that the values expressed in words and in figures are identical.
- If using cheques with a stub, first complete the stub including details of all bills—if more than one—being covered by the cheque; then complete the cheque.
- Identify the purpose of the cheque in the bottom left corner. Some cheques include a memo line for this purpose (see Figure 10-5).
- If using a **cheque register**, enter the details of the transaction.
- Whenever space remains on a line, such as after the payee's name or in the words or figures area of cheque, fill the space up with a line so that nothing else can be added.
- Ensure the individual name of the payee is correctly spelled. Courtesy titles (*Mr., Mrs.,* or *Dr.*) are unnecessary.
- Mistakes should not be erased or covered up with liquid paper. Write "VOID" in large letters across the face of the cheque and the stub and prepare a new cheque. Retain the cheque and stub in the files, or if using a register, record the cheque as "VOID" in the register and retain the cheque in the files.
- Obtain a signature from an authorized signatory. Ensure the signature is completed in ink.

The use of EFTs for business organizations is at the discretion of the financial institution, and with the exception of Revenue Canada payments for source deductions and goods and services tax (GST) remittance, may not be permitted for security reasons. Cheques can be "signed" only by those persons who have signing authority, usually executives. Therefore, granting access to online banking for the purpose of making payments to those who do not have signing authority presents a security concern. Some banks are now taking measures to correct this "loophole" using a password protection system.

Reconcile the Bank Balance

In the previous section on writing cheques, you saw how the cheque register is used to record and track the cheques written. The cheque register is also used to record deposits to the account as they are made. You can see in Figure 10-6 that entering both cheques and deposits and then calculating the current balance after each entry maintains the currency of both your financial data and the information about the balance of your account.

At the end of each month, you will print out (or your financial institution will provide) a statement of all activities on your account for that one-month period. The balance in the cheque register will not be equal to the balance shown on the bank statement. This difference exists for several reasons:

- All deposits made and entered into the register may not yet have been recorded by the bank.
- All cheques you have written and entered into the register may not yet have been cleared for payment.
- Interest or other credits may have been added to your account by the bank.
- Service charges may have been deducted from your account by the bank.
- An entry or calculation error may exist.

Accounting for the differences between the two figures is known as *reconciling the bank balance.*

If your financial institution sends you a hardcopy of the monthly bank statement, it may also include images of your cancelled cheques. These images are a record of the cheques you have written that have been cleared by the bank; that is, the amount has been deducted from your account and given to the payee. If you have hardcopy delivery, your online statement will include a link to the image of the cleared cheque, which can be downloaded and saved or printed for your file. Figure 10-9 shows the front page of a statement. You can see how the bank

FIGURE 10-9
Sample Monthly Bank Statement

First Settlers Bank of Alberta
Main Branch
Calgary, AB T5H 1L9

Rasmussen Realty Services
6030 – 5th Street SE
Calgary, AB T2H 1L4

STATEMENT OF ACCOUNT		ACCOUNT TYPE	STATEMENT FROM - TO	
Branch No.	**Account No.**	CURRENT CHEQUING	June 01, 20-- June 30, 20--	
123	456 987		Page 1 of 1	

DESCRIPTION	WITHDRAWALS	DEPOSITS	DATE	BALANCE
BALANCE FORWARD				8,821.88
PAYMENT TO 00864501355	486.29		June 01	
AVIVA/CGU INSURANCE	57.33		June 01	
CHQ 155	114.36		June 01	8,163.90
TERASEN GAS	148.00		June 06	8,015.90
ALBERTA HYDRO	68.00		June 15	7,947.90
TELUS	91.25		June 23	
DEPOSIT		750.00	June 23	8,606.65
INTEREST		11.28	June 30	
SERVICE FEE	9.95			8,607.98
	975.18	761.28		

itemizes deposits made, cheques that have cleared, interest payable if any, and any fees charged for the month.

The back of the statement may include a form that you can use to reconcile the final balance on the statement with the balance showing in your records. An example of such a form is shown in Figure 10-10; the four steps outlined in the figure will result in identical final balances being recorded on both the cheque register and bank statement. Your bank balance will be reconciled.

If your financial institution does not provide a reconciliation form, you can download one from the Internet or easily prepare one on your computer. See Figure 10-11 for a sample reconciliation form.

After you have completed the monthly reconciliation, the **cancelled cheques** or the images you retrieve from your online statement will provide legal proof of payment and should be stored in accordance with company policy.

Skills @ Work

The Conference Board of Canada has identified numeracy skills as a fundamental requirement in the workplace. Under the heading "Use Numbers," it lists:

- Decide what needs to be measured or calculated
- Observe and record data using appropriate methods, tools, and technology
- Make estimates and verify calculations

These skills can be developed at home, work, school, or in the community. Software programs such as Quicken or Sage 50 will reconcile the bank balance by prompting you to enter the amounts of the cancelled cheques, interest, and any fees that have been charged. Find a technology tool that is appropriate to assist in maintaining your specific type of financial records.

FIGURE 10-10
Sample Reconciliation Form Found on Back of Monthly Statement

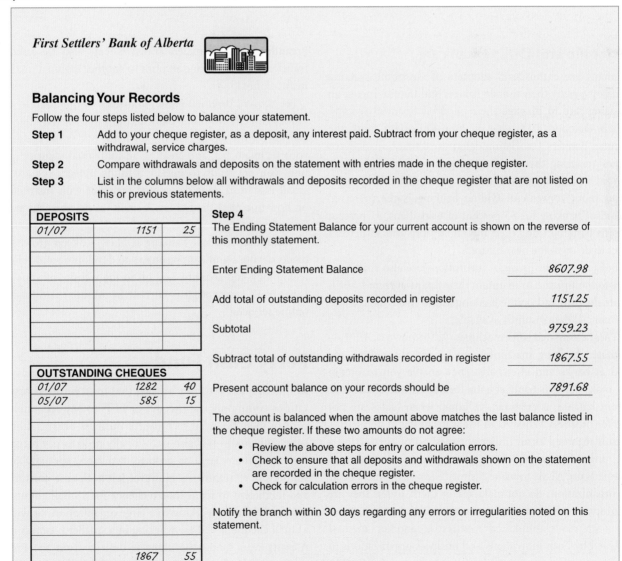

First Settlers' Bank of Alberta

Balancing Your Records

Follow the four steps listed below to balance your statement.

Step 1   Add to your cheque register, as a deposit, any interest paid. Subtract from your cheque register, as a withdrawal, service charges.

Step 2   Compare withdrawals and deposits on the statement with entries made in the cheque register.

Step 3   List in the columns below all withdrawals and deposits recorded in the cheque register that are not listed on this or previous statements.

DEPOSITS		
01/07	1151	25

OUTSTANDING CHEQUES		
01/07	1282	40
05/07	585	15
	1867	55

Step 4

The Ending Statement Balance for your current account is shown on the reverse of this monthly statement.

Enter Ending Statement Balance   8607.98

Add total of outstanding deposits recorded in register   1151.25

Subtotal   9759.23

Subtract total of outstanding withdrawals recorded in register   1867.55

Present account balance on your records should be   7891.68

The account is balanced when the amount above matches the last balance listed in the cheque register. If these two amounts do not agree:

- Review the above steps for entry or calculation errors.
- Check to ensure that all deposits and withdrawals shown on the statement are recorded in the cheque register.
- Check for calculation errors in the cheque register.

Notify the branch within 30 days regarding any errors or irregularities noted on this statement.

FIGURE 10-11
Bank Reconciliation Form

BANK RECONCILIATION
Rasmussen Realty Services
As of September 30, 20--

Cheque Register Balance		15,400.23	Bank Statement Balance		15,300.12
ADD:			ADD:		
Interest Earned		60.71	Deposit of 29/09		1,295.85
		15,460.94			16,595.97
DEDUCT:			DEDUCT:		
NSF Cheque—J.Lee	1,500.00		Outstanding Cheques:		
New Cheque Order	25.00		No. 206	1,272.10	
Service Charges	15.95	1,540.95	No. 207	1,403.88	2,675.98
Reconciled Balance		13,919.99	Reconciled Balance		13,919.99

Electronic and Online Banking

Canadians are enthusiastic adopters of electronic banking technology, using their mobile devices and the Internet at an increasing rate to manage their personal financial records. In their October 2014 issue of *How Canadians Bank*, the Canadian Bankers Association determined that Canadians of all ages are using the new technologies available from their financial institution to make their personal banking experiences more convenient. Online banking is the preferred method of banking for 55 percent of Canadians; 31 percent do some banking using their mobile device,[1] and 43 percent expect to do so in the near future.[2]

Banks and other financial institutions are also making it easier for companies to maintain their financial records. EFT, remote deposit, and online banking access make the company's financial data instantly available.

ATMs (automated teller machines) (also known as *ABMs*—automated banking machines) are located throughout the world at banks and elsewhere. They enable you to obtain cash, make deposits (only at bank locations), and check your account balance at anytime, including when banks are not open for business. While ATM use is declining in popularity, it is still regarded as an important method of conducting a wide range of personal banking transactions—85 percent of Canadians use ATMs to make cash withdrawals[3]—most business organizations do not make use of them, unless they are sole proprietorships or small partnerships.

Preauthorized automated transfer is another method employed by both individuals and business organizations to make payments on accounts that are invoiced each monthly.

Preauthorized automated transfers can also be used to transfer funds from one account to another within a financial institution.

E-cheques, or email money transfers, can be used to send money directly from one bank account to another. After registering for the service, adding the name and email address to your recipient list, and creating an individual security question, you are ready to initiate a funds transfer request. An email is sent to your designated recipient with instructions on how to collect the money. A small fee may be charged for this service.

Computer/Internet banking is likely to keep growing as banks devote significant resources to developing and refining technology and security. Log on to the website of your personal bank to see what is current in personal and business online services.

Petty Cash Fund

In this chapter, you have learned that most business organizations commonly use cheques or EFTs to pay accounts and control their financial records. All business organizations—large and small—will also occasionally need to pay for small incidental items such as postage, taxi fares, specialty office supplies, or refreshments. However, it is both time-consuming and inefficient to requisition a cheque for a small amount of money if you are working in a large organization, or writing a small cheque if you are working in a smaller business firm. A petty cash fund—the name is derived from the French word *petit,* for "small"—is usually established to handle the payment of purchases of small incidental items required by the office in the normal course of conducting business.

You can establish a petty cash fund to cover these expenses by writing a cheque on the current account of the business. The cheque can be for any amount. Usually the amount is based on either the estimated value or the actual calculated value of previous incidental expenses over a specific period, such as one month. A member of the department or office—often the administrative professional—is designated to monitor the fund. If you are given this responsibility, you should follow these guidelines.

- Keep on hand only sufficient funds to cover expenses for a specific period—two weeks, a month, or a quarter.
- Complete or obtain a petty cash voucher (see Figure 10-12) indicating the amount, date, and purpose of each expenditure.
- Retain receipts for all expenditures (attached to petty cash voucher).
- Record all transactions using a petty cash register (see Figure 10-13) or spreadsheet.
- Ensure you can account for all monies—cash on hand plus receipts and/or vouchers should equal the full value of the fund.
- Keep the cash and vouchers secure.

FIGURE 10-12
A Completed Petty Cash Voucher

No. 256	$50.75

PETTY CASH VOUCHER

DATE: May 30, 20--

PAID TO: First Class Computers

EXPLANATION: Graphics Tablet

CHARGE ACCT: Supplies

APPROVED BY: *M.A. Albertson* — Authorized Signature

RECEIVED BY: *Keri-An Mahar* — Recipient Signature

FIGURE 10-13
Petty Cash Register Page

PETTY CASH REGISTER

DATE	VOUCHER NO.	DETAILS	CREDITS	PAYMENTS
May 1			250.00	
May 5	250	Postage		15.75
May 9	251	Taxi to Spence and Associates		35.00
May 12	252	Toner		49.25
May 22	253	Cleaning supplies		8.56
May 24	254	Courier		10.45
May 29	255	Disk labels		7.95
May 30	256	Graphics tablet		50.75
Totals			250.00	177.71
June 1		Cash on hand	72.29	
		Cheque No. 135 to replenish fund	177.71	

FIGURE 10-14
Petty Cash Replenishment Request Form

RASMUSSEN REALTY SERVICES
Petty Cash Replenishment Request

Petty Cash Summary
May 1 – May 31, 20--

Postage and Delivery	26.20
Miscellaneous Office Supplies	107.95
Travel	35.00
Cleaning Supplies	8.56
Total Payments	177.71
Cash on Hand	72.29
Total Petty Cash Fund	250.00
Submitted by:	*Kaili Tanner*

- Prepare a petty cash fund summary on a regular basis.
- Replenish the fund before it gets too low by requesting a cheque for the amount needed to restore the total to its original (see Figure 10-14).

Payroll Accounting Procedures

Preparing employee payroll, a function of financial accounting, is usually handled by the accounting department of larger organizations. In smaller organizations, this service may be purchased from an accounting firm or bank or may be assigned to the administrative professional. If it is your responsibility, you can prepare payroll by using a spreadsheet or purchase software written specifically for calculating employees' **net pay**—gross pay less required and voluntary deductions. Companies are required by law to keep payroll records and to provide employees with a statement of earnings and deductions. To do this, you must know the federal and/or provincial or territorial regulations regarding minimum wages and maximum hours of work; how to calculate the amount of compensation due each employee; and the amounts that are required by law and must be withheld and then remitted to the respective governments on behalf of each employee.

Three compulsory deductions are required by law: personal income tax, employment insurance (EI), and Canada Pension Plan (CPP; or Quebec Pension Plan in Quebec). As an example, Figure 10-15 illustrates the gross pay, the required compulsory and voluntary amounts to be deducted, and the net pay for Guy LeBlanc, an employee at CanAsian Airlines. This example is based on the *payroll deductions online calculator* available on the Canada Revenue Agency (CRA) website. A link to this site can be found on the MindTap site that accompanies this textbook.

Each month, employers are generally required to remit to the federal government these amounts plus an additional amount that is equal to the employee's CPP contribution and an amount that is calculated at a rate of 1.4 percent (as of 2015) of the EI contribution. Deductions for CPP are age dependent, and the employer contribution for EI may be adjusted if employees are provided with a short-term disability plan. Rates may change periodically, or whenever new legislation is implemented, such as an increase to the minimum wage. In some provinces, health insurance and workers' compensation premiums are also a compulsory provincial government deduction.

Using EFT to process payroll is much more efficient than writing individual paycheques at the end of each pay period. The bank is provided with a list of employees and the amount payable to each, and the bank then uses EFT to transfer these funds to the individual employee accounts. Employees then receive a statement showing their gross pay, an itemized list of deductions, and the net amount that has been deposited to their account.

Financial Statements

Although no two business organizations are identical in their operations, all managers, owners, creditors, and investors generally rely on the same two financial statements as accurately representing the company's financial viability: the balance sheet and the income statement.

A **balance sheet** shows three things:
- A list of what the company owns—its *assets*
- A list of what the company owes—its *liabilities*
- The difference between the two—its *net worth*

The balance sheet is important because it gives a picture of the financial state of the organization on a specific day. It documents the ongoing liabilities for accounts payable, source deductions, GST, and the bank balance.

The **income statement** (also known as the profit and loss statement) summarizes an organization's income and expenses over a specific period of time—a month, a calendar quarter (three months), or a year. It shows the amount of money made (profit) or lost (loss) during that period. This information makes it possible to forecast future directions for the organization.

FIGURE 10-15
CRA Payroll Deductions Online Calculator

Payroll Deductions Online Calculator

Results

Employee's name:	Guy LeBlanc
Employer's name:	CanAsian Airlines
Pay period frequency:	Weekly (52 pay periods a year)
Date the employee is paid:	20---01-01
Province of employment:	Alberta
Federal amount from TD1	Minimum - 10,527.00
Provincial amount from TD1	Minimum - 16,977.00

Salary income		$ 1,350.00	
Vacation pay		$ 150.00	
Total Cash income			**$ 1,500.00**

Taxable income for the pay period		$ 1,475.00	
Pensionable earnings for the pay period		$ 1,500.00	
Insurable earnings for the pay period		$ 1,500.00	
Federal tax deduction	$ 226.47		
Provincial tax deduction	$ 109.07		
Additional tax deduction	$0.00		
Total tax deductions		$ 335.54	
CPP deductions		$ 70.92	
EI deductions		$ 26.70	
Amounts deducted at source		$ 25.00	
Total Deductions			**$ 458.16**
Net Amount			**$ 1,041.84**

Amounts deducted at source	
Union Dues	$ 25.00
Total	**$ 25.00**

Weekly Payroll for Guy LeBlanc of CanAsian Airlines

The Balance Sheet

A balance sheet provides information about an organization's net worth at a specific time of the year. The document itself has four main sections—the heading, the assets (current and capital), the liabilities (current and long-term), and the owner's equity. The assets section of the balance sheet should equal (i.e., should "balance" with) the liabilities plus owner's equity.

The *heading* identifies the who, what, and when of the statement. This information is displayed in three separate horizontally centred lines at the top of the page. The first line identifies the organization, the second the type of statement, and the last the period of time covered by the statement.

The *assets* includes two types of assets of the organization—the current assets and fixed assets. Current assets are cash or items such as accounts receivable or inventory that can readily be converted into cash on short notice. Fixed assets comprise land, buildings, or equipment that will be used over the length of the life of the organization, and are virtually permanent. On a balance sheet, listing current assets before fixed assets is known as using the liquidity order.

Liabilities are the debts of the organization. The *liabilities section* follows the assets section, and, like it, is presented in two parts—current liabilities and long-term liabilities. Current liabilities shows the ongoing commitment for CRA trust account liabilities such as GST/HST and source deductions, and will include items such as accounts payable and bank loans—items whose payment is expected to be made within the next 12 months or in the course of "current" operations. Long-term or fixed liabilities include mortgages and other debts whose payments will continue over a period of time longer than one year. While the format and content of a typical balance sheet will vary from firm to firm, it should remain the same from year to year. Figure 10-16 provides a sample balance sheet for a firm called Rasmussen Realty Services.

FIGURE 10-16
Example of a Balance Sheet

Rasmussen Realty Services
BALANCE SHEET
December 31, 20--

ASSETS

Current Assets

Cash		$60,500.00	
Accounts Receivable	$30,000.00		
Less: Allowance for Bad Debts	11,500.00	18,500.00	
Marketing Supplies		5,000.00	
Prepaid Taxes		7,450.00	
Total Current Assets			$ 91,450.00

Fixed Assets

Furniture, Fixtures, and Equipment	15,000.00		
Less accumulated depreciation	4,500.00	10,500.00	
Strata Unit	80,000.00		
Less accumulated depreciation	16,000.00	64,000.00	
Total Fixed Assets			74,500.00
Total Assets			$165,950.00

LIABILITIES

Current Liabilities

Accounts Payable	7,850.00	
Salaries and Wages Payable	23,600.00	
Provincial Taxes Payable	2,000.00	
GST Payable	4,500.00	
Total Current Liabilities		37,950.00

Long-Term Liabilities

First Mortgage Payable		75,000.00
Total Liabilities		$112,950.00

OWNER'S EQUITY

Mark Rasmussen, capital, January 1		45,500.00
December net income	15,000.00	
Less Drawings	7,500.00	
Excess of income over withdrawals		7,500.00
M. Rasmussen, capital, December 31		53,000.00
Total liabilities and owner's equity		$165,950.00

Professionalism @ Work

As an administrative professional your main responsibility may be to prepare financial statements. While the type of data contained in these documents is common, your firm may have adopted a specific format. You should review the files to determine the approved format or style used for previously prepared statements. Be sure to double-check all calculations and figures on reports or statements that you prepare. To help ensure accuracy while proofreading, have someone read the information to you.

The Income Statement

An income statement consists of two main sections—the heading and the body. The body of the income statement is divided into three subsections—the revenue section, the expenses section, and the profit or loss section.

As in the balance sheet, the *heading* answers the question, *who*, *what*, and *when* by identifying the organization, the type of statement, and the period of time covered. The *when* is very important. It may be for a one-month period only or for a longer period such as a quarter or a year. The example shown in Figure 10-17 identifies the type of financial statement—"Income Statement"; the name of the company—"Rasmussen Realty Services"; and the period of time—one month.

The *body* of the income statement is formatted in three vertical columns. The column at the extreme left, the widest, is used to describe listed revenue and expense items. The second or middle column (the first money column) is used when a section has more than one item. These detailed amounts are totalled in this column, and the total is entered in the third column (the second money column). The third column at the extreme right is the totals column. When the revenue or expense section has only one item, the middle column is not used and the amount is entered directly in the totals column. With the advent of computerized bookkeeping, the three offset columns are not as common as they once were, but the format depends on how the chart of accounts has been set up.

FIGURE 10-17
Sample Income Statement for a One-Month Period

Rasmussen Realty Services
INCOME STATEMENT
For Month Ending January 31, 20--

Revenue:		
Commissions Earned — Residential Properties	$25,000.00	
Commercial Properties	10,000.00	
Total Revenue		$35,000.00
Expenses:		
Salaries	10,000.00	
Computer Lease	2,000.00	
Utilities — Gas and Electric	250.00	
Telephone	125.00	
Advertising	4,500.00	
Total Expenses		16,875.00
Net Income		$18,125.00

The first section in the body itemizes all sources of revenue under the heading "Revenue" or "Income." The next section of the body details all expenses under the heading "Expenses." Last is the net profit or net loss section. This amount is calculated by deducting total expenses from total revenues. A positive result in this calculation corresponds to a net profit; a negative result, a net loss.

Whether or not you are routinely involved in financial recordkeeping, as an administrative professional you need to understand the role played by the company's accounting department, recognize the importance of current financial information, be able to interpret financial statements. Whatever role you play in maintaining financial records, remember that accuracy and confidentiality are critical.

People @ Work

Careers in Accounting

The field of accounting is a highly respected and valued profession. Three former national accounting designations—Chartered Accountant (CA), Certified General Accountant (CGA), and Certified Management Accountant (CMA)—have been united under a new single designation, Chartered Professional Accountant (CPA). CPAs are valued for their financial and tax expertise, strategic thinking, business insight, management skills, and leadership. As your business experience grows, you may decide to develop accounting expertise and become a CPA.

You can become certified as a CPA after successful completion of a series of required courses offered at your local college or online through the CPA Prerequisite Education Program (PREP) offered by CPA Canada plus practical experience.

You can learn more about the profession by talking to those in your organization who have earned this designation or by visiting the CPA website.

Soft Skills | Committed to the Community

In Chapter 3, you learned about business ethics and the characteristics of the ethical organization. Three high-profile situations illustrate what can happen when the procedures governing financial documentation are abused or ignored: the 2001 Enron scandal in the United States, the 2004 sponsorship scandal in Canada, and the Canadian Senate scandal over expense abuses, which began to be revealed in 2012 and went to trial in 2015.

In addition to ensuring that appropriate "checks and balances" are in place to protect financial integrity, the ethical organization understands that it has a social responsibility to the community. CIBC is one such organization that is "committed to investing in community initiatives that are important to our clients and employees through corporate donations and sponsorships. We support and encourage the passionate spirit of employees to volunteer."*

They do this through "three focus areas of Kids, Cures and Community" and "strive to make a significant social impact on

key national issues, such as poverty and homelessness, while still being responsive to local community needs."

Three of their five priorities include:
- Supporting the charitable and not-for-profit sector in Canada
- Linking their community investment program to tangible community needs
- Enabling employees to contribute[4]

The ethical organization is cognizant of the needs of its community and encourages its employees to participate in community activities. For example, you and other employees of your organization might
- Serve on local community boards and commissions
- Participate in the local chamber of commerce
- Provide leadership to solicit funds for worthy causes

Participating in professional or community activities could give you the opportunity to practise the financial recordkeeping skills discussed in this chapter.

* Courtesy of CIBC

Chapter Summary

The summary will help you remember the important points covered in this chapter.

- Every organization, regardless of size, must keep financial records.
- Routine banking activities include:
  - Preparing currency and cheques for in-person and/or remote deposit
  - Processing the payment of current accounts
  - Maintaining a register of all deposits made and payments processed

  Reconciling the bank statement with the register
- Funds should be deposited on a regular basis.
- The bank will not accept postdated or staledated cheques.
- Endorsing a cheque means signing it on the back; endorsement is done by the payee.
- There are three types of endorsements: blank, full, and restrictive.
- An invoice is a bill prepared by a vendor or seller.
- A monthly statement documents account activity such as purchases and payments.
- Quicken and Sage 50 are commercially available software programs used to manage accounting activities.
- Cheques are available in three formats—a chequebook with stubs, a chequebook with a register, and voucher cheques.
- Reconciling the bank balance will account for the differences between balances on the monthly statement and cheque register.
- A petty cash fund is established to handle purchases of incidental items.
- The petty cash voucher is a form used to record the amount, date, and purpose of incidental expenditures.
- Payroll may be prepared by the accounting department, as a service provided by an accounting firm or bank, or by the administrative professional
- Compulsory deductions to be remitted monthly to the government include income tax, CPP (Canada Pension Plan) premiums, and EI (Employment Insurance) premiums.
- A balance sheet is a list of the company's assets, liabilities, and net worth.
- An income statement is a summary of an organization's income and expenses over a specific period of time.
- Current assets include cash and assets that can readily be converted into cash.
- Fixed assets are assets that will be used up only over the lifetime of an organization.
- Liquidity order is current assets appearing before fixed assets on a balance sheet.
- Current liabilities include items on which payment is expected to occur in the course of "current" operations.
- Long-term or fixed liabilities include items on which payment will be made over a period of time longer than one year.
- Three former professional accounting designations—Chartered Accountant (CA), Certified General Accountant (CGA), and Certified Management Accountant (CMA)—have been unified under one designation, Chartered Professional Accountant (CPA).

Key Terms

deposit slip p. 171
cheques p. 171
postdated p. 171
staledated p. 171
endorsing a cheque p. 172
payee p. 172
drawer p. 172
blank endorsement p. 172
full endorsement p. 172
restrictive endorsement p. 172
e-deposit or remote capture deposit p. 172
invoice p. 172
monthly statement p. 173
voucher cheque p. 173
electronic funds transfer (EFT) p. 174

cheque register p. 175
cancelled cheques p. 177
preauthorized automated transfer p. 178
e-cheques p. 178
petty cash fund p. 178
net pay p. 180
balance sheet p. 180
income statement p. 180
net worth p. 181
assets p. 181
current assets p. 181
fixed assets p. 181
liquidity order p. 181
liabilities p. 181
accounts payable p. 181

Responses to Self-Check

1. A cheque is considered to be staledated if it is dated more than six months earlier. Although it may be refused by the bank or returned by the processing centre for that reason, the institution accepting may choose to contact the payer's financial institution to confirm whether the cheque will still be accepted. If so, it will be processed.

2. You should check the invoice against the price quoted or previously paid for similar items. Compare items listed on the statement against the invoices received, sales slips, and other records of account payments.

3. A cheque made out to "Cash" can be presented to a financial institution for payment by the bearer—that is, anyone holding it.

4. Restrictive endorsement provides the highest level of protection, as it limits what actions can be done with the cheque. Putting the words "For Deposit Only To" followed by the full account number on the back specifies that the cheque may only be deposited, in full, into the designated account. No cash can be obtained on it.

Discussion Items

These discussion items provide an opportunity to test your understanding of the chapter through written responses and/or discussion with your classmates and your instructor.

1. Explain how the role of an administrative professional might vary depending on the organization.
2. List and explain the purpose of each of the three different types of cheque endorsements.
3. What steps would you take to reconcile a bank statement with the cheque register? If the two are not equal, how would you try to resolve the issue?
4. List the three compulsory payroll deductions. What other payments must be remitted to the federal government?
5. Identify the major components of a petty cash fund and explain the steps you would take to establish such a fund.
6. Identify and explain the differences between an income statement and a balance sheet.

Critical-Thinking Activity

Each department of CanAsian Airlines operates and manages its own petty cash fund to cover the cost of incidental office-related expenses. In your department, Guy has been delegated the responsibility of maintaining this fund. As his supervisor, you are authorized to sign the requisition that is sent to the accounting department at the end of each month to replenish the fund.

Over the past few months, you have observed Guy opening the petty cash box and giving what appear to be small amounts to various individuals in the office. When you review the requests to replenish the fund, however, you notice that the requisition has no reference to these persons; nor are petty cash vouchers signed by these individuals

included with the requisition. The Policy and Procedures Manual, given to all new CanAsian employees, has a section on maintaining the fund. It states clearly that these monies are to be used only for office-related expenses.

While you have every confidence in Guy's ethics and integrity, and in his ability to maintain this fund, you suspect that Guy has been advancing monies to these individuals for personal use.

- How will you raise this issue with Guy?
- What questions will you ask him?
- What directions could you provide to help him resolve this issue?

Building Workplace Skills

Project 10-1 (Learning Outcome 1)

Online Project

Using the Internet browser of your choice, search for information on computer accounting, payroll, or money management software. Many vendors of software will include an online demo highlighting the best features of the software. Run the demos and compare the features of two software programs. Prepare a summary of your comparisons and submit it your instructor.

Project 10-2 (Learning Outcome 1)

Collaborative Project

Work with two of your classmates on this task. Choose from one of the following:

  a) Interview a bank manager to determine the automatic or electronic services the bank offers to its business clients. Prepare a presentation for your class.
  b) Interview an administrative professional about his or her responsibilities for financial recordkeeping in their business organization. Prepare a presentation for your class.
  c) Locate a business in your community where the administrative professional is responsible for preparing payroll. Interview him or her about this task and determine what software they use. Prepare a presentation for your class.

Background to Projects 10-3, 10-4, 10-5, and 10-7

CanAsian Airlines considers itself to be a good corporate citizen. The company's Mission and Values Statement encourage and support all company employees who wish to make a commitment to the community. CanAsian is a strong supporter of the United Way, which annually raises funds to support a variety of community health and social service providers. The annual United Way campaign is scheduled to begin soon, and you have volunteered to serve on the local CanAsian fundraising committee. You know that at the first meeting, a chairperson, a recording secretary, and a treasurer will need to be selected. You have decided to put your financial recordkeeping skills to use by volunteering to be the treasurer. At the meeting, your offer is accepted, and you will now begin to keep track of all income and expenses during the three-month campaign.

Complete Projects 10-3, 10-4, and 10-5 and submit them to your instructor.

Project 10-3 (Learning Outcome 2)

As a first step, you have opened a chequing account (215 331 789). You will deposit all funds received to this account and use it to make payments as necessary. The bank has provided you with a cheque register to document and record all transactions. The campaign officially begins the first week of October and in that week you receive several contributions. They included cheques as follows:

Martin Albertson	$1500	Luyin Wu	$120
Guy Beauchamp	$ 75	Keri-An Mahar	$500
James Robertson	$ 600	Greg Lee	$250

Each department at head office has held a 50/50 draw where the proceeds of ticket sales are divided equally between the winner and the fundraising campaign. At the end of the week, in addition to the cheques noted above, you also have the following cash to be readied for deposit: fifty $1 coins, thirty-five $2 coins, ten $5 bills, three $10 bills, and two $20 bills.

A cheque register, a deposit slip, and six cheques are available in files SCDP10-3a, 10-3b, and 10-3c. Use the information provided to complete the deposit slip. Be sure to put a restrictive endorsement on the cheques and record the deposit in the cheque register.

Throughout the month you continue to receive direct contributions and cash funds from raffles and 50/50 draws. The weekly deposit totals are as follows:

Week 2	$5346 (cash $346; cheques $5000)
Week 3	$2894 (cash $594; cheques $2300)
Week 4	$1785 (cash $285; cheques $1500)

Assume that you have made these deposits at the end of each week and that you have entered them into the cheque register. (In an actual situation, you would also issue individual receipts for each contribution.)

Project 10-4 (Learning Outcome 2)

The fundraising committee had some interesting ideas to encourage the widest possible involvement of the employees at head office. Implementing these ideas required the purchase of some items. You have received several invoices. At the beginning of the last week of the month, you have set aside time to pay the invoices. As you are the person who opened the bank account, you are authorized to sign the cheques.

Cheque forms are contained in file SCDP10-4. Use the following information to prepare these cheques. Be sure to also enter the amounts into the cheque register.

Lumiere Restaurant	$250	(raffle prize of a dinner for two)
Staples Office Supplies	$33.33	(raffle and 50/50 draw tickets)
The Casual Gourmet	$65.23	(fundraising committee lunch)
The Village Bouquet	$65.75	(floral arrangement—monthly raffle sales winner)
High River Rentals	$250	(rental of barbecue for luncheon)

Project 10-5 (Learning Outcome 3)

In the first week of November, you receive the first monthly statement from the bank (SCDP10-5a). The balance as of the end of October is $10 977.76, which includes interest of $20.84 and processing fees of $2.85. You notice that the last deposit you made was too late to have been captured in this statement, and that two of the cheques you wrote, for Staples and The Village Bouquet, do not appear on the list of cancelled cheques. Print a copy of the reconciliation form SCDP10-5b. Reconcile the bank statement with the cheque register you have created on the basis of the transactions recorded in Projects 10-3 and 10-4.

Project 10-6 (Learning Outcome 5)

Guy is taking an extended vacation and will be away from the office for the next month. Usually you would delegate the responsibility of maintaining the petty cash fund to another member of your staff, but because Luyin is still fairly new, you have decided to add this job to your other duties.

Guy has processed the replenishment request, so you will be starting a new petty cash register for this month. The balance is $150. Print out a copy of the petty cash register form SCDP10-6a. Record the amount of $150 on the first line of the "Credits" column. (Use the current month of the year in completing this exercise.)

The following were the cash payments you made from the petty cash fund during this month:

Day	Voucher No.	Description	Amount
1	115	Whiteboard pens	$ 7.34
5	116	BlueLine Taxi to airport	$15.00
8	117	Floral arrangement	$21.39
15	118	Coffee supplies	$18.48
25	119	Courier	$13.65
30	120	Plant fertilizer	$ 6.41

Total the cash payments and calculate the balance as of the end of the month. Forward the balance to the beginning of the next month and, using the petty cash replenishment form SCDP10-6b, summarize the month's expenses and prepare a request for funds.

Project 10-7 (Learning Outcome 6)

Fast-forward to the end of December and the conclusion of the United Way campaign at CanAsian's head office. It has been a very successful campaign, and employees at the head office location have been very generous in their direct contributions and participation in the various fundraising activities organized by the committee. It is now time to prepare a statement itemizing the revenues raised and the expenses incurred. As treasurer of the committee, you have this responsibility (see Figure 10-17 for an example).

Combine the information in Projects 10-3, 10-4, and 10-5 regarding revenues raised and expenses incurred in the first month of the campaign with the following data:

Month 2

Cheques from various individuals	1500.00
Barbecue lunch ticket sales	900.00
50/50 draw and raffle sales	1500.00
Purchase flowers—monthly prize winner	65.75
Paper napkins, etc.—barbecue	105.55
Bank Interest	25.32
Bank Service Charges	1.25

Month 3

Cheques from various individuals	2210.00
Karaoke night— ticket sales	3000.00
50/50 draw and raffle sales	985.00
Purchase flowers— monthly prize winner	65.75
Printing charges	210.00
Bank Interest	40.05
Bank Service Charges	1.25

Project 10-8 (Learning Outcome 4)

One of the other administrative assistants at CanAsian is about to return to work after being on maternity leave for the past year. She will be employing a live-in nanny to care for her child and asks you to provide her with some information on preparing payroll for this person. Based on the minimum wage for 40 hours per week in your province or territory, use the Online Payroll Calculator on the Canada Revenue Agency website to provide her with an example. She plans to pay her employee monthly and will include a portion of the amount required by your province or territory for vacation pay in each payroll. Print out a copy of the calculations and the Employer Remittance Summary that shows her the monthly amounts she will need to remit to the federal government for these three compulsory deductions.

Project 10-9 (Learning Outcome 6)

Add to your e-portfolio by describing how you can demonstrate a commitment to community involvement. For example, if you have an interest in assisting with the education of young children, you might volunteer to help in an elementary school; or, if you enjoy working with people who are ill or injured, you might volunteer to work in a hospital. The purpose of this project is to encourage you to think about your strengths and interests so you can assist your community. Remember, the ethical organization and individual seek to give back to the community in whatever way possible. Think futuristically and commit to working in your community in the future. You will not be engaging in this activity this semester unless you decide you want to do so. Save your reflections under an appropriate name in your e-portfolio folder.

Make the Grade with MindTap

MindTap®

Stay organized and efficient with **MindTap**—a single destination with all the course material and study aids you need to succeed. Built-in apps leverage social media and the latest learning technology. For example:

- ReadSpeaker will read the text to you.
- Flashcards are pre-populated to provide you with a jump-start for review—or you can create your own.
- You can highlight text and make notes in your MindTap Reader. Your notes will flow into Evernote, the electronic notebook app that you can access anywhere when it's time to study for the exam.
- Self-quizzing allows you to access your understanding.

Visit http://www.nelson.com/student to start using **MindTap**. Enter the Online Access Code from the card included with your text. If a code card is not provided, you can purchase instant access at NELSONbrain.com.

Endnotes

1. "How Canadians Bank," Canadian Bankers Association website, http://www.cba.ca/en/media-room/65-news-releases/718-canadians-embrace-value-and-convenience-from-new-banking-and-payment-technologies-cba-research, Accessed March 20, 2015.
2. "How Canadians Bank."
3. "How Canadians Bank."
4. "Community Investment" CIBC 2014 Corporate Responsibility Report and Public Accountability Statement, http://corporateresponsibilityreport.cibc.com/pdfs/social.pdf, Accessed May 16, 2015.

CHAPTER 11

Managing Physical and Electronic Records

LEARNING OUTCOMES

After studying the chapter, you should be able to ...

1. Define records management and explain how it is used within an organization.
2. Describe equipment, supplies, and media for filing physical and electronic records.
3. Describe types of records storage systems.
4. Apply the rules for indexing records.
5. Apply filing procedures for physical and electronic records.
6. *Demonstrate improved decision-making skills.*

Do I Qualify?

Administrative Assistant—Corporate Records

Fast-paced law office is looking for a hard-working and reliable administrative assistant to perform the following duties:

- Assist attorneys and paralegals with extended file searches
- Open files, and maintain a bring-forward system to ensure follow up and receipt of requested materials/documents
- Maintain a filing system; store, and retrieve files at the request of attorneys and paralegals
- Coordinate case transfers, including creating inventory lists for files
- Process files for off-site storage
- Independently review and process correspondence on a daily basis
- Communicate filing backlog and any other file-room issues to the team leader

Dependability, attention to details, effective decision-making skills, and ability to follow/interpret procedures are required for success in this job.

Technology has significantly impacted the handling of records within an organization. We have the ability to create, use, maintain, and store records electronically without ever making paper copies. However, we seem to want both, and as a result, we are seeing an explosion in the amount of paper records and electronic records being generated.

People will often read an email and then print out a paper copy even though an electronic copy can be easily maintained; or, a document is scanned for electronic storage and also stored in a physical file. We seem to have difficulty giving up paper even when we have excellent technological records management capabilities.

What does this situation mean for the administrative professional in today's workplace? It means you need to be proficient in both physical (paper) and electronic records management systems. It is important that essential physical or electronic information be quickly retrievable when it is needed. Whenever a record cannot be located or quickly retrieved, it is both a frustrating and costly process. Any delay in record retrieval can

- Cost the organization hundreds or possibly thousands of dollars
- Require decisions to be made on the basis of incomplete information
- Result in the loss of a valuable client

A record that cannot be found or is lost can have a more significant impact on an organization because it can

- Result in a lawsuit
- Negatively impact a legal case due to missing information

The administrative professional is the individual most often held responsible for locating a record and for doing so in a timely manner. An understanding of records management procedures and techniques can simplify the process for you and allow you to be known as the person who can locate needed materials instantly—a skill that can make you invaluable to your supervisor and the organization.

This chapter initially covers records management in general and detailed coverage of the management of physical records. It concludes with records management techniques related to electronic records.

Records Management

Because records are so valuable, they must be properly managed. **Records management** is defined as the systematic control of records from the creation of the record to its final disposition. A **record** is any type of recorded information. This information may be a printed document, such as a letter or report, or an electronic file, such as an email message or spreadsheet table. In some organizations, sound recordings, movies, photographs, and images on a variety of media may also be considered records. Successful organizations use the information in records to make decisions, handle daily operations, and plan for the future.

Records Value and Life Cycle

Records are important because they provide a history of a business or organization. Based on their content and purpose, records' value to a business or organization may be administrative, legal, or historical. (See Figure 11-1.)

After records are created or received by an organization, they are distributed manually or electronically, internally or externally to the appropriate individual or individuals. They have value for a period of time. During this time period, records are stored and may be retrieved for use. Eventually, most records are destroyed because they are

FIGURE 11-1
Records Values

Records Value	Description and Examples
Administrative	Records that are useful for decision making in daily business activities—procedures manuals, organizational charts, income statements, and balance sheets.
Legal/Legislative	Records that provide legal evidence of business transactions—contracts, agreements, and bylaws.
Historical	Records that document past operations—meeting minutes, public relations documents, and payroll records.

no longer useful. The records life cycle has five phases (Figure 11-2):

1. Creation or receipt of the record
2. Distribution of the record internally or externally to people who use the information
3. Use of the record (making decisions, locating information, etc.)
4. Maintenance of the record (storing and retrieving as needed)
5. Disposition of the record (retaining or destroying)

Records Management Components

The first step in establishing an effective records management system is the creation of a comprehensive set of

FIGURE 11-2
Life Cycle of a Record

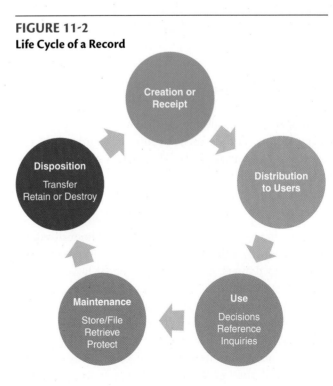

organizational policies and procedures for managing the life cycle of a record.

The records management department, or the person in charge of records management, must clearly document the policies and procedures for managing the records, either in a manual or on the organization's intranet. This document should include how records are to be stored, how long they are to be kept active, and how inactive records are to be stored and destroyed. Without such guidelines, personnel in different departments may store records differently, which can result in confusion, mishandling of records, and loss of important records. Following is a list of the essential components of a records management system:

1. An organizational set of policies and procedures for managing the life cycle of a record

2. Necessary equipment and media

3. Appropriate filing supplies

4. Record storage system or systems

5. Adherence to established indexing rules appropriate for the storage system

6. Retention schedules

7. Established procedures for moving files from active to inactive status, and guidelines governing their destruction

8. Procedures for maintaining and updating the records management system

9. Records management manuals and ongoing training for personnel

These components, explained in detail in the next sections, are necessary for a physical system, an electronic system, or a hybrid system that combines the two (prevalent in most organizations).

Managing Physical Records

Physical records include items such as traditional paper documents (forms, correspondence, contracts, reports, and hardcopy printouts of email or Web pages), microfilm rolls or microfiche sheets, films, videos, recordings, and photographs.

Equipment

Vertical files store physical records in traditional storage drawer cabinets, with the most common vertical file cabinets having four drawers. Lateral files are similar to vertical files except that the entire file drawer rolls out sideways, exposing the entire contents of the drawer at once. Less aisle space is needed for a lateral file cabinet than for a vertical file cabinet.

Movable-aisle systems consist of modular units of open-shelf files placed directly against each other. The cabinet has a wheel at the end of the unit that permits convenient and

safe movement. In the larger system pictured here, wheels or rails permit the individual units to be moved manually or electrically on tracks in the floor. Safety features may include an infrared photoelectric beam that automatically resets itself when the person or object is no longer breaking the beam. A key-operated carriage lock or a pressure-sensitive strip running the length of the file cabinet at floor level is another safety measure that prevents the system from moving. To ensure the security of records, magnetic identity access fobs are swiped through a reader, or a password code is entered, permitting only authorized personnel entrance to the system. These movable systems take up less space than standard files, making them a viable option for organizations with a high volume of active records. As many organizations have limited storage space, offsite storage can often be a good alternative. When implemented, it requires careful management by the administrative professional. A complete and accurate listing of all records stored offsite and the time required to retrieve these records must kept onsite. Advance notice (often 48 hours) is typically required to access and retrieve offsite records.

Lateral files use less space than vertical files.

Movable-aisle systems save space.

Supplies

Basic filing supplies for physical records include file guides, file folders (manila, hanging, or suspension type), and file folder labels.

File Guides

A file guide, usually made of heavy pressboard, is used to separate the file drawer into various sections. Each guide has a tab on which is printed a name, a number, or a letter representing a section of the file drawer in accordance with the filing system. Guides with hollow tabs in which labels are inserted are also available. The filing designation (known as the **caption**) is keyed on the label and inserted in the tab. Figure 11-3 illustrates one type of file guide. Guides are always placed in *front* of the folders.

File Folders

A file folder is generally made of manila (strong paper or thin cardboard) in one of two sizes—either letter size (8-1/2 × 11 inches, or 216 × 279 mm) or legal size (8-1/2 × 14 inches, or 216 × 356 mm). Folders are also available in a variety of colours.

The filing designation for the correspondence placed in the folder is keyed on a file folder label, which is then affixed to the tab of the folder. The tab may be at the top of the folder for traditional drawer files or on the side of the folder for open-shelf filing. Folders are made with tabs of various widths, called **cuts**, designated straight cut, one-half cut, one-third cut, and one-fifth cut. File folders may be purchased with these cuts in various positions. For example, if you are buying folders of one-third cut, you may want to have all the tabs in first position (on the left). Or you may want to also have the tabs in the second (in the centre) and third (on the right) positions. By choosing tabs in all three positions, you are able to see the file captions on three folders at once. Figure 11-4 illustrates the cuts in various positions.

FIGURE 11-4
Folder Cuts

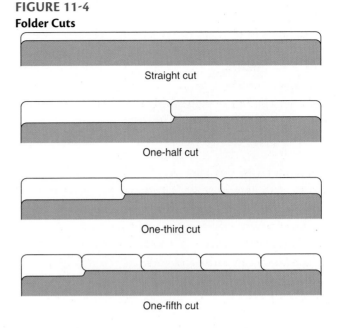

Straight cut

One-half cut

One-third cut

One-fifth cut

As the number of sheets in a folder increases, the records will tend to ride up in the folder and may begin to cover the label. To prevent this, use the score lines along the bottom edge of the folder to refold the folder, giving it a flat base on which the documents can rest. Each score line accommodates approximately 25 sheets of paper. A file folder can store a maximum of 100 sheets of paper, at which point it should be subdivided into two folders. Figure 11-5 illustrates the score lines and the flat base that is created when they are used.

Hanging or suspension folders are another choice in storage equipment. Small metal rods attached to the folders allow them to hang on the frame, which is placed in the file drawer. Using the precut slots on the folder, plastic tabs and insertable labels may be placed in any position on the folder. One or more standard folders can be placed in the hanging folder to group similar files together. Similar to score lines on standard folders, box-bottom hanging folders have cardboard inserts that fit into the bottom of the folder to expand the base of the folder (Figure 11-6). These are used for storing larger records (binders) or groups of manila folders.

FIGURE 11-3
File Guide

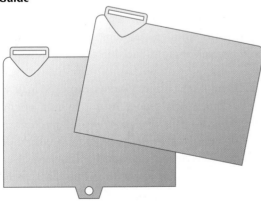

FIGURE 11-5
Score Lines

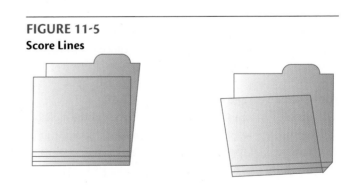

FIGURE 11-6
Box-Bottom Suspension Folders

Photo by Dick Hemingway

Score lines on folders or box-bottom folders provide a flat base for record storage.

File Folder Labels

File folder labels can be purchased as pressure-sensitive adhesive paper in continuous strips or sheets. Your computer software programs have features to format standard label sizes. Using the software features makes it easy to create and print labels.

Labels are available in white, a variety of colours, or white with a coloured strip at the top. Using colour on labels can speed up the process of filing and finding records, and can help to eliminate misfiling. Coloured labels may be used to designate a particular subject (green for budget items; blue for personnel items), to identify a project that extends past one year, to indicate geographic divisions of the country, or to designate particular sections of the file. It is then easy to spot a misfiled folder since its coloured label will stand out from the surrounding labels.

Records Storage Systems and Procedures

An important consideration in any records management system, whether that system is electronic or physical, is how the records are stored. *Records storage systems* can be alphabetic (alphabetical order), numeric (numerical order), or alphanumeric (containing both alphabetical and numerical symbols). Records in a physical or electronic system may be stored by any of these methods.

Alphabetic Storage Method

The alphabetic storage method uses the letters of the alphabet to determine the order in which a record is filed. This is the most common method used and is found in one form or another in every organization. An alphabetic system has many advantages:

Skills @ Work

Keying File Labels

Whatever format has been adopted by your organization, be consistent when preparing labels. Following are some suggestions to ensure consistency.

- Use the same style of labels on all folders. Whether you decide to use white labels, labels with coloured strips, or coloured labels, be consistent and use them on all folders.
- Use a font size large enough to read easily but small enough that the complete caption will fit on the label (12 to 14 points).
- Always key the name on the label in correct indexing order. (Indexing order is covered later in this chapter.)
- Key wraparound side-tab labels for lateral file cabinets both above and below the colour bar separator so the information is readable from both sides.
- Begin the caption as close to the left edge of the label as possible (two spaces, or approximately 0.5 cm); if the indexing units will not all fit on one line, the additional text can either align on the left with the first line or be indented two to five spaces (0.5 to 1.25 cm).
- Key captions in a consistent format. For example, use ALL CAPITAL letters for the key unit and a combination of upper and lowercase letters for other units, or ALL CAPITALS (or upper and lowercase) for the complete caption. Whatever format you choose—*be consistent*. Use punctuation such as a comma when necessary to separate units that could be easily confused. For example, the name Lee Jackson would be JACKSON, Lee.

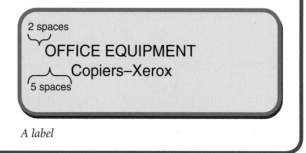

A label

- It is a **direct access** system. There is no need to refer to anything except the file to find the name.
- The dictionary arrangement is simple to understand.
- Misfiling is easily detected by alphabetic sequence.

Figure 11-7 illustrates an alphabetic file for physical records. Records are filed according to the basic alphabetic filing rules, which are introduced in the next section of this chapter.

In this example, the primary guides are placed in first position (at the left). Special guides, used to lead the eye quickly to a specific area of the file, are in second position (in the middle). Individual folders, such as ARNOUX GERALD, hold only records related to that individual or company.

A general folder (also known as a miscellaneous folder) holds records for names that do not have enough records

FIGURE 11-13
Terminal-Digit System

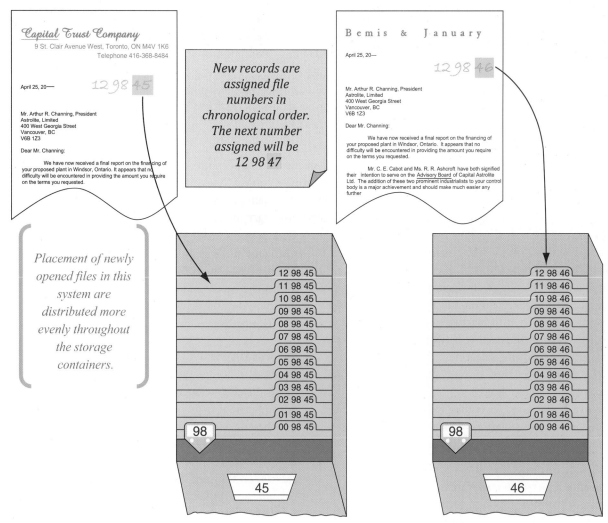

Alphanumeric Filing

Alphanumeric filing combines alphabetic and numeric characters. For example, RM-01 Records Management may be the main directory, with the subdirectories being RM-01-01 Physical Filing Methods and RM-01-02 Electronic Filing Methods.

Records Retention, Transfer, and Disposal

Retention Schedules

In both electronic and physical systems, it is important to know how long records should be retained by the organization. Knowing the various categories of records shown in Figure 11-14 will help you determine and understand records retention schedules.

The retention schedule should identify the period of time a record should be retained by determining:

- The length of time that a record should be retained in active storage

- The length of time that a record should be retained in inactive storage
- The process for destroying records that no longer need to be retained in inactive storage

As an administrative professional, you generally will not make decisions regarding the retention schedule. If your organization does not have a records retention schedule, check with your supervisor before making any decisions about how, when, and whether documents should be transferred or destroyed. You may need to consult with the legal counsel of the organization—or, if you are working in a small organization, an outside legal firm—before developing appropriate schedules for specific types of documents. A sample retention schedule is shown in Figure 11-15.

The Canadian government provides its employees with guidelines regarding records/information management, which are also relevant to a wide variety of other

FIGURE 11-14
Records Categories

Category	Description and Examples
Vital Records	Records that are essential for the continuation of the business and that are usually irreplaceable—copyrights, property titles, and mortgage documents—should never be destroyed.
Important Records	Records that support the continuing operations of the business that could be replaced at considerable cost in time and money—personnel files, inventories, and financial statements—may be transferred to inactive storage but should not destroyed
Useful Records	The records—letters, emails, and memos—are used in daily business and are replaceable with some delay or inconvenience.
Nonessential Records	These records—announcements and meeting agendas—have no useful value after their use. They are usually not considered to be a record.

environments. Links to this site can be found on the MindTap site for this textbook.

Records Transfer

At some point in the life of an electronic or physical record, on the basis of records retention information, you will decide to destroy it, transfer it to inactive storage, or retain it permanently. When distinguishing between active and inactive records, use the following categories:

- *Active records.* Used three or more times a month; should be kept in an accessible area.
- *Inactive records.* Used fewer than 15 times a year; may be stored in less accessible areas than active records.
- *Archive records.* Have historical value to the organization; are preserved permanently.

Two common methods of transfer are perpetual and periodic.

Perpetual Transfer

With the perpetual transfer, records are continuously transferred from the active to the inactive files. The advantage of this method is that all files are kept current, since any inactive material is immediately transferred to storage. The perpetual transfer method works well in offices where projects or tasks are completed. For example, when a lawyer finishes a case, the file is complete and probably will not need to be referred to at all or certainly not frequently. Therefore, it can be transferred to the inactive files.

Periodic Transfer

With periodic transfer, active records are transferred to inactive status at the end of a stated period of time. For example, you may transfer records that are more than six months old to the inactive file and maintain records that are less than six months old in the active file. You would carry out this transferring procedure every six months.

Records Disposal

In physical storage systems, the cost of maintaining documents that are no longer of any use can be significant, mainly due to the floor space necessary for the file cabinets.

When physical records have reached the end of their life cycle, they should be destroyed in accordance with organizational policies. If they are not confidential, they can be recycled; if they are confidential, they should be destroyed beyond any possible recognition. Chapter 10 includes information on shredders, which you may wish to review at this time.

Maintaining and Updating the File Management System

The records management needs of an organization change over time. Additionally, new physical and electronic systems, equipment, and storage possibilities become available. Organizations must keep current on what is available and change their systems as appropriate. Although changing systems can be expensive in the short term, new systems often

FIGURE 11-15
Retention Schedule

Record Category	Retention Period	Retained in Active File	Retained in Inactive File
Employee personnel records (after termination)	6 years	2 years	4 years
Payroll records	6 years	2 years	4 years
Patents	Indefinitely	Indefinitely	—

save money in the long term by offering improved speed and accuracy and requiring less staff time to operate.

People @ Work

Managing Electronic Records

The computer has become a major electronic records management component with records moving from computer to computer without ever being printed. Electronic records are document files created in specific software applications—word processing, spreadsheet, database, email, and others. These files are stored on computer storage devices where they can be easily accessed or changed. As the number of computer files increases, the need to organize and manage electronic records has become an important priority for businesses. As an administrative professional, you need to develop an effective and efficient method of storing and retrieving electronic documents.

Types of Electronic Records

Electronic records may be part of an electronic database or automated system. For example, customer names, addresses, and telephone numbers may be recorded in a database. Electronic records may also consist of individual word processing files (letters, reports, and contracts), spreadsheet files (budgets and cost analysis reports), and graphics files (presentations, drawings, and photos).

Automated Records

Electronic records are often created automatically. For example, when a customer enters an online order, the automated order system creates and stores a record of the order. The customer's contact and payment information are added to a customer database. When the customer orders from the company again, that information can be accessed by the order system so that the customer does not need to enter it again. An email order confirmation is automatically sent to the customer, and the order information is automatically sent to the warehouse. Once the items have been shipped, tracking information is available from the company's records or the delivery company's records.

Individual Records

Creating and receiving electronic records are routine processes for an administrative assistant. You will key letters, memos, and reports, and receive many email messages. Not all electronic documents that you create or receive should be treated as a record. Only those items that have continuing value for the organization should be considered records. An email from a co-worker reminding you about tomorrow's brown-bag lunch does not have continuing value and is not considered a record.

Database Records

A database is a collection of records about one topic or related topics. The records can be updated, copied, or deleted as needed. You can use queries and filters to find particular subsets of information and to create reports using the information. An electronic database may be made available to many users in an organization via a network or intranet, or it may be stored on a single computer for use by a few people. A database is often used to create an index or an accession log for a physical records system. While Microsoft Access is an example of a popular database program with many sophisticated features, you may also choose to use the database feature of a spreadsheet program to create a mini database. An Access database file with just a few records will consume significantly more storage space than a database file created using an Excel workbook.

Electronic Record's Life Cycle

An electronic record has a life cycle similar to that of a physical record. The life cycle has the following steps:

1. Creation and storage
2. Use and distribution
3. Retention and maintenance
4. Disposition

Creation and Storage

Electronic files are created using specific application software. These files can be stored on your hard drive (the "C" drive), on a network drive that might be designated by any letter of the alphabet from "G" to "Z," or some other storage media. Whatever storage device is being used, a unique file name must be determined—no other file in the folder can have an identical name.

The space available on the media being used can be quite large. Unless the files are organized in some way, it would soon be impossible to locate and retrieve anything—the files would be much like pieces of paper tossed randomly into a drawer. Organization is mostly achieved by creating electronic "folders" or "libraries" for storing related files. To further organize your files, you can also create folders (known as sub-folders) within these folders. While it is possible to create folders within folders within folders, it is best to keep the organization shallow (many folders at the same level) rather than deep (folders within folders within folders).

Many administrative professionals create a file-naming system for electronic files that parallels the physical records system. It might be alphabetic, subjective, or numeric, or a combination of these systems. The most important aspect of electronic file management is to create a system that makes retrieval quick and easy. Chose meaningful names for the files and folders you create, and be consistent in your naming procedure.

In addition to using a consistent naming procedure, many programs allow you to enter metadata (information about data) for records you create. Metadata can include such details such as title, author name, subject, and keywords that identify the document's properties—its topics or contents, as shown in Figure 11-16. These properties can be used to search for the document when you cannot locate it by name.

In a networked environment, the file server is divided into directories. You will be allocated a section of the network on which to store your files, similar to having a file cabinet by your desk. Within the networked environment, you will be granted access rights to this section of the network and to certain other directories/libraries; in some directories, you may be able only to read, and not modify or delete the file content. Often, master documents—documents that will be used by all employees of a department or organization—are placed in these restricted locations. They can be copied into your dedicated area and from there you can personalize and save them within your own file system, leaving the original unchanged. Figure 11-17 illustrates the file structure of network drives.

Use and Distribution

The use of electronic records is as varied as the use of physical records. You or the recipients of the record may use the information it contains to answer questions, make decisions, compile data, or complete other activities. Distribution may be accomplished through electronic channels such as email or shared folders on a network. In addition to printing and distributing through non-electronic channels such as mail or fax, files can be copied and distributed on removable storage devices—flash drives, CDs, or DVDs. When the record is sent

FIGURE 11-16
Document Properties

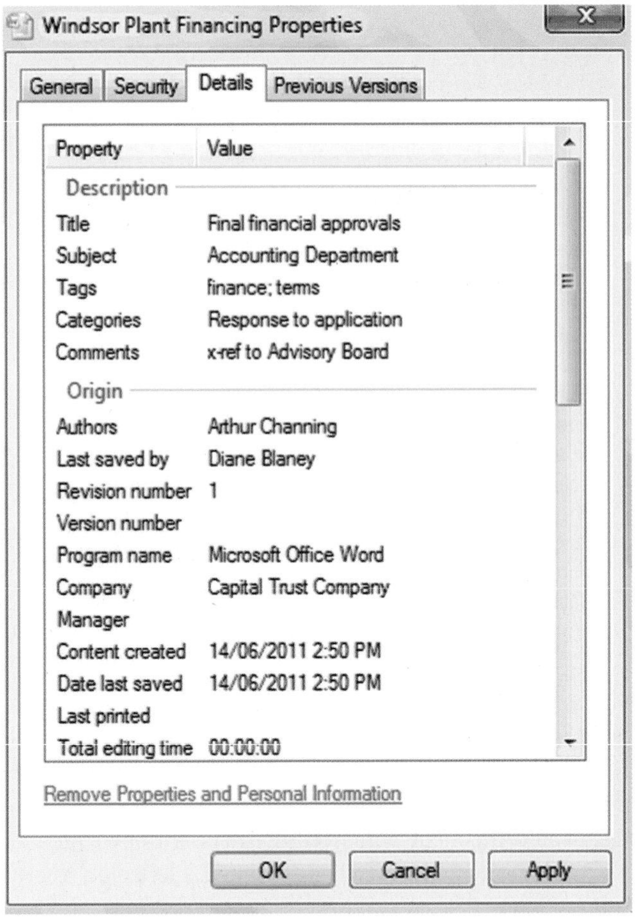

Used with permission from Microsoft.

as an attachment to an email, users can create folders in the email program where received files can be saved, organized, and managed.

Electronic records, like physical records, can inadvertently be stored in or moved to an incorrect folder, making them difficult to locate. When this happens, the search feature of your operating system can be used to help locate the file on any drive on the computer or on any drive to which the computer connects. You can search by filename, date, or specific text within a document file. Email programs also have a search component. You can use it to search by the name of the sender or recipient, by the approximate date, by the subject, or, by message text.

Automated records are created and distributed automatically. Knowing how to access use and maintain these records is important. For example, to answer a customer's questions, a customer order may be retrieved by searching for the customer's name, phone number, or order number.

Retention and Maintenance

While electronic storage is not nearly as space-intensive as physical record storage, some cost is involved in maintaining unneeded documents. Establishing a retention schedule for

FIGURE 11-17
File Structure of Network Drives

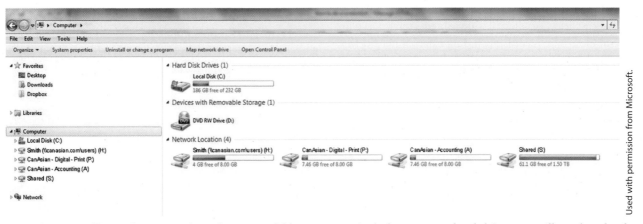

your electronic files and moving them from one folder to another or to a removable storage device (a process known as *data migration*) can help ensure storage space is occupied by files that have no continuing value to the organization. By using data migration to copy or move files and/or folders onto new media, and in new formats as they become available, you can ensure that today's electronic storage can be read with devices used in the future. Keeping your file structure clean by regularly deleting unnecessary files ensures more active files are easier to locate. Figure 11-18 provides suggested procedures you may wish to adopt.

In a large organization, maintenance of electronic files will likely be handled by your computer services department. Those staff will have an incremental and a full backup schedule in place. With *incremental backup*, new or changed documents are backed up daily. Complete network backups are usually scheduled at weekly, monthly, or quarterly intervals; this network backup is known as *full backup*. This protection does not include your own hard drive; you will need to develop a similar backup schedule yourself if you are storing important files locally.

Disposition

Generally, the disposition of records you create or receive will be at your discretion. When records are no longer needed, they should be deleted, or the storage medium should be destroyed. For electronic records such as automated records, someone in the company will be responsible for transferring the records to offline storage and eventually destroying them or placing them in permanent storage in accordance with company policy.

Whether electronic records are stored on your hard drive, the office network, or other media, they should be managed through the four phases of the electronic records life cycle: creation and storage, use and distribution, retention and maintenance, and disposition.

FIGURE 11-18
Procedures for Electronic File Retention

File Type	Retention Period	Tips
Daily correspondence	Five (or ten) days	Create five (or ten folders) named Day 1 to Day 5 (or to Day 10 for a two-week system). Store all correspondence in Day 1 on Monday of the first week, in Day 2 on Tuesday of the first week, etc. Once the designated period is over, return to the Day 1 folder and delete the documents that were created and stored one (or two) week(s) previously. You can then reuse the folder. This system will help to keep your directory active.
Weekly, monthly, quarterly, or annual reports	Retain until the next report is created	You may be able to use the format or some text of the previous document in the preparation of the current report.
Meeting agenda	Use the previous agenda to create the current agenda for a meeting	Updating the previous document is quicker than beginning from scratch every time you require an agenda for a regularly scheduled meeting.
Proposals and special reports	Retain until printed and distributed	Use the "versions" capability of your word processing software so you can return to a previous version of a document if necessary. Once the file is printed and distributed, delete it, or archive it.

Storage Media

Physical records are stored in file cabinets; electronic records are stored on electronic media. In addition to the hard drive of a computer, a variety of external storage media can be used for storage of electronic records, including external hard drives, CDs, DVDs, flash drives, and online file servers.

- Using an external hard drive, files can be saved, retrieved, copied, and deleted. The drive connects to a computer using a USB port, making the device and the files stored on it easily portable from one computer or office to another. External hard drives are useful for
  - freeing up and providing additional storage space on an internal drive
  - long-term storage of files
  - backing up files from a computer
  - storage of sensitive material that can be secured in a safe
- *CD (compact disc)* technology has become popular in digital archiving because information can be read any number of times but cannot be modified or erased. If information to be stored on a CD will need to be revised, then choose to use CD-RW (CD, rewritable) technology.
- *DVD (digital versatile disc)* technology is a popular choice for file storage. A DVD can contain video and sound files as well as data files, such as a word processing document. Unlike the CD-RW that records on only one side of the disc, a DVD disc may have one or two sides and one or two layers of data per side. The number of sides and layers determines the disc capacity.
- A *flash drive* is a storage device that contains a memory chip for storing data. Flash drives, also known as jump drives, thumb drives, and memory sticks, can hold anywhere from several megabytes to several gigabytes of data. They connect to a computer via a USB port. Once files are saved on the device, no power source is required for the device to continue to store files. Flash drives offer users the same options as external drives.
- Online storage options, or *cloud computing*, facilitate collaboration between employees while providing access to an organization's records from any Internet-connected desktop, laptop, tablet, or smartphone. One consideration facing many organizations in Canada is the location of cloud-based servers. Many cloud-based servers are physically situated in the United States, making them subject to the U.S. Patriot Act. Storage of personal data such as medical records and credit card transactions protected in Canada by the Personal Information Protection and Electronic Documents Act (PIPEDA) could be vulnerable to interception by U.S. authorities. For privacy considerations regarding electronic records, as well as commercial implications, many Canadian firms have chosen to not use cloud servers.

Microform is a general term for microimage media such as microfilm and microfiche. Most applications of microform storage are for inactive or infrequently accessed records such as personnel records of former employees and newspapers stored in libraries. Microforms were once the only way to store records in a compact way, but microfilm, microfiche, and the magnification equipment needed to read them now take up too much room and have all but been replaced by file conversion to digital formats.

Working with Database Records

As an administrative professional, you will be expected to work with existing databases, by adding, deleting, or editing records; answering questions; and preparing reports. While you may not be required to design and create a database, knowing the basics steps in doing so will help you understand how to use them.

A database contains tables of data. Data in each table are organized in fields—name, address, city, and province or territory. All fields related to one person make up a record, and a group of records related to one subject is stored in a table as illustrated in Figure 11-19. Additional tables with related data can be created and linked to one another.

Storing data in related tables eliminates the duplication of fields and allows you to create queries and reports based on data from several related tables.

When deciding which fields to use in a database table, consider the smallest unit of information you might use separately from the other information. For example, to create personalized letters using mail merge, only a person's last name is used in the salutation of a letter. This field would not be available in a database that allocates only one field for the customer name. By creating separate fields for the customer title, customer first name, and customer last name, you can easily create personalized salutations that correctly include only the customer's title and last name.

Word processing and spreadsheet software both contain features for creating simple database tables that are similar to the tables created in database programs. Whenever a document is created based on a database format, sorting on any field is possible. Fields can be sorted alphabetically or numerically, or, in ascending or descending order. It is possible to search and find an individual record or to apply filters to show only those records that match a specific criterion.

Records and information management (RIM) software is also available to assist you in managing electronic and physical records. These programs can help to automate many of the manual processes in records management. Rather than using word processing or database programs to create searchable databases, RIM software provides options for automating physical and electronic records throughout the life cycle. For example, using records information management software, paper documents can be digitized and stored online or on a variety of media, including CDs, hard drives, and flash drives. RIM software can provide the electronic tools needed to access your organization's information quickly and efficiently.

FIGURE 11-19
Database Table

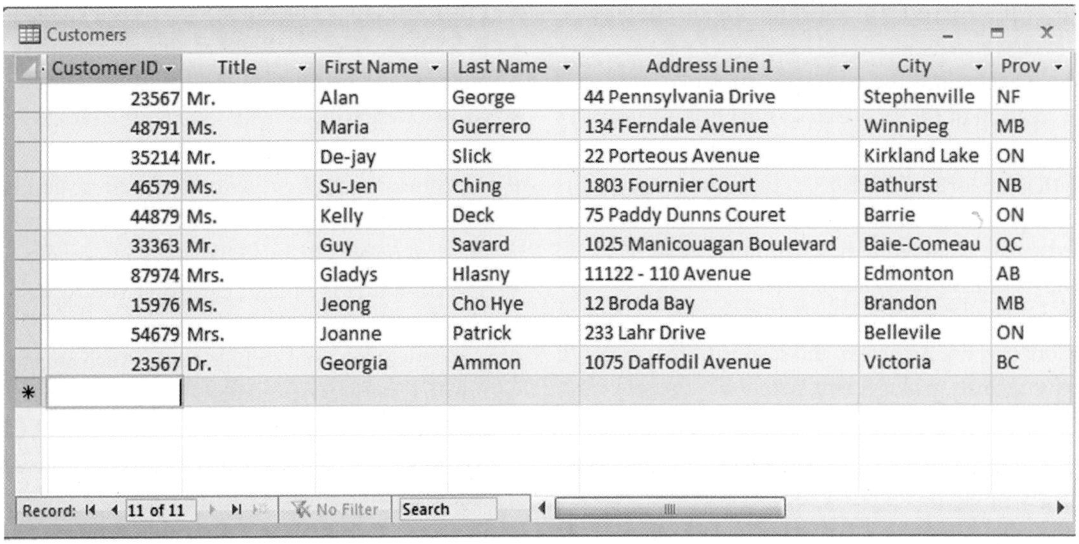

Customers							
Customer ID ▾	Title ▾	First Name ▾	Last Name ▾	Address Line 1 ▾	City ▾	Prov ▾
23567	Mr.	Alan	George	44 Pennsylvania Drive	Stephenville	NF
48791	Ms.	Maria	Guerrero	134 Ferndale Avenue	Winnipeg	MB
35214	Mr.	De-jay	Slick	22 Porteous Avenue	Kirkland Lake	ON
46579	Ms.	Su-Jen	Ching	1803 Fournier Court	Bathurst	NB
44879	Ms.	Kelly	Deck	75 Paddy Dunns Couret	Barrie	ON
33363	Mr.	Guy	Savard	1025 Manicouagan Boulevard	Baie-Comeau	QC
87974	Mrs.	Gladys	Hlasny	11122 - 110 Avenue	Edmonton	AB
15976	Ms.	Jeong	Cho Hye	12 Broda Bay	Brandon	MB
54679	Mrs.	Joanne	Patrick	233 Lahr Drive	Bellevile	ON
23567	Dr.	Georgia	Ammon	1075 Daffodil Avenue	Victoria	BC

Record: ◄ ◄ 11 of 11 ► ►► No Filter   Search

Used with permission from Microsoft.

The features of RIM software include the following:

- Faster retrieval of documents
- Reduction in the labour costs involved in processing files
- Ability to view, print, fax, email, or annotate any document from your PC
- Recovery and repurpose of space previously used for manual filing and storage
- Safe storage of backup copies of all files
- Generation of activity reports by department and user
- Generation of guidelines for records retention and disposal

The Future of Records Management

The field of records management is becoming increasingly complex. Emerging technologies affect our access to information and the speed and accuracy with which this access is possible. Increasing the security and protection of your organization's vital records will be critical for both physical and electronic records. As an administrative professional, you will want to monitor these changes and adapt your system to meet these challenges.

Soft Skills   Effective Decision Making

Effective decision making is important in all areas of your work as an administrative professional, including records management, which is more than just arranging items in alphabetic order—it is an exercise in making decisions.

A *decision* is the outcome or product of a problem, a concern, or an issue that must be addressed and solved. The process by which a decision is reached includes five steps, which are shown in Figure 11-20. You should systematically follow these steps when making a decision.

FIGURE 11-20
Effective Decision-Making Steps

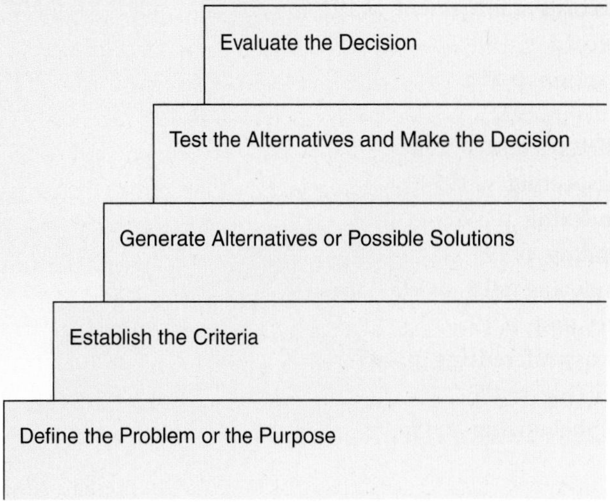

Evaluate the Decision

Test the Alternatives and Make the Decision

Generate Alternatives or Possible Solutions

Establish the Criteria

Define the Problem or the Purpose

Chapter Summary

The summary will help you remember the important points covered in this chapter.

- Records management is the systematic control of records from the creation of the record to its final disposition.
- A *record* is any type of recorded information including emails, letters, reports, spreadsheets, personnel records, or any other type of organizational record.
  - Records are considered to have administrative, legal/legislative, or historical value.
- The records life cycle has five phases: creation or receipt, distribution, use, maintenance, and disposition.
- An effective records management system has the following components:
  1. An organization-wide records structure
  2. Necessary equipment and media
  3. Appropriate filing supplies
  4. Records storage system or systems
  5. Adherence to established indexing rules appropriate for the storage system
  6. Retention schedules
  7. Established procedures for moving files from active to inactive file status and guidelines governing their destruction
  8. Procedures for updating the management system
  9. Records management manuals and ongoing training for personnel
- Vertical and lateral drawer cabinets are the traditional storage equipment for physical records. Basic filing supplies for physical records include file folders, file guides, and file labels.
- Records in a physical or electronic system may be organized in alphabetical order, numerical order, or a combination of both.
- Procedures for filing physical records include inspecting, indexing, coding, sorting, storing, and preparing cross-references as needed.
- Cross-referencing is necessary when a record may be sought under more than one name.
- Alphabetic indexing rules based on those developed by ARMA International are used for indexing and coding physical records in an alphabetic filing system.
- The computer is a major electronic records management component. Electronic records may be stored online or on a variety of external storage media, such as external hard drives, CDs, DVDs, and flash drives.
- Retention schedules (indicating the length of time a record should be maintained) are essential to effective records management systems.
- Records are classified as Vital, Important, Useful, or Nonessential.
- Records may be transferred to inactive files through perpetual or periodic transfer.
  - Organizations may have specific guidelines on document destruction.
- Records and information management systems may be manual, electronic, or a combination of the two.
- Effective decision making follows five steps:
  1. Define the problem or the purpose.
  2. Establish the criteria.
  3. Generate alternatives or possible solutions.
  4. Test the alternatives and make the decision.
  5. Evaluate the decision.

Key Terms

records management p. 191
record p. 191
caption p. 193
cuts p. 193
direct access p. 194
inspecting p. 195
indexing p. 195
coding p. 195
indexing units p. 195
key unit p. 195
cross-referencing p. 195
sorting p. 196
alphabetizing p. 196

storing p. 197
retrieving p. 197
index p. 204
keywords p. 205
accession log p. 206
vital records p. 208
important records p. 208
useful records p. 208
nonessential records p.208
perpetual transfer p. 208
periodic transfer p. 208
metadata p. 210

Responses to Self-Check A

Name	Key Unit	Second Unit	Third Unit	Fourth Unit
Henry Hubert Bowers, Jr.	Bowers	Henry	Hubert	Jr
Roger Alan Driver	Driver	Roger	Alan	
Elite Autobody Shop	Elite	Autobody	Shop	
The $ Store.	Dollar	Store	The	
Z. T. Glasier, III	Glasier	Z	T	III
U-R Rental Company	UR	Rental	Company	
CBC Television	CBC	Television		
Sister Mary Vanetta	Vanetta	Mary	Sister	
Physicians' Hospital	Physicians	Hospital		

Responses to Self-Check B

Name	Key Unit	Second Unit	Third Unit	Fourth Unit
Moncton Cleaners	Moncton	Cleaners		
3rd Street Movie	3rd	Street	Movie	
43–47 Rogers Road Materials	43	Rogers	Road	Materials
7 Seas Restaurant	7	Seas	Restaurant	
Etienne Laberge, 712 Royale, St. Augustin, Quebec	Laberge	Etienne	Saint Augustin	Quebec
Ministry of Health and Welfare	Canada	Government	Health	
Department of Skills Training, Province of Saskatchewan	Saskatchewan	Province	of	Skills

Discussion Items

These discussion items provide an opportunity to test your understanding of the chapter through written responses and/or discussion with your classmates and your instructor.

1. List the essential components of a records management system.
2. Identify and explain records storage methods.
3. What is the difference between the indexing and coding filing procedures?
4. What is the purpose of a cross-reference?
5. How does the terminal-digit numeric storage method differ from the consecutive numeric storage method?
6. What is the advantage of entering metadata for electronic records that you create?

Critical-Thinking Activity

CanAsian has a relatively good company-wide records management program. Both physical and electronic management systems are maintained, with individual offices filing their records manually as long as they are active and then moving their records to electronic storage after the active period has passed. CanAsian has not produced a company-wide records management manual. The records manager has encouraged individual offices to move to electronic filing for most active records; however, most offices have not followed the recommendation. You have moved to electronic filing for almost all the records you oversee. Several of the other administrative professionals have seen your system and have asked for your help in transferring their files to an electronic system. Mr. Albertson has given his permission for you to work with them.

Using the decision-making model presented in this chapter, describe the problem and the steps you would take to assist the others in filing and managing their records. What suggestions, if any, would you make to the records manager?

Building Workplace Skills

Project 11-1 (Learning Outcomes 1, 2, and 3)

Collaborative Project

Team up with three of your classmates on this task. Interview one administrative professional concerning records management; your interview may be done by email. Ask the following questions. Report your findings orally to the class.

1. What records management system(s) do you use (manual, electronic, or a combination of these systems)?
2. What storage methods do you use (alphabetic, numeric, or alphanumeric)?
3. If you use an alphabetic method, do you also use subject and/or geographic methods?
4. What is your role in document management?
5. Does your company have a records retention schedule? If so, may I have a copy?
6. What aspect of records management is the most difficult for you?
7. What suggestions do you have for the beginning administrative professional in terms of how to handle records management?

Project 11-2 (Learning Outcomes 4 and 5)

Access SCDP11-2. For each group of names, indicate the indexing units and sort the names in correct alphabetical order. The correct response is given for the first group as an example. Using the form provided, key your responses; submit your work to your instructor.

Project 11-3 (Learning Outcomes 4 and 5)

Access SCDP11-3a. Print out the document and cut on the cut lines to create index cards. Index and code the units on each card. Arrange the cards in correct alphabetic sequence. Access SCDP11-3b. Use or print out the document to record the number printed in the top right corner of each card as they appear from top to bottom (front to back) when arranged in alphabetic order. Submit a copy of your work to your instructor.

Project 11-4 (Learning Outcomes 4 and 5)

Access SCDP11-4a. Print out the document and cut on the cut lines to create index cards. Index and code the units on each card for a geographic classification system. Arrange the cards in correct order for a geographic system. Access SCDP11-4b. Use or print out the document to record the number printed in the top right corner of each card as they appear from top to bottom (front to back) when arranged in geographic order. Submit a copy of your work to your instructor.

Project 11-5 (Learning Outcomes 4 and 5)

Access SCDP11-5. Indicate the subject you would use for storing the correspondence listed. Mark your answer to the right of each item. Print out and hand in your answers to your instructor.

Project 11-6 (Learning Outcome 5)

Using the index cards from Project 11-4, create a database. Enter the customer information. Also add a field for the customer number. (The number is in the top left corner of the card.) Retrieve the list by province; print out a copy of the list. Next, retrieve the list by customer number; then print out a copy of the list. Turn in both printouts to your instructor and, if you wish, place one copy in your e-portfolio.

Project 11-7 (Learning Outcome 4)

Physical records that you are to store in a terminal-digit numeric filing system have been assigned the numbers listed below. Using SCDP11-7, code the numbers in the form provided for Part A. Then, in preparation for placing the records in the files, determine the correct sort order. Use the form provided for Part B to enter the numbers that you have determined would be the correct order for storage.

06 24 79	06 75 23
06 25 79	06 75 22
08 19 45	06 24 78
07 02 98	08 92 15
08 54 79	08 93 15
08 19 23	07 01 14

Project 11-8 (Learning Outcome 5)

Online Projects

a) Several companies provide file hosting and backup services for personal or business files via the Internet. Search the Internet using a search term such as "online storage." Access several links on the search results list and read the information provided. Access SCDP11-8a; write a memorandum to your instructor describing the services provided by one company. Identify the Web sources you used.

b) Records and information management (RIM) software is introduced in this chapter. Search the Internet using this search term or the term "document management software." Read about the features of the software. Select one of the features and write a brief paragraph summarizing the information provided. Access SCDP11-8b and submit your findings in a memo to your instructor.

Project 11-9 (Learning Outcome 6)

Add to your e-portfolio by determining how you will continue to increase your decision-making skills. File your plan on your plan under an appropriate name in your e-portfolio folder.

Make the Grade with MindTap

MindTap®

Stay organized and efficient with **MindTap**—a single destination with all the course material and study aids you need to succeed. Built-in apps leverage social media and the latest learning technology. For example:

- ReadSpeaker will read the text to you.
- Flashcards are pre-populated to provide you with a jump-start for review—or you can create your own.
- You can highlight text and make notes in your MindTap Reader. Your notes will flow into Evernote, the electronic notebook app that you can access anywhere when it's time to study for the exam.
- Self-quizzing allows you to access your understanding.

Visit http://www.nelson.com/student to start using **MindTap**. Enter the Online Access Code from the card included with your text. If a code card is not provided, you can purchase instant access at NELSONbrain.com.

CHAPTER 12

Developing Customer Focus

LEARNING OUTCOMES

After reading this chapter, you should be able to …

1. Develop effective techniques for receiving workplace visitors.
2. Define customer focus and describe strategies for developing customer focus.
3. Develop skills for providing effective customer service.
4. Describe how to handle difficult customer service situations.
5. Describe and apply methods for calendaring and scheduling.
6. Apply guidelines for scheduling and cancelling appointments.

Do I Qualify?

Executive Assistant

Highly organized and professional, you will report to the President providing administrative support to the executive team. Booking appointments for all executive officers, preparing confidential materials, and assisting with board and industry meetings are some of the functions that will require your expertise.

Your strong interpersonal and communications skills make you confident liaising with a wide range of stakeholders, from executive personnel and board members to government officials, clients, and personnel at all management levels. Your attention to detail, computer proficiency with Microsoft Office applications, ability to multi-task, and strong team commitment will make you the successful candidate.

Customer Focus

While organizational goals may vary from business to business, the major goal of all organizations is to make a profit. To achieve this goal, customer service is vitally important in every organization. A **customer**, also known as a *client* or *buyer*, is someone who buys or uses the products or services of a company or organization. **Customer service** is often defined as the ability of an organization to consistently give customers what they need AND what they want. As an office worker, you may feel that "customer service" does not apply to you, that it applies only to those working in retail or sales. However, this is not the case. Successful businesses and organizations

are those that are committed to providing high-quality customer service to all their customers. This attitude and commitment is called **customer focus**. Organizations with a customer focus know the importance of providing excellent customer service to attract and maintain customers. Customer service is not simply a job or a department; it is a way of thinking within an organization.

One such organization is the Disney Corporation where the basis of its philosophy is providing quality customer service that not only meets but exceeds expectations. Applying this philosophy to other businesses is easy—whatever you do, it must be of the highest quality and always with the needs of your clients foremost in your mind. Make every contact with clients or customers one that makes them feel valued and important. Over the years, many companies from around the world have sent their managers to the Disney Institute to learn how to adapt the Disney approach to their own organizations. You may want to consult a book published by the Disney Institute, *Be Our Guest: Perfecting the Art of Customer Service* by Theodore Kinni; many other books are available on the topic of customer focus.

As an administrative professional, a significant part of your day-to-day activities will involve interacting with external customers or clients as well as with members of your own organization (internal customers). Good communication skills in your personal interactions are an important aspect of projecting a positive image of your company.

Before beginning this section, take a few moments to think about your experiences of good or excellent customer service. Then consider situations where you experienced inappropriate reception techniques or poor customer service. Now complete the following Self-Check.

Disney is well known for its customer-first philosophy.

SELF-CHECK

Identify your experiences of good or excellent customer service or reception techniques. Describe your experiences and how they made you feel. Next, list your experiences of inappropriate or poor reception techniques. Indicate how the receptionist might have handled the situation better.

External Customers

Everyone within an organization has a role to play in developing an environment that is focused on the customer or client. The most recognized external customers of a business or organization are the people or other organizations that buy or use the products and services provided by the organization. Other visitors to the workplace may be representatives of other businesses who wish to provide a service or sell a product to your firm. In all cases, these visitors to your workplace should be treated courteously.

You should know your supervisor's preferences and expectations regarding how to handle visitors. For example, your supervisor will usually want immediate access to be granted to certain people, such as the president of the organization, the chairperson of the board, a valuable client or customer, or a distinguished civic official. Learn about your supervisor's preferences by determining:

- who will be seen immediately regardless of how busy your supervisor is at the time
- whether friends or relatives should be included in this group
- whether there are certain people your supervisor *will not* see under any circumstances
- how to handle job applicants or sales representatives (e.g., referring them to the human resources or purchasing department)
- when introductions should be made for visitors new to the office
- whether a particular time of day is set aside for seeing visitors

Greeting the Visitor

In many large organizations, a receptionist initially greets all external visitors to the workplace. Other than through telephone communication, this initial contact may be the first experience that the customer or client will have with the company, so it is important that it is a positive one. The receptionist may record the name of the visitor, her or his company affiliation, the nature of the visit, the person the visitor wishes to see, and the date of the visit. The receptionist may then bring the visitor through or notify the administrative professional that the visitor has arrived. If it is a first-time visit, your job may involve going to the reception area and then escorting the visitor to your supervisor's office.

Even though the receptionist may already have greeted the visitor, your role as an administrative professional is to welcome him or her to the organization. Greet the person graciously and use the visitor's name if you know it. Everyone appreciates being called by name, and doing so informs visitors that you care enough to make an effort to remember their name.

If you have never met the visitor, stand, introduce yourself, and identify your position as "Mr. Albertson's administrative assistant." Extend your hand to the visitor as you do so. If the person seems to back off, simply drop your hand to your side, smile, and ask the client to be seated.

Business greetings in North America have become relatively informal and may even begin with a hug if the person is a close friend or long-time acquaintance. You may find that your supervisor greets some individuals in this informal manner. As an administrative professional, you do not initiate such an intimate greeting with someone entering your office; if the visitor initiates it, do not recoil in surprise or embarrassment, as this response can be awkward for both parties. If a frequent visitor to your office insists on this greeting and it makes you uncomfortable, then mention it to your supervisor. He or she can politely tell the visitor that you are uncomfortable with such a greeting.

In small companies, you may be on the front line, greeting all visitors to your workplace and directing them to the correct individual within the organization. Always give a visitor your immediate attention. If you are on the phone when a visitor arrives, make eye contact and, when appropriate, ask the caller to hold while you greet the visitor. Tell the visitor you will assist him or her in just a moment. Return to your telephone call and finish as quickly as possible. It is discourteous to leave someone standing at your desk while you finish filing papers, preparing a report, or talking on the phone. If you must answer the telephone when a visitor is at your desk, excuse yourself.

Greet people with a smile and a handshake.

If confidential information is on your desk or computer screen when a visitor arrives, be certain the visitor cannot read it. You might casually place the papers in a folder on your desk or remove the information from the screen. You can handle these situations nonchalantly while smiling and greeting the visitor appropriately.

In the course of your duties, if provincial, territorial, or federal government officials visit your office, greet them using the title of whatever office they hold followed by their last name (for example, *Senator Marchand*, *Minister Laing*, or, as is the case with the Prime Minister or provincial premiers, *Mr. Prime Minister* or *Ms. Premier*).

Determining the Purpose of the Visit

When a scheduled visitor (one who has an appointment) comes to the workplace, you will probably already know the purpose of the visit. When you receive an unscheduled visitor, however, you must find out why the person is calling. Your job is to learn the name of the visitor and why that visitor wants to see your supervisor. Be wary of a visitor who tries to avoid your inquiries by using evasive answers, such as "*It's a personal matter*," or, "*I have reason to believe Mr. Albertson will be interested in what I have to say.*"

Your initial greeting may be "Good morning (or afternoon). How may I help you?" Such a greeting gives the person a chance to respond with his or her name and the reason for the call. If the visitor does not volunteer the information you need, ask for it but *avoid* the following blunt questions:

- What is your name?
- What do you want?
- Where do you work?

Keeping a register of workplace visitors is a polite way to obtain the information you need. Merely ask visitors to record their name and affiliation, person visited, and purpose of the call on the register. The register shown in Figure 12-1 also includes space to record the date and time of the visit. Most visitors to large organizations regard registering as routine, and do not object to providing the information. In fact, some administrative professionals such as those working in law offices are required, for billing purposes, to keep a register of the time their employer spends with clients. If you use a register frequently, you may want to transfer the information to a computer file for ease of use.

Another easy, convenient method to gather the information you require is to ask for the person's business card, which will include the person's name, title, company name, address, and telephone number. The business card will not, however, provide the reason for the visit. You can then say, "May I tell Mr. Albertson the purpose of your visit?"

You will save the visitor and your supervisor time by determining the reason for the visit and referring the visitor to the most appropriate individual in the organization. If the visitor refuses to reveal the purpose of the visit, you may respond "*I'm sorry, but Mr. Albertson sees callers only by appointment.*

FIGURE 12-1
A Register of Workplace Visitors

REGISTER OFFICE VISITORS				
Date	**Time**	**Name and Company**	**Person Visited**	**Purpose of Call**
06/11/—	9:00	John Paterson, Apex Security	M.A.	Security system
06/11/—	9:45	Gabriel Sierra	K.M.	Interview
06/11/—	10:15	Don Heinrich, Crowfoot District News	D.B.	Sales rep

If you tell me the purpose of your visit, I'll check to see if Mr. Albertson can see you at another time." You may also offer the visitor a sheet of paper and suggest that he or she write a note; you can then take the note to your supervisor. Your supervisor will let you know whether he or she will see the visitor. If your supervisor is in a conference or meeting, you might suggest that the visitor write a letter requesting an appointment at a later date.

Be considerate if you must refer the visitor to someone else. Call the office of that person to determine her or his availability. If the person can see the visitor immediately, escort the visitor to the other office if possible. If you are unable to leave your desk, give the visitor specific instructions on how to find the office. If an appointment must be made for another day, check with the visitor to set a mutually convenient time.

Do not disclose specific information about the organization or your supervisor to unidentified visitors. If a person comes to your office and asks for specific information, your response should be *"I'm sorry. I don't have that information."*

Making the Wait Pleasant

If the visitor has to wait, part of your job is to make the visitor comfortable and ensure that wait is as pleasant as possible. Explain the reason for the delay—particularly if the visitor had an appointment—and let the visitor know approximately how long the wait will be. Try not to be too specific about the length of the delay unless the visitor asks specifically. For example, you might say, *"I'm sorry, but Mr. Albertson had an unexpected meeting; he will be available shortly."* Such an approach lets the visitor know you are concerned but that the delay is unavoidable. Offer the visitor some reading material, such as a current business publication, a local or national newspaper, or an

organizational publication, and some refreshment if it is available. Then the wait will not seem so long.

You should then return to your work, keeping the visitor updated on whether the wait will be longer than anticipated so that he or she can choose to come back later or see someone else in the organization if that is suitable and can be arranged.

Remembering Names and Faces

Remembering the names and faces of frequent visitors to the workplace makes your customers and clients feel valued. It is not always easy to do so when you are new to an organization. The following pointers will help you learn and remember names:

- Listen carefully to the person's name when it is pronounced; write it phonetically if the pronunciation is difficult.
- If you do not understand a name, ask the person to repeat it.
- Use the name when you first learn it. For example, you might say, "I'm very happy to meet you, Ms. Woods."
- Use the name again before the person leaves. Repeating the name helps you remember the name for future meetings.
- Ask the person for a business card and enter the details (and other notations, such as a description that will help you remember the visitor) into your contacts database.

If you receive a visitor who has been in the office before but whose name you have forgotten, be tactful and say, *"It's good to see you again."* At least you will let the person know that you remember him or her. If the person has an appointment, there is no reason not to be able to use their name. Check all appointments each day on your supervisor's calendar, and, if you keep a separate one, on your calendar as well. If your electronic calendars are not synchronized, doing so helps you identify any appointments scheduled without your knowledge and ensures that you know the names of all visitors, the reason for the appointment, and whether or not your supervisor will need an introduction.

Handling Interruptions

You may need to interrupt your supervisor with a message when visitors are present. Do so as unobtrusively as

Professionalism @ Work

Making Introductions

Have you ever been in a business situation where you were the only person in the group who did not know everyone present and no one introduced you? If you have, you know how awkward it is. The most important rule concerning introductions is this: *Make them*. Do not let someone feel ignored.

In making introductions, follow the one basic rule: *The most important person is named first, regardless of gender*. If you have some additional information about the person you are introducing, mention it; it helps to put people at ease. While you should always use the title *Dr.* and government titles such as *Senator* when making introductions, it is not always necessary to use courtesy titles such as *Mr., Mrs., Miss*, or *Ms.* Use the first and last names of the individuals when introducing them unless your supervisor prefers the use of these courtesy titles. Here are some examples.

- A customer/client is more important than your supervisor.
  "Mr. Paterson, president of Apex Security, this is Mr. Albertson."
- A government official is more important than your supervisor.
  "Senator Marchand, this is Mr. Albertson."
- Your supervisor is more important than a new employee who is at a lower level on the organizational chart.
  "Mr. Albertson, this is Connor Englund, who will be taking over from Jasmine in accounting."
- When introducing people of equal rank in business situations, the social rules for introductions apply. A man is introduced to a woman.
  "Amy Sierra, this is Casper Lin."
- When introducing business associates, mention something about the other person.
  "Mr. Arar, I would like you to meet Mr. Albertson. Mr. Arar is the head of marketing at Phillips International and a Vancouver Canucks fan."
- A younger person is introduced to an older person.
  "Grandad, this is my friend Gabriel."
- When introducing a government official, present the person within the organization to the government official.
  "Senator Marchand, this is Keri-An Mahar, our Director of Human Resources."

When being introduced you should
- Stand up. (Both men and women should stand.)
- Make eye contact with the person, and move toward them.
- Use a firm but not crushing handshake.
- Repeat the person's name when you are introduced.

"I'm very glad to meet you, Mr. Yarzab," or "Hello, Thomas" in a less formal situation.

possible. Depending on your supervisor's preference you could:
- telephone or
- knock on the door, enter quietly, and hand your supervisor a note. (The visitor should not be privy to the information; never give the information verbally.)

When a visitor overstays the time allocated to the appointment, this same approach can be used. It provides your supervisor with a convenient means of letting the visitor know other people are waiting or other responsibilities require his or her attention.

Handling the Difficult Visitor

It is not always easy to be pleasant to visitors. Some people will be difficult no matter how helpful and professional you are. Sometimes a visitor is upset or angry for reasons that have nothing to do with you or the company. Something may have happened on the way to your office, and the person is venting his or her frustrations on you. When that happens, do not take it personally; take a deep breath and tell yourself to stay calm.

Although you CAN control your own behaviour, you cannot control the actions of others. Try to defuse the anger by
- Listening—let the visitor talk.
- Empathizing—put yourself in the visitor's place and try to understand his or her viewpoint. Most of the visitor's anger or frustration will be released through talking.
- Questioning—ask what you can do to solve the problem or make the situation better. Sometimes just asking the question will get the situation back under control.
- Apologizing—sometimes making an apology is the best approach. At such times, you must keep foremost in your mind your role as an ambassador of goodwill—your role is to be even-tempered and tolerant.

Dealing with Abusive Visitors

Some visitors go beyond simply being angry or frustrated and become abusive. Usually, you cannot help an abusive customer until she or he calms down. As you would with someone who is difficult, do not let yourself become angry, as this behaviour can merely escalate the situation.

Look for points of agreement with the customer and voice your agreement. This technique generally works well, and you can then begin to help solve the problem with the customer. If the customer continues to be abusive, you may have to ask the customer to call back later when he or she can discuss the issue calmly.

Many organizations have a policy concerning difficult or abusive telephone situations. Find out what the policy is and observe it. Some companies have a recorded announcement telling callers that the call may be recorded for customer service quality or training purposes. Customers may be less likely to make threats or inappropriate comments when they know the call might be recorded.

Maintaining a Customer Focus

External customers who are not satisfied with the service they receive are likely to take their business elsewhere in the future; customers who are pleased with the service they have received are more likely to buy from the company again. Increased sales and profits can be a major benefit of providing effective customer service. Excellent external customer service can lead to customer satisfaction, customer loyalty, and customer retention.

A successful administrative professional understands the importance of customer focus in all business relationships. Some strategies (plans of action for achieving goals) for developing a customer focus include showing respect for customers and going out of your way to seek their input in resolving problems and issues. Taking responsibility for errors or mistakes, providing a complete explanation, and following up on issues will ensure that you maintain effective relationships with your customers or clients.

Showing Respect for Customers

You may have heard the statement "The customer is always right." Although the intent of the statement is to show the importance of customers, the statement should not be taken literally. Customers are people, and people are not always right. If a customer does come to you with a concern, give it your serious attention.

The customer deserves to be treated fairly and with respect, to have his or her complaint or question heard, and to be provided with an explanation if there is a question about a product or service. Show the customer that you are sincere and serious about providing assistance.

Seeking Customer Input

Problems can provide learning opportunities for you or your organization. An effective customer focus strategy is seeking input from customers. A customer concern or complaint is really a request for action. If you listen to the customer, he or she will often have ideas about how to solve the problem. Doing something special or extra that is not required of you as part of your job or obligations to the customer can help the company maintain a valued external customer and may also help you to build a good relationship.

Have you ever been disappointed in a product or service that you purchased? When you brought your concerns to the attention of a customer service representative, did he or she listen intently to your concern? Were you offered a solution to your problem and perhaps given something extra for your trouble? Perhaps you purchased a sweater from an online store, and the company sent the sweater in the wrong colour. When you called the customer service line, the representative explained how to return the incorrect merchandise and gave you a voucher for 20 percent off your next order. This positive interaction likely made you feel valued and that your continuing business was important to the company.

Use problem situations to obtain information from customers. Asking for a customer's feedback gives her or him an opportunity to participate in the process of improving a situation. Sometimes a customer will recognize issues that you may not see and suggest ideas about how a problem can be avoided in the future. Allowing the customer to participate in solving a problem is a positive step toward re-establishing goodwill. Customers today access social media and company websites to provide unsolicited feedback. Accessing the same databases that are available to customer services representatives, they are often able to search and locate answers to their problems. As an administrative professional, one of your roles may be to monitor your social media sites and feeds, and to acknowledge and respond to customer concerns.

Taking Responsibility

When you make a mistake, do you admit it or try to hide that you have made a mistake? If you answered honestly, you probably had to say that there have been times when you did not admit you had made a mistake. Everyone occasionally makes an error or mistake, and admitting it can be difficult for anyone. However, refusing to admit to being wrong can damage your reputation and label you as being dishonest.

When you or your company makes a mistake, the key is to apologize quickly for the error and then solve the problem. When a mistake is made, take the time to determine what went wrong and how you can prevent the same mistake in the future. If you skip this step, it's possible you will repeat the mistake in the future.

Learn from the positive situations as well; take time at the end of the day to think through what went right. Document the procedures or strategies that worked well; use them in similar situations in the future.

Explaining the Situation

Have you ever been in a situation in which you spoke clearly, articulated well, and gave details, and yet the individual to whom you were talking still did not understand you? For most people, the answer is "yes." Why did the person not understand your meaning? Perhaps the person is not using the same frame of reference as you. Explain issues or points clearly and fully to your customers. Do not assume the customer already has all the information related to the issue or problem. Apply effective listening techniques and give the person an opportunity to let you know whether she or he understands by asking, "Does this make sense to you?" This question gives the individual an opportunity to tell you whether or not you have been clear in your communication.

Following Up on the Issue

Once a problem has been solved, it is imperative to follow up by checking with the customer to determine whether the solutions have been implemented. The most effective problem solving has little or no value if the solution was never implemented.

A customer remembers the end result. Despite receiving excellent service throughout the resolution process, if the problem is not resolved, that is all the customer will remember. If you need more time to implement a solution, phone to let the customer know you have not forgotten the issue; doing so will go a long way toward maintaining customer satisfaction.

A positive customer service encounter starts and ends with a positive attitude. The attitude you display is often as important as the answers you give and the actions you take. Show your positive attitude by attempting to help customers even when you do not have all the answers

Internal Customers

Although many people are aware of the importance of providing service to external customers, individuals sometimes forget the importance of internal customer service and that all of the techniques and strategies that make for effective external customer focus apply equally to internal customers. Internal customers are departments or employees within an organization who use the products or services provided by others within the organization.

People @ Work

Print Shop Employees

Employees in the printing services department of a company serve the needs of other employees, who represent the internal customers of the workers in the printing services department. Without the services this department provides, others in the company would not be able to do their work. For the entire organization to be effective, a customer service focus must be projected by all employees, even those employees who have no direct contact with external customers, such as those in the printing services department.

For a business to provide good external customer service, effective internal customer service is essential. The relationships among managers, employees, associates, and peers are all important when developing an internal customer focus. Developing strong relationships with those who depend on you to provide answers or services is essential to creating an environment that puts customers first. By developing positive relationships with internal customers, you show that you value their importance to the organization. Excellent internal customer service can lead to employee satisfaction, employee loyalty, employee retention, and a higher level of external customer service.

Greetings between co-workers are less formal than with external visitors. When meeting a co-worker for the first time, stand and offer your hand when introducing yourself or being introduced. Consider the occasion and the setting before greeting a co-worker with a more informal greeting such as a hug. Never hug someone who is at a higher or lower rank in the company than you are as it can look as if you are currying favour or you are taking advantage of someone.

If a co-worker drops by your office for a quick question, you do not need to offer the person a seat unless he or she is your superior; doing so will probably prolong the visit. If you are visiting a co-worker who has a modular workspace (rather than a standard office), either knock or say the person's name from the entrance to the workspace.

Maintaining Calendars

Working as an administrative professional, you may find yourself providing administrative support to more than one executive in the firm. It may be that, as a member of a team, you will be responsible for maintaining the calendars of several people in your group. When this is the case, you should consider yourself not a member of a group but rather a member of a "team of two"—you plus each individual supervisor. It is important to be aware of the personal preferences of each member.

Just as your supervisor may have a preference for handling visitors to the office, he or she may also have a preference for dealing with the daily routine. He or she may wish to maintain his or her own calendar and just let you know what is scheduled each day, or may wish you to maintain the schedule on his or her behalf. As an administrative professional, you may be responsible for scheduling appointments, maintaining a record of the appointments your supervisor has personally scheduled, and coordinating these appointments with other scheduled activities.

Commonly, two types of information are recorded when maintaining calendars—appointment data and reminder information. Usually at the end of a year, when it is time to set up a calendar for the next year, the previous year's calendar serves as a source of information about regularly scheduled events. When a new regular commitment is undertaken, enter that into the calendar for the balance of the year.

As an administrative professional managing your supervisor's calendar, you will enter not only business appointments and events but also other, more personal events, such as birthdays, anniversaries, and so on. If you are using an electronic calendar, it is easy to edit details of an appointment. If you are using a paper-based calendar, it is a good idea to use a pencil to record these and other events so that it is easy to make adjustments when commitments need to be changed.

The calendar is also useful for identifying blocks of time dedicated to work on major projects or reports. Your supervisor may also ask you to schedule a daily or weekly planning session for the two of you to meet and organize upcoming activities. If he or she does not do so, suggesting this option yourself demonstrates your professionalism and illustrates that you are proactive and responsible. Spending time discussing these anticipated activities and updating the calendar is a good way to avoid conflicts in the schedule. If your supervisor uses a mobile device to record appointments while out of the office and if that mobile calendar is not synced with yours, you can use a planning session to update the main calendar with appointments your supervisor may have made while out of the office.

As discussed in Chapter 2, the calendar can also be used for noting reminders to yourself or your supervisor. Check the reminders daily and again at a specific time each week to see that everything has been done. If using a paper-based calendar and an item has not been attended to that day, transfer it to the reminder activities for the next day so that it is not forgotten.

As an administrative professional, your most important responsibility in maintaining your supervisor's calendar is to ensure that conflicts are avoided and that the calendar is constantly updated.

Scheduling Appointments

An **appointment** is a time set aside for people to discuss an issue. When it comes to scheduling appointments, understand your supervisor's preferences and know which appointments should be given preference and how much time should be allocated for each appointment. If you have entered regularly occurring appointments/meetings into the calendar, when a request for an appointment is received, you can be sure to avoid conflicts in the schedule.

Requests for appointments are usually received in one of three ways—by telephone, by email/mail, or in person.

- *When appointments are requested by telephone*, determine the purpose of the appointment to ascertain whether your supervisor is the most appropriate person. To reduce any margin of error, confirm that you and the caller have identical information by repeating the time, date, and place of the appointment to the caller as you enter it into the calendar. Obtain and record the caller's telephone number and/or email address in the event you might need to change any of the details of the appointment. If required, provide the caller with directions to your office.

- *Appointments requested by email or mail* will normally contain the requisite information of who, what, when, and where, and as a result you may be able to enter the specifics into the calendar and provide a confirmation to the sender that the appointment has been scheduled. Incoming mail or email may contain announcements about meetings or conferences of interest to your supervisor. Make a note of these on the calendar and draw them to your supervisor's attention.

- *When an individual is in the office personally making the request*, you can provide a reminder of the date and time established as mutually convenient.

Skills @ Work

Guidelines for Scheduling Appointments

When scheduling appointments for your supervisor it is important to know his or her preferences. Then you should do the following:

- Record the exact time (beginning and end), location, and purpose of the appointment.
- Ensure that scheduled appointments do not overlap by providing unstructured time (15 minutes) between appointments.
- Accurately record the name, company, and phone number/email address of the visitor on the calendar, in the event that changes are necessary at a later date.
- Avoid scheduling appointments on Monday morning, as many people use this time to plan activities for the week.
- Avoid making appointments the day before your supervisor leaves on a business trip, the day before an important report is due, or very early or very late in the workday.
- Schedule any away-from-the-office appointments either early or later in the day.
- Provide a client or visitor with more than one option for an appointment so that she or he may choose a specific time.
- Specify the beginning and end times for an appointment if it is shorter than normal so that the visitor is aware of the time frame.
- If you must refuse a request for an appointment, offer an alternative time and a legitimate reason for doing so.

Confirming appointments is a regular activity for administrative professionals working in medical or law offices. Check the policy in your office or the preference of your supervisor to learn whether you are expected to confirm appointments.

Cancelling Appointments

If your employer cannot keep an appointment, your responsibility is to cancel it. Appointments may be cancelled by a telephone call or by an email. Be sure to give a reason, and offer to reschedule. A detailed explanation is not necessary. For example, you might say, "Mr. Albertson has been called out of town unexpectedly, and he will be unable to keep the appointment. May I schedule another appointment for next week?"

List of Appointments

Depending on your supervisor's preference, you may be expected each day to prepare a list of appointments and gather the necessary materials. This task can be done either at the end of the previous day or first thing every morning. Reviewing this list serves as a quick reminder for you and your supervisor when you arrive at the office, and should include the time, purpose of the appointment, name and affiliation of the caller, and any necessary reminders or materials. If you are using an electronic system, the list of appointments can be quickly and easily printed out along with any recorded daily reminders.

Electronic Calendars and Online Appointment Systems

In a networked environment, it is possible to link all calendars (or just those relating to a specific group) within the organization, giving each person access to multiple calendars. You will find the task of maintaining current schedules for your supervisor and yourself is much more efficiently accomplished using the networked calendar since you can enter appointments, tasks, and reminders; maintain histories, agreements, and connections with clients; cancel appointments; and easily rearrange schedules as events change.

One of the advantages of networked or shared calendars quickly becomes evident when attempting to arrange a meeting with a larger group. For example, arranging a meeting of four or five people means you must first choose a time when all the required people will be available and when a meeting room is available. This step may require a phone call or email to each person. Next you need to read the replies and compare them to determine which time is mutually convenient before confirming with everyone.

Using scheduling software in a networked environment makes finding a meeting time and place simple. You enter the names of the participants, the tentative date, the tentative time, the length and location of the meeting, and any resources that may be needed. The software reviews the calendar of each potential participant—whether there are two or twenty-two—as well as the required resource (the meeting room). If there are conflicts, you are notified. You can then decide whether to schedule the meeting as tentatively planned or leave the program to determine a time suitable to all. Some advantages and disadvantages of using electronic calendars are listed in Figure 12-2.

Larger organizations generally install **networking software** such as Novell GroupWise 2014 or IBM SmartCloud Notes. Although networking software is costly, it may be a more cost-effective option for large organizations than "free" online cloud-based solutions. Networking software includes a flexible and powerful set of applications that provide the members of a large organization with the tools to organize, schedule, collaborate, and assign tasks. For example, with GroupWise 2014 WebAccess, auto-refresh notifies the WebAccess user when new messages have arrived, and IBM SmartCloud Notes can be configured to integrate between on-premises systems and the cloud.

Using OfficeCalendar, organizations of any size are able to create and share with other Microsoft Outlook users on the network Outlook personal and group calendars, contacts, tasks, and email folders. This affordable software application is an Outlook add-in that can be easily installed on a single computer dedicated as a network server or on a basic peer-to-peer

FIGURE 12-2
Advantages and Disadvantages of Using Electronic Calendars

ADVANTAGES
- Can be easily edited—appointment details can be quickly revised or cancelled
- Provides a visual or audible reminder of an upcoming scheduled event
- Can be minimized while using other programs
- Unlimited additional details can be included. You are not restricted by space, as is often the case with paper-based calendars.
- Integrates with the mail program—notices and agendas can be automatically sent to meeting participants. Participant acceptance or rejection automatically generates a response to the sender.
- Automatically generates a list of appointments, tasks, and reminders that can be printed
- Recurring events are entered more easily—one entry is automatically copied throughout the calendar
- Includes task list—incomplete tasks are automatically forwarded to the next day

DISADVANTAGES
- Provides details about your scheduling procedures and calendar information to others in the office
- If you are to rely on the information in the electronic calendar, everyone must be diligent in keeping entries up-to-date; otherwise, it can be frustrating when attempting to schedule meetings.

Windows-based network. With OfficeCalendar Online, Web access using a laptop, notebook, or other mobile device, is convenient anytime anywhere. Two-way synchronization means that Outlook folders, calendars, contacts, and tasks online always match those in Outlook and vice versa. In other words, you, or perhaps your supervisor working remotely over an Internet connection from home or while travelling, can schedule an appointment or meeting while your supervisor is away from the office. Since all changes made to a calendar, contacts, and tasks from any location essentially update a single version of the calendar, your supervisor will be able to view this entry in her or his calendar when it is accessed. No matter where or how it is accessed, it will always be current. See Figure 12-3 for an illustration of OfficeCalendar Online. When the owner of a calendar has approved access by others, clicking on the name of a shared calendar owner provides access to the contents of that shared calendar.

Figure 12-4 illustrates Outlook Calendar in one-week view with current/next month and new appointment screen displayed.

The electronic calendar options mentioned here are but a few that are available. Search the Internet for *electronic calendars* or *online calendaring tools* to locate additional current information. Vendors often offer an online video or a trial version of the software to download and try before you buy.

and their guests found two of their seats occupied, they turned to Leslie for assistance.

Mr. Bronson indicated that he had purchased four season tickets. After checking on the computer, Leslie noticed that two of the tickets were returned in January and a credit was issued. When she relays this information to Mr. Bronson, he indicates that the tickets that were returned were for a show two months ago, not for today's performance. Although Leslie wants to be helpful, there is not a lot she can do. Once the original tickets were released (and the credit issued), the tickets were resold. In addition, the table seating for today's matinee performance is sold out. All Leslie can do is offer the Bronsons and their guests four seats in the gallery at the back of the theatre.

Mrs. Bronson is angry and insists on sitting in their original seats. She insists that Leslie remove the individuals from her seats. How should Leslie handle the situation?

Building Workplace Skills

Project 12-1 (Learning Outcomes 1 and 3)

You receive the following visitors in your office today. How would you deal with each situation? Write a memorandum to your instructor, using the memorandum form on the MindTap site (access to which is provided with the printed access card on the inside cover of your textbook) file SCDP12-1, and state what you would do.

1. A sales representative comes in and asks for an appointment to see your supervisor; your supervisor has told you he does not like to see sales representatives.
2. Your supervisor has been called out of town unexpectedly. He scheduled an appointment with Mr. Chlebovec for 11 a.m. but failed to tell you about this appointment. You forgot to check his calendar. Mr. Chlebovec comes in at 10:50 for his appointment.
3. A woman comes in to see your supervisor. She refuses to give her name or the purpose of her visit. However, she says the matter is urgent. She seems upset.
4. Ms. Nicole Botha comes in to see your supervisor. Ms. Botha has an appointment at 11 a.m., and it is now 10:55 a.m. Your supervisor has had an extremely busy morning, and he is now in a conference that will last until 11:20 a.m.
5. R. T. Yip is in your supervisor's office. He had an appointment at 2 p.m. It is now 3 p.m., and your supervisor has an appointment with Ms. Carol Haile. Ms. Haile has arrived.
6. George O'Casey arrives at 3 p.m. for his appointment with your supervisor. Upon checking your appointment book, you find that Mr. O'Casey's appointment is for 3 p.m. tomorrow.

Project 12-2 (Learning Outcome 5)

Online Project

Browse the Web for information on various online and electronic scheduling and calendaring software. Identify and compare the features offered by the various suppliers marketing this type of software. Prepare a short summary of your findings, giving the Web addresses; submit your summary to your instructor.

Project 12-3 (Learning Outcome 6)

Your supervisor, Mr. Albertson, relies on you to keep his schedule up to date at all times. On the MindTap site, file SCDP12-3, you will find a calendar. Monday is a statutory holiday, so the calendar pages are for the balance of the week, from Tuesday to Friday. Today is Tuesday; the following activities occur on Tuesday. Make the appropriate adjustments to the calendar.

1. A letter arrives in the mail announcing the grand opening of a new location of the company that supplies your office with weekly floral arrangements. The letter invites Mr. Albertson to a wine-and-cheese celebration at 5:30 on Thursday the 8th.
2. Jim Rosza calls to say he will not be able to keep the luncheon appointment on Thursday. He asks if it could be changed to Friday. You check the calendar and see that Mr. Albertson is meeting his daughter and her fiancé for lunch. You let Mr. Rosza know about the conflict, and tell him you will check with Mr. Albertson and call Mr. Rosza back to confirm.

    Later in the day, you check with Mr. Albertson. He lets you know that he cannot cancel the luncheon with his daughter and suggests you find another time that is mutually convenient. You call Mr. Rosza to ask whether Wednesday would be suitable, and he agrees.
3. Judy Hafey, the secretary of the Board of Governors at Mount Royal University, calls to say the board meeting has been cancelled for this week.
4. Mr. Albertson asks you to find an hour and a half in his schedule this week when he and you can meet to organize the materials he will need for the trip to China next week.
5. Keri-An Mahar calls to see whether Mr. Albertson can see her today to review interview questions to be used when interviewing applicants on Thursday for the sales representative position. You suggest 1 p.m. and she agrees. She feels one hour would be sufficient.
6. On Wednesday morning, you receive a call from John Paterson. It is 8:15 a.m., and he tells you he is stuck in traffic because of an accident on the highway. He asks whether Mr. Albertson will still be available to see him if

he is 45 minutes late. After looking at the calendar, you confirm that this rescheduling is fine.

7. At the end of the day on Wednesday, on his way out the door, Mr. Albertson asks you to remind him on Thursday that he needs to book reservations for dinner with his wife and to order flowers to celebrate their anniversary.

If you are able to do so, transfer these details to an electronic calendar such as Microsoft Outlook or one of the online calendaring tools you may have discovered in Project 12-2. If not, use the paper-based calendar provided.

Submit the revised calendar to your instructor.

Make the Grade with MindTap

Stay organized and efficient with **MindTap**—a single destination with all the course material and study aids you need to succeed. Built-in apps leverage social media and the latest learning technology. For example:

- ReadSpeaker will read the text to you.
- Flashcards are pre-populated to provide you with a jump-start for review—or you can create your own.
- You can highlight text and make notes in your MindTap Reader. Yourotes will flow into Evernote, the electronic

Project 12-4 (Learning Outcomes 1, 2, and 3)

Create a newsletter that includes tips and strategies for providing effective customer service. The newsletter should be one to two pages in length. Use the contents of this chapter and any other sources of information on this topic you can find on the Internet or other publications. Note the source information for these articles. Review newsletters you have received or examples you find online to help you format the document. Design and create an appropriate masthead (the block of identifying information usually positioned at the top of the page). Include at least two graphics and one bulleted list in the body of your newsletter. Follow instructions provided by your instructor for submission of this project. Add this document to your e-portfolio.

MindTap®

notebook app that you can access anywhere when it's time to study for the exam.

- Self-quizzing allows you to access your understanding.

Visit http://www.nelson.com/student to start using **MindTap**. Enter the Online Access Code from the card included with your text. If a code card is not provided, you can purchase instant access at NELSONbrain.com.

Planning and Organizing Meetings and Other Events

CHAPTER 13

Do I Qualify?

Administrative Assistant

Growing company seeks an administrative assistant with good planning and organizational skills: a people person who is resourceful, creative, and detailed-oriented. The successful candidate will possess strong communication and listening skills and will be able to think outside the box, multi-task, and troubleshoot when problems arise. Job duties include:

- Handling telephone and written communications
- Working collaboratively with co-workers and managers
- Planning meetings and handling related tasks
- Doing research and creating documents and presentations
- Delegating responsibilities as appropriate and providing direction to co-workers when organizing meetings and other events.

LEARNING OUTCOMES

After studying this chapter, you should be able to …

1. Describe types of business meetings and appropriate formats for various situations.
2. Describe the roles and responsibilities of the meeting leader, the administrative professional, and participants for meetings and conferences.
3. Identify types of virtual meetings—teleconferences, video conferences, and web conferences.
4. Plan meetings and prepare related materials.
5. Prepare agendas and minutes.

Meetings in the Workplace

Meetings are a way of life in the workplace. In an environment where businesses are downsizing, you might expect fewer meetings; however, the opposite is actually closer to reality. Resolving issues and making decisions by working collaboratively in teams has become more common. This collaborative approach has effectively increased rather than decreased the number of meetings that are being held. Even estimating conservatively, administrative professionals could spend an average of four hours a week in meetings; managers could possibly spend 50 to 80 percent of their workweek in meetings. Since time is money, these meetings can be very costly to business.

Meetings can be a good means of generating ideas, sharing information, and making decisions. However, it is imperative that meetings be both effective and necessary, and that meeting time be spent as productively as possible. Unfortunately, many meetings are unnecessary and/or unproductive, thereby wasting the time of both the individual participants and the organization. Unnecessary meetings

FIGURE 13-1
Criteria for Determining When a Meeting is Necessary or Unnecessary

A meeting is considered *necessary* when:	A meeting is considered *unnecessary* when:
• Advice is needed from a group of people. • A group needs to be involved in solving a problem or making a decision. • An issue needs clarification. • A group needs to receive information that may be difficult or confusing and may require discussion. • A problem exists but it is not clear what the problem is or who is responsible for dealing with it. • Quick communication is necessary with a large number of people.	• The purpose of the meeting and/or the appropriate people to attend are not clearly identified. • Confidential or sensitive personnel matters need to be addressed. • There is inadequate data for the meeting. • There is insufficient time to prepare for the meeting. • Group members feel considerable anger or hostility among themselves, and need time to calm down before coming together. • One-way information needs to be shared.

generally occur when no clear purpose or agenda has been defined or when no follow-up action has been identified. You may have attended a meeting where it seemed as if the major purpose was to avoid making a decision or to engage in small talk with other participants. Such occasions often result in participants wondering why the meeting was called in the first place. Consider the criteria above in Figure 13-1 when determining whether a meeting is necessary or unnecessary.

This chapter will help you develop the knowledge and skills needed to assist your supervisor in planning, organizing, and facilitating meetings that are effective and productive for all. This chapter will also help you develop the skills to be a productive team member and to run an effective meeting.

Types of Meetings

A variety of informal meetings are regularly held within an organization, such as *staff meetings* or meetings with customers and clients of the business; some meetings may be more formal in nature, such as *board meetings, committee* or *task force meetings*, and *project team meetings*. As an administrative professional, you need to to understand these different types of meetings.

Informal Meetings

An executive may meet informally with the staff who report to him or her. The purpose of staff meetings may be to review directions, plans, or assignments, or to handle routine issues. These meetings may be scheduled on a regular basis or arranged as needed. Informal meetings with customers or clients are generally small, including only two or three people.

Formal Meetings

Most large corporations and organizations operate with a board of directors that meet once a month or less often. The chairperson of the board leads the meeting, and the conduct of these formal meetings is defined by procedures outlined in the bylaws—the organization's written policies and procedures. If the organization is a public entity required by law to hold meetings that are open to the public, a notice of the meeting is posted according to legal procedures. An agenda indicating the items to be discussed is distributed before the meeting and participants generally follow parliamentary procedures documented in *Robert's Rules of Order*.

In most organizations, an ad hoc committee (also known as a *task force* or *project team*) may be formed to deal with a specific issue or problem. Established for a specific purpose or project (such as planning, producing, and marketing a new product) the committee is disbanded once the purpose has been accomplished or the project has been completed. A standing committee is generally established for an ongoing purpose. For example, one standing committee may be a safety committee that meets regularly (perhaps every month) to identify and address safety concerns. While the standing committee continues to function from year to year, its members may change periodically.

Face-to-Face Meetings

Even with the variety of technology that is available today, the traditional face-to-face meeting format where participants gather at a common location is an important means of conducting business. Some advantages and disadvantages of the face-to-face meeting format are listed in Figure 13-2.

Virtual Meetings

An alternative to face-to-face meetings, virtual meetings use telecommunication technology so that individuals at different locations can participate in a meeting as if they were in the same room. Through a variety of technology-assisted, two-way (interactive) communications, participants can choose from teleconferencing, videoconferencing, or web conferencing, each one of which provides a different communication advantage.

Teleconferences

A teleconference, also known as a conference call, is a meeting in which more than two individuals at different locations

FIGURE 13-2
Advantages and Disadvantages of Face-to-Face Meetings

Advantages	Disadvantages
• An informal setting creates a relaxed atmosphere that allows participants to deal more effectively with a difficult issue. • Participants have an opportunity to communicate informally with one another before, during, and after the meeting. • A creative, interactive group discussion is more likely when people are together in the same room. • More group members are likely to participate. • People can see and hear all group members, and observe and respond to the body language of others.	• Travel to another city, province or territory, or country can be costly, particularly when those costs include local transportation and accommodation. • Productive work time is lost when travelling. • A rental cost may be incurred if an appropriate meeting space is not available in-house. • Conflicts may occur when booking an in-house meeting room that is also used for other purposes. • A cost may be incurred for refreshments if the meeting is longer than two hours. • Socializing can consume a major part of the meeting time unless controlled by the chairperson. • Creativity could suffer if individuals (particularly those who work together daily) rely on their colleagues' suggestions or solutions.

attend and communicate with each other via a telecommunications network. The communication device may be as simple as a standard telephone or a speakerphone around which a small group may gather. A small group conference call can be easily arranged by pressing the appropriate button on your telephone and following the instructions provided by your service provider to connect all participants. A conference call can also be organized through your local telephone service provider, which will set up the call and make sure all participants are on the line at the appropriate time. For larger groups, you can arrange for a meeting room with microphones, speakers, and bridging technology. Bridging services, supplied by telecommunication service companies, provide individuals or groups of participants in multiple locations with access to a single phone number that is used to dial in and connect with each other.

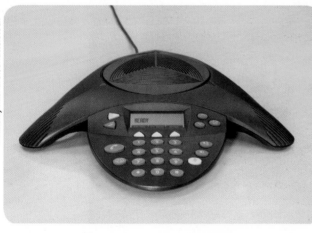
Bridging equipment is used to connect participants at multiple locations through dial-in access to a single phone number.

In addition to local telecommunications providers, several teleconference service providers can also assist you in arranging a conference call. Using the key term *teleconference service providers Canada*, search the web to locate companies that provide these services in Canada and review some of the services they provide by accessing their websites.

One of the main advantages of a teleconference is the ability to gather participants on short notice (assuming their schedules allow). Other advantages include:

● Connecting individuals at any location
● Using familiar, readily available, and inexpensive telephone technology
● Reducing expenses related to travel and administrative support
● Increasing the number of meeting participants
● Receiving digital recordings of meetings

Although a very effective method of group communication and collaboration, the conference call has some disadvantages. The primary disadvantage is the lack of visual input. Because participants miss the visual clues that come from body language, misunderstandings can arise over something that has been said. It can be difficult to determine who is speaking, especially when some group members are not known to one another. During the call, the following guidelines will help make conference calls more effective:

● Identify yourself whenever you speak.
● Take turns speaking; ask whether anyone else wishes to speak.
● When sharing the site with others
   – Place the microphone as close to the speaker as possible.
   – Avoid side conversations—these sounds can be picked up by the microphone and are distracting to all.
● Mute the microphone when you or others at your site are not speaking.

Video Conferences

A **video conference,** similar to a teleconference, is a meeting in which two or more people at different locations use telecommunication technology—computers, video/web cameras, and/or microphones—to participate in a virtual "face-to-face" meeting where they can SEE and HEAR each other in real time. Small group video conferences can be easily arranged using a computer or mobile device that has video-conferencing software such as Skype, IBM Sametime, or Yahoo! Messenger. On a larger scale, groups of participants may gather together in dedicated video-conferencing rooms where audio and video connections are provided for several people at different locations.

Video conferences allow for individuals at distant locations to HEAR and SEE one another while discussing issues.

Web Conferences

Web conferences include three types of virtual meetings: the web meeting, the webinar, and the webcast. Using text, audio, and/or video, interactive communication happens in real time over the Internet. As with other types of virtual meetings, web conferences save the time and expense of travelling. A web conference can be between just two people but is usually held with numerous participants. It can have either a two-way video component—commonly known as a web meeting—or a one-way video component, known as a webinar or webcast.

A **web meeting** is a meeting where groups of people anywhere in the world connect to exchange ideas and information via computers and an Internet or a local area network connection. This technology provides people the opportunity to work collaboratively and productively in **real time**, simultaneously creating documents such as presentations, spreadsheets, reports, and proposals. Microsoft *Skype for Business* is a cloud-based instant messaging and meeting service (see Figure 13-3). Participants can move quickly and easily from instant messaging to online meetings with audio-, video-, and screen-sharing capabilities.

In a **webinar,** a presenter can share information and conduct question-and-answer sessions with participants. A webinair does not, however, provide the same level of interactive possibilities as a web meeting.

A **webcast** is primarily a presentation tool; because it is broadcast simultaneously to hundreds of recipients, it can be compared to a television broadcast except it takes place over

FIGURE 13-3
Skype for Business

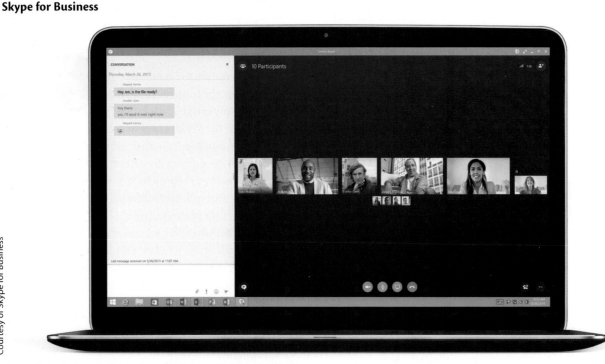

See, talk, and share information with Microsoft Skype for Business.

the Internet. The one-way nature of this type of conferencing means that there is little opportunity for the presenter and the audience members to interact.

All types of virtual meetings have several advantages:

- Individuals can participate in a meeting or conference anytime from anywhere.
- Participants save time and the costs of meals and accommodation.
- A considerable amount of information can be presented concisely through the use of sophisticated audio and video technology.
- People who have expertise in a number of different areas can be brought together.
- A recording of the meeting can be provided to individuals who were not in attendance.
  Virtual meetings also have some disadvantages:
- Participants have less opportunity for effectively brainstorming ideas.
- The structured environment leads to less spontaneity between individuals.
- Small nuances of body language are less likely to be picked up over the monitor.
- Participants have less opportunity for interaction before or after the meeting, which is a benefit in face-to-face meetings.

Videoconferencing Tips

The following guidelines will help make any video conference an effective and productive experience for all.

Be prepared:

- Designate a central contact person to be responsible for organizing the video conference.
- Develop a plan to handle any technical issues that may arise.
- Prepare an agenda, a list of attendees, and an outline of the meeting objective(s); distribute these and other relevant materials prior to the meeting.

During the meeting:

- Begin and end on time. Introduce all participants (consider using name tents) and use their names when directing questions to specific people. Announce when participants enter or leave the meeting.
- When speaking, make eye contact with the camera and allow for transmission delays. (Pause at the end of comments to allow other participants to respond, pose a question, or make a comment.)
- Practise standard meeting etiquette:
  - Be on time, courteous, and professional. Turn off cellphones, beepers, and watch alarms.
  - Be present—when your microphone is on, avoid side conversations, shuffling papers, or other distracting activities that can be picked up; mute the microphone when not speaking.
  - Dress professionally—as if you are attending a face-to-face meeting; avoid jewellery and bright or boldly patterned clothing that could cause audio or visual distraction.

Whether the meeting is face-to-face or virtual, in the office with employees or colleagues, or on the road with clients and prospects, the same principles apply—be respectful of people's time, have an agenda, focus on what needs to be achieved, begin and end on time, and conclude with action items. Carefully analyze the meeting's purpose and the outcomes expected. This will help to determine the most appropriate meeting format. By following the guidelines presented here, you can ensure the meeting is effective.

Before the Meeting—Roles and Responsibilities

As you help plan and organize a meeting, remember that before, during, and after a meeting, everyone has a role to play: the person who initiates and usually leads or facilitates the meeting; the administrative professional who assists in planning for the meeting, making the necessary arrangements, and preparing the required materials; and the meeting participants. Each individual or group has specific roles and responsibilities that help ensure an effective and productive meeting.

The Meeting Leader's Responsibilities

The meeting leader is responsible for determining the purpose of the meeting, setting the objectives and planning the agenda, deciding who should attend, and determining the number of attendees. He or she may work closely with the administrative professional in accomplishing these tasks.

Determine the Purpose and Objectives

Every meeting must have a purpose; without it, there is no need for a meeting. Generally, your supervisor will call the meeting, so it is his or her role to state the purpose. Unless you as the administrative professional are calling the meeting, it is generally not your responsibility to determine the purpose of the meeting. However, you do need to understand the purpose of the meeting in order to make appropriate arrangements. If your supervisor does not tell you the purpose of the meeting, ask. Your asking may help your supervisor define the purpose; in other words, it may help crystallize his or her thinking regarding the meeting.

Every meeting should also have specific written objectives. Objectives should clearly define the purpose and state what is to be accomplished. For example, if the purpose is to establish a strategic plan for the following year, the objectives might be

- to evaluate the accomplishment of objectives for the current year
- to establish objectives and timelines for the following year, based on the organization's three-year strategic plan

- to determine the resources needed to meet these objectives
- to determine the responsibility for carrying out all objectives

When meeting notices clearly state both the purpose and objective of the meeting, all participants will understand why the meeting is being called. Sharing the objectives with the participants beforehand also allows them to be prepared for the meeting. If they have questions about the purpose, they will have an opportunity to ask their questions before the meeting.

Plan the Agenda

The agenda is a document that lists the topics to be discussed at a meeting and may include the time allocated to each item (see Figure 13-4). Distributed before the meeting, a well-planned agenda saves time and increases productivity in a meeting. It is the responsibility of the meeting leader to plan the agenda. The administrative professional's responsibility is to produce and distribute the agenda to all participants.

Identify Participants

Identifying participants is generally not determined by the administrative professional unless you are chairing or leading the meeting yourself. While it is your supervisor's responsibility, you may be asked for suggestions, especially if you have worked for a company for a considerable amount of time.

People invited to the meeting should be individuals

- who can contribute to the objectives,
- who will be responsible for implementing the decisions made, or
- who represent a group affected by the decisions.

FIGURE 13-4
Meeting Agenda

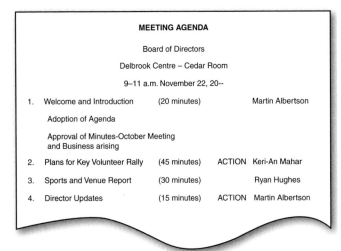

MEETING AGENDA

Board of Directors

Delbrook Centre – Cedar Room

9–11 a.m. November 22, 20--

1.	Welcome and Introduction	(20 minutes)		Martin Albertson
	Adoption of Agenda			
	Approval of Minutes-October Meeting and Business arising			
2.	Plans for Key Volunteer Rally	(45 minutes)	ACTION	Keri-An Mahar
3.	Sports and Venue Report	(30 minutes)		Ryan Hughes
4.	Director Updates	(15 minutes)	ACTION	Martin Albertson

For example, in the previous situation, where the purpose is to establish a strategic plan for the next year, all managers in the department should be invited to the meeting.

In another example, where the objective is to brainstorm ideas for international expansion, the people who should attend are the officers of the company since this decision will eventually be presented to the board of directors for approval.

Consideration should also be given to the background of the individuals being invited. For example, the diversity found in a **heterogeneous group** (a group having dissimilar backgrounds and experiences) can often solve problems more satisfactorily than a **homogeneous group** (a group with similar backgrounds and experiences). A heterogeneous group often brings varying points of view to the problem. Creative thinking through the diversity of participants present is more likely to occur than with a homogenous group. However, a more heterogeneous group may require a skilled facilitator in order to make the meeting productive.

The ideal number of participants is based on the purpose of the meeting and the number of people who can best achieve that purpose. A good size for a problem-solving and decision-making group is from 7 to 15 people. This size group allows for creative **synergy** (the ideas and products of a group of people developed through interaction with each other). There are enough people to generate divergent points of view and to challenge each other's thinking.

Small groups of six people or fewer may be necessary at times. For example, if the purpose of the meeting is to discuss a personnel matter, only the human resources director and the supervisor may be in attendance. If the purpose of the meeting is to discuss a faulty product design, only the product engineer, the manager of the engineering department, and the line technician may be present. Having only a few people in a meeting has advantages:

- Participants may be assembled more quickly.
- The meeting can be informal, resulting in more spontaneity and creativity.
- Group dynamics are easier to manage.
  A small group also has disadvantages:
- Points of view are limited.
- The participants may not generate enough ideas to create the best solution to the problem.
- Participants may not be willing to challenge each other's point of view, especially if they are a close-knit group.
- Participants may lack some of the details surrounding the issue.

Establish the Time and Place

The meeting leader is responsible for suggesting or establishing the approximate time of the meeting and identifying its general location. The administrative professional will check with participants to determine the most appropriate

record the specific details about who will do what, when, and how. Write "Action" or "Agreed" beside items when discussion concludes and/or after the vote has been taken.

- If a committee is being created or officers elected, record their names and positions.
- Record the date, time, and place for the next meeting, and the time that the meeting ends or adjourns.

If you have used a tablet or laptop, you need only read over your notes, make necessary changes to the file, format the file, and distribute the document. Such an approach is faster than taking notes by hand or making an audio recording of the meeting and then having to key everything after the meeting.

The Participants' Responsibilities

Participants are responsible for arriving on time and contributing thoughtful, well-considered, or well-researched comments. Participants should demonstrate appropriate meeting etiquette by:

- respecting the chair's role,
- giving their full attention to the meeting,
- being courteous to other participants,
- listening non-judgmentally to others,
- participating in discussions without dominating them,
- turning off pagers and cellphones so that text messages, emails, and phone calls cannot be answered during that time, and
- taking notes.

Participating in a meeting may sound simpler to do than it actually is—your mind may wander and you could find yourself focusing on other work-related tasks or on personal issues. However, your positive contributions could provide the perspective that brings the meeting back on track when discussions stray, or they could help the chairperson keep the meeting focused.

If a meeting does go longer than scheduled, it is perfectly acceptable as a participant to excuse yourself and leave the meeting. In doing so, let the meeting leader and others know you have a previous commitment, but that you will review the minutes and be prepared for the next meeting. This comment demonstrates your desire to fulfill your commitments and lets the other participants know you are being responsible, not inconsiderate or rude—but rather that you are fulfilling another obligation.

After the Meeting—Roles and Responsibilities

The Meeting Leader's Responsibilities

Evaluate the Meeting

Generally, with informal meetings within an organization, no formal evaluation is necessary. However, an informal evaluation can be done by the chairperson (and possibly by the participants). If attendees are forthright, they may tell the chairperson they found the meeting to be a waste of time.

When attendees make such a statement, the chair should seek clarification on exactly what they meant. The chair may also want to ask two or three individual participants how the meeting went. In either case, the chair will also want to consider the following questions to help evaluate the meeting:

- Did everyone in attendance take part in the meeting?
- Was the nonverbal behaviour positive?
- Were participants creative problem-solvers?
- Did participants exhibit a high energy level?
- Was the purpose of the meeting satisfied?
- Were appropriate decisions made?
- Can I improve the way I handled the issues, the people, or the meeting?

If the meeting is relatively formal, the chairperson may ask participants to complete an evaluation form. See Figure 13-9 for a sample.

FIGURE 13-9
A Meeting Evaluation Form

Meeting Evaluation
Place a check mark in the "Yes" or "No" column. Attach any additional comments you may have to this form.

1. Was the purpose of the meeting accomplished?
Yes ☐ No ☐

2. Was the agenda received in time to prepare for the meeting?
Yes ☐ No ☐

3. Was the room arrangement satisfactory?
Yes ☐ No ☐

4. Did the chairperson help the group accomplish the goals of the meeting?
Yes ☐ No ☐

5. Did the chairperson adhere to the agenda?
Yes ☐ No ☐

6. Were the appropriate people included in the meeting?
Yes ☐ No ☐

7. Did all attendees participate in the discussion?
Yes ☐ No ☐

8. Did attendees listen to each other?
Yes ☐ No ☐

9. Did the chairperson encourage participation?
Yes ☐ No ☐

10. Did the meeting begin on time?
Yes ☐ No ☐

11. Did the meeting end on time?
Yes ☐ No ☐

12. Were decisions that were made consistent with the purpose of the meeting?
Yes ☐ No ☐

The Administrative Professional's Responsibilities

After a meeting, review with the meeting chairperson what did and did not go well. Such a review helps you plan more effectively for the next meeting. Your duties after the meeting include ensuring that the meeting room is left in order, preparing the minutes, and handling other details.

Routine Tasks

These routine tasks are essential after a meeting:

- Return all equipment. See that additional tables and chairs are removed and/or returned to their proper location.
- Clean up any food or beverage leftovers, or notify the cleaning staff if the room needs a general cleaning.
- On your task list or calendar, make a note of items that require future attention by you or your supervisor.
- Send out any necessary follow-up correspondence.
- Evaluate the meeting. Review what happened and consider how you might improve the arrangements for the next meeting; if you used a caterer, was the quality of the food acceptable? Were the staff helpful?
- Keep notes on meetings for an appropriate length of time so that you are able to refer to them when planning the next similar meeting. Keep the names and telephone numbers of contact people. These notes will help ensure future success.
- If the chair has decided on a formal evaluation, you may be expected to prepare and administer the evaluation and summarize the results.

Prepare the Minutes

Minutes are not necessary for all meetings; however, the record they provide reminds participants of the discussion that occurred and the responsibilities they may have agreed to as a result of the meeting. The overview of discussions, decisions, and action items provides the information needed so that non-attendees, too, can be well informed prior to the next meeting.

Minutes are required in the following situations:

- When decisions are made that affect a large number of people
- For formal meetings, such as board of directors' meetings
- When participants act upon a list of different topics and a record is necessary to recall the events
- When the same type of meeting is held on a regular basis and a record is needed of the group's continuing activities
- When meeting results need to be reported to the president or other officers of the organization

If minutes are necessary, they should be prepared and distributed within 24 to 48 hours of a meeting. Prompt preparation and distribution of minutes reminds participants of their responsibilities before the next meeting and gives those who were unable to attend a sense of what occurred and what decisions have been reached. Non-participants (those who are not members of the group but who are interested or affected) may also receive a copy of the meeting minutes. For example, minutes from a company board meeting may be made available to all executives within a company.

Although there is no set format for writing minutes, checking previous minutes of the group will provide you with a sense of the format followed in your organization. Your word processing program will have a variety of templates from which you can chose, or your organization may use templates that include the preferred formatting and the standard information common to all minutes. Minutes generally include the following information:

- The title *Minutes*, the group's name and type of meeting, and the date
- The names of the meeting leader, members present and absent, and, optionally, those who arrived late and whether or not a quorum was established.
- Minutes are usually single-spaced. Margins should be at least 1 inch (about 2.54 cm). If the minutes are to be placed in a bound book, the left margin should be 1-1/2 inches (about 3.81 cm).
- Numbered paragraphs or subject captions that usually correspond to the agenda items can be used as paragraph headings.
- Motions made, names of the mover and the seconder (if there is one), and the outcome of the motion—whether it passed or failed.
- A concise summary of the important discussion points, the items on which action needs to be taken, and the name(s) of those responsible.
- The date and time of the next meeting if one has been scheduled.
- The time the meeting adjourned or ended.
- Minutes of informal meetings do not require signatures; the minutes of board meetings and professional organizations are generally signed. When minutes are to be signed, a signature line should be provided.
- Store minutes electronically or in hardcopy form in a binder or notebook. Retain them for future reference with the agenda and all pertinent materials that were presented.

Minutes from a meeting are shown in Figure 13-10.

The Participants' Responsibilities

Your responsibilities as a participant do not necessarily end once the meeting is over. For example, you may be responsible for undertaking some research or other action before the next meeting; or you may have been asked to work with one or two other people to bring back a recommendation to

FIGURE 13-10
Meeting Minutes

MINUTES

Summer Games Association

MONTHLY MEETING - BOARD OF DIRECTORS

Delbrook Centre – Cedar Room
November 22, 20--

PRESENT: Martin Albertson (Chairperson), Keri-An Mahar (Recorder), Sabina Burrell, Sarah Chung, Ryan Hughes, Dean Kvanstrom, Dianne Lyons, Annika Strilchuk

ABSENT : Mae Michaluk, Jeremy Siu

1.   The meeting was called to order at 9:00 a.m. Attendees were asked to introduce themselves, Chairperson Albertson welcomed new members Sabina Burrell and Dianne Lyons.

       The agenda was approved by consensus with the following addition:

       ➢ Approval of Logo; added as item 5

       Minutes of the October meeting were approved as circulated with one amendment. Under item 7, the prizes donated for the Key Volunteer Rally were from "Towne and Country Sports" and not from "Country Sports".

       Business Arising
       Sabina confirmed the process for registering as a Non-Profit Society has been completed. As a result a bank account has been opened and funds can now be deposited.

       Dean indicated that confirmation for a location for the Opening Ceremonies has been received from the hotel at Lonsdale Quay.

2.   Keri-An reported on the plans for the Key Volunteer Rally, Since she does not have a Chair for the Reception Committee, she will assume responsibility for this function but will need help from other Directors. Martin volunteered to help with beverage purchases, Sarah with name badges and Dianne with equipment rentals. Martin indicated he would need a projector for a video he will be presenting. Keri-An asked other Directors to contact her if there was anything else she needed to arrange.   **ACTION ALL**

3.   Ryan reported on the determination of the sports to be involved. To date 23 of the 28 of the activities have been confirmed with 5 sport specific associations still to reply. He is arranging for a sport venue tour sometime early in the spring, Date TBD. All Directors will be expected to attend.   **ACTION RYAN**

4.   All Directors reported on their progress in recruiting chairs for their various directorates. Still needed a Director of Communications and Director of Promotions. Names of any potential candidates should be forwarded to Martin to contact.   **ACTION ALL**

5.   Three examples of a logo for the games were circulated. Considerable discussion produced no consensus Item tabled to next meeting.

Next meeting December 20, 20-- in the Committee Room at City Hall.

The meeting adjourned at 11:00 a.m.

---

the next meeting. Whatever the task, it must be completed in a timely manner; others are depending on it.

International Meetings

In international organizations, upper-level managers commonly meet with staff in locations outside of Canada. Also, as organizations in Canada continue to broaden their international scope, meetings to pursue international opportunities are held with business leaders in many other countries. You may be involved in setting up and/or participating in electronic meetings with individuals from other countries, or the meetings may be held in other countries. In international meetings, remember that cultural differences do exist, and these differences must be understood and respected. Otherwise, you may be dealing with an international incident rather than achieving a resolution on an important contract or issue. It is important that you do your homework before the meeting.

Find out as much as you can about the culture or cultures that will be represented. Then, be sensitive to the needs of the individuals in the meeting. Remember to consider the differences in time zones; when it is noon in Halifax, it is the following day in Beijing. Use the time zone calculators on the Internet to help you find a suitable time when everyone can meet electronically.

International meetings are typically more formal in nature than local meetings. Learn and use the proper greetings. Follow accepted practices for exchanging business cards and giving (or not giving) gifts or other amenities.

Professionalism @ Work

Etiquette for International Meetings

- Learn and use proper greetings in all meetings. Greetings become doubly important in a virtual meeting so do not ignore them in such a situation.
- Do not use first names of participants. Even though using first names is common in North American meetings, it can be considered inappropriate in other countries.
- Acknowledge the leader of the other group(s). For example, if the presidents of companies are involved, they should be recognized first and should speak first.
- Remember the hierarchical nature of the international participants and show respect for everyone but especially for those in positions of authority.
- Disagree agreeably; some cultures consider it offensive to be contradictory.
- Avoid gesturing with your hands. In another cultural context, such gestures may mean something you do not intend. Also, some people are offended by gestures.
- Watch your body language; remember that body language has different meanings in different cultures.
- Do not mistake a courteous answer for the truth. "Yes" does not always mean "yes," and "no" may not mean "no."
- Understand the concept of time; in some cultures it is precise, while in others it is more fluid.

Conferences and Other Events

Executives may belong to a professional organization in a particular field of expertise, such as accounting, engineering, or human resources. Many of these organizations hold at least one major conference each year. Most companies encourage their executives to participate in conferences as a means of broadening their knowledge. As a member of a professional organization such as the International Association of Administrative Professionals (IAAP), ARMA International, the Canadian Information Processing Society (CIPS), or some local organization, you too may attend or perhaps help to plan some of their conferences. While a conference, convention, or special event is much larger in scope and has more participants than a meeting, many of the principles of organizing effective meetings can be applied to organizing these larger events. Event planning is a skill that many employers seek in their administrative professionals. Your program of study may include a complete course devoted to this topic.

Your role as an administrative professional may be to assist your supervisor in planning a conference. Similar to planning for a meeting, you will have a variety of responsibilities before, during, and after the event. In doing so, you may use event planning software. You may also work with a professional meeting or event planner.

Before the Event

Preparing for a regional or national conference takes months of work. Good planning ensures a smooth, successful event. Poor planning can result in a disorganized, ineffective event. Event management software such as *Smartsheet*, a spreadsheet, or Microsoft OneNote can help you to keep the details organized and ensure important arrangements are not overlooked.

Similar to planning a meeting, when planning a conference, one of the major responsibilities is to determine the location and meeting facilities. Contact the chamber of commerce in the city being considered. Ask for information about the city and appropriate conference facilities. Request conference planning guides from the hotels and conference centres that give floor plans of the facilities, dining and catering services, price list of rooms, and layout of meeting rooms. Once the city and hotel have been selected, detailed arrangements need to be made for meeting rooms, guest rooms, meals, and so on.

Your task will not be to invite someone to speak unless you are working on a conference where you are a member and assisting with the planning (an IAAP conference, for example). However, you may contact presenters to make travel and lodging arrangements before the conference. If you are responsible for making hotel arrangements for a presenter, you should determine the types of accommodations the presenter would prefer (within the cost limitations of the budget), as presenters' expenses are usually covered, at least in part, by the host organization. For example, does the presenter need an accessible room? If the conference is not at a hotel, you might give the presenter a choice of two or three area hotels (within your price range). If you are making flight reservations, you need to know the person's desired arrival and departure times and any other transportation needs.

	0	■	i	Done	Task Name	Start Date	End Date	Sep 14	Sep 21	Sep 28	Oct 5	Oct 12	Oct 19
1		🔒		☐	⊟ Section 1	09/16/14	09/30/14				Section 1		
2	0			✓	Sub-task 1	09/16/14	09/23/14		Sub-task 1				
3	💬	🔒	📑	✓	Sub-task 2	09/24/14	09/25/14			Sub-task 2			
4	💬			☐	Sub-task 3	09/26/14	09/30/14				Sub-task 3		
5	0		⚖	☐	⊟ Section 2	09/27/14	10/09/14				Section 2		
6				☐	Sub-task 1	09/27/14	09/27/14			Sub-task 1			
7				☐	Sub-task 2	09/29/14	10/01/14			Sub-task 2			
8				☐	Sub-task 3	10/02/14	10/08/14				Sub-task 3		
9				☐	Milestone	10/09/14	10/09/14				◆ Milestone		
10				☐	⊟ Section 3	10/14/14	10/28/14						
11				☐	Sub-task 1	10/14/14	10/16/14					Sub-task 1	
12				☐	Sub-task 2	10/17/14	10/21/14						Sub-task

Event planning software provides a visual timeline that helps keep event details organized and ensures important arrangements are not overlooked.

Preregistration is typically held before the conference; you may be involved in setting up the preregistration in addition to actually registering individuals. Most registration is now done online, and your role may be to design the online registration process and post the appropriate information online. Also, you may be involved in preparing packets of information for the registrants. Registration packets often include program information, a list of participants, and a small gift or two.

During the Event

Your responsibilities during the conference may include running errands, delivering messages to participants, and solving any problems that may occur. Other responsibilities may include checking the room arrangements, equipment needs, meal arrangements, and a multitude of other last-minute details as they arise. Since you are a representative of the company for which you work or the organization of which you are a member, it is imperative that you present a positive image at all times. Keep a smile on your face, and handle even the most difficult situations with poise and confidence.

After the Event

After the conference, your basic duties involve cleaning up and following up. These responsibilities include seeing that all equipment is returned, presenters are assisted with transportation to the airport, letters of appreciation are sent to presenters and others, expense reports are completed, and bills are paid. You may also be responsible for seeing that the proceedings of the conference are published and made available to participants. You may not be responsible for writing the report, but you may be responsible for working with the conference reporters in assembling and distributing it. At many conferences, the sessions are recorded and made available to participants on the conference website. You may be responsible for assembling presentations from different presenters, and uploading them to the website.

A post-conference evaluation session should be held with all individuals who worked on the conference. At this meeting, you will need to review the areas that were successful and those that were not. The participants may have completed a formal evaluation of the conference. If so, the evaluations need to be tallied and summarized in the post-conference evaluation session. Take note of all issues and/or problems, which should be passed on to the appropriate organization or company personnel so that people involved in the next conference will have the benefit of your experiences. No one ever wants to make the same mistake twice. A record of the problems or issues and their solutions or outcomes will help the next group avoid some mistakes.

People @ Work

Meeting or Event Planner

Meeting or event planners coordinate the details of a meeting or conference as requested by a client. The client may be a business, an organization, or an individual. A meeting planner typically handles tasks such as these:

- Determining and/or arranging for the meeting location at a hotel or convention centre
- Handling lodging arrangements and coordinating transportation requirements for participants
- Arranging for meals and other food and beverage services, possibly in conjunction with a caterer
- Arranging for necessary telecommunication services
- Arranging for any necessary audiovisual equipment
- Assigning exhibit space and working with exhibitors to resolve any issues related to the exhibits

Your company may hire a meeting planner to coordinate the details of a large meeting or conference. You may work with the planner to explore ways to meet your company's needs and stay within your budget.

Chapter Summary

The summary will help you remember the important points covered in this chapter.

- Meetings can be a good means of generating ideas, sharing information, and making decisions. Unnecessary and unproductive meetings waste the time of both the individual and the organization.
- A meeting is considered unnecessary when its purpose and/ or the appropriate people to attend have not been clearly identified, when there is inadequate data or insufficient time to prepare, when one-way information could be better communicated by other means, when there is a need to discuss confidential or sensitive personnel matters, or when a considerable amount of anger or hostility exists.
- Meetings may be informal, such as staff or customer/ client meetings, or formal, such as a board, committee, or project/task force meeting.
- Meeting formats may be face-to-face or virtual. Teleconferences, video conferences, or web conferences— web meetings, webinars, and webcasts—are examples of virtual meeting formats.
- The meeting leader is responsible to determine the purpose and objectives of the meeting, plan the agenda, determine the participants, and establish the time and place. The administrative professional may assist with these tasks.
- The administrative professional is responsible, in consultation with the meeting leader, to select, reserve, and prepare the meeting room; determine the seating arrangement; prepare and distribute the meeting notice, agenda, and meeting materials; order equipment and food and beverages; handle duties during the meeting; and follow up after the meeting.
- During the meeting, the chairperson is responsible for determining the procedures, adhering to the agenda, managing time, encouraging participation, and reaching decisions.
- The participant's responsibilities include reading material before the meeting, being on time, adhering to the agenda, making contributions, listening thoughtfully to other participants, and carrying out any responsibilities assigned during the meeting.
- When planning and conducting international meetings, the chairperson and the administrative professional should become familiar with the customs and culture of the participants.
- Compared with meetings, conferences are much larger in scope and have more participants. The administrative professional may be involved in planning a conference; carrying out duties during the conference, such as solving problems, running errands, and assisting with registration; and follow-up activities such as writing letters of appreciation, filling out expense reports, and paying bills after the conference.

Key Terms

bylaws p. 234
ad hoc committee p. 234
standing committee p. 234
teleconference p. 234
conference call p. 234
video conference p. 236
web meeting p. 236
real time p. 236
webinar p. 236
webcast p. 236
heterogeneous group p. 238
homogeneous group p. 238
synergy p. 238

rectangular arrangement p. 240
circular and oval arrangements p. 240
semicircular or U-shaped arrangements p. 240
agenda p. 241
speaker's list p. 244
Robert's Rules of Order p. 244
amendment p. 245
minutes p. 245
motion p. 245
parliamentary procedures p. 245
quorum p. 245
resolution p. 245
verbatim p. 246

Responses to Self-Check

1. Consider its size, arrangement, temperature, and ventilation, and whether the room is large enough to accommodate the equipment needed.
2. U-shaped and semicircular are the most effective arrangements for informal meetings.
3. An agenda should include the name of the meeting or the group, date of the meeting, start and end times, location, order of topics and activities, person responsible for presenting each topic or activity, action expected on each item, and background materials (if necessary).

4. Determine whether other equipment, such as a projection device and/or screen or a podium/lectern, is required and, if there is to be a head table, whether it should be skirted. Depending on the length of the meeting, arrangements for refreshments should be made. Be prepared with extra agendas, meeting materials, pads of notepaper, and pens to take to the meeting.

Discussion Items

These discussion items provide an opportunity to test your understanding of the chapter through written responses and/or discussion with your classmates and your instructor.

1. When is a meeting unnecessary?
2. Identify and describe three types of virtual meetings.
3. What are the responsibilities of an administrative professional when preparing for meetings?
4. What is considered good etiquette when participating in an international meeting?
5. From the board of directors to the office staff, meetings are commonplace in companies and other organizations. For each of the following situations discuss the type of meeting described and the format(s) that could be used for the meeting.

a. The persons responsible for the overall direction of a company are meeting to discuss long-range plans and policies.
b. A group of employees from one location are meeting to discuss the ongoing issue of office safety.
c. A group of employees from locations around the country are meeting to write a recommendation for a new flextime work policy for the company.
d. The manager of the human resources department is meeting with people who work in that department to discuss the progress of work assignments.
e. Company representatives and customers from the United States, Germany, and India are meeting to learn about new products the company will introduce next quarter.
f. A new flextime work policy has been approved by the board. Employees need to be informed.

Critical-Thinking Activity

CanAsian Airlines is planning an online conference for its Calgary and Beijing executives. The meeting is being held to begin discussion of the strategic direction of the airlines for the next five years. You have been asked to coordinate with the various offices on agenda items. Once you receive the agenda items, you will be working with Mr. Albertson to send out the necessary materials and the agenda. You have contacted the appropriate administrative professional in each office to discuss these details. To date, you have received agenda items from two of the three executives in the Calgary office and one of the three executives in the Beijing office. You have emailed a reminder to the administrative professional in each office, asking for the executive's agenda; you have received no response. The meeting is only a month away, and you are becoming anxious. You know you must get the agenda out soon. You do not want to go to Mr. Albertson with the situation, but you do not know how to handle it. What should you do?

Building Workplace Skills

Project 13-1 (Learning Outcomes 1, 2, 3, 4, and 5)

Collaborative Project

Mr. Albertson is planning a meeting with not-for-profit groups and several large businesses within the Calgary community to consider ways in which the organizations might work together on these major issues affecting the city: transportation, crime, inner-city housing, and public education. The not-for-profit groups involved in this meeting are the Department of Social Services, the Calgary Foundation, the Chamber of Commerce, the Asian-Pacific Coalition, the Junior League, and the First Nations Council. The businesses are Talisman International, MDS Health Care, Clark Associates Inc., Godwin Tools, and Lowell Granite. The group's work will take approximately one year; recommendations from this group after one year of operation will go to the mayor for action.

The first meeting will be an organizational one to develop a mission statement and to establish goals for the group. Mr. Albertson has already contacted the community leaders, and they have agreed to serve on the task force. Mr. Albertson has asked you to handle several of the arrangements for him. Since this project is fairly extensive, you ask your two assistants to work with you. (Assemble a group of three for this project—you and two of your classmates.) Mr. Albertson is considering a virtual meeting. He asks you to research the advantages and disadvantages of teleconferencing and web conferencing. Prepare a memorandum to Mr. Albertson, using the memorandum form SCDP13-1 on the MindTap site (access to which is provided with the printed access card on the inside cover of your textbook), summarizing the results of your findings; include copies of the articles you found. Then draft a letter for Mr. Albertson, inviting participants to the first meeting; use the letterhead in SCDP13-1a on the MindTap site. The meeting will be held two days—Thursday, November 15, beginning with lunch at noon and ending at 4 p.m., and Friday, November 16, beginning with breakfast at 8:30 a.m. and ending at 11 a.m.

Prepare an agenda. The agenda on November 15 should include a welcome to the group from Mr. Albertson; lunch; an introduction of the participants; and a video conference with Dr. Peter Sigman, who has been working with inner-city issues for over 15 years. Dr. Sigman will be in Toronto; the participants at the meeting will have a chance to interact with him after his presentation. The remainder of Thursday afternoon will be devoted to writing a mission statement for the group. On Friday morning, the group will begin to develop their goals. Mr. Albertson will facilitate both sessions.

Plan a team meeting with your two classmates to determine who will be responsible for each task. (Optional – Use Doodle or some other evite application to poll your classmates to determine when you can meet.)

At your meeting determine how you will work together as a team. Use the team evaluation form SCDP13-1c from the MindTap site. Discuss it with your teammates so everyone understands what evaluation criteria are being used. Once you have completed the project, each member of your team should complete the evaluation form.

1. Refer to the section in this chapter that discusses the administrative professional's responsibilities in assisting with meetings. Make a list of the things your group must do. Include menus for lunch and breakfast.
2. Write a memorandum to Mr. Albertson summarizing these details using the memo form SCDP13-1.
3. Prepare a draft of a letter inviting the not-for-profit groups and the businesses to the meeting. Include an agenda. Give the draft to your supervisor for approval. (In this case, the supervisor will be your instructor.) The meeting will be held in the Board Room at CanAsian. Once your instructor has approved the letter and the agenda, prepare letters and envelopes for the invitees. Include the agenda for the two days. Addresses are given in SCDP13-1b.
4. Complete the team evaluation form separately, and then discuss your evaluation with your team members. Next, prepare a team evaluation that consolidates the opinions given by each team member. Submit it to your instructor.

Use the form file SCDP13-1c. (Provide each member of your team with a copy one for your collective evaluation.)

Project 13-2 (Learning Outcome 5)

Attend or view on television a meeting of a local club, governmental body, or civic organization. For example, municipal council meetings are often broadcast on local television channels. YouTube also has meeting videos that can be used for this activity. Take notes as the meeting is conducted. Prepare minutes of the meeting. As a guide, you can use the minutes in Figure 13-10 or some other style suggested by your instructor. Write a short report that describes the behaviour and comments of the meeting leader and the participants. Evaluate the success of the meeting and the effectiveness of the leader and the participants.

Project 13-3 (Learning Outcome 4)

You belong to a professional association for administrative assistants in Calgary and have been asked to work on a committee planning a conference. You have been asked to create a flyer that will be posted on the conference website. Preliminary details for the flyer can be found in file SCDP13-3. Use graphics, different fonts, and any other design elements you feel appropriately represent the activities. Place a copy of this flyer in your e-portfolio.

Project 13-4 (Learning Outcome 4)

Online templates for agendas and other meeting documents are available that can assist you in creating these typical meeting documents. Access these templates and download several different styles of documents that you think might be useful. Save these templates as part of your e-portfolio.

Project 13-5 (Learning Outcome 3)

Many software programs are available for purchase or free trial download that can be very useful for administrative professionals when planning/conducting meetings and other events. Some of following programs offer an opportunity for a free demo or a video demonstrating the features of the program. Search the Internet for these and other programs. Choose one to download and try it or view the demo provided. Discuss these features with your classmates. Some suggestions follow:

Meetings

WebEx, GoToMeeting, or Skype for Business are three software programs that makes it possible for business people to meet from any location using a tablet, laptop, or smartphone with a camera, headset, and microphone.

Scheduling

Doodle has a feature that makes it possible to survey a group of people that may not be on the same calendar or network to obtain individual input on selecting an appropriate date and time for a meeting. For example, you can use Doodle to set up a meeting with members of your IAAP executive who work for various organizations. Invitations to respond to a poll can be sent to their respective email addresses.

Make the Grade with MindTap

Stay organized and efficient with **MindTap**—a single destination with all the course material and study aids you need to succeed. Built-in apps leverage social media and the latest learning technology. For example:

- ReadSpeaker will read the text to you.
- Flashcards are pre-populated to provide you with a jump-start for review—or you can create your own.
- You can highlight text and make notes in your MindTap Reader. Your notes will flow into Evernote, the electronic

Event Planning

Smartsheet provides templates for all the activities needed in organizing and planning events, tracking projects, and maintaining marketing reports.

MindTap®

notebook app that you can access anywhere when it's time to study for the exam.

- Self-quizzing allows you to access your understanding.

Visit http://www.nelson.com/student to start using **MindTap**. Enter the Online Access Code from the card included with your text. If a code card is not provided, you can purchase instant access at NELSONbrain.com.

CHAPTER 14

Arranging Business Travel

Do I Qualify?

Travel Administrative Assistant

The ideal candidate will have at least three years of office experience and the ability to work in a fast-paced team environment. Duties include:

- Reviewing travel request forms prior to booking travel
- Making travel arrangements for air, hotel, and rental cars using approved lists and websites
- Handling revisions to travel arrangements
- Following company guidelines for securing the best rates
- Preparing travel expense forms in accordance with company policies, coding expenses in accordance with company guidelines, and obtaining appropriate approval of expenses before submitting to Accounting

Travel is a way of life for many business executives, and with the growth of our global economy, the amount of international travel has increased dramatically. Many North American businesses are now multinational, having locations both within Canada and abroad; and many international companies now have locations within Canada. The car industry is a good example of international locations. Ford, Honda, Mazda, Toyota, Mitsubishi, and Nissan are some of the car manufacturers from abroad who have manufacturing or assembly plants in North America. The United States and other countries take advantage of land, labour, and technical expertise available in other parts of the world to decide where to produce and/or assemble a product.

Having offices or subsidiaries in other cities may require the company's executives to travel. Executives, and possibly yourself and other administrative professionals, are often members of professional organizations that conduct provincial or national conventions at least once each year. As an administrative professional, you too may occasionally need to travel. In order to handle travel arrangements effectively, you need to become familiar with the types of services available. This chapter will first introduce you to this variety of services and help you to understand your options, and will then focus on making travel arrangements and helping you understand your responsibilities while the executive is out of the office.

Air Travel

Time is an extremely important commodity for busy executives. As a result, travelling by air rather than car or rail is generally the preferred choice.

A traveller can fly from Toronto to Vancouver in approximately five hours or from Winnipeg to Dublin in approximately seven hours. During a flight, travellers can use their time productively by reading newspapers, journals, or periodicals. Travellers are instructed to turn off computers and cellphones during take-offs and landings. However, during the flight, travellers can use their laptops, tablets, or smartphones to write letters and reports, to connect to the Internet to communicate with colleagues and clients, and to stay current on news or investments.

Flight Classifications

While different airlines may use slightly different names for their flight classes, all airlines offer essentially three broad classes—first class, business class, and economy class. International flights generally offer all three classes. Longer national and some international flights offer business class and economy class. Since 1991, when EVA Air first introduced the premium economy class category, this new flight class has grown in popularity and is now available from many carriers.

First-class accommodations are the most expensive of the three classes and the most luxurious. First-class travellers typically have individual "pods" where they are able to lie down and get a restful sleep. The quality of food, choice of entrees, and service time are personalized. Meal presentation may include cloth napkins, tablecloths, silverware, and china dinnerware.

Tablets, smartphones, and laptops allow us to continue to be productive as we travel regionally, nationally, and internationally.

Complimentary alcoholic beverages and headsets for listening to music or viewing movies are provided. There are more flight attendants per passenger than in the other classes, which means greater attention is given to each flyer. First-class customers have access to a private lounge in the terminal while waiting for their flight departure. They exit the aircraft first and board at any time during the boarding process. All first-class travellers have no-cost access to individual power ports, Wi-Fi access to the Internet, and the airline entertainment app for personal mobile devices.

Business-class accommodations provide a level of service between first class and economy. The business-class section is located in front of the economy class—either directly behind first class or at the front of the plane if first class is not offered. Designed especially for passengers travelling for business purposes, business class is not available on all aircraft or on all flights. Typically, this class is offered on international and long-distance domestic flights such as those between Toronto and Vancouver. Services provided include many of those offered to first-class travellers, such as complimentary Wi-Fi and entertainment app access for personal mobile devices, more spacious and comfortable seating or pods, more legroom than economy class, complimentary alcoholic beverages, and, when offered, better food than economy class. Like first-class travellers, business-class travellers also have access to a lounge in the terminal while waiting for their flight departure and are allowed to exit first and board at any time during the boarding process.

Many companies recognize the effects of **jet lag** (the feeling of exhaustion following a flight through several time zones) on the international traveller. For example, many companies have implemented policies that approve first-class or business-class travel for executives who travel long distances, so that they have the opportunity to sleep while travelling. This means business travellers are often able to be productive immediately upon arrival at their destination.

Economy-class accommodations are typically the lowest-priced seats on the airplane. Also known as coach or tourist class in other countries, seats are closer together than either business or first class, and fewer flight attendants are available to serve the needs of the travellers. Some airlines may offer complimentary snacks; some will charge a fee. Complimentary beverages usually include pop, fruit juice, water, tea, and coffee. Many airlines also provide economy-class travellers with Wi-Fi access to the Internet and entertainment apps for use with personal mobile devices. Customers may be required to pay a fee for this access, and they can buy or rent a headset if they have not brought one with them. When available, premium economy offers the flyer some benefits similar to business class, including larger more comfortable seats, complimentary refreshments, increased baggage allowance, and priority boarding.

© auremar/Shutterstock

The events of 9/11 had a severe impact on airlines worldwide. Some airlines ceased operating. Of those airlines that continued to operate, the costs associated with the implementation of increased security procedures led them to eliminate some services and start charging additional fees. Some airlines have eliminated refreshment service altogether on short-haul or regional flights, and have introduced fees for all checked baggage. Food providers in airports saw a business opportunity here, and began providing carry-on meals in specially designed bags. To avoid checked baggage fees, many people travel with only carry-on luggage.

Because of the increased emphasis on reducing the expense of air travel, many airlines have added regional jets, which are smaller in size than the planes that fly longer routes within Canada or internationally. Regional jets generally have 30 to 100 seats, fly shorter distances (for example, from Calgary to Kelowna or from Halifax to Moncton), and offer only one class of flight—economy. They may offer drinks and snacks or small boxed lunches. They can typically charge less because they have eliminated many traditional passenger services. In addition, low-fare airlines may offer limited flight schedules, serve only secondary airports, or serve fewer destinations than other airlines.

Company-Owned and Chartered Planes

Large corporations may lease their own plane or fleet of planes if the amount of travel by company employees makes it advantageous to do so. Smaller business may contract with one of the small airlines that specialize in privately chartered jet service, renting an entire airplane rather than purchasing individual seats on a commercial flight. Generally small in size, chartered planes are usually located adjacent to regular airports and use the same runways as the major airlines. Food may be available on these jets for an additional cost; flight attendants are generally not available.

Relatively new to the scene is Ubair, whose goal is bridge the divide between private and commercial aviation using an app to make chartering a private plane as simple as requesting a taxi. Available in Canada, the United States, and the Caribbean, Ubair has access to a significant number of planes through a variety of aircraft management companies. As an option, when compared with commercial flights, chartering through Ubair may prove to be both surprisingly affordable and much more convenient for the business traveller.

Airline Loyalty Programs

For the frequent business traveller, membership in a frequent traveller program may be worthwhile. Membership is available through individual airlines, which typically provide a comfortable lounge for members who are awaiting the departure of their flight or have a layover between flights. Membership fees vary, and entry is not based on your chosen flight classification. First-class and business-class travellers automatically have access to these lounges. Economy-class travellers may pay a fee for access to these lounges at the time of booking. A variety of services are available in the lounges, including:

- High-speed and wireless Internet access for mobile devices; a PC workstation; and equipment to print, fax, and scan documents
- Conference rooms, lounge space, and showers
- Reading material
- Complimentary alcoholic beverages, pop, juice, and coffee
- Hot and cold refreshments
- Assistance with airline reservations

Parking Services

Large airports generally provide a free shuttle service from a parking lot or rental car location to the airport gate. However, you are charged for parking your car, with the fee based on how long your car is parked. Since parking at an airport for an extended period of time can become expensive, large cities generally provide frequent private shuttle services to the airport from various locations around the city. Paying for a shuttle to and from the airport may be cheaper than paying for parking at the airport for an extended time.

Ticketing

Reservations for air travel can be made online or by telephoning the airline directly. Once the reservation is completed, a trip confirmation email message is sent to the traveller. This document contains the basic information needed—the confirmation or receipt number and the departure and arrival times. Using this information, travellers are able to access their reservation on the airline website within 24 hours of a flight. Once they have checked in, they can choose to print a hardcopy of their boarding pass or have it sent electronically to a tablet or smartphone.

Use a touch-screen check-in kiosk to print your boarding pass.

It is also possible to check in at the airport. Travellers present their e-ticket to the ticket agent at the airline ticket counter, where a boarding pass is printed and checked baggage can be dropped off. Alternatively, travellers can use a touch-screen check-in kiosk at the airport, by inserting a travel document such as a passport or entering the confirmation/receipt number onto the screen. The e-reservation information is retrieved from the airline database and a boarding pass is printed. Travellers can then proceed directly through security and on to the departure gate, with just a short stop to drop any tagged checked baggage onto a conveyor belt. Most airlines have implemented a charge for checked baggage for travellers in economy class. This fee can be paid during the online check-in.

On occasion, it may be necessary to cancel or change a flight reservation. It is a good idea when booking a flight to confirm the airline policy for cancelling or changing the reservation. The policy for cancellations, which varies depending on the class of flight booked, is described on the airline's website and may include a charge. If the ticket is non-refundable or non-transferable, it can usually be used at a later date to travel to either the same or a different destination. These airline policies may influence an organization's policy regarding the preferred flight class to be used when arranging business travel. For example, your organization's policy may recommend booking only travel that is flexible, even though doing so may not result in the least expensive fare. Another option is to purchase flight passes that can be used by a pool of travellers; cancelled bookings simply go back into the pool and are used as required by any traveller.

When mechanical problems or other issues cause a flight to be changed or cancelled, passengers are not charged. The airline tries to make the situation as painless as possible. To help offset the inconvenience being experienced by their passengers, airlines may provide vouchers for food, or a hotel room if the change involves an overnight stay.

Airline Security

Everyone who travels by air must go through airport security checkpoints. Carry-on baggage, and in some cases checked baggage, must also go through security checkpoints. These checkpoints were developed after 9/11 to help prevent passengers from bringing anything on a plane that would enable them to take over or damage the plane. A variety of security precautions such as full-body scanners are currently in place at airports around the world. As new incidents of potential terrorism occur, these security precautions will continue to be constantly revised. Being knowledgeable about current security measures is important for business travellers; check for changes before travelling. The following general suggestions will help business travellers expedite their security clearance and cope with the security procedures at airports:

- Arrive early. Most airlines advise arriving at the airport up to two hours, and in some cases three hours, before the scheduled departure. Travellers who have special needs or concerns may be advised to arrive even earlier.
- Carry proper identification. Acceptable government-issued photo identification such as a passport is required for all international travel and when crossing the U.S.–Canada border by air.
- When possible, check in and print a boarding pass or request an electronic confirmation sent to your mobile device before arriving at the airport. By taking this step and having only a carry-on bag, you can proceed directly to security, bypassing the queue at the ticket counter.
- Inspect your bags and remove any prohibited items. A list of currently prohibited items is available on the airline website.
- Follow the screening guidelines. Keep your identification and boarding pass in a location that is easy to access; wear shoes that can be easily removed. If you are travelling with a laptop computer, you may need to take it out of the carrying case for screening. No two airport security areas process travellers in exactly the same way. Be prepared to make adjustments to what is required.

AIR CANADA

A STAR ALLIANCE MEMBER

ABC HYPHEN

ECONOMY CLASS

CANCUN
CUN > **TORONTO** **YYZ**

Gate	Zone	Seat
N/A	**5**	**16A**

Flight	Boarding	Date
AC1811	**11:30**	**22 MAY**

Remarks   Airline Usage
                                              0001

Booking Reference   Ticket Number
NQPDVI   **0142147522114**

OPER BY/PAR AIR CANADA ROUGE

Air Canada Electronic Boarding Pass sent to a mobile device enables a traveller to board a flight paper free.

Relaxed security measures, dedicated lanes, and kiosks are available in some airports for travellers with membership in Trusted Traveller Programs such as *Nexus* and *TSA Pre✓*. Details can be found at www.cbsa-asfc.gc.ca/prog/nexus/menu-eng.html and www.dhs.gov/trusted-traveler-programs. Low-risk travellers who qualify are not required to remove their coats or shoes, or to present their toiletry bag at security.

Ground Transportation

Once executives arrive at their destination, they may need some type of ground transportation to their hotel. That transportation may be a taxi or shuttle bus. When making arrangements, check taxi costs and the availability of shuttle services to the destination hotel. Some hotels provide a free shuttle service to and from the airport. Shuttle services are also available from private vendors, which may be less expensive than taxi service. Limousine service is also available at many airports, the cost being approximately the same as taxi service.

If executives must attend meetings at several locations during their stay, renting a car may be the most economical and convenient method of ground transportation. Car rental agencies are available at most airports. Cars may also be rented through airlines or travel agents or on the Internet. When renting a car, specify the make and model preferred; the date, time, and location the car will be picked up and returned; and always request a vehicle navigation system—Global Positioning System (GPS). Most car rental agencies have age restrictions; depending on the agency, the person renting the car must be at least 21 or 25.

Hotel Reservations

Hotel reservations can be made by telephone, through travel agents, and online through hotel and/or travel websites. Always check for booking fees or cancellation restrictions when making reservations. The lowest room rate may require immediate payment and may not be refundable if the reservation must be cancelled. Some hotels provide breakfast at no additional charge, and most have business centres with computers, copiers, fax machines, and other equipment for use by business travellers. Tablets, smartphones, and other mobile devices are standard equipment for travelling executives. Wireless Internet access from a traveller's room is generally available in most hotels. Meeting rooms are also available in many hotels. If you are making hotel reservations directly with the hotel, let the reservations clerk know the equipment and/or meeting rooms that are needed and whether the traveller will arrive late. You can simply ask the hotel to "guarantee" the room for late arrival; this procedure ensures that the hotel room is not released to someone else. You will, however, be charged for the room should the traveller not arrive and/or not call the hotel to cancel within the time permitted in their cancellation policy guidelines.

Car Travel

If an executive is travelling only a few hundred kilometres, he or she may prefer to travel by car. Some executives use cars furnished by the company; the company pays gasoline expenses. Other executives are reimbursed on a per-kilometre basis for any job-related car travel. Your responsibilities for a trip by car may include determining the best route to follow, making hotel reservations, and identifying restaurants along the way. You can find this information yourself on the Internet by using Google Earth, Google Maps, or Yahoo Maps. Smartphones with a navigational application installed can be used to locate "just-in-time" information related to restaurants, tourist sites, and other attractions within the proximity of the mobile device. Members of the local affiliate of the Canadian Automobile Association (CAA) can choose to obtain maps and hotel and restaurant information from them rather than from the Internet.

Rail Travel

Long-distance rail travel is a seldom-used option in most parts of Canada, as it can potentially take more time than travelling by air. Travelling short distances by rail, such as the Via Rail run between Montreal and Toronto or the Amtrak service in the United States, may be faster than flying when you factor in the extra time required to drive to the airport and pass through security. Train stations are generally located close to the city centre, and their fares are usually less expensive than airfares. Travel by train allows the executive the freedom to work during a trip using a mobile device. First-class and sleeping accommodations are available on trains, along with coach accommodations for more economical travel. Reservations and information on routes, schedules, and rates are available on the *Via Rail Canada* site for Canada and the *Amtrak* site for the United States.

International Travel

Because of the increasingly global nature of business, executives must sometimes make trips abroad. As an administrative professional, you need to know how to make arrangements for international travel. You should also know something about the business culture of the country the traveller is visiting.

Flights and Appointments

We covered various flight classifications earlier in this chapter; however, travellers should be aware that on international flights, weight and size restrictions for luggage may vary from one airline to another. International travellers must arrive at the airport earlier than domestic travellers; most airlines suggest arriving two to three hours before the flight to allow sufficient time for check-in, which can be more involved for international flights.

If you are involved in setting up appointments or meetings for the executive, remember the time zone differences. Jet lag can limit an executive's effectiveness. Since it takes the body about a day to adapt to the new environment for each time zone crossed, try to give the traveller an extra day to recover from the trip before scheduling meetings.

If possible, you should not schedule appointments in the office for the day before the executive leaves on a trip, or for the day the executive returns. The day before a trip is usually busy in preparation for the trip, and when the executive returns from a trip, he or she must again contend with time zone changes.

Travel Documents and Currency

International travellers need a passport. Travellers may also need a visa, health-related documents, and local currency.

Passports

A Canadian **passport** is an official travel document issued by the Government of Canada that certifies the identity and citizenship of an individual and facilitates their travel abroad. A passport is required to enter most countries; even if a country does not explicitly require a passport, having one in your possession when you cross any border is a good idea because it shows proof of your identity and citizenship. For many years, Canadians were not required to present passports when entering or travelling within the United States. Since the events of 9/11, however, border security procedures have become more rigorous. Official government identification is required of citizens who are crossing the Canada–U.S. border by car for any length of time. A passport, a Nexus identification card, or an enhanced driver's licence (which is currently available in four provinces) is acceptable when crossing the Canada–U.S. border by land or sea. Possession of a Nexus card gives the holder access to designated priority crossing lanes at many Canada–U.S. border crossings. When all occupants of a car have a Nexus card, the vehicle occupants can often bypass a long queue of waiting vehicles at busy border crossings.

Passport application forms can be obtained from a regional passport office or a designated Service Canada receiving agent location. However, it is recommended that you visit Canada.ca/passport for the most updated version of the passport application forms; there, you can open and complete online a PDF-fillable form to download, print, and submit. Applications submitted in person before an agent can be processed within two weeks (10 business days); applications submitted by mail or through a designated receiving agent can be processed within four weeks (20 working days). Canada.ca/passport has more information on the complete passport

Courtesy of Citizenship and Immigration Canada

FIGURE 14-1
Simplified Renewal Application Process

When you use the Simplified Renewal Application Process, you do not need to submit your proof of Canadian citizenship, supporting identification, or guarantor information, as you would have required in the general application process. However, you must submit your previous passport with your Simplified Renewal Application. To be eligible for Simplified Renewal you must have been 16 years of age or older at the time of your previous application, and the name on the form must be exactly the same as it appears on page 2 of the submitted passport. Along with your application form, the required fee, and two photos (taken within six months of the date the application is submitted with the name and address of the photographer and date the photos were taken stamped on the back), you must submit a previous Canadian passport that:
- was/is valid for five (5) or ten (10) years;
- is not damaged;
- was never reported lost or stolen; and
- is still valid or expired for no more than one year.

application process. Figure 14-1 details the Simplified Renewal Application Process.

Travellers are responsible to ensure that their passport is valid for travel. Many countries require that your passport be valid for several months after the date you plan to leave; otherwise, the traveller may be refused entry. Each country sets its own rules, so you should consult the travel advice and advisories at travel.gc.ca/advice to confirm the requirements of each of your destination countries.

Adult applicants can choose to apply for a passport that is valid for five or ten years from the date of issue. As soon as it is received, sign it to render it valid and enter your personal information and emergency contacts. Keep the passport with you while travelling in foreign countries; do not leave it unattended in your luggage, vehicle, hotel room, or elsewhere. It is also a good idea to photocopy page 2 of your passport to carry separately from your passport. You can also email it and other important travel documents to yourself, send it to your epost account if you have one, or upload it to your cloud storage so that you can access the documents quickly if they are lost or stolen while you are travelling.

Since 2013, all Canadian passports have been issued as 36-page electronic passports, or ePassports. These ePassports reduce the risk of tampering and identity fraud by including a digital facial image and other digital security features unique to the Government of Canada. Details about the passport holder appear in multiple places that can be scanned and compared with the personal data stored on the ePassport chip. Extra security features reduce processing times at border crossings and other Canadian entry points by enabling machine-assisted verification, where available. This technology helps border officials determine that the passport is authentic and confirms the identity of the holder.

A link to Canada's Passport Program site is provided on the MindTap site that accompanies this textbook.

Visas

A visa is a document granted by a foreign government that permits a traveller to enter and travel within a particular country. It is usually in the form of a stamped notation on a passport, indicating that the bearer may enter the country for a certain period of time. Rules and restrictions for visas vary from country to country. Some countries require the traveller to apply for and obtain a visa prior to the trip. Be sure to check with the consulate of the country in question sufficiently in advance of the executive's trip. To assist you, Passport Canada provides links to consulates (diplomatic missions) on its website.

Health-Related Documents and Precautions

Some countries require people entering the country to have had specific vaccinations or health tests, such as testing for contagious diseases. Records documenting these tests or vaccinations may be required for travel to the country. The entry requirements for a particular country should be checked before every trip in case of changes; for example, many countries have enacted specific practices in response to the 2014 Ebola outbreak. The Passport Canada website provides current travel reports on safety and security, local laws and customs, entry requirements, health conditions, and other travel warnings. A travel agency or the website of the country to be visited can also supply information about required vaccinations or tests.

Before leaving for a foreign country, the traveller should check with a physician concerning any medical issues. Travellers who take prescription medicine should order enough medicine to cover their needs while they are away and take some extra medicine as a backup in case some of the medicine is lost or the trip lasts longer than planned. Do not pack prescription medicine in checked baggage; use your carry-on luggage for your medication, written prescriptions, and the contact information for the doctors who prescribed the medication and the pharmacists who filled the prescriptions.

The environmental factors in foreign countries can differ from those in Canada, and it is easy to develop some type of illness as a result of another country's food, water, or climate. A physician can prescribe medications for colds or stomach-related illnesses.

Tap water in another country may be safe for local residents; however, it may contain different microbes from the water in Canada, thus causing possible digestive problems. To be safe, use purified water at all times, even when brushing your teeth, washing your hands, or rinsing raw foods. For the same reasons, you may want to avoid consuming ice served in drinks. Many restaurants and markets serve and sell purified water.

Currency

Before leaving Canada, money can be exchanged at banks and currency exchange offices for the currency of the country being visited. If tipping is expected in the destination country, it is useful to have a supply of small-denomination notes in the appropriate currency. More money can be exchanged as needed upon arrival at the destination country. Any currency left over at the end of a trip can be exchanged back into Canadian currency. The rate of exchange for various countries is published in the newspaper and is available online. Several websites provide currency converter utilities that show equivalent amounts in two or more currencies. To find such a website, search the Internet using the term "currency converter." It is always a good idea to be aware of the exchange rates before travelling to another country and, once in the destination country, to pay attention to the exchange rates, which can change daily. Exchange rates are not always the same; for example, the rate at a bank may be more favourable than at an airport or less favourable than at a money exchange.

The proliferation of ATMs (automated teller machines) throughout the world has made it much easier to obtain funds while travelling. Cash in the currency of the country is dispensed from the ATM. The exchange rate is automatically calculated, and the traveller's account is debited in Canadian currency. Many companies establish accounts for executives to utilize while travelling on business. When you use a credit card to make purchases quoted in a foreign currency, the credit card company will automatically apply the current daily exchange rate to the charge on your account.

Transportation Arrangements

You may need to make local travel arrangements within a country. Hotel and rail arrangements should be made before arriving. Car arrangements may be made after arriving.

International Car Rental

Travel agencies can arrange for car rentals before executives arrive in a country, or cars can be rented after they have arrived. In most countries, a Canadian driver's licence is sufficient. You may obtain an International Driving Permit from a local CAA office. Travellers must have appropriate insurance. They should also familiarize themselves with the driving regulations of the country they are visiting. Driving conditions are often quite different in other countries. For example, the steering wheel may be mounted on the right side of the car, or the country's custom may be to drive on the left side of the road.

International Rail Travel

Many countries, particularly those in Europe, have excellent rail service. Service is frequent, relatively inexpensive, and a traveller can get from one European city to another in a relatively short period of time with limited inconvenience. The trains are clean, and the accommodations are comfortable. Underground rail and bus transportation are also convenient and are inexpensive ways to travel in many European countries.

Cultural Differences

Travellers need to be knowledgeable about and sensitive to the customs and culture of the country they are visiting. Business practices can differ greatly from country to country. For example, in some countries, business gifts are expected. In others, business gifts are not particularly welcomed. If a gift is given it should be small: a nice pen or a memento representative of Canada. Executives must be aware of customs and taboos when giving gifts to avoid inadvertently offending someone. Figure 14-2 lists some gift taboos.

A basic understanding of the culture of the people in the country where the executive is travelling will help you make appropriate travel arrangements. Information about other countries may be obtained from a variety of sources:

- *Consulates of the country to be visited.* (A **consulate** is an office of a government in a foreign city that acts to assist and protect citizens of the consul's country.) These offices usually have printed materials and information available on their websites. They are also willing to answer questions about local customs and culture.
- *Travel books.* These books, available at libraries and bookstores, generally contain information about local customs and business practices.

Books about doing business with a particular country being visited. These books are also available at libraries and bookstores.

- *Seminars and short courses.* The company may arrange for consultants to assist personnel in understanding the culture abroad. Local colleges and universities often provide short courses or one-day seminars on the culture of various countries and tips on doing business with particular countries.
- *The Internet.* Numerous articles are available that review cultural differences internationally. It is also a good source for finding books concerning cultural differences.

Here are some general rules that apply to international travel:

- Learn the appropriate greeting for the country you will be visiting.
- Learn how to say "please" and "thank you" in the language of the country.
- Have business cards printed with your name and your company name in both English and the language of the country you are visiting.
- Do not criticize the people or customs of the country you are visiting. Show appreciation for the music, art, and culture of the country.
- Remember that business generally is more formal in other countries than it is in North America.
- Dress appropriately: business suits for men and conservative dresses or suits for women. Although dress in North America has become more casual than in the past, you cannot assume that the same is true for international organizations. Casual business dress generally does not imply a professional image. It may be seen as sloppy dress. It is also important to be well groomed.
- Eat the food that is offered you; do not ask what you are being served; show appreciation to your host. (If you do have allergies or religious limitations, try to communicate your restrictions to your host in advance or politely inform them of foods you cannot eat but suggest that you could try other items.)
- Be courteous and respectful at all times.

Answer the questions about international travel in Self-Check A.

FIGURE 14-2
Understanding Gift Etiquette

- In English-speaking countries, including Britain, Ireland, and Australia, gifts are not expected and might even be considered inappropriate. Business gifts are also rarely exchanged in Spain and France.
- Gift giving is important in China, Japan, the Philippines, Russia, and Eastern European countries.
- When visiting China, present your gift to the Chinese official at your first meeting.
- In Korea, it is rude to open a gift in front of the donor.
- When giving gifts, be certain the gift is made in Canada. For example, it would be inappropriate to give a gift to someone from China that was made in that country.
- Appropriate gifts include pens, pen-and-pencil sets, or other desktop items such as a small box or paperweight. Items from your home province and books of historical areas of your province are also appropriate.
- Photo albums containing pictures of the people you met on your trip are appropriate gifts.
- Flowers are *not* a universally acceptable gift to take to someone who is hosting you in their home. If flowers *are* acceptable, the colour and type of flower are important. For example, in Italy, chrysanthemums are displayed mainly at funerals. In Brazil, purple flowers signify death.
- In France, it is appropriate to take flowers to a dinner host. Chrysanthemums (primarily funeral flowers) or red roses (indicating romantic intent) should not be sent. Chocolates are also an acceptable gift for the French dinner host.

Travel Procedures

How travel arrangements are made depends on the company where you work. Large organizations may have a travel department that follows administrative guidelines to organize and book travel for all employees. Smaller firms may expect that individuals will make their own travel arrangements, while others will use a travel agency to schedule all company travel. This agency becomes knowledgeable about the needs of the company, thereby providing the unique services the company requires. Whether you contact the travel agency on your supervisor's behalf or make the arrangements yourself, as an administrative professional you will likely have a role in making travel arrangements.

If an executive is travelling by air, you need to know the name of the preferred airline (if the executive has a preference) along with the frequent flyer number. A **frequent flyer program** is an incentive program offered by most airlines that provides a variety of awards after the accumulation of a certain number of mileage points. Awards may include upgrades from economy to first class and free airline tickets.

You should also determine whether the flight is to be direct (if possible) or whether the executive is willing to change planes. Budget may be a consideration and less expensive flights are sometimes available if the executive is willing to change planes. The downside of changing planes is the hassle of getting from one flight to another and the increase in travel time. If the change occurs in the United States, it may mean collecting baggage, clearing customs, and repeating the boarding security check once again.

You should also know the seating preference of the executive—aisle or window—as well as the preferred class of flight—first class, business class, premium economy, or economy—which may be dictated by company policy.

If you are making arrangements for more than one top-level executive to travel to the same location at the same time, company policy may dictate that the executives fly on separate airlines. In case of a serious accident, both executives would not be lost to the company.

If an executive is travelling by rail, you need to know similar information: type of accommodations (coach or first class), sleeping accommodations (if travelling on the train for more than one day), and ticket delivery (whether tickets will be picked up at the train station, mailed, or delivered).

Skills @ Work

The first time you help to plan a trip for an executive, talk with the person about his or her travel preferences. If you are to be an effective agent, you must have the following information:

- Flight preferences—class of accommodations, seating, meals
- Hotel preferences—price range, number of nights, single or double room, size of bed (full, queen, king)
- Car rental preferences—type of car, size, make, model, number of days of usage, and pickup and drop-off locations
- Reimbursement policies of the company—whether a **per diem** rate (daily food allowance for which no receipts are required) is in effect or receipts are required for meals and other travel expenses
- Arrangements for transportation to airport or train station
- Appointments to be made—where, when, and with whom
- Materials—business cards, smartphone, laptop, and so on
- Person in charge while the executive is away
- Correspondence and calls—how they will be handled in the executive's absence
- The executive's credit card number or company account number for charging tickets, hotel, car rental, and so on

When you are first made aware of an upcoming trip, open a file folder where you can store notes and other information relating to the trip. Create an electronic folder for documents and/or open a new section in OneNote to track your preparations. Details of the trip are then available for instant referral when needed.

Arrangements by a Travel Agency or Travel Department

Travel agencies are companies that offer travel advice and make travel arrangements for clients. They book flights and arrange for online delivery of confirmations, make hotel reservations, arrange car rentals, and perform specialized services that the executives may need (such as obtaining workspace or meeting space at the destination). They prepare an itinerary, which lists airlines, flight numbers, departure and arrival times, hotel reservations, and car rental arrangements. Travel agencies invoice the company directly for the cost of tickets and any other expenses that they may have incurred on a behalf of a client, such as a deposit to guarantee a hotel reservation for late arrival. Since they no longer receive commissions from airlines, a fee will be charged if the service provided is limited to making flight arrangements. Commissions received by travel agencies from hotels and other service industries when services are booked may help to minimize charges to the client. Travel agencies may also provide 24-hour assistance to travellers who encounter problems such as cancelled or delayed flights.

In a large organization, a travel department will provide many of the same services. They do not usually offer travel advice but will have an in-depth knowledge of organizational policy and traveller preferences.

People @ Work

Travel Agent

A travel agent is a person who makes travel arrangements, such as airline, hotel, and car reservations, for clients. Travel agents provide information and offer advice on travel destinations as well as information on travel documents (passports, visas, and certificates of vaccination), travel advisories, and currency exchange rates. Most travel agents work for travel agencies or tour operators; some are self-employed. As an administrative assistant, you may provide information on the travel needs of executives or co-workers to a travel agent who will make the travel arrangements.

Arrangements by the Assistant

If your organization does not work with a travel agency, you may have the responsibility of making the travel arrangements directly.

Making these arrangements online is the most efficient method of doing so, although in some instances, you may find it necessary to telephone the airlines, hotels, and car rental agencies directly. All major airlines have a website where you can check flight availability and compare costs. One-stop online travel-booking sites such as Expedia and Travelocity can be used to compare not only costs but also the airlines offering the most direct route for a particular trip.

Both sites negotiate and consolidate fares directly with major airlines and offer below-market deals to consumers. Before confirming arrangements, ensure that you are familiar with any limitations linked to these special fares. Can they be changed or upgraded at a later date? Are they valid for standby on other flights? Can points on a frequent flyer program be accumulated?

You may assist executives with travel arrangements by determining passport and visa requirements, checking on currency needs, researching health issues in the country to be visited, making hotel reservations, arranging car rental, and arranging rail transportation. You may also be responsible for the following:

- Preparing a complete itinerary
- Completing a Travel Advance Fund form to obtain funds in advance of the trip
- Preparing and assembling materials for the trip
- Checking the calendar
- Confirming appointments
- Determining how matters are to be handled while the executive is away

Prepare an Itinerary

Once you have determined where and when the executive is to travel and after you have made the appropriate travel arrangements, you need to prepare an itinerary. The itinerary is a must for you and your employer. The **itinerary**, a detailed outline of the trip, is a record of all trip arrangements for you and the executive. An itinerary should include flight numbers, airport names, departure and arrival times, hotel arrangements, car rental information, appointments, and any other pertinent information. If you are working with a travel agency, it will provide an itinerary that includes flight, hotel, and car information. However, an agency does not have the information on appointments and other special information. The executive needs an itinerary that reflects *all* the activities on the trip. You are responsible to compile all the details into one document. It is a good idea to prepare multiple copies of the itinerary:

- One for the executive
- One for the executive's family
- One for the person who will be in charge while the executive is away
- One for your files

Figure 14-3 (on page 267) shows an itinerary prepared by the administrative professional. If the executive is travelling from one time zone to another, time zones should be included on the itinerary; otherwise, they are not necessary.

Another option for creating an itinerary is to use software applications like TripIt and Flight Tracker to consolidate all travel details. TripIt automatically creates an itinerary, provides links to maps for hotels, and when used with Flight Tracker, advises the traveller of flight interruptions or delays. The itinerary can be shared with other people, and as the travel organizer, you can make changes that are automatically communicated to the traveller. You can also print out a hardcopy of the itinerary as backup for the mobile application. Check it out. A link to Tripit.com is on the MindTap site accompanying this textbook.

Obtain Travel Funds

Companies differ in how they handle funds for trips. Airline tickets may be charged directly to the company, or the

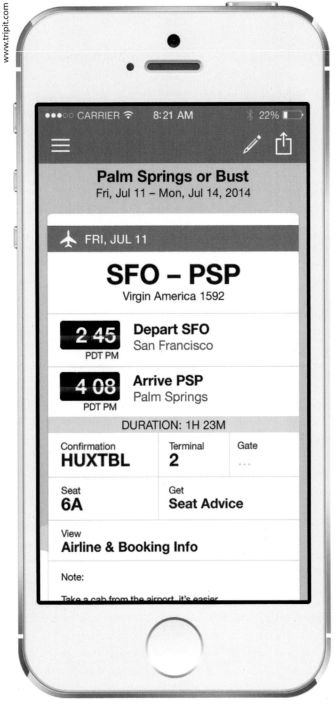

Use TripIt to organize all trip details into one comprehensive itinerary.

she leaves on the trip. Another practice is for the executive to use a credit card or, when he or she needs cash, an ATM to pay the expenses; reimbursement is then arranged by the company upon returning from the trip. Most company policies require employees to turn in a receipt for an expense above a certain amount.

Prepare and Organize Materials

Several items may be needed for a trip. If it is an international trip, items such as passports, medications, business cards, and small gifts may be necessary. Whether the trip is domestic or international, several items usually must be prepared, such as reports for meetings and presentation materials.

Once the materials are prepared, the administrative professional assembles the appropriate number of copies and gives them to the executive. The traveller needs items such as the following:

- E-ticket confirmation and possibly a boarding pass
- Passport and visa if travelling to a country where a visa is required
- Itinerary
- Hotel and/or car rental confirmation
- Credit cards and currency
- Business cards
- Special materials, reports, or contacts for appointments
- Presentation materials
- Laptop, tablet, or smartphone and the necessary accessories:
  - charging cables and voltage adapter for destination country if voltage is different
  - updated data plans to cover the period and destination of travel
  - SIM card(s)—advise relevant parties of new phone numbers
  - research on how the traveller can quickly and easily obtain necessary data plans/SIM cards in the destination country or top up the account balances
- Reading materials

Check Appointments

Check both your supervisor's calendar and your calendar, to see whether any in-office appointments have been scheduled for the period when your supervisor will be away. If so, find out whether they are to be cancelled or whether someone else in the company will handle them. Then, notify the people involved. Also check other files, such as reminder files or pending files, to see whether any matters need to be handled before the executive leaves.

Email or call people the executive plans to see during the trip to confirm the appointments. Obtain or verify addresses and make a note of these addresses on the itinerary. Update your supervisor's electronic calendar to include any additional

traveller may pay for the tickets and be reimbursed later. Hotel, meals, and car rental may be charged on a credit card provided by the company. Another practice is for the individual to be given a cash advance to cover all expenses of the trip. To do so, the individual fills out a travel fund advance form or requisition before leaving, indicating how much money he or she will need for lodging, meals, and so on. The company advances the money to the employee before he or

Sometimes when a manager is away and we are not sure how to handle something, we find ourselves thinking we cannot do the job. We may even become frustrated and negative about our abilities. Soft skills have been stressed throughout this book. We know that people lose their jobs more often due to a lack of "soft skills" rather than a lack of knowledge or technological skills. We also know from research that one of the most significant differences between high and low achievers is their attitude. High achievers maintain a positive attitude. They believe they can perform their job well, make a difference on the job, and solve problems. People with a negative attitude often believe they cannot perform their job well so they do not really try. Do not confuse a positive attitude with a Pollyanna attitude (a foolishly or blindly optimistic attitude). People who have a positive attitude do not see everything in life as wonderful. However, they do see ways to change a bad situation.

Think now about your attitude. Is it generally positive or generally negative? Answer the questions in Self-Check B.

Assuming you accept the importance of achieving and maintaining a positive attitude, answer the following questions:
- What is a positive attitude?
- How do you go about achieving and maintaining a positive attitude?

Attitude is defined as "a state of mind or feeling with regard to some matter or position." A positive attitude merely means that you believe in yourself; you believe that you have the power to make positive things happen in your life. Even though you might believe you have a positive attitude, consider these situations:
- Do you procrastinate in your coursework, putting off homework to the last minute and then doing a poor job?
- Do you engage in activities harmful to your health even though research shows the behaviour to be harmful?
- Are you extremely critical of everyone, including yourself?

If you answered yes to any of these questions, chances are your actions do not always reflect what you believe is a positive attitude. So how do you go about achieving and maintaining a positive attitude? Here are some suggestions:
- Practise visualization. Picture yourself in positive situations where you are achieving your goals and solving your problems.
- Listen to yourself talk. Do you often say, "I don't think I can do that" or "I know I won't be successful on that job"? Control your inner voice. Say to yourself—silently or out loud—"I didn't mean that. I know I can do the job well and be successful, and here is how I will be successful." Then think through the ways that will make you successful in the particular situation you are confronting.
- Remind yourself often of your past successes.
- Surround yourself with positive people and ideas. Do not spend time with negative people. They can sap your energy and positive resolve.
- Continue trying to achieve whatever is important to you until you are successful.

SELF-CHECK B

1. Do you think of yourself as successful in most situations? _____

2. Do you expect to do a good job? _____

3. Do you think about your failures often? _____

4. Are your best friends positive or negative people? _____

5. Now think of a time when you had a negative expectation of an action or event. Describe that expectation. Did it come true? _____

Chapter Summary

The summary will help you remember the important points covered in this chapter.
- Airlines offer three broad flight classifications—first class, business class, and economy (or coach).
- First-class accommodations are the most expensive and most comfortable of the three flight classes, typically offering individual "sleeping pods," power ports and Internet access, better food, personalized service, and complimentary alcoholic beverages.

- Business-class accommodations are slightly more expensive than economy and offer sleeping pods or more spacious seating, power ports and Internet access, complimentary alcoholic beverages, headsets, recliner seats, and more legroom.
- Economy-class accommodations provide complimentary pop, fruit juice, water, tea, or coffee, and may provide snacks and, for a fee, meals. Seats are closer together and less service is provided. Economy class is the least expensive flight class.

- Premium economy offers benefits similar to business class, including larger and more comfortable seats, complimentary refreshments, increased baggage allowance, and priority boarding.
- In addition to flying, the executive may also travel by car or by rail. A local affiliate of the CAA can provide information for car travel, and the appropriate railroad can provide information about rail travel.
- When travelling internationally, the executive needs to be sensitive to different customs and cultures. The executive should take business cards with his or her name and the company name printed in both English and the language of the country being visited.
- Jet lag can be a factor in international travel; it should be considered when scheduling appointments.
- Small business gifts may be appropriate for business associates when travelling abroad.
- A passport is necessary when travelling by air to the United States and anywhere internationally.
- A visa is a document granted by a foreign government that permits a traveller to enter and travel within a particular country.
- Automated teller machines dispense cash in the currency of the country being visited; the currency exchange is calculated automatically and the account is debited in Canadian currency.
- Before leaving for an international trip, the executive should check with a physician or health authority about health problems that may occur due to the food, water, or climate of the destination country, and/or vaccinations that may be required.
- Rail and bus transportation are other alternatives to renting a car when travelling internationally.

- In helping the executive to schedule travel, the administrative professional must know the dates and times of travel, the cities to be visited, hotel preferences, car rental preferences, appointments to be scheduled, materials needed, and so on.
- If the executive is travelling by air, the administrative professional must know the executive's preferences in terms of airline, class of flight, aisle or window seat, meal choices, and so on.
- Arrangements for travel can be made through travel agencies or by the administrative professional by calling the airline, hotel, and car rental agency directly or by booking online on airline websites or one-stop travel-booking sites.
- The administrative professional has several responsibilities before the trip, including preparing an itinerary, obtaining travel funds, preparing materials for the trip, checking the calendar, confirming appointments, and understanding how matters are to be handled while the executive is away.
- While the executive is away, the administrative professional should handle messages, appointments, and correspondence; make the appropriate decisions; maintain a positive attitude; and use time wisely.
- When the executive returns, the administrative professional must bring the executive up to date on significant happenings while he or she was away and assist with any correspondence and reports that need to be prepared as a result of the trip.
- Expense-tracking apps for smartphones can assist the executive in the tedious chore of collecting receipts.
- When completing the expense report, verify all receipts and ensure prohibited items such as alcoholic beverages are not included in the request for reimbursement.

Key Terms

first-class accommodations p. 257
business-class accommodations p. 257
jet lag p. 257
economy-class accommodations p. 257
passport p. 261
visa p. 262
ATMs p. 262

consulate p. 263
frequent flyer program p. 264
per diem p. 264
itinerary p. 265
Pollyanna attitude p. 271
attitude p. 271

Responses to Self-Check A

1. Contributions to the increase in international travel include the global economy; countries taking advantage of land, labour, and technical expertise available in all parts of the world; international markets; and technology.

2. You can find information concerning customs and cultures of other countries through consulates of the country to be visited, travel books, books about a particular country, the Web, and seminars and short courses offered at local colleges.

3. Six general rules that apply to international travel include the following (students may list any six items below):
   - Learn the appropriate greeting for the country you will be visiting.
   - Learn how to say "please" and "thank you" in the language of the country.
   - Have business cards printed with your name and your company name in both English and the language of the country you are visiting.
   - Do not criticize the people or customs of the country. Show appreciation for the music, art, and culture of the country.
   - Remember that business generally is more formal in other countries than it is in North America.
   - Dress appropriately; business suits for men and conservative dresses or suits for women. Be well groomed.
   - Eat the food that is offered you; do not ask what you are being served; show appreciation to your host.
   - Be courteous and respectful at all times.
4. Since the body generally takes about one day to adapt to the new environment for each time zone crossed, allow an extra day to recover from the trip before scheduling meetings.
5. Prescription medication should be packed in carry-on luggage in case checked luggage is lost. Take some extra medicine as a backup in case of loss or the trip lasting longer than planned. It is also a good idea to take written prescriptions and the contact information for the doctors who prescribed the medication and the pharmacists who filled the prescriptions.

Discussion Items

These discussion items provide an opportunity to test your understanding of the chapter through written responses and/or discussion with your classmates and your instructor.

1. Why do many business travellers travel by air? List and describe the three broad classes of airline flights.
2. Describe how an e-ticket for air travel works.
3. List eight general rules that apply to travelling internationally.
4. What are five guidelines that will help business travellers cope with the security procedures at airports?
5. List four responsibilities of the administrative professional during trip preparation.
6. Explain why a positive attitude is important, and list five steps to achieving a positive attitude.

Critical-Thinking Activity

Numerous groups of Chinese administrators from the Beijing office of CanAsian visit the Calgary office, and Mr. Albertson often serves as a host for these groups. Mr. Albertson has asked you to visit China with Keri-An Mahar, who has recently been made vice-president of human resources, to learn more about the Chinese culture so you can be of greater assistance to him when he hosts these groups. You will be in the Beijing office for one week. In preparation for your trip, you do some reading about culture and talk with one of the administrative professionals (who was born in China) about the culture. You think you are fairly well prepared. However, during the trip, some situations occur that make you feel embarrassed about your lack of preparation:

- The Chinese officials always offer you their business cards. You notice immediately that the cards have their names, addresses, and so on, in Chinese on one side and English on the other. You do have business cards, but your name and pertinent information are in English only.
- Small gifts are given to you in each office but you have nothing to offer in return.

- The Chinese officials take many photos of your visit; as you leave, they present both you and Ms. Mahar with photo albums.
- Since the trip was one week long, you took three bags with you. However, you were embarrassed as you went from the airport to the hotel because the Chinese host who met you insisted on carrying your bags.
- In the first meeting at the Beijing CanAsian office, you immediately extended your hand in greeting to each member of the Chinese group. Although they were very polite, you felt you had done something wrong.
- In an effort to show your friendliness, you immediately made small talk with the Chinese. An interpreter was present at all sessions. People were polite to you, but you sensed you had said or done something inappropriate.
- The Chinese hosts provided you with all lunches and dinners. The tables were filled with food, but you were not familiar with many of the dishes; the food was very different from Chinese food you had eaten in Canada. You politely refused several of the dishes offered. You wonder whether you made an error.

Respond to the following questions. Before you do, read the information in SCDCTA-14, found on the MindTap site (access to which is provided with the printed access card on the inside cover of your textbook). Additionally, discuss your answers with your classmates.

- What errors did you make, and what should have been done?
- What could you have done to prevent these errors?

Building Workplace Skills

Project 14-1 (Learning Outcomes 1 and 2)

Online Project

Mr. Albertson is visiting CanAsian's China office in Beijing from November 11 through November 16. Determine flight times and hotel arrangements by checking a website. The executive vice-president of the Beijing office, Pai Ying, will pick Mr. Albertson up at the airport. He will not need a car. He wants to leave the morning of Monday, November 11 and return the afternoon or evening of Saturday, November 16. He will fly first class and prefers low-calorie meals. He wants a nice hotel that includes a queen-size bed, a room for non-smokers, and exercise facilities. Mr. Albertson does not speak Chinese. His appointments while in China include the following:

November 14, 9 a.m., appointment with Chan Yi
November 14, 2 p.m., appointment with Sheng Mo
November 15, 10 a.m., appointment with Kuo Lu
November 15, 1 p.m., appointment with Niu Chih

Use a one-stop travel booking site such as Travelocity, Expedia, and/or your favourite booking site to determine the most appropriate flight times and hotel. Prepare an itinerary incorporating all details including the appointments. Note the number of hours on the itinerary for travel time; also note the time difference from Calgary to China. Submit the itinerary to your instructor.

Project 14-2 (Learning Outcomes 3 and 5)

While Mr. Albertson is in China, you ask one of your assistants, Luyin Wu, to sort the mail every day and ask the other assistant, Guy Beauchamp, to take care of telephone calls. You are devoting your time to a report that will take you several days to complete; you must have it finished by the time Mr. Albertson returns. Mr. Albertson calls in after being away three days to see whether any urgent items may need his attention. You tell him there is nothing. However, after hanging up, you decide to check the mail and the telephone calls. You discover that he should have been informed of two calls and three letters. You thought you were clear in your instructions to both Luyin and Guy that they should call your attention to any important items. You are upset with

them and call them in to voice your concerns. "I should have known you two would make a mess of the job." Both Luyin and Guy say they did not understand your instructions. You tell them you will take care of the mail and phone calls yourself. They are both concerned; Guy apologizes profusely and Luyin looks down and says nothing. The situation is tense in the office for the next few days.

Answer these questions:
- How should you have handled the situation?
- Did you demonstrate a positive attitude?

Once you have answered those questions, describe your role during Mr. Albertson's absence.

Project 14-3 (Learning Outcome 4)

On his return, Mr. Albertson gives you the receipts from his trip and asks you to complete the travel expense report for him. Use the expense form file SCDP14-3 and enter the following data. You may print the form and fill in the items by hand or, if available, open the form in Excel and complete it on the computer.

- *Hotel rate (including continental breakfast).* $225.63 each night (November 12 to November 15)
- *Taxi charges.* To Calgary airport—$25.75; to hotel—$55; to appointments on November 14—$75.12; to appointments on November 15—$92.15; to Beijing Airport—$30.55; To home—$65
- *Meals.* November 13—lunch $25.25; dinner $65.84. November 14—lunch with Chan Yi $105.25; dinner $50.55. November 15—lunch $30.33; dinner with Niu Chih $225.66

Project 14-4 (Learning Outcome 3)

Mr. Albertson has returned from a recent trip to B.C., during which he met with several people. He has asked you to write a follow-up letter to a potential client, Mr. Cai, who lives in North Vancouver.

- Use SCDP14-4 to prepare the letter.
- Writing as Mr. Albertson, thank Mr. Cai for meeting with you and indicate that you thought the meeting was very productive. Tell the client that the information he requested is provided in an enclosed brochure. Invite him to call you if he has any questions about the information. Indicate that you will call next week to discuss the information further.
- The client's name and address are shown below

Mr. Raymond Cai
Cai Inc.
1501 Eastern Avenue
North Vancouver, BC V7L 3G2

Project 14-5 (Learning Outcome 3)

You have been asked to find information about currency conversion amounts for three currencies: the euro, the U.S.

growth and career path; sometimes, changing jobs is a part of that growth. Ask yourself the questions posed in Self-Check A.

Now you are ready to begin thinking about the steps you need to take to identify a job that fits your skills and interests, apply for that job, and succeed at that job.

Sources of Job Information

One of the first things to do as you look for a job is to gather all the information you can about available job opportunities. Information is available through:

- The Internet
- Networking
- College and university placement offices
- Newspaper advertisements
- Employment and recruitment agencies—public, private, and temporary
- Professional organizations
- Direct contact

The Internet

A variety of resources for job seekers are available on the Internet. In addition to job listings, you will find tips for résumé and cover letter preparation and for interviewing. You are also able to research companies in which you have an interest and actually post your résumé on the Internet for employers' review. Check out some of the best-known big Canadian online job boards:

- WowJobs (www.wowjobs.ca) consolidates job postings from other job boards, classified ads, and company sites across Canada and around the world.
- Indeed (www.indeed.ca) will post your résumé for review by prospective employers.
- WorkBC (www.workbc.ca) lists job opportunities in British Columbia. Similar sites exist for each province in Canada.
- Public Service Commission of Canada (www.jobs-emplois.gc.ca) hosts a job board that posts positions available in the federal public service and provides

information on procedures about their regularly scheduled testing.

- Job Bank (jobbank.gc.ca) is Canada's one-stop online job board for employers, businesses, and job seekers. It provides listings of current job openings from coast to coast.
- Monster.ca (www.monster.ca) offers a career centre where you can gain access to career advice and tips on preparing a résumé and interviewing; you can also view job openings, employer profiles, and post your résumé online. Use the mobile app to search for jobs anytime, anywhere.
- Workopolis (www.workopolis.ca) allows you to post your résumé, save job searches, and receive job notices by email for positions in a variety of job categories. The online Resource Centre offers advice on résumé writing, interviewing, and networking
- CanadianCareers.com (www.canadiancareers.com) provides information on marketing yourself, exploring careers, and finding work.

These job boards provide some very useful job-search information and can be used to jump-start your job search by providing information on the kinds of jobs available and the skill sets employers are seeking. Using these big job boards, you can continue your search for jobs on individual corporate websites, on professional association websites, and on specialty sites such as CareerMBA.com.

Networking

Despite the millions of job listings available on the Internet, getting the job often depends on personal contacts. **Networking**, which is defined as "the process of identifying and establishing a group of acquaintances, friends, and relatives who can assist you in the job search process," has long been one of the best strategies for finding a job. In fact, some studies have shown that as many as 80 percent of jobs are obtained through some form of networking. Why? Employing and training a new employee costs an organization a considerable amount of money, so the organization wants to hire the right person. When human resource directors hear about potential employees from respected existing employees, they are more confident of the applicants' abilities and believe they can hire an excellent employee with limited risk.

How do you go about this traditional form of networking? If you have a part-time job, let management know you are ready for a full-time position. If you take part in a co-op program, let the organization know you are interested in a full-time job. Talk with friends in your community or church, or with associates in professional organizations to which you belong. You also might give them a copy of your résumé.

Networking is an excellent way to obtain job information.

Networking has migrated from the traditional to the online environment with membership in business-focused online social networking organizations such as LinkedIn. Joining is free with the option to upgrade later to premium paid services. Once you have joined, you create a profile that includes as much or as little information about your professional history as you wish to include; this profile acts like an online résumé. You can then build your own professional network by inviting your business and professional contacts to join you.

LinkedIn also maintains a job board that provides you with a listing of available positions that, based on your individual past searches, could be of specific interest to you.

College and University Placement Offices

Most colleges and universities maintain a placement office. Visit this office. Your school may not receive enough calls from employers to provide positions for all students, but counsellors are usually well informed about job opportunities in the community. They know the employers who need entry-level workers, and they can match a job to your qualifications and abilities.

Newspaper Advertisements

Employers and employment agencies list available positions in local newspapers. These ads describe the positions and the qualifications required and may provide information about the salaries offered.

Employment Agencies

There are two types of employment agencies: public and private. **Employment and Social Development Canada** is the national public employment agency. You can visit their local office to speak with a counsellor in person or access their job postings online. An advantage of this federally funded government agency is that its services are provided free to Canadian job seekers.

Private employment agencies charge either you or the employing firm a fee. The employer pays the fee when an applicant is hired. When you are responsible for the fee, you will be asked to sign a contract with the employment agency. Ensure you understand how the fee is calculated (usually 5 to 10 percent of your first year's salary) and how it is to be paid.

Private employment agencies will generally administer standard tests on behalf of employers. Be prepared to demonstrate your abilities and skills with the following:

- Specific software packages, such as Microsoft Word, Excel, and PowerPoint
- Keyboarding speed and accuracy
- Grammar, punctuation, and proofreading
- Mathematical operations and problem solving

A **temporary agency** (one that offers temporary work) is not a source of job information in the usual sense. A temporary agency can place you in numerous different companies. Some organizations also use temporary agencies in a similar manner. Without either party having any long-term commitment, you can gain an understanding of where you want to work as a full-time employee, and potential employers get first-hand knowledge of prospective employees. Often, full-time employment can result from a temporary placement—a "win-win" situation for all involved.

Professional Organizations

If you are a member of a professional organization, in addition to networking at meetings and other functions, check whether the organization maintains a listing of jobs in your area. You can also ask other members whether they are aware of any openings.

Direct Contact

If you are interested in obtaining a position with a certain company or in a particular type of business, the **direct contact** or **cold call** (going directly to an organization without having an appointment, or sending a letter and résumé without knowing whether a job is available) is sometimes successful. Especially if you have a gift for selling yourself, you might find this approach beneficial. However, before you engage in the direct-contact approach, find out as much as you can about the company. Never restrict your job search to walk-ins only. It can be time-consuming, and often has little likelihood of success.

Researching and Applying for Jobs

Once you have identified sources of information about jobs, you are ready to research the organizations and apply for jobs. Having information about an organization will help you tailor your résumé and cover letter to illustrate how your qualifications meet their expectations. Do not focus your research on just one organization; rather, select several organizations that interest you.

Researching Organizations

Before applying for any job, spend some time learning about the organization—its mission and vision, its financial history, its products or services, its reputation, the length of time it has been in business, and how it treats its employees. How do you do this? There are several possibilities.

Since many organizations have websites, that is probably the best place to start your research. Review everything on the site—read about the history of the organization, its philosophy, its mission and values, its strategic direction, and information about its products or services. You can also follow these suggestions:

- Read periodicals, such as *Canadian Business*, which often profile some of the largest businesses in the country.
- Ask friends, relatives, and acquaintances what they know about the organization.
- Review an annual report of the company; most companies' annual reports are available online.
- Consult your local chamber of commerce or Better Business Bureau.
- Ask your college or university placement office for information.
- Check online to view the listing of *Canada's Top 100 Employers*—a link to this site can be found on the MindTap site for this textbook.
- Access Glassdoor (www.glassdoor.com) and LinkedIn to find out more about companies and the people who work at these companies.
- Use informal channels such as association blog sites or topic-specific blog sites to research an organization and its culture (i.e., the culture that organizations typically don't advertise).

Preparing a Résumé

The **résumé**, a concise statement of your background, education, skills, and experience, is an important part of your job application packet. Just as the letter of application is a sales letter, so is the résumé. It represents a very important product—YOU. The sections of a résumé may vary; there is no one perfect model. How you set up your résumé depends on your situation and how you want to present your qualifications. The following sections are common to most résumés though their placement may vary depending on the format you choose to use.

Heading

This section, much like a letterhead, is at the top of your résumé and contains your full name and contact information—address, personal telephone number, email, and social network profile if appropriate. Enhance the formatting of your name with a different typeface or font size; possibly use a graphic line to separate it from the next sections.

Objective

This section informs the reader the position you are seeking. It should be concise and give your résumé focus, and can be labelled *Career Objective*, *Job Objective*, or simply *Objective*. See the following examples.

Career Objective: A challenging position as an administrative professional with opportunities to use my technology and human relations skills.

If you know the area of work you want or the specific job title, use it. If you are interested in a specialized field or have a long-term goal, include it.

Job Objective: Legal Administrative Assistant with a long-range goal of being a law office manager.

Relevant Skills

In this section, identify your skill strengths. For example, list your computer skills, including your keyboarding skills and the various software packages in which you are proficient.

Education

List the schools you have attended and, if pertinent, the qualifications you have acquired. You might also list the specific courses, workshops, or programs of study you have taken, that pertain to the position you are applying for.

Employment History

List the companies where you have worked, the dates of employment, and your duties. You may want to reverse the order in which you present the education and experience sections on your résumé, presenting your most recent education and job experience first. When you have experience that directly relates to the job for which you are applying, list it first. Remember that the résumé is a sales piece. You want to call attention to your best-selling features first.

Accomplishments

This section allows you to detail your leadership and interpersonal skills, and provides evidence to future employers that you are a well-rounded person. If you have participated in special activities, maintained memberships in professional organizations, or achieved specific honours, list them here.

References

A reference is a person who can verify your academic ability and/or your work skills and habits, and is both willing and available to recommend you to employers. Choose your references carefully. Select those individuals who know your qualifications well and will take the time to respond to a reference request. It is inappropriate to include names of close relatives or personal friends.

Generally you should not list references on your résumé; the résumé is a place to highlight work experiences and skills. However, you may choose to include a heading "References" and the statement "References will be furnished on request."

Be sure to contact your references before beginning a job search. Let them know what you are doing and ask whether you can use them as a reference. Verify the addresses and phone numbers of your references, their current employment, and their job titles and duties. Keep your list of references current by contacting them periodically, especially when changing jobs, addresses, or your surname. An accurate list of references can be a determining factor in the hiring of one applicant over another.

While you may carefully select your references and confirm they are available to support your job application, remember that job recruiters may research Internet user groups and join discussions, "Google" your name, search for you on Facebook, and check out your LinkedIn profile to see what others say about you.

Your Online Image

Social media takes the personal and makes it public. The information you reveal, the words you use, and the images you post are there for everyone to see; be sure that the online profiles you created as a teenager in high school do not come back to haunt you when you enter the workforce. Showing yourself in silly or compromising situations may seem like harmless fun at any time, but such images can reflect badly on you in the workplace—causing you to miss a great job opportunity, or even to lose your job.

In the spring of 2011, a riot broke out after the Vancouver Canucks lost the last game in the Stanley Cup final. Smartphone images of the riot were instantly posted around the world and were later used to identify many of the individuals who participated. Some of these individuals lost sports sponsorships, educational scholarships, or jobs, and many of them were prosecuted. While you cannot control everything comprising your online image, make every possible effort to monitor it to ensure you have no online trail of illegal activities,

Professionalism @ Work

The Professional Résumé

Whichever style of résumé you prepare, keep these guidelines in mind.

- Always be accurate and honest when listing information on your résumé.
- Keep the résumé short—preferably one or two pages. If your résumé is longer than one page, be sure to include your name at the top of each page.
- Target your résumé to each job. Highlight those areas of your background or work experience that fit the position you are applying for.
- If you are a recent graduate and have held only part-time jobs, list them.
- If you have not had any paid work experience, list volunteer jobs or leadership positions you have held.
- Do not use personal pronouns (*I*, *me*, *you*). They are unnecessary and detract from the impact of the résumé.
- Describe your qualifications and skills in specific terms using action verbs; avoid vague language.
- Check your spelling and grammar usage. Read and reread the résumé several times. Ask someone who is a good proofreader and grammarian to review it.
- Avoid using abbreviations, with the exception of a degree designation.
- Use keywords in your résumé. Your document may be scanned by a computer that has been programmed to pick up on certain words that have been used in the advertisement; review the job ad for keywords and ensure you use them in your résumé. An administrative assistant should list specific software programs such as Microsoft Word, Corel Draw. Use "collaborative" or "team player" as keywords in your résumé; employers often seek people who work well with others.
- Take advantage of professional help when writing your résumé. Check Web sources, talk with your college or university placement representatives, and visit a bookstore or library for materials on résumé preparation.
- Avoid the use of résumé templates. Sell yourself and your skills by creating your own personalized templates with matching letterhead and résumé headings.
- Use high-quality, white, letter-sized paper for your résumé. Print on one side of the paper only. Do not fold or staple.
- Use a professional, neutral email address, such as rlsmith@yahoo.com. Never use an email address such as fungirl@me.com, partyhappy@look.com, or some equally unprofessional address.
- Include a link to your social networking site, especially when you know that the contents will present you in a positive light.

embarrassing party pictures, or rude or politically insensitive comments by or about you.

Depending on the type of job you seek and your employment history, you will likely choose one of three commonly used résumé formats—the **chronological résumé**, the **functional résumé**, or the **combination-style résumé**. Once your résumé has been created, you can publish it in a hardcopy or electronic format. In determining the format to use for your résumé, consider your purpose and background, and the requirements of the potential employer.

Chronological Résumé

Figure 15-1 (on page 284) illustrates the chronological résumé—the format most frequently used by job seekers. Education and experience are listed in separate sections in reverse date order, with the most recent entries listed first. This format is easy to read and interpret, and is best used when it relates directly to the job you seek, or when the jobs you have listed reflect increasing responsibility, which demonstrate your progress and growth.

Functional Résumé

The functional résumé works well for individuals who have good educational backgrounds and skills but little or no work experience. Rather than focusing on work experience, the functional résumé documents those skills and abilities that are most applicable to the specific job you are seeking. While the information included is the same as in a chronological résumé, the organization of content is different—your education, experiences, and activities are clustered into categories that support your career goals. This format is usually appropriate when you have developed skills that are more relevant to the job than to the heading labels, or when you have had periods of time when you did not work; for example, you took a break from your career to have or care for a child or to travel. The functional résumé allows you to de-emphasize these gaps and emphasize your skill sets. A functional résumé is shown in Figure 15-2 (on page 285).

Combination-Style Résumé

The combination-style résumé works best for the experienced worker who has held several different jobs and when skills, titles, and heading labels are equally impressive. The chronological format with functional subheadings allows you to present your experiences in reverse chronological skill set order. This format is not the best choice when you do not have numerous experiences that match a number of skills, or when you have multiple skills but a small number of different experiences (job titles or organizations for which you have worked).

Preparing Electronic Résumés

Human resources departments and recruiters use a variety of methods to process résumés. In addition to receiving hardcopy, print-based résumés, they, like job seekers, are using technology extensively. Not only do you need a traditional résumé with its bullets, bold headings, different font styles, and graphics to take with you to interviews, but you also need to prepare a version that can be submitted electronically to prospective employers. Many organizations have added sections to their home page that allow you to submit your résumé online. The content of your **electronic résumé** (statement of background and experiences submitted online) should be based on your hardcopy version. Résumé systems do NOT read résumés directly. They first convert the résumés to plain text and then read and process the plain text. Remove all the formatting enhancements and graphics from your résumé and save it as a plain text (.TXT) file so that résumé system software can then be used to search for keywords in stored résumés. This process helps the organization to narrow its search to the most suitable candidates. The plain text version of your résumé can either be embedded in the body of an email or sent as an email attachment.

Your attachment can also be formatted in Word or WordPerfect or converted to a PDF (portable document format) file. Converting it to a PDF file ensures that all the formatting enhancements you have used will be viewed by the reader just as you intended. PDF files cannot, however, be scanned by résumé software. When submitting your résumé and/or cover letter by email, check with the employer to determine which of these formats is preferred. It is possible that the employer will not open attachments due to the risk of a virus being present. If this is the case, use the job title in the subject line of the message and submit only one email message that contains both your cover letter and résumé in plain text format embedded in the body of the email.

FIGURE 15-1
Chronological Résumé

Colette Soros

2520 Boswell Avenue
North Vancouver, BC V7H 1L7

604-555-0113
e-mail: csoros@hotmail.com
linkedin.com/in/colettesoros

JOB OBJECTIVE

Administrative assistant with the opportunity to use technology and human relations skills

COMPUTER SKILLS

Keyboarding at 90 wpm; proficient in Windows, Word, Excel, PowerPoint, Access, Internet research,
and Web page design

EDUCATION

Capilano University, North Vancouver, BC, September 20-- to May 20--

Diploma in Administrative Systems (two-year program)

Courses studied: Business communications, organizational behaviour, management, accounting, English, psychology,
administrative procedures, and computer software

EXPERIENCE

Intern, Admissions Department, Capilano University, September 20-- to May 20--

- Prepared spreadsheets using Excel
- Keyed correspondence using Word
- Prepared first drafts of letters to students
- Filed correspondence on hard drive and discs
- Handled student inquiries
- Answered the telephone
- Assisted in designing class schedule

Receptionist, Martin Paper Company, June 20-- to August 20--

- Greeted visitors
- Answered the telephone
- Keyed correspondence

HONOURS

- Dean's List
- Lieutenant Governor's Silver Medal

REFERENCES

Furnished on request.

Arrange jobs in reverse chronological order and format job titles in bold for readability

Use bulleted lists to make résumé easier to read

You can also post your electronic résumé online to job boards or directly to the website of a specific organization, where you will find instructions for completing an online application form and uploading your résumé. Follow the guidelines for preparing a professional résumé and adapt it as follows for your electronic version. Remember, you are not creating a different résumé, merely altering the formatting of the print version:

- Use a single-column format; maximum of 65 characters to each line.
- Be sure your name is the first line on your résumé.

FIGURE 15-2
Functional Résumé

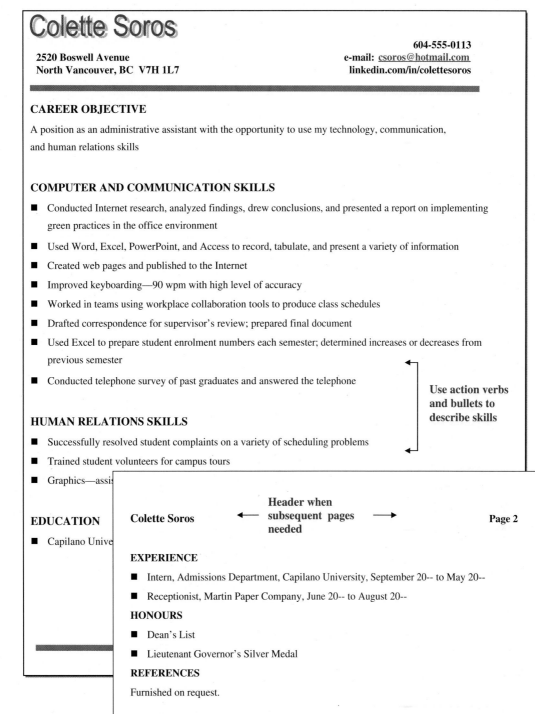

Colette Soros

2520 Boswell Avenue
North Vancouver, BC V7H 1L7

604-555-0113
e-mail: csoros@hotmail.com
linkedin.com/in/colettesoros

CAREER OBJECTIVE

A position as an administrative assistant with the opportunity to use my technology, communication, and human relations skills

COMPUTER AND COMMUNICATION SKILLS

■ Conducted Internet research, analyzed findings, drew conclusions, and presented a report on implementing green practices in the office environment

■ Used Word, Excel, PowerPoint, and Access to record, tabulate, and present a variety of information

■ Created web pages and published to the Internet

■ Improved keyboarding—90 wpm with high level of accuracy

■ Worked in teams using workplace collaboration tools to produce class schedules

■ Drafted correspondence for supervisor's review; prepared final document

■ Used Excel to prepare student enrolment numbers each semester; determined increases or decreases from previous semester

■ Conducted telephone survey of past graduates and answered the telephone

Use action verbs and bullets to describe skills

HUMAN RELATIONS SKILLS

■ Successfully resolved student complaints on a variety of scheduling problems

■ Trained student volunteers for campus tours

■ Graphics—assis

EDUCATION

■ Capilano Unive

Colette Soros   ← **Header when subsequent pages needed** →   Page 2

EXPERIENCE

■ Intern, Admissions Department, Capilano University, September 20-- to May 20--

■ Receptionist, Martin Paper Company, June 20-- to August 20--

HONOURS

■ Dean's List

■ Lieutenant Governor's Silver Medal

REFERENCES

Furnished on request.

- Use standard address format for the balance of your contact information (street, city, province or territory, postal code) placed on separate lines.
- If you have more than one telephone number, use a separate line for each.
- Use a basic, plain font (Times New Roman or Arial) and a font size of 11 to 12 points for the body.

- Use all caps for headings with a maximum size of 14 points rather than italics, bold, script, or underlining.
- Use well-known abbreviations; minimize the use of unfamiliar ones.
- Use keyboard characters such as asterisks (*), equal signs (=), tildes (~), and vertical separators (|) rather than bullets, graphic lines, shading, or boxes.

All of these techniques will mean that your résumé will be entered into the company's system in the "cleanest" format possible. The résumé software will then read the text to identify and extract important information about you such as your name, address, phone number, work history, years of experience, education, and skills. See the example in Figure 15-3.

Preparing a Cover Letter

The cover letter is generally the first contact you make with an organization and is the key to obtaining an interview. It is a sales letter; along with your résumé, it introduces you to the organization, attempts to arouse the prospective employer's interest, and gives you an opportunity to request an interview. Prepare it thoughtfully. Present your most relevant selling points, including your skills and your background. Its appearance, format, accuracy, arrangement, and content are extremely important in making a good impression on the reader. Follow these guidelines:

1. Start by introducing yourself; open with a brief statement of your qualifications. Let the person know you are

FIGURE 15-3
Electronic Résumé

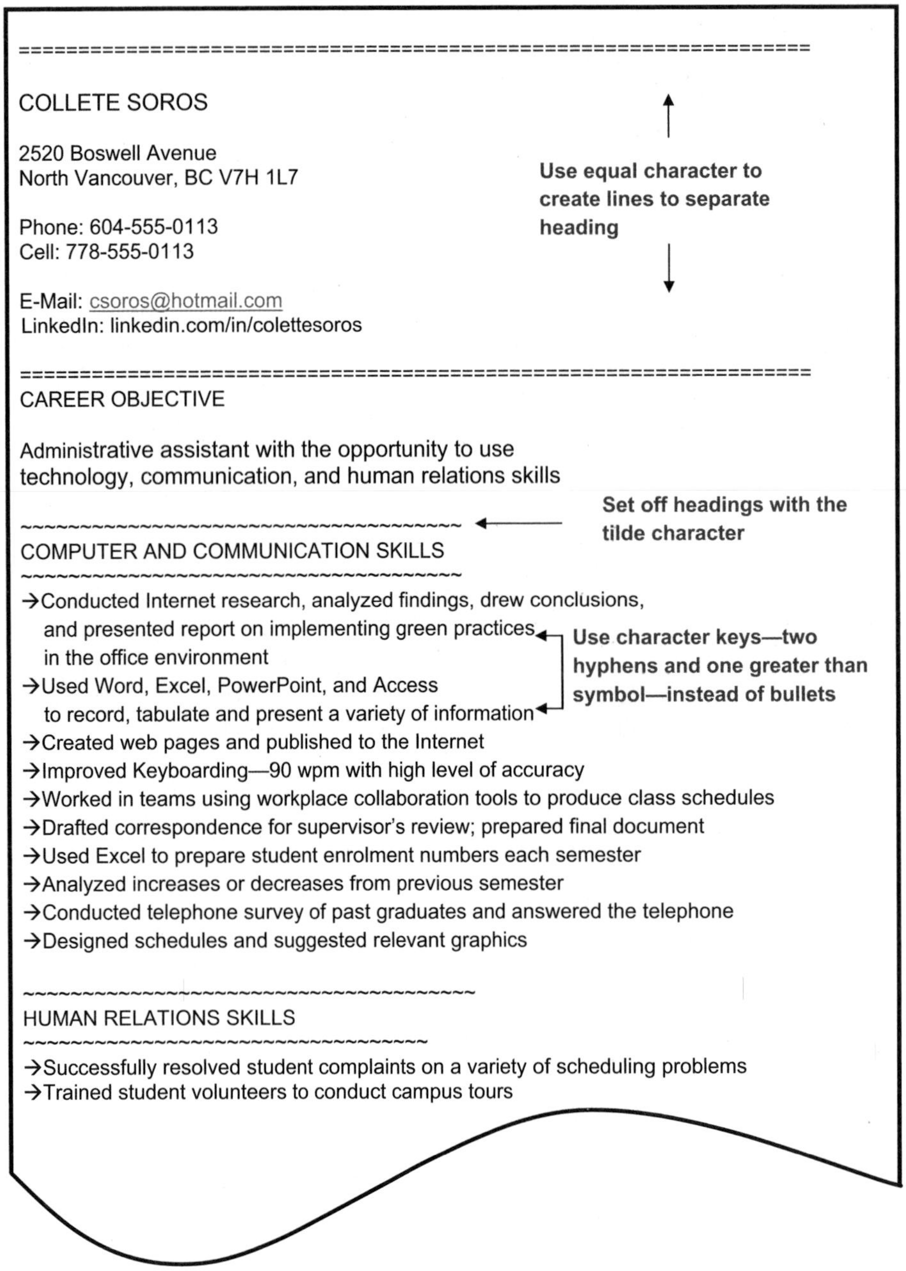

```
================================================================

COLLETE SOROS

2520 Boswell Avenue
North Vancouver, BC V7H 1L7

Phone: 604-555-0113
Cell: 778-555-0113

E-Mail: csoros@hotmail.com
LinkedIn: linkedin.com/in/colettesoros

================================================================
CAREER OBJECTIVE

Administrative assistant with the opportunity to use
technology, communication, and human relations skills

~~~~~~~~~~~~~~~~~~~~~~~~~~~~~~~~~~~~~~
COMPUTER AND COMMUNICATION SKILLS
~~~~~~~~~~~~~~~~~~~~~~~~~~~~~~~~~~~~~~
→Conducted Internet research, analyzed findings, drew conclusions,
   and presented report on implementing green practices
   in the office environment
→Used Word, Excel, PowerPoint, and Access
   to record, tabulate and present a variety of information
→Created web pages and published to the Internet
→Improved Keyboarding—90 wpm with high level of accuracy
→Worked in teams using workplace collaboration tools to produce class schedules
→Drafted correspondence for supervisor's review; prepared final document
→Used Excel to prepare student enrolment numbers each semester
→Analyzed increases or decreases from previous semester
→Conducted telephone survey of past graduates and answered the telephone
→Designed schedules and suggested relevant graphics


~~~~~~~~~~~~~~~~~~~~~~~~~~~~~~~~~~~~~~
HUMAN RELATIONS SKILLS
~~~~~~~~~~~~~~~~~~~~~~~~~~~~~~~~~~~~~~
→Successfully resolved student complaints on a variety of scheduling problems
→Trained student volunteers to conduct campus tours
```

Use equal character to create lines to separate heading

Set off headings with the tilde character

Use character keys—two hyphens and one greater than symbol—instead of bullets

Multiple, Team, and Virtual Interviews

You may have more than one interview for a particular position. For example, a human resources professional may interview you first. Next, you may interview with your prospective supervisor. Finally, you may have a group interview with your prospective team members.

A team interview may be with two or three or even five or six people. Although this type of interview sounds intimidating, it need not be. Follow these additional tips specifically for a successful team interview:

- When introductions are made, pay careful attention to the individuals' names—if you can do so unnoticed, jot down their names or initials to assist you during the interview.
- Focus on each individual as the person asks a question.
- Listen carefully to the question, jot down a few notes to remind yourself of key points, and answer the question succinctly.
- Make eye contact with people and, if possible, use their name when responding to a question.
- When you ask a question, ask it of the group. If one member of the group has asked a question or said something that you need clarified, address that individual.
- If you find yourself getting nervous, glance occasionally at people who have given you positive feedback—those with a friendly face, open body language, and positive reactions to your responses. Say to yourself, "This person likes me; I am doing well."
- Thank the group when the interview is completed. Use their names, if possible; it shows you were paying attention.

Occasionally organizations will conduct a **virtual interview** (using telephone or videoconferencing tools, a candidate is interviewed by an interviewer at a distant location). If you are applying for a job in another city in Canada or for a national firm with its head office in a city other than yours, it is not necessary for you or the interviewer to meet in the same city for an interview. A telephone conference call or computer conferencing with WebEx or Skype can easily be arranged. You can be interviewed by one or more interviewers via the telephone or participate in a virtual video interview from any location in the world.

If you are scheduled for a virtual interview, you need to be well prepared. When a camera is involved, most people get a little nervous. However, your goal is to relax and treat the situation as if the person interviewing you is in the same room.

Virtual interviews require similar preparation to face-to-face interviews. In addition to the previous hints, consider the following additional suggestions when participating in a virtual interview.

You may be interviewed by a team.

- Greet the interviewer warmly and with a smile, just as you would in person, and use the interviewer's name. For example, you can say, "I'm happy to meet you, Mr. VanDoss."
- Sit in the chair provided; sit back in the chair, not on the edge of your seat. Sitting on the edge of the chair can connote nervousness.
- If you are wearing a suit jacket, tuck it underneath you so that the jacket shoulders sit flat and you project a polished and professional image.
- Try to forget the camera is there; do not concentrate on it. Concentrate on the interviewer and the questions you are asked.
- Dress in colours that look good on you and on camera. Black or grey generally does not come across well on camera. Do not wear jewellery that jingles. The noise on camera is even more noticeable than in person.
- Pay attention to body language and small nuances of the interviewer. Do not spend an inordinate amount of time answering any one question. Be warm and informative but also be concise.
- Enunciate carefully. Poor enunciation is more pronounced on camera than in person.
- Once the interview is over, thank the person and terminate the program.

Interview Follow-Up

Promptly after the interview, follow up by writing a letter or email thanking the employer for the interview and reviewing points of special interest. Figure 15-7 is an example **follow-up letter**. Adapt the content if you are sending an email.

If you have heard nothing in regard to your application, a second follow-up message may be advisable a week or two after the first one. The second message should merely remind the employer of your continued interest in the job and express

FIGURE 15-7
Follow-Up Message

Colette Soros

2520 Boswell Avenue
North Vancouver, BC V7H 1L7

604-555-0113
e-mail: csoros@hotmail.com
linkedin.com/in/colettesoros

June 15, 20--

Ms. Keri-An Mahar
Human Resources Department
CanAsian Airlines
2300–888 3rd Street SW
Calgary, AB T2P 4C4

> Begin by thanking the interviewer.
>
> Follow with a recap of your skills and abilities, and indicate your continuing interest in the position.
>
> Close with a reminder of the next steps you agreed to at the conclusion of the interview.

Dear Ms. Mahar:

Thank you for giving me the opportunity to interview for the administrative assistant position that is open in the Human Resources Department. I appreciate the time you spent with me, and I enjoyed learning more about CanAsian Airlines.

Because of my education and experience, I am confident I can be an asset to the company. My skills in technology, communications, and human relations will help me perform at a high level. The interview today reinforced my interest in joining your team; I was extremely impressed with what I heard from you about CanAsian's philosophy of management and the directions the company is taking. I welcome the chance to become a part of the organization.

You may reach me at home by calling 604-555-0113 or by e-mail at csoros@hotmail.com.

Thank you again for your kindness, and I look forward to hearing from you within the next two weeks.

Sincerely,

Colette Soros

Colette Soros

a willingness to return for another interview if necessary. Depending on the situation, you may want to make a third contact with the organization. Being persistent shows your interest in the job, and the organization may view it as a plus. You do not want to risk annoying the employer, so use good judgment in determining how many follow-ups are appropriate in each job situation.

After an interview, you may decide you are not interested in the position. In this case, you should promptly send a courteous message expressing your appreciation for having been considered and explaining why you do not wish to remain a candidate. Although you are not interested in the present position, you may be interested in the future in another position within the company. If so, the courteous way you decline the first position may help when being considered a second time. You always want to keep the doors open.

Interview Evaluation

You may feel you did very well in the interview but you did not get the job. There simply may have been someone more qualified or with more experience than you. Organizations will usually provide you with a generic reason why this is so; most do not give exact reasons because of legal problems that may occur.

In any case, do not lose confidence in your skills and abilities. Play back the experience in your mind. Note the questions you had trouble answering, questionable reactions from the interviewer, and any errors that you believe you made. Think also about what went well and about how you can correct errors before the next interview. Review these thoughts with a trusted adviser and ask for some suggestions. Maintain a positive attitude, learn from each interview situation, and turn a job rejection into a positive learning opportunity.

Job Offer Evaluation

When deciding whether or not to accept a job offer, you need to ask yourself whether the organization lived up to your expectations. Ask yourself, the following questions:

- Do my skills and the position match?
- Is the work environment one in which I will be happy and will have an opportunity to grow?
- Will I have a chance to work with people I can respect and admire?
- Will the work be interesting?
- Will I be able to learn from the job duties and the people?
- Are the benefits and compensation packages acceptable?

You will be spending a major part of each week on the job—be certain you have found a position that will make you feel happy and productive in your job.

Job Advancement and Changes

Once you have successfully completed the interviewing process and accepted the job offer, your task is to perform the job well by applying your skills and knowledge. Listen to what co-workers and supervisors tell you. Observe and learn what is expected and accepted in the office. Make sure you have a clear understanding of your job duties and how you will be evaluated. Most companies provide job descriptions that detail the responsibilities of particular jobs. If you are not given one, ask for it. If a job description does not exist, ask your supervisor to review your duties with you.

Performing Successfully

Listen to what your supervisor and co-workers tell you. Pay attention to what is happening in the organization and learn daily from the people with whom you work and your supervisors within the organization.

It is your responsibility to know what your job is and not wait for your employer to describe every aspect of it. Do your job with commitment and professionalism. As a professional, you are responsible to not only meet but also exceed expectations and consistently produce quality work in a timely manner. You may wish to review the section on professionalism in Chapter 1.

Soft Skills   Living Your Values

In Chapter 5, you spent some time clarifying your values. Think back now to the values you identified as most important to you. In Project 5-5, you were asked to keep a list of your values. You may want to look back at that list now. Ask yourself this question: How can I live my values in the job I have now or in a future job? For example, assume you identified *dependability* as one of your values. How do you live *dependability* on the job? You report to work on time. If your job requires eight hours of work each day, you work all of those eight hours. You do not spend an hour and a half for lunch every day when the organization allows an hour. You complete all projects in the time frame given you. If you know you will have trouble completing a project on time, you immediately let your supervisor know your reservations. You establish a plan for getting the work done when it is needed.

Consider two more values you may have identified—perhaps *cooperation* and *tolerance*. How do you live *cooperation* at work? You cooperate with your supervisor and your co-workers. If an assignment requires overtime, you put in the hours graciously. You do not complain or look for excuses. How do you live *tolerance* at work? You do not judge other people. You listen openly to what they have to

say. You do not evaluate people based on their gender, age, or ethnicity.

Think about your own values and how you will live them on the job by responding to Self-Check C.

SELF-CHECK C

List three of your values. How will you daily live these values on a job? If you determine it is impossible to live your values, what steps will you take?

1. _____
   _____
   _____

2. _____
   _____
   _____

3. _____
   _____
   _____

Growing from the Performance Appraisal

The frequency of **performance appraisals** varies from company to company and even from position to position. As a new employee, this appraisal may occur during the first three to six months and then annually or semi-annually thereafter. Some organizations provide information on evaluation procedures during the orientation for new employees. If you do not receive information concerning evaluation procedures, ask your supervisor. Your employer may also use the same performance appraisal form for all employees in your classification. If a form is used, ask for a copy. Figure 15-8 shows a portion of a performance appraisal form. Another method of evaluation may be meeting with your supervisor to discuss your work performance, which is followed by a formal written evaluation document that becomes part of your personal file.

A fairly common procedure during the performance evaluation is to ask you to evaluate yourself, paying attention to the job description that you were provided when you first took the job and any planning documents of the company that detail the goals that need to be accomplished. For example, if your unit has a planning document, you and your supervisor may have used it as a basis to determine your job responsibilities and establish your goals. Then, during the evaluation period, the planning document is used to determine whether you have accomplished your goals. Figure 15-9 offers some tips to help you during the evaluation process.

Advancing on the Job

Advancing on the job may mean doing your present job more effectively and efficiently. Learn your job well, work well with others, and learn new ways of doing your job better. Remain current on new equipment, software, and procedures related to your job. Work on improving your verbal, nonverbal, and written communication skills. Remember that you gain valuable work experience from whatever job you are assigned. Concentrate on doing each task of your job to the best of your ability.

FIGURE 15-8
Sample Performance Appraisal Form

CanAsian Airlines
PERFORMANCE APPRAISAL

Employee Name _____

Job Title _____

Supervisor _____

Assessment

4 Performance demonstrates consistent and important contributions that surpass defined expectations of the position.

3 Performance demonstrates attainment of the defined expectations of the position.

2 Performance has not reached a satisfactory level. Improvement is needed.

1 Performance demonstrates deficiencies that seriously interfere with the attainment of the defined expectations of the position.

Skills	Assessment
Organization	
Prioritizes tasks	
Plans steps to accomplish tasks	
Meets deadlines	
Attends to detail	
Communication	
Conveys ideas effectively	
Responds to ideas conveyed by others	
Demonstrates appropriate professional courtesy	
Demonstrates sensitivity to a diverse staff	
Problem-Solving Skills	
Demonstrates ability to identify problem	
Demonstrates ability to select best solution	
Follows through on chosen solution	
Takes action to prevent future problems	

FIGURE 15-9
Evaluation Tips

Read the evaluation tips below to help you understand how to conduct yourself during an evaluation and ways that you can grow and learn from the experience.
- Discuss the issues openly and honestly.
- Maintain a calm and professional demeanour.
- Provide the evaluator with important information relating to your performance that the evaluator may not have.
- Accept negative comments as a criticism of your performance, not criticism of you as an individual.

- Resolve to correct your mistakes. Tell the evaluator you will do so.
- Discuss with your evaluator how you can improve your performance.
- If the evaluator is not clear about the direction you should take for the future, ask for clarification. Writing objectives that fit the unit's strategic plan can help you know what you should accomplish.
- Accept praise with a smile and a thank-you

Advancing on the job may also mean taking advantage of promotional opportunities that come your way. Remember that promotions usually come to those individuals who have performed well at their position in the company. Be ready for a promotion should the opportunity present itself. Learn as much as you can about other jobs in the company. Know how your present position fits into the organizational structure of the company. Stay informed about job openings in the company.

Leaving a Job

You may decide to leave a job voluntarily, or you may be given no choice. Whatever your reasons for leaving (being unhappy with a position and deciding to leave on your own, looking for greater opportunities, or being forced to leave), you must handle your departure in a professional manner.

The Exit Interview

Most companies conduct an **exit interview**—a meeting between the departing employee and a company representative who is usually a staff member in the human resources department, not your immediate supervisor.

The purpose of the meeting is for the company to learn the departing employee's impressions of the company and possibly the reason why the employee is leaving. It is not a time for you to get even, to make derogatory remarks about your supervisor, or to unduly criticize the company. Regardless of your reason for leaving, you will probably need a reference from the company. Be honest and professional, not vindictive.

For example, if you are leaving for a job that has greater opportunities for growth, you can say, "I've decided to accept a position with greater responsibility." You do not need to give all the reasons for your move. Keep in mind the adage about not burning your bridges. If you are leaving of your own choice, you may wish to return some day. A sample exit interview form is shown in Figure 15-10.

A Layoff or Termination

At some time in your career, you may have to face the situation of being laid off or fired. Assume first you are being laid off. The situation may be a downsizing of the company where other jobs are being eliminated in addition to your own. Keep in mind that you did not cause the situation. Even though the situation is difficult, the skills, abilities, and experience you gained from your job will help you to find another one. Remain positive and begin to think about what you want to do next. As one door closes, another opens.

What if you have been fired? Your feelings of fear, rejection, and insecurity are normal. However, it is no time to blame or feel sorry for yourself. It is time to take a hard look at your skills. Listen to what your employer tells you about your performance. What can you learn for the future? What steps do you need to take to ensure that you do not find yourself in the same situation again? In what areas do you need to improve? Talk with family, friends, and your closest advisers. Realize that the job may not have been the best one for you. Commit to finding a job that will better match your skills and abilities.

FIGURE 15-10
Exit Interview Form

EXIT INTERVIEW/TERMINATION FORM

TO BE COMPLETED BY SUPERVISOR

Name _____   Social Insurance No. _____
           Last   First   M.

Job Title _____   Eligible for Rehire _____ Yes _____ No

Date of Hire _____ Termination Date _____   Comments _____

_____

TO BE COMPLETED BY EMPLOYEE LEAVING				
	Satisfactory	Unsatisfactory	No Opinion	Comments
1. Workload/ responsibilities				
2. Working conditions				
3. Satisfaction received from work				
4. Attention to employee ideas				
5. Supervision				
6. Employer benefits				
7. Advancement opportunities				
8. Other				

Reason for Termination _____

_____

Postemployment Plans _____

_____

Additional Comments _____

_____

_____

_____ _____
Supervisor's Signature   Date

_____ _____
Employee's Signature   Date

Chapter Summary

The summary will help you remember the important points covered in this chapter.

- Seek employment opportunities through networking, professional organizations, direct contact, the Internet, placement offices, and employment agencies.
- Research and learn as much as you can about the organization before applying for a jobs.
- The résumé is a concise statement of your background, education, skills, and experience arranged in chronological or functional order and prepared in either hardcopy or electronic form, or both.
- The four goals of a cover letter are to introduce you to the organization, to describe your skills and background, to transmit your résumé, and to request an interview.
- The interview is extremely important. Most interviews are in person but they can also be conducted via teleconference or web conference. Prepare carefully and present yourself to the best of your ability.
- Read an employment application form completely before filling in each blank. Be truthful; state your background and experience accurately.
- After a job interview, send a follow-up message thanking the employer for the interview and reviewing points of special interest.
- To advance on the job, you must combine your skills and knowledge, listen to what co-workers and supervisors tell you, and observe and learn from performance appraisals and informal feedback.
- Formal performance appraisals are usually done within three to six months after you begin work. After that time, appraisals are done annually or semi-annually.
- If you decide to leave a job (either on your own or due to a layoff or termination), handle the situation professionally. Do not make negative comments about your supervisor, the job, or the company.
- If you are fired, remember that feelings of fear, rejection, and insecurity are normal. Take some time to analyze your skills. Listen to what your employer tells you about your performance. Learn from your mistakes.

Key Terms

networking p. 279
Employment and Social Development Canada p. 280
private employment agencies p. 280
temporary agency p. 280
direct contact or cold call p. 280
résumé p. 281
chronological résumé p. 283
functional résumé p. 283
combination-style résumé p. 283

electronic résumé p. 283
cover letter p. 286
employment application p. 287
job interview p. 288
virtual interview p. 291
follow-up letter p. 291
performance appraisals p. 294
exit interview p. 295

Responses to Self-Check B

1. Briefly talk about your education and job experiences. Do not spend more than a minute or two on your answer. Be concise; this question should not take up much time in the interview process.
2. Make several positive statements, such as "My previous employer would say I am a hard worker and I complete my tasks in a timely manner. My co-workers would say I am easy to work with and I care about them."
3. Briefly describe the computer courses you took and the software packages in which you are proficient. Talk about how your English and communication courses improved your writing skills and your ability to interact with others.
4. You might say you have an outgoing personality and you enjoy working with people.
5. You might mention your computer skills, writing skills, human relations skills, critical-thinking skills, and problem-solving skills.

Discussion Items

These discussion items provide an opportunity to test your understanding of the chapter through written responses and discussion with your classmates and your instructor.

1. What are some common sources of information about job openings?
2. What is the purpose of a résumé? What different styles are used? What should be included in a résumé?
3. What is the goal of a cover letter?
4. List five hints for making a good impression during the interview.
5. What is the purpose of a follow-up message?
6. What is the purpose of performance appraisals? What might you be evaluated on in a performance evaluation?

Critical-Thinking Activity

Arturo Herrera has just finished a two-year business course in college. He has done well in school. He is proficient in Microsoft Word, Excel, and PowerPoint. His math and English skills are good, and he works well with people. He has applied at five different companies for administrative assistant positions, but he has been turned down for all of them. Arturo knows he has the skills necessary to handle the jobs; he does not understand why he has not been hired. Here is what happened on his last job interview.

Arturo was 10 minutes late for the interview. He left home in time to get to the interview, but he had trouble finding a parking space. When he went in, he told the receptionist he was sorry he was late but he could not find a parking space.

The first question the interviewer asked him was "Could you tell me a little about yourself?" Arturo thought he did a thorough job with the question. He spent 10 minutes telling the interviewer about his life, starting from grade school. When the interviewer asked him if he had worked before, he said he had only had summer jobs. He told the interviewer he had recently been on five interviews and he believed the interviewers were unfair when they did not offer him the job.

What mistakes did Arturo make? How can he correct these mistakes in the future? How should he prepare for the next job interview?

Building Workplace Skills

Project 15-1 (Learning Outcome 1)

Online Project

Using the Internet, identify three sources of job information; at least one site should include jobs available for administrative assistants. Report your findings, including your sources, in a memorandum to your instructor. Include the information available on each website. List details for several administrative assistant job openings, including the city, province or territory, company, and salary (if given). Use the memorandum form SCDP15-1 to report your findings to your instructor.

Project 15-2 (Learning Outcome 2)

Using one of the administrative assistant job listings you found in Project 15-1, apply for the position. Prepare a résumé and a cover letter. Use either a chronological or functional format, whichever better fits your background and experience. Save your résumé using an appropriate file name. Print out a copy. Then prepare that same résumé as an electronic résumé, making the necessary changes to fit the electronic format and save using an appropriate file name. Print out a copy of your electronic résumé. Submit your chronological or functional résumé, your electronic résumé, and your letter of application to your instructor. Include these documents in your e-portfolio.

Project 15-3 (Learning Outcome 3)

Collaborative Project

Work in teams of four on this project. Before beginning this project, review the pages in your textbook on interviewing. Using the position you applied for in Project 15-2, assume you are going on an interview. Role-play that interview with your classmates with one of you being the employer, one being the interviewee, and the other two observing. When you have finished, the two observers will critique your performance. Repeat through the steps again until each member of the team has played every role.

Project 15-4 (Learning Outcome 4)

Collaborative Project

As a team of three or four, interview an employed administrative professional. The interview may take place by email rather than in person. Ask the individual these questions:

- To what do you contribute your success in this position?
- What advancement opportunities are available in your company?
- What skills do you believe are necessary in order to be promoted?

Report your findings to the class.

FIGURE 16-2
Different Invoicing Options

Hourly	The virtual assistant and client will generally discuss the type and amount of work to be done before setting a mutually agreeable hourly rate.
Flat Rate	Virtual assistants who have an established client base may negotiate a fee that is based on a certain number of hours, days, or even weeks.
Per Project	In this method, it does not matter how long it takes to complete the project, the fee remains the same. When setting this type of fee, it is important that the virtual assistant and client have mutual trust in identifying the scope of the work.
On-Call	Rather than working specific days of the week or weeks of the month, the virtual assistant accepts work on an as-needed basis for a client with whom they have a long-standing relationship.

Personal Traits and Skills

To be an effective virtual assistant or teleworker, you must be productive. To accomplish the job tasks to the satisfaction of your clients or customers, you need to be certain you understand their expectations—when the job is to be completed and the timeline for completion. Repeat your understanding of the expectations. Then, if you have misunderstood something, the client or customer has an opportunity to correct you. To be productive, you need to be disciplined, a self-starter, organized, technologically proficient, and possess excellent oral and written communication skills.

Being Disciplined

Certainly a large part of your discipline is driven by external sources, such as your paycheque or remuneration. As an independent worker, you understand the relationship between discipline and productivity. Those who are not disciplined enough to deliver the product or service the customer or client needs will soon find themselves with no customers or clients.

For the home-based worker, distractions are numerous—household chores, other family members, and errands, to name a few. Do not let distractions interfere with your focus. Being disciplined means formulating a plan for dealing with distractions. Here are some suggestions:

- Establish specific times during the day to initiate communications with clients or customers.
- Tell both family and friends in a nice way that you cannot be interrupted—you have deadlines to meet; ask whether

you or they can call back at a better time. Be pleasant but firm; they will soon understand the situation.

- If you have young children, you may need to hire some help during the day, or, when your children are of school age, you will need to help them to understand when you can and cannot be disturbed.
- Be disciplined about when to quit work. High achievers may be tempted to work 14 hours a day. You might be able to keep up that schedule for a few days, but burnout and sleep deprivation will eventually occur.

Self-management is no small task for anyone. It requires constant attention and self-nurturing. Take a few minutes now to evaluate your self-management skills by completing Self-Check B.

SELF-CHECK B

Answer these questions with a yes or no.

1. I am able to articulate my goals.
   Yes ❑   No ❑
2. I know my strengths.
   Yes ❑   No ❑
3. I understand my weaknesses.
   Yes ❑   No ❑
4. I seek to minimize my weaknesses.
   Yes ❑   No ❑
5. I maintain an appropriate balance between my work and my personal life.
   Yes ❑   No ❑

Soft Skills   Self-Management

Self-management is the Soft Skills objective for this chapter. What does self-management mean? It means that you
- Have self-knowledge—you know your personal and professional strengths and weaknesses
- Manage your time effectively
- Handle stress appropriately
- Balance your work and your personal life
- Understand your values
- Can articulate your goals

A Self-Starter

Having the initiative to begin a project and follow it through to completion is the trademark of a self-starter. Working as a virtual assistant or teleworker means you must rely on your own sense of pride and satisfaction in the accomplishment of a job well done. No one but you is responsible for setting the goals and timelines. A self-starter is the opposite of a procrastinator. Self-starters do not wait to the last minute to begin a project or task but organize themselves early in the process, creating timelines and setting deadlines. It is a trait you must possess if you choose to join the virtual workforce.

Being Independent

In the traditional office setting, you generally have someone you can go to for help in solving problems. You are part of a team that can help you, and you soon learn each team member's strengths and weaknesses. You know which individual to go to for help. Not so in most remote working situations. You have to be independent and a creative problem-solver. You need to figure out how a report should be written, the format that is most effective, and the appropriate graphs and charts to include. The old proverb "Necessity is the mother of invention" is particularly true for the virtual assistant or teleworker. Whatever occurs, you must be creative enough to find a solution.

Being Well Organized

When working at home, it is important to establish a routine; each day, set objectives for yourself. Before you quit work each afternoon, record the objectives you need to accomplish the next day on your to-do list or computer notes program. It also helps to put timelines by each objective. Some projects will take more or less time than you had envisioned, but estimates help keep you focused the next day. You may wish to review the time management techniques covered in Chapter 2.

Technological Proficiency

Technology skills are essential for all administrative professionals. Using telecommunications to work from remote locations means that a teleworker performs his or her job in isolation, with no help readily available when problems with technology occur. Manufacturers of telecommunications equipment offer online services. Using these services demands more understanding of telecommunications on the part of the teleworker than is demanded of the worker in the traditional office. As a virtual assistant or teleworker, you need to be able to understand the problem well enough to describe it accurately and to follow instructions from the telephone or from an online or instant messaging assistant. You will need to be able to apply what you have read in manuals to prevent problems from occurring—in other words, you need to be your own troubleshooter.

As telecommunications equipment becomes more sophisticated, you, as a teleworker, must continue to upgrade your knowledge and skills. You can do so by reading computer periodicals, checking upgrades on equipment through the Internet, and talking with other teleworkers about what they are using.

Being an Excellent Communicator

As a virtual assistant, you may never see your clients or customers face to face. The importance of being a good communicator and continuing to develop your communication skills is crucial. Communicating by telephone means your verbal skills are just as important as the written ones you will use in email and when preparing reports and other documents for your clients. You may wish to review the chapters in Part 2 that focus on verbal and written communication skills.

Virtual Workplace Challenges

Being a successful teleworker demands that you conquer isolation, noise, and family issues. You also need to develop an appropriate balance between home and work responsibilities.

Isolation

To a great degree, the environment of a virtual assistant or teleworker is one of isolation. If you have been accustomed to working in a traditional office environment, you will understand the differences immediately. You are not able to get a cup of coffee and exchange small talk with a co-worker, nor do you have someone with whom you can discuss a work problem. You miss little things, such as taking a walk with a co-worker at lunchtime. The degree to which isolation bothers you depends to some extent on your personality traits, such as whether you are an introvert or an extrovert. If you are more extroverted, you can still enjoy being a successful virtual assistant or teleworker—you just need to be more proactive at connecting with others than someone who is introverted. You can follow these suggestions:

- Join a health club; exercise with people; sign up for an aerobics class or arrange to jog or walk with a neighbour.
- Go to a deli or coffeehouse where you can chat with people or occasionally have lunch with someone in a similar business.
- Take advantage of any professional development activities or events that are held in your area or even online webinars.

As a part-time teleworker, you will have other opportunities to connect with colleagues. You can follow these suggestions:

- Arrange for regular contact with your supervisor or other colleagues by phone, Skype, email, or instant messaging.

- Be available for phone or Skype calls. Email is not always the best medium when collaborating on projects.
- Participate in any company-sponsored professional development activities and social events.
- When visiting the office, be sure to make a personal connection with the colleagues with whom you collaborate.

If you are extremely introverted, you probably need to work on enjoying interactions with others. For example, if your business involves working with clients or on teams, you may need to work on communicating with your contacts and enjoying your interactions.

Noise

Since noise can be a distraction when you are trying to work, you should do what you can to try to lower the noise level around the house. Adding more insulation to your home by installing acoustic foam on your walls, double-pane glass windows, and wall-to-wall carpeting are all costly but effective solutions. Less costly but almost as effective is to install noise-reducing ceiling tiles and self-stick foam weatherstripping to windows. Some of these costs may be defrayed by taking advantage of some personal income tax incentives when working from your home—claiming a portion of the costs of establishing and running a home office, and the costs of necessary supplies, repairs, equipment, and/or furniture.

Family Issues

If you have decided to become a virtual assistant or teleworker and you have a family, or live with other family members, you must talk with your family members about this arrangement. Many people have misconceptions about what it means to work from home. You need to talk with your family and explain that working from home does not mean you have time to take on additional responsibilities around the house, but that you are serious about your work and cannot be a full-time parent while maintaining a full-time work schedule. Everyone needs to understand his or her role and responsibilities in the new arrangement. Once the responsibilities have been determined, write them down and post them in a place that is readily accessible to all family members. The following are some additional suggestions for keeping family issues to a minimum:

- When you need someone to help with the children either full-time or after school, use a childcare referral service and/or ask friends for recommendations.
- Do not expect perfection from your family—keep the lines of communication open. When you believe someone is not doing his or her fair share, communicate your feelings.

Ensure both family and friends know your working hours just as if you were going to the traditional office each day. Referring to your home office as your workplace and dressing for your office each day as if you were working outside of your home can help you to get in the "mood" for work. You can help your family understand when you are working and should not disturbed by posting your work schedule on a bulletin board in a place the family uses frequently, putting out a "Do Not Disturb" sign, or closing your office door.

Do not let family and friends think you can take on extra community projects because you are working from home. Give a business reason for your refusal, for example, by saying, "I am sorry but I have an important project to finish. I simply do not have the time." Answer your business phone professionally with your name and/or your company name.

Work/Life Balance

Just as you cannot let family and friends interrupt your work to the point that you get nothing done, you also cannot ignore family and friends to the point that all you do is work. You must find a balance between family and work. What is that balance? You must answer that question for yourself. What is important is that you understand what a healthy balance is and maintain that balance. You may have heard the old saying "All work and no play makes Jack [or Jill] a dull person." The statement has great validity. If you allow work to become all-consuming, you can develop stress levels that make you physically and emotionally sick. If you never read a book, listen to a news program, read a magazine, or learn something new outside of your job, you may find that you have fewer good ideas and less creativity in your work projects. Review the questions about balancing work and life in Figure 16-3.

People @ Work

Depending on the type of work you choose to do as a virtual worker, you may come in contact with more than the clients and customers who have contracted your services. You may have a client who is planning an event—which may mean that the people in your work environment could include hotel and catering staff, representatives of multimedia rental agencies, and potential speakers. All of the skills you have acquired in this course of studies that qualify you to be an administrative professional will play a role. Working effectively with a wide variety of people in a variety of different and challenging situations can be very rewarding.

FIGURE 16-3
Work/Life Balance

1. Have you stopped seeing friends because it seems like a waste of your time?
   Yes ❑   No ❑

2. Are family members complaining that they see too little of you?
   Yes ❑   No ❑

3. Have you missed important family occasions because of work?
   Yes ❑   No ❑

4. Do you see fewer movies/concerts/plays/sporting events and so forth because of work?
   Yes ❑   No ❑

5. Do you find yourself feeling bored or empty when you're not working?
   Yes ❑   No ❑

6. Are you unsure of what to do with yourself when you're not busy?
   Yes ❑   No ❑

7. Does relaxing make you feel guilty or nervous?
   Yes ❑   No ❑

8. Do you have trouble making conversation that isn't about your job?
   Yes ❑   No ❑

9. Do you work to the point where you are simply too tired to do anything else?
   Yes ❑   No ❑

10. Do you have trouble saying no to work-related requests?
    Yes ❑   No ❑

11. Do you evaluate your day strictly by the amount of work you accomplished?
    Yes ❑   No ❑

12. Have you been wondering recently what the point of all this work is?
    Yes ❑   No ❑

Did you answer yes to four or more of these questions? If so, your life may be out of balance.

Source: Alice Bredin, *The Home Office Solution* (New York: John Wiley & Sons, 1998), p. 126.

Creating an Effective Home Workspace

Deciding to become a virtual assistant or teleworker means that you will need to create a space in your home where you can work—a place you can call your office. Before considering the type and size of workspace you need, ask yourself these questions: What type of work will I be doing? How much space do I need to accomplish this work? What furniture and equipment do I need? What should I consider when selecting furniture and equipment so that I avoid ergonomic health-related problems? Will I be working on highly technical material that requires a distraction-free workspace? Will I be meeting clients or customers in my workspace? What environmental factors are important to me? For example, do I need to be close to a window?

Once you ask and answer these questions, you are ready to consider the location and size of your workspace.

Workspace Size and Location

If you need a distraction-free workspace, locate your office away from the family living area of your home—perhaps in a spare bedroom or a basement room. If clients, customers, and/or co-workers will be meeting with you occasionally, try to locate the space close to an outside entrance. If you have concerns about external noise, try to locate your workspace as far away as possible from the noise. How large the space needs to be depends on whether you are working from home full- or part-time. If you are a teleworker working at home only one or two days per week, you can be less concerned about workspace. Your space may be a small area in a corner of a room that can be set up with a minimum amount of equipment.

If you are working as a virtual assistant, you must consider the type and size of desk you need and the space required for all the necessary equipment and supplies. Your location needs to have space for file cabinets and bookshelves, and sufficient electrical outlets and telecommunications connections in proximity to your equipment—stringing extension and other cords across a room can be dangerous. Chapters 2 and 3 include several suggestions for setting up a workspace that is both safe and ergonomically sound. Some key points are repeated in Figure 16-4.

You may wish to refer to these chapters and suggestions again. As a virtual assistant, you will have more control over creating your workspace than when working as an administrative professional in the traditional office.

Hardware and Software

Whether you are working from home or from some other remote/mobile location, you will need a computer. A desktop or

FIGURE 16-4
Workstation Checklist

- Eliminate glare from your computer and your workstation.
- Be certain you have adequate light for reading without squinting.
- Adjust your chair height so that your feet are flat on the floor.
- Be certain your chair is sturdy—a base with five legs is more stable than four legs.
- Place your computer keyboard five centimetres below your desk surface.
- Eliminate loud noises from your workstation environment.
- If the colour of your workstation is depressive, change it.

laptop computer is a likely choice if working from a home office; a notebook, laptop, or tablet may be more suitable when working in a mobile environment. If you have ergonomic concerns about working exclusively with any of these mobile devices, remember that peripheral equipment such as a standard keyboard and mouse can be connected wirelessly to a notebook, laptop, or tablet. Your other equipment purchases should include a printer, fax machine, copier, and scanner, or a multi-function machine that also includes a telephone. Identify your needs and then follow these suggestions to help you in your selection:

- Read or subscribe to digital versions of computer periodicals such as *Computer Shopper*, *PCWorld*, *Wired*, and *Maximum PC*.
- Conduct online research; equipment and software manufacturers advertise their products on the Web. Enter the search string "*home office computing*" to locate readings and other online resources.
- Shop your local computer stores and try the equipment.
- Talk with people who use the technology. For example, discuss the best buys with other teleworkers, computer technicians, or friends who are computer-literate.

The type of work you will be doing as a virtual assistant or teleworker will define the type of software you will need. Certainly you will need appropriate software to enable you to connect with clients, customers, or colleagues. Email, instant messaging, and teleconferencing software such as Skype, Google Hangouts, or FaceTime may all be necessities. Unlike these software applications, which are designed with a "calling mode," is another option—Perch. This always-on video portal is a downloadable app that connects office spaces and facilitates natural unscheduled face-to-face communication among team members.

Some features such as Skype are built in to "suite" programs such as Microsoft Office and Corel Office, which can also include programs for word processing, spreadsheets, databases, presentations, and personal management. Virus protection, firewalls, spyware protection, and system maintenance software will also be necessary to protect your client's or employer's electronic data.

Skills @ Work

In addition to determining and obtaining the software you need to complete projects for your clients, you may need to develop skills working with accounting software. Quicken, a popular personal and small business finance management software, may suit your needs. You can use it to customize estimates, track your income and expenses, create invoices, and process payments. It tracks federal and provincial taxes and identifies eligible tax deductions. A link to the Quicken website can be found on the MindTap site for this textbook. Take a look the demos and videos to see what it can do for you and how easily you can develop the skill to manage your finances.

Other Equipment and Supplies

Once the location of your home workspace has been determined, a desk and ergonomic chair selected, and your hardware and software in place, you need to consider what other furniture will be required. You will also need file cabinets to store hardcopy documents, bookshelves, and other storage containers for supplies and business records. Personalized stationery and business cards are supplies you can design yourself using your word processing or desktop publishing program. With all this in place, you are ready to open for business as a virtual assistant.

Overall, to be productive as a virtual assistant or teleworker you will need a space that is not only functional but also safe.

Workplace Safety

Be conscious of the need for security. Since you are often working home alone using computer technology and other expensive hardware, you want to do what you can to maintain a theft-proof environment. Here are several suggestions for keeping your workplace safe:

- Install simple locks on windows so they cannot be forced open from the outside.
- Install a security system that contacts the police if a break-in occurs.
- Install a deadbolt on the office door. Draw the shades when you are working at night.
- Be certain your office furniture and equipment is insured for the proper amount.

Health, Life Insurance, and Retirement Benefits

If you are a virtual assistant, you need to arrange for health and life insurance coverage and set up a program for retirement. Talk with several health and life insurance companies, and research the benefits available. If you have a friend who has a trusted insurance agent, you might start with that person. You must be concerned about providing adequately for you and your family during your retirement years. Options include **RRSPs** (registered retirement savings plans) and investments in **mutual funds** (funds that include a combination of stocks and bonds purchased through a mutual fund company) or individual **stocks** (ownership in a company) and **bonds** (a debt owed by an organization). Consult with a certified financial planner about your long-term plans and needs.

If you are a teleworker, ensure that you are covered by the organization's wellness plans. Check workers' compensation coverage in your province or territory. If you fall and injure yourself during established working hours while working in your home, will you be covered for the injury just the same as you would be as an employee in the traditional office?

Survival Strategies

Once you have created your office workspace and begin to work as a teleworker, you will find that creativity, self-management, productivity, and continual learning are essential skills for you to possess.

Certainly, these skills are many of the same skills demanded in the traditional workplace, but in that environment, you have the luxury of receiving input from your co-workers about your strengths and weaknesses and taking advantage of organization-sponsored staff development events. As a virtual assistant or teleworker, these opportunities are not as easily available to you; you must be sure to take care of yourself. You cannot keep up a pace of constant, effective work production if you do not also give yourself the opportunity for renewal. You do not want to become insular (narrow or provincial in outlook). How can you take care of yourself? Here are some suggestions.

Take a Break

Give yourself breaks—breaks of 30 minutes or an hour or two do not reduce your productivity; they improve it by giving you a chance to renew, reflect, and think more creatively. Leave your cellphone at home and get out in the fresh air. Take yourself and your dog, if you have one, for a walk; notice the beauty of nature wherever you find it around you. Find someplace to walk where you can let your mind be free of the stresses of work for a period of time.

Reward yourself with longer breaks where you have the chance to work at the same time you enjoy a beautiful setting. That setting may be Long Beach on the west coast of Vancouver Island, a cottage on the shores of Lake Ontario, or the beach in Mexico. Remember, the teleworker can work from almost any setting as long as he or she has access to telecommunications. You may be surprised at how much work you can actually accomplish and how creative and refreshed you feel for allowing yourself the opportunity for renewal. Growth comes when we let ourselves thoroughly experience the world.

Schedule Relaxation

If you are not very good at taking that impromptu walk in the park—you never quite find the time or you just forget about it—schedule the walk, along with other relaxation activities, on your calendar. Actually enter that 30 minutes to read or watch television on your calendar and set an alarm as a reminder, or schedule a time at a local club every week to play tennis with a friend. Although "scheduled relaxation" appears to be an oxymoron (a combination of contradictory terms), many of us have become so conditioned to accomplishing what is on our calendars that the only way we take advantage of a relaxing activity is to schedule it.

Exercise

Numerous studies have shown the importance of regular exercise for our bodies and minds. Yet most of us fail to exercise on a regular basis. Exercise is so important; it is the task of the cardiopulmonary system to pump oxygen into your blood and then to pump the blood to all parts of your body. When you are sitting and breathing quietly with your heart at rest, less oxygen and blood are flowing to your brain than when you exercise. Your brain activity naturally slows because blood and oxygen are in lower supply.

Aerobic exercise is best since the body uses oxygen to produce the energy needed for the activity. For an activity to be aerobic, it must meet three criteria: it must be brisk, sustained, and involve a repeated use of large muscles. Examples of aerobic exercise include walking, jogging, swimming, stationary cycling, and jumping rope.

Both starting and maintaining an effective exercise program are difficult tasks but well worth the effort—the payoff being a healthier body and a more creative, productive brain. To sustain an exercise program, write on a calendar the days you plan to exercise each week, mark off the days you exercise as the week goes by, and at the end of the week count up the number of times you exercised to determine whether or not you met your goal. Make arrangements for family or friends to exercise with you, and find an indoor location where you can exercise in extreme weather conditions.

Eat Properly

Eating properly may be more of a challenge for the teleworker than the traditional office worker because it is easy to take a break, go to the kitchen, and reach for whatever snack is available. It is easy to get involved in a project and reach for a snack to break the tension.

One of the tricks to keeping your eating under control is to refrain from buying unhealthy food and snacks at the grocery store. If the food is not in the house, you cannot eat it. Put fruits and vegetables on the weekly grocery list; cut out a major part of the fat that is in your diet; and reduce sugar and caffeine, excessive consumption of which contributes to poor health and to certain diseases such as hypertension and heart disease. The average cup of regular coffee contains 100 to 150 milligrams of caffeine. Nervousness, insomnia, and headaches have been related to as little as 250 milligrams of caffeine. Consume caffeine in moderation.

Sleep

The proper amount of sleep is essential to mental and physical health. Studies show that many people have sleep deprivation; their bodies have been denied the proper amount of sleep for so long that it is affecting their physical health. Although the amount of sleep an individual needs varies, studies show that most people should sleep from seven to nine hours per night.

Many of us have problems getting the proper amount of sleep due to our busy schedules and stressful lives. The teleworker may go back to the "office" at the end of the day for another three or four hours of work. Teleworkers may also go to bed thinking about the projects they worked on that day or the projects planned for the next day and find that sleep does not come easily. Practising the following techniques may help you fall asleep:

- Set aside the hour before bed for quiet activities such as reading.
- Take a warm bath.
- Turn off the TV in the bedroom and/or turn down the TV in an adjoining room.
- Practise deep-breathing exercises.
- Create a relaxing scene in your head—waves rolling up on a beach or a walk along a mountain stream.
- Be certain your mattress and pillow are right for you—the proper firmness or softness.
- Pay attention to the amount of coffee, tea, cola, and chocolate you consume; these stimulants can lead to sleep deprivation.

Reward Yourself

In the traditional work setting, rewards can come from your supervisor or from your co-workers in the form of a smile and a thank you or a pat on the back, being told you have done a good job, or a promotion and/or increase in salary. When you are a virtual assistant or teleworker, you must remember to reward yourself. That may not be easy to do. Being successful in life demands that you not only should recognize your strengths, but also reward yourself for them. You can feel good about your work and your accomplishments by doing the following:

- Making a to-do list of what you plan to accomplish each day then marking off your accomplishments at the end of the day. Mentally thank yourself for your ability to stick to the task.
- Sharing your accomplishments with others. Tell your spouse, your children, and your close friends about what you have achieved. For example, if you have completed a complicated project and the public response has been favourable, brag about it a little. Your family and close friends will also be proud of your accomplishments and share your successes.
- Rewarding yourself. Give yourself a night out at the theatre or buy something for yourself you have been wanting. Take the time to read a novel, go to a concert, or enjoy a meal at a restaurant with family or friends.

Chapter Summary

The summary will help you remember the important points covered in this chapter.

- Advantages of telework for the individual include fewer distractions from co-workers; more flexibility with the organization of daily tasks; savings in time, commuting, and other costs; and higher job satisfaction.
- Disadvantages of telework for the individual are isolation, lack of separation between home and work, more distractions from family, potential for excessive working hours, less awareness of changes in the company, and a fear of being forgotten by colleagues and supervisors.
- Advantages of telework for the organization include improved employee retention; higher productivity; fewer hours lost due to traffic problems; savings in costs of office space, maintenance, and housekeeping; an increased pool of candidates for positions; and reduced absenteeism.
- Disadvantages of telework for the organization include contacting the employee, maintaining adequate communication between other employees or with customers, and possible delays in customer service.

- Societal advantages of telework include increased entrepreneurial activity, increased community stability, and less pollution.
- To be successful in telework, the individual must be productive, disciplined, a self-starter, independent, well organized, technologically proficient, and possess excellent oral and written communication skills.
- Telework success can be undermined by isolation, noise, family issues, and work/life imbalance.
- The teleworker must consider the home workspace and equipment and furniture needs.
- The teleworker must also consider workplace safety and health, life insurance, and retirement benefits.
- The teleworker must follow ergonomic guidelines in selecting and setting up the furniture and equipment in a home workspace.
- Survival strategies include both short and long breaks, relaxation, exercise, proper nutrition, sleep, and self-rewards.

Key Terms

virtual assistants p. 301
extroverts p. 301
introverts p. 301
virtual teams p. 302
sleep deprivation p. 303
self-management p. 303
RRSPs p. 307

mutual funds p. 307
stocks p. 307
bonds p. 307
insular p. 308
oxymoron p. 308
aerobic p. 308

Responses to Self-Check A

Explanation of Score

12–20 Strong Introvert. You may need to get out more than you are doing now. The critical aspects of working at home, such as communicating with customers or co-workers, may feel like chores to you.

21–30 Moderate Introvert. You probably do not have many problems coping with the relative isolation of working at home. However, make regular interaction breaks a priority.

31–35 Introvert/Extrovert. You enjoy solitary and social time in a balanced way. You have trouble with isolation when a deadline or major project keeps you from your usual regimen of socializing.

36–41 Moderate Extrovert. You often feel cooped up and lonely. The good news is that you are not likely to let that happen very often. As an extroverted person, you probably initiate contact whenever you feel you need it.

42–48 Strong Extrovert. You may have trouble handling the isolation that comes with working at home.

Discussion Items

These discussion items provide an opportunity to test your understanding of the chapter through written responses and/or discussion with your classmates and your instructor.

1. Define telework. List three advantages and three disadvantages of telework for the individual. List three advantages of telework for the organization.

2. List and explain four qualities and skills necessary for success in telework.
3. Explain what is meant by self-management.

4. List the considerations when setting up a home office.
5. List and explain five survival strategies for the teleworker.

Critical-Thinking Activity

Ryan Stapleton has been working for A&I Telecommunications as an administrative professional for five years. His work involves researching and preparing reports, managing a website, providing computer and software training, and working on TQM teams. Recently, he was offered the opportunity to work two days per week from home, with the rationale that researching and preparing reports plus managing a website require a work environment free of interruptions. The company believes he can be more productive by working on these projects from a home office. A&I will provide him with the computer equipment he needs.

Ryan is married and has two children—one 10 years old and one 2 years old. Ryan's wife works full-time away from the home. Ryan has now finished his first two weeks of work as a teleworker. Although Ryan thought his wife understood that he has a full-time job the two days he is home, she began making additional demands of him. She suggested that he keep the 2-year-old on the two days he is home. She also expects him to cook on those two nights. He tried keeping

the 2-year-old at home, but he cannot get any of his work done. However, since his wife is insisting on the arrangement, he is going to give it more time.

Ryan considers himself an extrovert. Although he enjoys the freedom of working on his own the two days each week, he misses the hubbub of the workplace. He also is receiving a lot of email and telephone calls from his supervisor and co-workers about work issues. The report he prepared during his first two weeks took more of his time than usual. He had to work from 8 a.m. until 10 p.m. every day to finish the report; his childcare duties and meal preparation also interfered with his work time. He believes his productivity is decreasing rather than increasing. Ryan wants to continue telework but he is not sure the hassles he is facing are worth it.

What advice would you give Ryan? Using critical thinking, suggest how the issues Ryan is facing should be handled.

Building Workplace Skills

Project 16-1 (Learning Outcomes 1, 2, and 3)

Online Project

Find and study at least three articles on the Internet to discover the advantages and disadvantages of working as a virtual assistant/teleworker, the current telework outlook, statistics, and the qualities and skills needed by the virtual assistant/teleworker. Use the Web addresses provided on the MindTap site for this textbook and any additional resources that you discover. Write a short summary of your findings, listing your sources. Submit your keyed report to your instructor.

Project 16-2 (Learning Outcome 5)

Research two articles using periodicals such as *Computer Shopper, Wired,* and *PCWorld*; the website of the Canadian Centre for Occupational Health and Safety (www.ccohs.ca); or the Ergonomics section of Chapter 2 to determine how to properly configure a workspace and how furniture and equipment should be used. Submit a short, keyed summary of the articles to your instructor, listing the resources you used, and place a copy in your e-portfolio.

Project 16-3 (Learning Outcomes 2 and 3)

Collaborative Project

With two or three of your classmates, search the Internet for information on the advantages and disadvantages and qualities and skills necessary for success as a virtual assistant or teleworker. If you know someone who is a virtual worker, talk to this person; however, an interview is not a requirement because you may not have access to such a person. If you are able to talk to a virtual worker in your area or on the Internet ask some of following questions:
- Why have you chosen to be a virtual assistant or teleworker?
- What education or experience prepared you for this job?
- What characteristics and skills do you feel are most important for a teleworker?
- Where is your workspace located? If it is at home, what challenges have you had to overcome?
- In what ways can virtual assistants be effectively utilized?
- What tips would you give a potential virtual assistant?

Prepare a presentation of your findings to share with the class. Place a copy in your e-portfolio.

Make the Grade with MindTap

MindTap®

Stay organized and efficient with **MindTap**—a single destination with all the course material and study aids you need to succeed. Built-in apps leverage social media and the latest learning technology. For example:

- ReadSpeaker will read the text to you.
- Flashcards are pre-populated to provide you with a jump-start for review—or you can create your own.
- You can highlight text and make notes in your MindTap Reader. Your notes will flow into Evernote, the electronic notebook app that you can access anywhere when it's time to study for the exam.
- Self-quizzing allows you to access your understanding.

Visit http://www.nelson.com/student to start using **MindTap**. Enter the Online Access Code from the card included with your text. If a code card is not provided, you can purchase instant access at NELSONbrain.com.

Endnote

1. Alice Bredin, *The Home Office Solution* (New York: John Wiley & Sons, 1998), pp. 38–42.

Leading with Confidence

CHAPTER 17

Do I Qualify?

Medical Assistant Supervisor

Community health clinic seeks experienced medical assistant with strong administrative skills and a background in primary care. Duties include:

- Training and supervising medical assistants
- Performing patient intake procedures
- Assisting in supervising clinic flow and activity
- Ensuring supply stocks and equipment maintenance
- Representing the clinic at local meetings as requested
- Promoting opportunities for feedback from medical staff to improve service

Candidate must have discretion, good judgment, organizational or management ability, initiative, and excellent communication skills.

LEARNING OUTCOMES

After studying this chapter, you should be able to …

1. Describe the characteristics of effective leaders.
2. Define the essential management responsibilities.
3. *Determine your own leadership values.*

Leading and Managing

Whatever form leadership takes, most of us find ourselves in leadership roles or have the opportunity to take on leadership roles at numerous times in our lives. If you assume positions of greater responsibility in the workplace, you may have one or more people reporting to you. While you may not choose to become a manager or supervisor, you may still have opportunities to assume leadership roles by leading teams within the workplace, or becoming involved as an officer in a professional organization. Leading with confidence is an important ability to develop as you grow in your career. It will serve you well throughout life, regardless of the profession you choose.

Defining Leadership and Management

Leadership within an organization can be defined as the act of inspiring and motivating people to achieve organizational goals. The verb *to lead* has been defined as "to guide on a way especially by going in advance," "to direct on a course or in a direction," and "to direct the operations, activity, or performance of."[1] The capacity to lead well is more than filling a position or an office—it is a philosophy, an attitude, and a practice in the workplace. An effective leader keeps the long run in mind, stimulating employees to do more than they thought they could.

Management in a business setting is the act of organizing and directing people to accomplish organizational goals. Chapter 1 identified the responsibilities of management as a subset of leadership. Often overlapping, these responsibilities are complementary but different in concept, purpose and process. This chapter will help you understand some of the practical concepts of leadership and management.

Leadership Traits and Qualities

You probably have encountered people whom you consider to be good leaders. What makes you put someone into that category? Is it a person's effectiveness at getting things done? Is it the respect he or she shows others, the ability to guide people, or the level of trust and rapport that person establishes with others? In addition to integrity and emotional maturity (see the Professionalism @ Work box), the following are several other important qualities of an effective leader.

Professionalism @ Work

Integrity and Emotional Maturity

Integrity, the firm, consistent application of ethical standards at a personal level is considered the most important factor in leadership and is the cornerstone of good leadership. Leaders with integrity set the standards in their organizations. They earn people's trust because they can be relied upon to "do the right thing" and to "walk the talk" (do what they say they will do). Doing what they say they will do, however, may not necessarily be "right" for everyone. Having the goal to be "fair" may not always be nice or easy, but it is an important characteristic in leaders with integrity.

Emotional maturity is an important part of leading others. Effective leaders are not driven by emotion. They understand the kinds of occurrences that tend to make them angry or irritated or that trigger other negative feelings. Rather than simply reacting, they choose how they will respond. Good leaders have developed ways of managing negative emotions so that their work is not affected, nor are their emotions visible to others.

Understands Self

Good leaders know themselves. They capitalize on their strengths, concentrate on developing those strengths, and try to make their weaknesses immaterial. We are all shaped by our background and experiences, learning through life how we should behave and what we should value. Individuals change as a result of new experiences and new knowledge.

Making a mistake is not unique or even unforgivable. What is unforgivable is continuing to make the same mistake and refusing to learn from our mistake and accept responsibility for it. Acquiring self-knowledge is a lifetime process. If we are to understand ourselves, we must continue to explore our own potential, to reflect on our experiences, and to seek new challenges.

Builds a Shared Vision

Visionary leaders work with and involve employees at all levels of the organization to create a shared vision of the organization. They do this by asking questions like the following:

- What values does the organization have? What values should it have?
- What contributions should the organization make to the community?
- What reputation does the organization have? What reputation should it have?
- Who are the clients and customers of the organization?
- How do people work together within the organization?
- Do the values of the individuals within the organization match the values of the organization?
- What contributions do individuals within the organization make to the community?

Effective leaders help employees understand the organization's vision and how their individual goals and objectives support that vision. Effective leaders publish the organization's vision statement so employees are aware of it. Many organizations publish their value/vision statement on their website to inform the general public about what is important to the organization.

Lives by a Set of Values

Ethical behaviour is the accepted practice in business. Leaders must work within the organization to identify and define the principles of ethical behaviour, and then ensure that they are carried out in the daily activities of the organization. Even though it can be difficult to determine what is and is not ethical in specific instances, few of us would disagree that our leaders must stand firmly on moral principles. When difficult decisions need to be made, leaders must follow a thoughtful decision-making process like the one outlined in Chapter 2. Effective leaders understand that establishing and living a set of values must begin with the top leaders and that living the organizational values must permeate every level of the organization.

Commits to Service

Effective leaders consider service to others as primary. More than just being concerned with their own career, effective leaders understand how they can serve the organization and its employees, as well as the external community. The values

interview. A link to PI Worldwide where you can find out more about Predictive Index assessment can be found on the MindTap site that accompanies this textbook.

Orientation

Once a person is employed, the next step is an orientation to provide that individual with the knowledge necessary to be successful on the job. The new employee will possess the skill set outlined in the job posting but know little about how your organization works. As a manager, you are responsible to inform new employees about the history of the organization, its policy and procedures (perhaps provide them with a policy and procedures manual), and its job evaluation procedures (frequency and criteria). Routine day-to-day procedures of the job (records management and technology) also need to be explained. Also include in your orientation any information on additional training, as a result of changes in technology, available through company-sponsored seminars, tuition-reimbursed courses at local colleges or universities, or job internships.

Assigning another experienced employee to "mentor" a new employee will help the new employee to learn the routine procedures that may be unique to the organization. A mentor can be the new employee's "go to" person who will answer any initial questions, introduce the employee to other members of the organization and generally help this person feel part of the team from the outset.

Team Training

If a team is to be successful, a manager working with teams must take on the following responsibilities:

- *Empower the team.* Give them the information needed to get the job done.
- *Trust the team.* Once the team has the information it needs, trust the team to produce the best possible solutions to problems.
- *Take a strong stand with the team when needed.* If the team is not accomplishing the task and is getting bogged down in personality issues, let them know that such behaviours are not acceptable.
- *Check on the team's development.* Are team members communicating with and trusting each other? Do they understand the goals of the team? Do they understand individual roles? Is every member involved in the process and product?
- *Do not micromanage.* To **micromanage** is to direct every small detail of another person's work.

Teams often cannot function effectively without acquiring some interpersonal skill development. As a result, managers may need to be involved in team training. The following skills

Ongoing training is essential.

are generally necessary for all team members as they work together:

- *Listening.* Summarizing, checking for understanding, and giving and receiving feedback
- *Resolving conflicts.* Identifying and resolving conflicts within the team or with individuals outside the team
- *Influencing others.* Gaining respect as a team and as individuals
- *Developing solutions.* Creatively generating and sorting through alternative solutions to issues
- *Ensuring ongoing quality.* Determining how results will be measured

Motivating Others

People are generally motivated to do work and to do it well for a variety of reasons. In Chapter 1, you considered initiative and motivation and whether you are extrinsically or or intrinsically motivated. Knowing and understanding your own motivation can help you to determine the factors that will motivate others. Find out what motivates other individuals and use that knowledge to encourage each employee to have a positive attitude about their job and to do their best work. Figure 17-3 identifies several motivational factors for you to consider.

Delegating

Delegating means giving the responsibility for tasks to others and then empowering them to get the job done. Think carefully about the tasks you will delegate. Work out the details of what you want the person to do and write down your directions so the person can refer to them later. Provide the necessary information and let them do the planning and organizing. They might not do it the same way that you would, but who knows, they might find a better way, and everyone would learn something valuable in the process.

FIGURE 17-3
Motivational Factors

- *Set objectives.* Help the employees you supervise to establish challenging, measurable objectives. Then help them commit themselves to achieving the objectives. This approach requires follow-through and planning on the part of the supervisor. You must not only know the objectives, but also follow up to see that the employee has achieved the objectives.
- *Recognition.* As a supervisor, you need to become sensitive to the accomplishments of others. You can give recognition in a number of ways: verbal praise for a job well done, a thank-you letter written to an employee, and recognition in the organization's newsletter.
- *Develop a team.* Individuals need to be an accepted member of a group. As a supervisor, you can capitalize on this need by building a team of people who work together well. Productivity can be increased when every person in the group contributes to the overall effectiveness of the team.
- *Financial reward.* As a supervisor, know what your employees do and then pay them fairly for their work. Reward employees who consistently give you outstanding performance with good salary increases.
- *Delegate work.* Employees enjoy doing meaningful and challenging work. Provide them this opportunity by delegating important projects to them.

Arrange for the employee to check in with you periodically, and make yourself available for these exchanges. Try to anticipate questions but ensure the employee knows to approach you with any problems, questions, or requirements for additional support as they arise.

Delegating can be challenging. It requires you to relinquish control and allow others to make mistakes. Give them the authority they need and trust team members to complete their assignments responsibly.

Evaluating

Informal feedback can be invaluable to productivity, morale, and motivation. Taking the time to provide frequent, constructive feedback shows employees how you expect work to be done and helps them to improve. In Chapter 15, the topic of formal performance appraisal/evaluation was introduced. Formal appraisals assess long-term performance against a set of previously established goals. They are conducted as a method of identifying performance that is inadequate and recognizing performance that is exceptional. Most companies have formal evaluation periods in which personnel are evaluated every six months or every year. These evaluations may be individual evaluations, team evaluations, or work-group evaluations.

Individual evaluations are essential even if team evaluations occur. The human resources department may have developed forms and procedures for individual evaluations; the manager completes an evaluation and the employee completes a self-evaluation. At the evaluation conference, both evaluations are discussed and a final evaluation document is prepared. Once these processes have been developed, they should be implemented consistently with all employees throughout the organization. Figure 17-4 provides some techniques that will help you understand how to effectively evaluate employees.

Team evaluations are used by some companies; employees who work together as a team are asked to evaluate each other. These evaluations may be administered by the team's supervisor or discussed among the team members only. Guidelines should be given to the team beforehand to ensure that the session does not become one of fault-finding or blaming others. The team leader should stress that the evaluation is meant to determine whether tasks have been successfully completed by the team and to acknowledge the contributions made by individual members.

FIGURE 17-4
Evaluation Techniques

- *Evaluate performance on a day-to-day basis.* Give employees immediate feedback on their performance. If a report or letter is not written or formatted correctly, inform the employee immediately. Praise a job well done; do not wait for a yearly evaluation session.
- *Allow adequate time for the evaluation.* Set aside enough time on your calendar to do a thorough evaluation. Hold it in an appropriate place where you are not likely to be interrupted.
- *Give credit where credit is due.* When work is done well, tell the responsible employees. Look at the total work of the employee; do not treat the evaluation as a time just for criticism. Express to employees the areas in which they are performing in an exemplary manner, in an average manner, and below expectations.
- *Be fair.* Analyze the employee's work objectively on the basis of established performance criteria not on how well you like or dislike the employee. When discussing errors, word your comments positively; suggest how the work could have been performed satisfactorily. Give the employee an opportunity to suggest possible alternatives. For example, you might say, "You are doing well in…but you need to improve in…" rather than, "Your performance is a problem."
- *Listen to what the employee is saying.* Too often we listen to others with only half an ear. By providing the employee with an opportunity to speak, he or she will be able to release much of his or her anxiety and thus be more receptive to constructive criticism. Let the person talk.
- *Avoid personal areas.* Do not try to counsel an employee about his or her personal problems that should be handled by a qualified professional.
- *Establish attainable objectives for improvement.* Help the employee develop a plan of action for improvement, which should include setting target dates for the accomplishment of each objective. Recognize any resulting improvement; this plan of action is meant to be a growth plan for improvement.

Work-group evaluations should set measurable objectives that are related to the overall goals established by the organization. The manager and the work group might also use a total quality approach to identify ongoing improvements by asking:

- What needs to be improved?
- What actions should the work group take to improve the areas identified?
- Who does what and when is it done? Develop an **action plan** listing tasks to be achieved, identifying who is responsible for them, and when each will be completed.
- How do we know the action is working? Monitor the action plan to determine whether the desired results have been achieved.

- How can we ensure that the problem will not recur? Implement training and other necessary measures to ensure that the problem does not happen again.
- What have we learned? Areas where difficulties occurred should be reviewed so performance can improve.

As a manager you may also be responsible for identifying and preparing employees for promotion. Promoting qualified personnel from within the organization can improve employee morale. You should watch for promising employees and use every opportunity to encourage them and further develop their skills. Using these evaluation techniques can help you to identify those employees who have potential for promotion.

Soft Skills Earning the Right to Lead

You have learned in this chapter that the effective leader has certain traits and is willing to follow a set of values to help the organization and its employees to learn and grow. You have learned that several management responsibilities are necessary in order for an organization to function efficiently. You have learned that a definite link exists between good leaders and good managers. Although management tasks are more concrete, effective managers must have leadership characteristics—those traits that keep the organization focused on doing what is fair.

Needless to say, not all people have the leadership traits mentioned in this chapter, and not all are interested in developing them. The process of learning how to lead is ongoing. No one is born with the right to lead; leadership is earned. It is individuals who consistently demonstrate a commitment to the skills defined in this chapter who earn that right.

Chapter Summary

The summary will help you remember the important points covered in this chapter.

- Regardless of the profession you choose, the ability to lead with confidence will serve you well throughout life.
- Leading well is a practical philosophy where an individual motivates and inspires others as the organization achieves its goals.
- Reading the work of respected writers in the fields of leadership and management will help you become a more effective leader.
- Effective leaders have integrity and emotional maturity, understand themselves, work to build a shared vision, live by a set of values, commit to service, empower others, reward risk-taking, model appropriate conduct, and know how to follow.
- Leadership styles include autocratic, democratic, and laissez-faire.
- The effective manager is also an effective leader.
- Management responsibilities include planning, organizing, recruiting and employing, orienting, training, motivating, delegating, and evaluating.
- The process of learning how to lead is continual. No one is born with the right to lead. Only those who demonstrate a commitment to develop needed leadership characteristics earn that right.

Key Terms

leadership p. 313
management p. 314
power p. 315
empowering p. 315
autocratic leadership p. 316
democratic leadership p. 316
laissez-faire leadership p. 316
MBO p. 317
tactical planning p. 317

strategic or long-range planning p. 317
span of control p. 317
job analysis p. 318
work periods p. 318
nine-day fortnight p. 318
micromanage p. 319
delegating p. 319
action plan p. 321

Discussion Items

These discussion items provide an opportunity to test your understanding of the chapter through written responses and/or discussion with your classmates and your instructor.

1. List the traits and qualities of an effective leader.
2. Explain the difference between leadership and management.
3. Define the essential responsibilities of management.
4. Describe the three most common leadership styles.
5. List five motivational factors.

Critical-Thinking Activity

Two months ago, CanAsian offered you a position as records manager. You accepted the offer since the position matches your skills and career goals. Five individuals report to you. During the two months, two staff members have committed what you believe to be serious ethical violations. The situations are as follows.

Situation 1

One of your first responsibilities was to develop an electronic document system for personnel records. You asked two of your staff (Nazira and Theodore) to work with you on the project. As your team started to work, you reminded them of the confidential nature of the project, stating that no information could be shared with anyone. Two weeks into the project, Nazira reported she overheard Theodore discussing project details with two administrative professionals in the accounting department. He gave them details of three executives in the company, including their ages, salaries, and employment history.

Situation 2

Kami, one of the five members of your staff, worked overtime one evening on a project you assigned. You left the office at 5 p.m., but returned at 8 p.m. Kami was not working when you returned. She provided the completed assignment the next morning. When Kami submitted her overtime hours for the week, she claimed overtime from 5 p.m. until 11 p.m. on that evening; overtime is paid at time-and-a-half.

How should you handle each situation? As you respond, ask yourself whether you are living your values.

Building Workplace Skills

Project 17-1 (Learning Outcomes 1 and 2)

Collaborative Project

Work as a team with four of your classmates on this assignment. Interview two top-level executives (presidents or vice-presidents, if possible). Ask them the following questions:

- What are the characteristics of an effective leader?
- How did you develop your leadership skills?
- How is planning conducted in your organization?
- Do you provide ongoing training for your employees? If so, what types of opportunities do you provide?
- What process do you use to evaluate employees?

Summarize your findings and report them to the class.

Project 17-2 (Learning Outcome 3)

Mr. Albertson is heading an effort to promote leadership in the organization. He has asked you to research the theories of two leading writers on leadership or management and to create a Web page or a set of Web pages. This material will be posted on the company intranet for managers and other employees to review.

Choose two of the leadership and management writers mentioned in this chapter, or choose other writers with the approval of your instructor. Research the writers' leadership or management theories. Use Word, Web design software, or a free website design site to create Web pages or a website about their ideas. You should have at least two pages with images and summaries written in your own words. Place a copy of this material in your e-portfolio.

Project 17-3 (Learning Outcome 3)

Assuming you are in a leadership position, identify and record the leadership values you would uphold and demonstrate to your employees. Save this document in your e-portfolio folder.

Your e-portfolio should now be nearing completion. Review the *Employability Skills 2000+* chart you created in Chapter 1. Did you successfully acquire all these skills? Write a summary of what you intended to accomplish. Include an evaluation of your actual accomplishments and your future plans. Submit this summary to your instructor or arrange a meeting to review your e-portfolio.

Make the Grade with MindTap

MindTap®

Stay organized and efficient with **MindTap**—a single destination with all the course material and study aids you need to succeed. Built-in apps leverage social media and the latest learning technology. For example:

- ReadSpeaker will read the text to you.
- Flashcards are pre-populated to provide you with a jump-start for review—or you can create your own.
- You can highlight text and make notes in your MindTap Reader. Your notes will flow into Evernote, the electronic notebook app that you can access anywhere when it's time to study for the exam.
- Self-quizzing allows you to access your understanding.

Visit http://www.nelson.com/student to start using **MindTap**. Enter the Online Access Code from the card included with your text. If a code card is not provided, you can purchase instant access at NELSONbrain.com.

Endnotes

1. "lead," Merriam-Webster Online, http://www.merriam-webster.com/dictionary/lead, accessed May 15, 2015.
2. "laissez faire," Merriam-Webster Online, http://www.merriam-webster.com/dictionary/laissez_faire, accessed May 15, 2015.
3. Peter F. Drucker, *The Practice of Management* (New York: HarperBusiness, 1993).

Glossary

A

accession log A document that records the numbers that have been assigned. p. 206

accountable items Express items; for example, items sent via FedEx, UPS, Purolator, and registered mail. p. 153

accounts payable The amount owed to a supplier or vendor for goods or services purchased on credit. p. 181

achievement The act of accomplishing or finishing a task. p. 38

action plan A plan that includes specific tasks to be achieved, who is responsible for each task identified, and when the task will be completed. p. 321

active listening *Listening* for the meaning as well as to the words of the speaker. p. 85

ad hoc committee A special committee that is formed to deal with a specific issue or problem; also known as a *taskforce* or a *project team*. p. 234

administrative assistant See *administrative professional*. p. 10

administrative professional Workplace support person. This occupation was formerly referred to as *secretary*, *receptionist*, and by such specialized titles as *legal secretary* and *medical secretary*. Although these titles are still in use, shifting roles have led to the more common use of *administrative assistant*, *executive assistant*, *marketing assistant*, *payroll assistant*, *human resources assistant*, and *office manager*. p. 10

aerobic Exercise that causes the body to use oxygen to produce the energy needed for the activity; it must be brisk, sustained, and involve a repeated use of large muscles. p. 308

agenda An outline of what will occur at a meeting. p. 241

alphabetizing Comparison of units in a *caption*, unit by unit and letter by letter, to determine a difference. p. 196

amendment Used to change the wording of a *motion* that has been made. p. 245

amoral Lacking moral judgment or sensibility; neither moral nor immoral. p. 57

annotate To make notations on a piece of mail concerning a previous action taken or facts that will assist the reader. p. 150

APA style Documentation guidelines established by the American Psychological Association. p. 107

appointment A time set aside for people to discuss an issue. p. 225

assets A list of what a company owns. p. 181

ATMs Automated teller machines. p. 263

attitude Position, disposition, or manner with regard to a person or thing. pp. 79, 271

autocratic leadership A controlling leadership style in which the leader directs and closely supervises the work that is done; employees have no input into the decisions. p. 316

B

balance sheet A financial statement showing a company's *assets*, *liabilities*, and net worth. p. 180

BCS Bar code sorter. p. 154

bill of lading A document that itemizes a shipment's contents, quantity, and the delivery destination. It accompanies items such as parcels or packages being shipped from a supplier to a customer. p. 159

bit The basic unit of information in computer storage. p. 65

blank endorsement The signature of the *payee* of a financial instrument. p. 172

blog Also called a *weblog*, a Web-based journal in which participants express their opinions, thoughts, and feelings. p. 143

body language Various meaningful body motions or gestures. p. 86

boilerplate text Standard text used in documents. p. 109

bonds Debt owed by an organization. p. 307

brainstorming Engaging in problem solving. p. 110

broadband A *telecommunications* service that uses cable, DSL, wireless, and satellite connections. Short for "broad bandwith," as in a high-speed network able to carry video as well as voice; *bandwidth* describes the throughput of a network per unit of *time*, and is measured is kilobits, megabits, or gigabits per second. p. 68

building blocks Parts of a document or text that are often used in a particular type of document, for example a cover page. p. 109

business-class accommodations A mode of air travel slightly more expensive than *economy class*, but less expensive than *first class*; located in front of economy class or directly behind first class. p. 257

bylaws The rules and procedures that govern the operation of an organization. p. 234

byte A unit of computer storage comprising eight bits. p. 65

C

Canada Post Corporation (CPC) Canada's postal service. p. 148

cancelled cheques Written *cheques* that have been cleared by the bank. p. 177

caption One or more *filing units*, such as the entire name or a part of the name by which the *record* will be stored. p. 193

carpal tunnel syndrome A major occupational illness that occurs due to the compression of a large nerve, the median nerve, as it passes through a tunnel composed of bone and ligaments in the wrist. p. 35

casual listening Hearing and trying to understand what is being said with the objective of relating to others. p. 84

CEO Chief Executive Officer. p. 9

CFO Chief Financial Officer. p. 9

channel A means by which a *message* is sent, such as a letter, speaking in person or by telephone, or electronically by email. p. 83

cheque register A log used to record the details of all *cheques* written and deposit made. p. 175

cheques Legal documents authorizing the bank to pay a specific sum to a designated *payee*. p. 171

chronic stress Occurs when a distressful situation is prolonged, allowing no rest or recuperation for the body; it can cause physical and emotional problems. p. 36

chronological résumé A *résumé* that lists a person's credentials in reverse chronological order, with the most recent entries listed first. p. 283

CIO Chief Information Officer. p. 9

circular and oval arrangements Two effective seating arrangements for minimizing status positions. Works well for small groups of from six to eight people. p. 240

cloud computing Storing and accessing of applications and computer data through a Web browser that provides computer services to computers and mobile devices on demand. p. 66

coding Marking a *record* by the name, subject, location, or number determined in the *indexing* process. p. 195

coherence In writing, the sense of being interrelated, when all sentences in a paragraph are related to each other in terms of content, grammatical construction, and choice of words. p. 101

cold call See direct contact. p. 280

collating Assembling, in chronological order, the pages in a multiple page document. p. 162

combination-style résumé A *résumé* that presents experiences in reverse chronological skill set order. p. 283

communication Occurs when a message is sent by one person and received and understood by another person. p. 82

communication barrier Anything that interferes with successful *communication*; can be internal or external. p. 84

compressed workweek A work arrangement in which employees work the usual number of hours (35 to 40), but the hours are compressed into four days. For example, a 35-hour week consists of three days of nine hours each and a fourth day of eight hours. p. 8

computer virus A program with unauthorized instructions that is introduced without permission or knowledge of the computer user. p. 69

computer vision syndrome A health problem that develops from screen glare. p. 35

conciseness Saying what is needed without cluttering the correspondence with irrelevant information, needless words, or flowery phrases. p. 94

conference call A meeting in which more than two individuals at different locations attend and communicate with each other via a telecommunications network; also known as a *teleconference*. p. 234

confidentiality Secrecy of the information received or the confidences shared. Many firms require employees to sign a

confidentiality agreement to highlight the importance of this aspect to new employees. p. 14

conflict of interest When private interests of a member of the board of directors conflict with the duties they owe the company. p. 9

conflict resolution Addressing and dealing with conflicts in a positive manner. p. 37

consulate An office of a government in a foreign city that acts to assist and protect citizens of the consul's country. p. 263

continuous quality improvement (CQI) See total quality management (TQM). p. 7

COO Chief Operating Officer. p. 9

copyright The exclusive right granted to the author or creator of an original body of work to reproduce or authorize someone else to reproduce the material. p. 163

corporations Legal entities formed by following a formal process of federal or provincial incorporation; may be publicly or privately owned. p. 9

cover letter A letter that is used when applying for a job, with the *goal* of arousing the prospective employer's interest, describing the abilities of the person writing the letter, and requesting an interview. p. 286

cpm Copies per minute. p. 161

creativity Having the ability or the power to cause to exist. p. 118

credible Believable or trustworthy. p. 126

critical thinking Conscious and deliberate inquiry. "Critical" comes from the Greek word *krinein,* which means "to separate, to choose." p. 12

cross-referencing A method of identifying an alternate name that could be used when a record is requested. p. 195

current assets Cash, or *assets* such as accounts receivable or inventory, that can readily be converted into cash in a short period of time. p. 181

customer Also known as a *client* or *buyer,* someone who buys or uses the products or services of a company or organization. p. 281

customer focus A commitment to providing high-quality *customer service* to all customers. p. 218

customer service The ability of an organization to consistently give customers what they need and want. p. 218

cuts Tabs of various widths on folders. p. 193

D

delegating Assigning tasks to others and then *empowering* them by providing the necessary information to get the job done. p. 319

democratic leadership A leadership style in which employees share in authority, decisions, and plans. p. 316

demographics Characteristics such as age, gender, race, education, and income level. p. 120

dependability Trustworthiness. Examples are being at work on *time* if you are working at an established location; being productive when engaged in *telework*; a willingness to put in additional time on important assignments; doing what you say you will do, and when you say you will do it. p. 14

deposit slip A form that accompanies a deposit and itemizes the amount of cash and/or the value of cheques being deposited. p. 171

die An engraved metal stamp used for impressing the postage. p. 156

digital subscriber line (DSL) A technology that provides high-speed data communications over analogue phone lines. p. 68

direct access A system that does not require referring to anything but the file to find the name. p. 194

direct approach Used when the *message* is favourable or neutral; it begins with the reason for the correspondence, continues with any needed explanation, and closes with a thank-you for the action that has been taken or with a request that action be taken by a specific date. p. 93

direct contact or cold call Going directly to an organization without having an *appointment* or without knowing whether a job is available. p. 280

discrimination Treatment or consideration based on class or category rather than individual merit. p. 48

diversity competency Specifically learned behaviours that can be actively practiced to promote equity and inclusion. p. 87

downsize To reduce the number of employees within a business. p. 36

downsizing Streamlining an organization so that it is more manageable and cutting overhead costs. p. 8

drawer The organization or person who has written the *cheques*. p. 172

DSL See digital subscriber line. p. 68

due process The requirement of managers to impose sanctions on employees only after offering them a chance to correct the organizational grievance. p. 50

duplexing In *reprographics*, copying on both sides of a sheet of paper. p. 162

E

e-cheques Also known as email money transfers, these electronic payments are used to send money directly from a personal bank account to anyone with an email address and a personal bank account at one of many Canadian financial institutions. p. 178

ecologically Pertaining to the relationship between human groups and their physical and social environment. p. 162

economy-class accommodations The least expensive of the three classes of flight; seats are closer together, there is less legroom, and service is not as good as in first class or business class.

e-deposit or remote capture deposit An image of a cheque is captured by scanning (or taking a picture) and is then electronically delivered to a financial institution for deposit to an account. p. 172

editing Reviewing and revising a *message* to improve its form and content. p. 94

EFT See electronic funds transfer. p. 174

electronic funds transfer (EFT) A method whereby a bank uses computer technology to effect a transfer of funds. p. 174

electronic résumé An online statement of one's background and experiences. p. 283

emoticons Simulated faces produced by using the characters on the basic keyboard, used to communicate emotion, *tone*, or *attitude* in keyed text. p. 102

emotional intelligence The capacity to develop self-awareness, self-discipline and empathy in ways that impact on relationships with others. p. 14

empathizing Attempting to feel or think how another person is thinking or feeling. p. 222

empathy mentally entering into the feeling or spirit of a person. pp. 38, 93

emphatic listening Used to hear, understand, and offer *feedback* that shows you have understood the *message*. p. 85

Employability Skills 2000 + A profile developed by the Conference Board of Canada and updated regularly that identifies critical skills needed in the workplace. p. 211

Employment and Social Development Canada The national public employment agency whose services are provided free of charge to Canadian job seekers. p. 280

employment application A form used by companies to obtain information about prospective employees' education, background, and experience. p. 287

employment at will The doctrine that allows employees to be fired for no valid cause, if the employer wishes to do so. p. 50

empowering The passing on of authority or responsibility. p. 315

endorsing a cheque Signing a *cheque* on the reverse. p. 172

epost A free, secure, online personal digital mailbox that allows individuals and businesses to access, view, and pay bills online. p. 149

epost Connect A secure service linked to an *epost* account that provides private and confidential online secure communications services for business customers through Bulk and Collaboration options. p. 149

ergonomics The study of the fit between people, the tools they use, and the physical setting in which they work. For example, ergonomics can help in the design of office furniture and equipment that is physiologically sound so that the user remains healthy while using it. The Greek words *ergoes* and *nomos* were combined to coin the word. p. 33

e-stamps Electronic postage purchased via the *Internet* and downloaded to a PC. Also known as *PC postage*. p. 156

ethics The systematic study of moral conduct, duty, and judgment. p. 46

evaluative listening Used to hear, understand, and judge what is being said. p. 85

executive summary A one or two-page summary of a report. p. 107

exit interview An interview done by the employer when an employee leaves the company. p. 295

extranet A private network that belongs to an organization such as a bank, and requires the authorization of selected external people for them to use it. p. 67

extrinsic motivation An impulse to action that comes from outside a person, such as a possible salary increase or a promotion. p. 15

extroverts People who prefer to be energized by the outside world. p. 301

F

fax machine Short for *facsimile machine*; electronically sends an image of an original document from one location to another via communication networks. p. 144

total quality management (TQM) The principle of continued improvement in an organization; developed by Dr. W. Edwards Deming, an American statistician. p. 7

touchpad A small pad that uses motion and pressure by a finger to control the mouse pointer. p. 64

touch screen A computer screen that allows the user to input data by touching the screen with a finger or a pointer. p. 64

U

unity In writing, the sense of being united, when all sentences in a paragraph clarify, relate to, or help support the main idea, which is usually expressed in the *topic sentence.* p. 98

useful records *Records* that are useful for the smooth, effective operation of an organization. p. 208

USB An external port on a computer for connecting peripheral devices. p. 65

V

values Our beliefs that determine how we live on a day-to-day basis. p. 79

verbal communication The process of exchanging ideas and feelings through the use of words. p. 85

verbatim A word-for-word record of what has been said. p. 246

video conference A meeting in which two or more people at different locations use *telecommunication* technology—computers, video/web cameras, and/or microphones—to participate in a virtual "face-to-face" meeting in real time. p. 236

virtual assistants Entrepreneurial self-employed freelance administrative assistants. pp. 7, 301

virtual interview The use of telephone or videoconferencing tools to enable a candidate to be interviewed by an interviewer at a distant location. p. 291

virtual office The operational domain of any organization that includes remote workers. p. 7

virtual teams Dispersed workers who come together through *telecommunications* technology to accomplish a task. p. 302

visa A document granted by a government abroad that permits a traveller to enter and travel within a country. p. 262

visual aid An object or image that listeners can see and that will help them understand a message. p. 122

vital records *Records* that cannot be replaced and should never be destroyed. p. 208

voice mail An efficient method of managing incoming calls when call recipients are unavailable and when broadcasting messages (sending the same message) to multiple voice mail boxes. p. 139

voice over Internet protocol (VoIP) Software and hardware that allow voice signals to be carried over an IP-based network, with *POTS* quality and reliability; also known as *IP telephony.* p. 133

voucher cheque A *cheque* that includes a form for recording the details of the payment. p. 173

W

Web browser Software that provides a way to look at and interact with all thxve information on the World Wide Web in a single unified interface. p. 67

webcast A type of broadcast that is similar in nature to a television broadcast, except it takes place over the *Internet.* p. 236

webinar A seminar presented over the *Internet.* p. 236

web meeting A meeting that utilizes technology to enable groups of people anywhere in the world to exchange ideas and information via computers and an *Internet* or LAN connection. p. 236

Wi-Fi Abbreviation for *wireless fidelity*, the popular term for a highfrequency LAN that connects users of portable computer devices to the *Internet.* p. 64

Wiki A website or group of Web pages on which anyone can add, edit, or delete content. p. 143

work ethic An inner drive to work hard and well. p. 15

work periods The third factor in organizing work; the time in which the work is to be performed. p. 318

X

Xpresspost A Canada Post service that offers next-business-day delivery to local or regional destinations and two-day service between most major Canadian locations. p. 158

Y

***you* approach** A communication method that requires the communicator to put the recipient at the centre of the *message*; *you* and *your* are used rather than *I* or *we.* p. 93

Index

Box-bottom hanging folders, 193–194
Brainstorming, 110
Breaks, 308
Brevity, in written communication, 96
Bridging services and equipment, 235
Briggs, Katharine, 301
Bring forward (BF) notation, 195–197
British Columbia Institute of Technology, 277
Broadband, 68
Brokaw, Tom, 82
Building blocks for documents, 109
Business documents. *See* Written communication
Business organizations, 8–9
Business Reply Mail, 157
Business travel. *See* Travel
Business-class accommodations, 257
Bylaws, 234, 245
Bytes, 65

C

CAA (Canadian Automobile Association), 260, 262
Cable Internet connections, 68
Caffeine, 39–40, 308
Calendaring and scheduling, 224–229
    cancelling appointments, 225
    electronic calendars, 226–227
    lists of appointments, 225–226, 229
    online appointment systems, 228
    paper-based calendars, 228–229
    scheduling appointments, 225
Call forwarding, 134
Call holding, 134
Call management features of phones, 133–134
Call management skills, 133–136
    attentiveness, 135
    discretion, 135
    problem calls, 136
    proper English, 135
    slang, 135
    smiling, 134–135
    speaking distinctly and clearly, 136
    tactful questions, 136
    taking messages, 135
    using caller's name, 136
Call parking, 134
Call waiting, 134
Caller display, 134
Calling in sick, 55
Canada Labour Code (CLC), 48–49, 51
Canada Pension Plan (CPP), 180
Canada Post Corporation (CPC), 148–149, 154, 157, 174. *See also* Mail
Canada Revenue Agency (CRA), 180–181
Canada's Top 100 Employers, 281

Canadian Association of Virtual Assistants (CAVA), 302
Canadian Automobile Association (CAA), 260, 262
Canadian Bankers Association, 178
Canadian Business, 281
Canadian Centre for Occupational Health and Safety (CCOHS), 36, 53, 301–302
Canadian Copyright Act, 56
Canadian Information Processing Society (CIPS), 250
Canadian Occupational Safety and Health (CanOSH), 51
Canadian Postal Code Directory, 154
Canadian Union of Public Employees (CUPE), 50
CanadianCareers.com, 279
Cancelled cheques, 177
CanOSH (Canadian Occupational Safety and Health), 51
Capacitive technology, 64
CAPs (Certified Administrative Professionals), 17, 131
Captions, for file folders, 193
Car rental, 260, 262, 264–266
Car travel, 260, 262
Carpal tunnel syndrome, 35
Casual listening, 84
Catalysts, 316
CAVA (Canadian Association of Virtual Assistants), 302
CCOHS (Canadian Centre for Occupational Health and Safety), 36, 53, 301–302
CD (compact disc) technology, 212
CEOs (chief executive officers), 9
Certified Administrative Professionals (CAPs), 17, 131
Certified Human Resources Professionals (CHRPs), 277
Certified Records Managers (CRMs), 17
CFOs (chief financial officers), 9
Chairpersons (meeting leaders), 237–239, 244–247
Chairs, 33–34, 307
Change
    ethical, 57–58
    job changes, 294–296
    openness to, 14
Change tracking, 97
Channels of communication, 83
Chartered planes, 258
Chartered Professional Accountants (CPAs), 184
Cheque registers, 173–176
Cheques
    cancelled, 177
    defined, 171
    e-cheques, 178
    endorsing, 172

    formats for, 173–174
    postdated, 171
    preparing for deposit, 172
    staledated, 171–172
    voucher, 173, 175
    writing, 175
Chief executive officers (CEOs), 9
Chief financial officers (CFOs), 9
Chief information officers (CIOs), 9
Chief operating officers (COOs), 9
Chronic stress, 36–37
Chronological résumés, 283–284
CHRPs (Certified Human Resources Professionals), 277
CIBC, 184
CIOs (chief information officers), 9
CIPS (Canadian Information Processing Society), 250
Circular seating arrangement, 240
Clarity, in written communication, 94
CLC (Canada Labour Code), 48–49, 51
Clichés, 96
Click-N-Ship, 156
Clothing, 16, 125, 237
Cloud computing, 65–67, 212
COD (collect on delivery), 159
Code of Conduct, 47
Coding records, 195–196
Coherence, in written communication, 101
Cold calls (direct contact), 280–281
Collaboration tools, 141–144
Collaborative writing, 109–110
Collating, 162
Collect on delivery (COD), 159
College of Physicians and Surgeons of Nova Scotia (CPSNS), 131
College placement offices, 280
Colour, in workplace, 53
Combination-style résumés, 283
Communication, 11, 76, 78. *See also* Collaboration tools; Telecommunications
    age issues and, 81–82
    attitudes and, 79
    barriers to, 83–84
    collaboration tools, 141–144
    cultural differences and, 79–81
    defined, 82
    effective, 86–87
    gender issues and, 81
    good techniques, 33
    ineffective, 27
    listening, 84–85
    nonverbal, 86–87
    presentations, 118–127
    process of, 82–83
    values and, 79
    verbal, 85–86
    virtual assistants and, 304
    written, 91–113